T0270341

ILLINOIS
POLITICS

ILLINOIS POLITICS

*A Citizen's Guide to
Power, Politics, and Government*

Melissa Mouritsen, Kent D. Redfield,
and James D. Nowlan

Library of Congress Cataloging-in-Publication Data

Names: Mouritsen, Melissa, author. | Redfield, Kent, author. | Nowlan, James Dunlap, author.
Title: Illinois politics : a citizen's guide to power, politics, and government / Melissa Mouritsen, Kent D. Redfield and James D. Nowlan.
Description: Fully revised and expanded edition. | Urbana : University of Illinois Press, [2024] |
Identifiers: LCCN 2023054140 (print) | LCCN 2023054141 (ebook) | ISBN 9780252045875 (cloth : acid-free paper) | ISBN 9780252087974 (paperback : acid-free paper) | ISBN 9780252056758 (ebook)
Subjects: LCSH: Illinois—Politics and government. | BISAC: POLITICAL SCIENCE / American Government / State | POLITICAL SCIENCE / Civics & Citizenship
Classification: LCC JK5716 .N68 2024 (print) | LCC JK5716 (ebook) | DDC 320.4773—dc23/eng/20240316
LC record available at https://lccn.loc.gov/2023054140
LC ebook record available at https://lccn.loc.gov/2023054141

Contents

Preface

This book is about the politics, government, and public policies of Illinois. We authors find that many works about American government deal with one or another of these topics, but seldom all together. We consider the topics inseparable, indeed interwoven: politics is the serious game of getting one's candidates into government, where they can implement public policies that reflect the values of the successful participants.

This book is a substantial revision of two earlier iterations: *Illinois Politics and Government: The Expanding Metropolitan Frontier* (Nebraska, 1996), by Samuel K. Gove and Nowlan, and *Illinois Politics and Government: A Citizen's Guide* (Illinois, 2010), by Nowlan, Gove, Richard J. Winkel Jr., with a major chapter by Redfield. The authors of the present book are Mouritsen, former chair of the political science department at the College of DuPage and a specialist in suburban politics and political corruption; she has run for Democratic Party office in Cook County and is now on the Berwyn North School District 98 Board. Redfield is an emeritus professor of political science at the University of Illinois at Springfield; he is the most widely quoted observer of Illinois politics in the media, in Illinois, and the nation. Nowlan is a jack-of-all-trades in Illinois politics and government, having served as a Republican state legislator, worked for three unindicted Illinois governors, and made observations about Illinois in more than 600 newspaper op-ed pieces and in books such as this.

The earlier editions emphasized an individualistic Illinois political culture in which self-interest dominated and political corruption was tolerated, but that chicanery appeared to be on the wane. The authors also contended that a rapidly expanding metropolitan region outside Chicago would likely come to dominate Illinois politics and government. We now find it hard to support the case that corruption has abated. In 2006, both Illinois governor George Ryan and, separately, his campaign committee were convicted of corruption. In 2009, Governor Rod Blagojevich suffered an unprecedented legislative impeachment, conviction, and removal from office. In 2023, high-profile lobbyists and a utility company CEO were found guilty of public corruption, as was, in a separate trial, a longtime aide to former Speaker of the Illinois House Michael Madigan. And, as of the print date of this book in 2024, Democratic Chicago alderman Edward Burke and former Speaker of the Illinois House and state Democratic Party of Illinois chair Michael Madigan, both political powerhouses for fully half a century, face trial on multiple indictments for political corruption.

Nor had political dominance shifted toward the suburbs beyond Chicago and Cook County. Indeed, the once-Republican collar counties around Cook had tilted toward the Democratic Party, largely as a result of increased population diversity. In the early 2020s, however, leadership in both chambers of the Democrat-dominated legislature shifted, for the first time in decades, from Chicago lawmakers to those living in suburban Cook County. Since 2000, political observers and presidential candidates have concluded that Illinois has become a solidly "blue," or Democratic, state. Two decades ago, Republican presidential campaign directors conceded the Illinois electoral vote outcome to the Democrats and bypassed Illinois to focus their efforts on battleground states. More important to Illinois politics, continuously since 2009, all statewide offices, both US Senate seats, most Illinois congressional representatives, as well as the two top posts in the Democrat-dominated legislature have been members of the Party of the Donkey.

This book frequently uses the chronological frame of 1970–2020 (or later) for several reasons. Coauthors Redfield and Nowlan began their academic and political careers around 1970, so while this year may seem like ancient history to students, it is but a flashback to these authors. The following factors are of course much more important: In 1970, Illinois adopted a new constitution, which gave local governments more power and expanded the powers of both the governor and legislature. Further, Governor Richard Ogilvie (1969–73) served back then as an arguably "modernizing" Illinois governor, leading the adoption of a state income tax, advocating for the new constitution, and providing an activist approach to state government that has generally been followed by most of Ogilvie's successors.

In this edition, we observe that over the past half century, Illinois has been largely rearranging itself—in terms of its population, economy, and politics—across all three traditional geopolitical regions of the state (Chicago, the six-and-a-half suburban "collar counties," and the remaining ninety-five "downstate" counties). Indeed, because of population shifts and increased diversity chronicled in our first chapter, we contend the primary Chicago-suburbs-downstate regions should be replaced by Chicago/Cook County—suburban collar counties—downstate geopolitical regions. We believe this ongoing rearrangement and increased population diversity are causing a transition of Illinois from a moderate to a liberal polity, and to increased political polarization of the kind seen nationally, among other consequences that we develop in this book. Our book is divided into three sections: Politics, Institutions, and Policy. We think of politics as the struggle to get one's adherents into government and then to help build their influence, even power. Once inside government, the successful political players shape the policies that in turn determine how we live our lives, and of who gets what, which is after all what politics is mostly about.

There are new, separate chapters in this edition. Previous units on taxing and spending as well as on education are now accompanied by chapters on social policies, or "people services," where most of state spending is to be found, and on "state regulation of our behavior." The "regulation" chapter discusses the many ways our state government guides or behavior, all spelled out in the 23,000(!) pages of our Illinois Compiled Statutes. There is also a separate chapter, for the first time, on political corruption. We find this focus important, as Illinois cannot seem to free itself from a political culture that treats government as simply another marketplace in which to do business, and where too many citizens are willing to take unearned personal gain at public expense. The result is a general perception among citizens across the nation and within our state that corruption in Illinois is simply endemic. Such perceptions may well harm the vitality and attractiveness of this state, which otherwise has great strengths, which we will speak to in the chapters that follow.

Acknowledgments

The authors owe a significant debt of gratitude to Jessica Gray for development of the tables and charts in this book, and for additional research. The author's express their deep appreciation to Richard J. Winkel Jr. for his major contributions to the 2010 edition of this book, many of which are reflected in this edition. Many friends and colleagues deeply experienced in Illinois and its politics and government made valuable contributions to this book. They include Allen Andersen, Jason Anderson, Bob Barry, Judge Harry Bulkeley (ret.), Bruce Dennison, David Dyer, Sherry Eagle, Kevin Fanning, Representative Brad Fritts, Phil Gonet, Ray LaHood, Representative Lindsey LaPointe, Ann Lousin, Judge Michael McCuskey (ret.), Ken McMillan, Rich Miller, Laurence Msall, Representative Michelle Mussman, Alderman Rob Pabon, John Shaw, Judge Kent Slater (ret.), State Senator Win Stoller, Don Udstuen, and Dixie Zietlow. We also thank Dick Simpson for his careful consideration of our chapters, helpful edits, and general counsel. And to David Goldberg and Jeanne Schroeder, thank you for helping us polish our words. The authors thank Carl Sandburg College in Galesburg, Illinois, for permission to use throughout several of the timeless editorial cartoons of the late Bill Campbell. Finally, we appreciate the thoughtful guidance provided by University of Illinois Press editors Martha Bayne and Mariah Mendes Schaefer.

Responsibility for any errors of fact or interpretation resides with the authors.

PART I
POLITICS

1

ILLINOIS IN PERSPECTIVE

The "Tall State," as it was called in a 1960s tourism campaign, stretches almost four hundred miles from its northern limit at the Wisconsin line to its southern tip at Cairo (pronounced *kay*-ro), nestled between Kentucky and Missouri. The northernmost latitude is on a line with Portsmouth, New Hampshire, and at Cairo, its latitude is close to that of Portsmouth, Virginia.

The state's rich diversity and significant population is due in great measure to U.S. territorial delegate Nathaniel Pope, who in 1818 succeeded in passing an amendment to the Illinois Enabling Act that moved the new state's northern boundary forty-one miles to the north. This area of eight thousand square miles—mostly empty at the time—today encompasses metropolitan Chicago and almost 80 percent of the state's population; without it, Illinois would never have become one of the top six states in population and wealth that it is.[1]

When the first French explorers came to Illinois they were met by Cahokia, Kaskaskia, Michigamea, Peoria, and Tamaroa Native American tribes who together with others made up the Illini Nation. "Illinois" was the French spelling for these people. Tens of thousands populated the state until disease and war, brought first by the French and later the British colonists, decimated their numbers.

European settlement of the state was facilitated by natural factors, ingenuity, and human achievements. The Ohio River offered a convenient water superhighway, and the state's generally level topography made the prairie relatively easy to traverse on foot. The opening of the Erie Canal in New York in 1825 facilitated the flow of Yankees and European immigrants via the Great Lakes. The early development of Illinois as a railroad center helped disperse the newly arrived throughout the state; later, the main line of the Illinois Central Railroad, running from New Orleans, would bring tens of thousands of Blacks to jobs in Chicago.

The platting, or dividing, of Illinois into townships of thirty-six uniform parcels of one-mile squares, as decreed by the U.S. Congress in the Northwest Ordinances of 1785 and 1787, was designed to transfer public lands efficiently into private hands.[2] This it did. Each mile-square represented a "section" of land of 640 acres. Township roads were laid out along the sections. The township plats made it simple to survey and sell land with a minimum of confusion and dispute. Even today, for the airplane traveler crossing Illinois, a geometric checkerboard pattern rolls out below.

There was a hunger to develop this rich flatland, but, first, transportation infrastructure was needed to get the settlers in and the bounty of the fields to market. When Abraham Lincoln and Stephen A. Douglas served as state lawmakers in the 1830s, the legislature embarked on an ambitious scheme of "internal improvements," but the dreamed-of network of wood-plank roads, canals, and railroads collapsed under the weight of poor planning, a weak national economy, and a lack of both capital and engineering capacity.[3] Lincoln and Douglas later became U.S. congressmen and revived the idea, this time convincing the federal government to assist by providing huge land grants for private investors. In 1851, the federal government offered 3.75 million acres of railroad right-of-way and adjoining land to investors in the Illinois Central Railroad. Within five years, 705 miles of track had been laid from Cairo to Galena, with a spur to Chicago. The Illinois Central became the longest railway in the world and the nation's largest private venture to that date.

Railroads served as the interstate highways of the nineteenth century. If a town was on a rail line, it generally prospered; if not, the town was often abandoned. Railroad trackage in Illinois increased from 111 miles in 1850, to 2,800 miles in 1860, to 7,000 miles by 1875. In part because of its railroad network, Illinois was the fastest-growing territory in the world by the middle of the nineteenth century.[4] The thirty-six million acres of land in Illinois were enough for about a quarter-million quarter-section (160-acre) farms. One-fourth of those farms had been taken by 1850 and nearly all by 1875. Three in four farms were within five miles of a railroad, and only 5 percent were more than ten miles distant.[5]

Early Triumph for the "Modernizers"

In the free-for-all environment of the state's early days, no one culture held sway. This northern state had been settled first by southerners, primarily poor, land-hungry northern British and Scots Irish pioneers from the uplands of Virginia and the Carolinas and from Tennessee and Kentucky.[6] James Simeone describes the first settlers as the "white folks" who saw the West (Illinois Territory) as a place of opportunity and feared the reestablishment of an economic aristocracy of English and old Virginia families.[7]

A second surge came in the 1830s via the new Erie Canal, primarily from New England and the Middle Atlantic states. These Yankees, who mostly settled in the central and northern parts of Illinois, generally brought more assets with them and put down roots into richer farmland than did those farther south.

These settlement patterns set the stage for a struggle between the "white folks" in southern Illinois and the "modernizers," primarily Yankees, in the north.[8] The genius of the modernizers, according to author Richard Jensen, lay in a combination of values: faith in reason and equal rights, a drive for middle-class status, and the sense of having a mission to transform the world in their image. Education was their remedy, efficiency their ideal.

Everyone in Illinois recognized the difference between modernizers and white folks, or "traditionalists," as Jensen identifies them, although nobody used those words. Each group thought the other peculiar. Fast-talking Yankee peddlers were distrusted—one county even set a prohibitive fifty-dollar-per-quarter license fee for clock peddlers. One Yankee woman was amused by the drinking, horse trading, and quaint, slow drawl of the southerners. She talked with one who allowed that "it's a right smart thing to be able to read when you want to" but who didn't figure that books and the sciences would "do a man as much good as handy use of the rifle."[9]

Strong commitment to education was the hallmark of the modernizers. By 1883, the northern part of the state provided its children with one-third more days of schooling than did the schools in "Egypt," as deep southern Illinois was called, with its towns of Cairo, Karnak, and Thebes.[10] Jensen quotes a nineteenth-century governor on the values in northern Illinois: "Is a school house, a bridge, or a church to be built, a road to be made, a school or minister to be maintained, or taxes to be paid? The northern man is never to be found wanting."[11]

By 1860, the Yankee modernizers dominated northern Illinois politics, while traditionalists held sway in the south. Central Illinois became the uncertain political battleground. With Lincoln's election and the Civil War, the modernists triumphed and, through the Republican Party, controlled Illinois politics almost continuously for the following seventy years. (In order to emphasize that generalizations about traditionalists and modernizers are just that, we note that Lincoln, the modernizer, came from southern traditionalist roots, while Stephen A. Douglas, who represented the traditionalist viewpoint in the 1860 presidential election, came from upstate New York.)

Chicago and the Great Midwest

In a compelling synthesis of the organic relationship between a great city and the vast prairie that envelopes it, William Cronon explains that neither Chicago nor the rich countryside of the Midwest would have developed its great wealth if not for the symbiosis between the two: the urban center contributing creativity, energy, and capital and the farmers and small towns providing ambition, intelligence, and the harvest from incredibly fecund soils.[12] Plentiful water and easy waterborne transportation provided further economic stimulus. The Wabash, Ohio, and Mississippi Rivers formed Illinois's natural boundaries, while the Illinois River traversed the middle, positioning the state at the heart of the young nation's economic expansion.[13]

At the southern tip of Lake Michigan, Chicago sat astride the boundary between East and West. Chicago's meatpackers, grain merchants, and manufacturers showed extraordinary drive and creativity, not to mention a knack for attracting capital. The railroads were eager to carry their goods, and these capitalists put the Midwest's natural resources to use to create an unprecedented hive of economic development by the end of the 1800s.

Chicago's Yankee capitalists, such as the meatpackers Philip Armour and Gustavus Swift, systematized the market in animal flesh. Building on the adage that "the hog is regarded as the most compact form in which the Indian corn crop . . . can be transported to market," they created hog-slaughtering lines that were the forerunners of the assembly line.[14] Cattle were standardized as grade no. 1, 2, or 3. Rail cars were refrigerated so that dressed beef from Chicago could be marketed in the East.

According to Cronon, the overarching genius of Swift and Armour lay in the immense, impersonal, hierarchical organizations they created, operated by an army of managers and workers who would outlive and carry on after the founders. By 1880, Chicago had more than seventy-five thousand industrial workers, the largest such labor force west of the Appalachians.[15] To quote the muckraker Frank Norris: "The Great Grey City, brooking no rival, imposed its dominion upon a reach of country larger than many a kingdom of the Old World."[16]

By 1890, Chicago, with more than one million residents, was the nation's second-largest city. It promoted itself in 1893 by presenting the World's Columbian Exposition to twenty-seven million visitors. From a one-square-mile tract of marshes and scrub pines on the south side of Chicago arose a fairy city that hosted the exhibits of forty-six nations, a single exposition building said to seat three hundred thousand persons, and an amusement park ride built by George Ferris that could carry forty persons in each of thirty-six cars on a 250-foot-high revolving wheel.[17] Visitors were equally impressed by the real-world development a few miles up the lakefront in the city center. At twenty-one stories, the Masonic temple was the world's tallest building, a so-called skyscraper.

There was a tension between the fairy city of the exposition and the real city that surrounded it, a tension that persists to this day. Rural visitors from "downstate" (the portion of Illinois outside of Chicago and its suburban ring) were agog at the artificial White City but "afeared" of the perceived dangers and tumult of Chicago. Many Chicagoans, in fact, had already become eager for the tranquility of the country. In 1868, the urban planner Frederick Law Olmsted designed Riverside, west of Chicago, as a new community where families could enjoy the country while the breadwinner could take the train to his job downtown. Skyscraper and suburb created each other, said Cronon, and the railroad made both possible.[18]

By 1930, Chicago had 3.4 million inhabitants—almost half the state's total—and was the fourth-largest city in the world and the second largest (after New York) in the United States. By 1945, Chicago's population peaked at 3.6 million, as the suburban era began. Auto ownership doubled between 1945 and the early 1950s, and expressways were being built, foreshadowing massive suburban growth. According to Jensen, "Comfort, security, and the promise of continued progress . . . made the suburban era a time of placid complacency."[19]

With Chicago leading the way and many downstate communities still thriving with mixed industrial and agricultural economies, Illinois was a relatively strong state through most of the twentieth century. But driven as it was by commercial achievement and with a succession of local and statewide leaders who worked closely with and profited from business interests, Illinois became a place where the wealth of opportunity was matched only by the ruthlessness of those pursuing it.

The writer Nelson Algren, in his prose poem *Chicago: City on the Make*, identified two key characteristics of the culture that came to dominate Illinois. First, leadership and success were highly prized; and second, if the success involved a bit of shady dealing, so be it. "If he can get away with it I give the man credit," Algren said of a safe-blower. The same culture has always looked askance at weakness, brooking no sympathy for a woman reduced to prostitution or a jobless man numbing himself with beer. Warned Algren: "Wise up, Jim: it's a joint where the bulls and the foxes live well and the lambs wind up head-down from the hook."[20]

Downshift in the Economy

The state is characterized by its diversity. At the center of the nation, Illinois is sometimes referred to as a microcosm of the country. In 2007, for example, the Associated Press tagged Illinois "the most average state" in the nation, based on how closely the states matched national levels with regard to twenty-one demographic and economic factors. According to the AP, "Illinois' racial composition matches the nation's better than any other state. Education levels are similar, as are the mix of industry and the percentage of immigrants."[21]

Though average, perhaps, among the states, Illinois has throughout its history been significantly wealthier than the nation as a whole. This has made it easier to provide decent schools and good public universities than has been the case for poorer states, even if the poorer states tax their citizens more heavily than has Illinois. The state continues to have a big economy; Illinois's gross domestic product topped $1 trillion in 2022.[22] This would make Illinois about the seventeenth largest economy in the world, just ahead of Saudi Arabia, the Netherlands, and Switzerland.[23]

According to former state economic development director Jim Schultz, Illinois arguably ranks among the top three states in each of the six Rs he considers critical to economic development: rails, rivers, runways, roads, routers, and research. To illustrate, in addition to being the freight railroad hub of the nation, Chicago and Illinois boast 2,100 miles of interstate highway, more than any states other than California and Texas, which are much larger geographically. Go to any highway map and observe the dense webbing of interstate highways in Illinois.

Since World War II, however, Illinois has experienced a gradual yet persistent slowing in its rate of economic growth relative to the nation, which creates problems for elected officials who would like to fulfill the high expectations of citizens but find that their revenue stream cannot always keep up. Republicans tend to blame what they consider high taxes and strong labor unions for the relatively slow growth; Democrats retort that the Illinois economy has indeed been growing, but faster growth in recent decades in poorer states in the South and Southwest has been converging toward that of Illinois.

In fact, the relatively slow growth in the Illinois economy appears to roughly track the state's relatively slow growth in population. Figure 1.1 shows that on a per capita basis, Illinois income continues to be above that of the nation. Yet, as figure 1.2 reflects, Illinois's population has been growing more slowly than that of the nation.

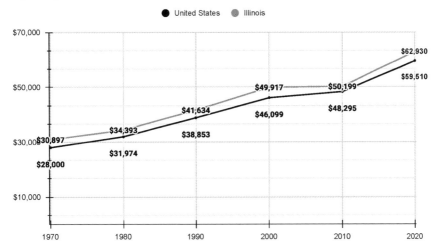

Per Capita Income, Illinois vs United States, 1970–2020

Figures adjusted for inflation to 2020 dollars

Figure 1.1. Per Capita Income. Source: Illinois Regional Economic Analysis Project (IL-REAP) with data provided by the U.S. Department of Commerce, Bureau of Economic Analysis, November 2021. Obtained October 11, 2022.

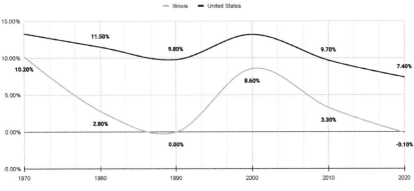

Illinois vs. United States Population

% change in population from decade to decade, 1970–2020

Source: "Historical Population Change Data, 1910–2020," U.S. Census Bureau, April 26, 2021

Figure 1.2. Illinois vs. U.S. Population. Note: Since the release of the 2020 census, a May 2022 report from the U.S. Census Bureau on the Post-Enumeration Survey revealed that the population of Illinois was undercounted by 1.97 percent.

INTO THE SUNSET

Figure 1.3. "Into the Sunset." Cartoon by Bill Campbell.

In 1958, per capita personal income in Illinois was 116.3 percent of the national average. This figure declined to 110.3 percent in 1970, and 105.8 in 2021.[24] Since 1990, total non-farm employment growth in Illinois has fallen behind that of both the United States and the rest of the Midwest. On a scale with a starting point of 100 in 1990, the U.S. economy reached 132 by 2016, and that of the Midwest (minus Illinois) reached 117, while Illinois stood at 113.[25]

Prosperity continues to elude much of rural Illinois. During the 1980s, jobs and wealth declined in rural western Illinois for the first time since the Great Depression. In 2019, the highest rate of poverty was not in Cook County, where Chicago is located (13 percent), but in Jackson County (25.4 percent), Alexander County (24 percent), both in deep southern Illinois, and McDonough County (23.3 percent) in the west central part of the state.[26] One measure of the economic desperation in small communities is their willingness to pursue jobs that would have been shunned in better times. In the 1960s a corrections department official would have been tarred, feathered, and run out of town if he had proposed building a prison in a community. By the 1980s, downstate communities were literally begging to be the sites for new prisons to hold Illinois's inmate population, which was burgeoning at the time.

Division by Demographics

"Illinois stands at the geo-historical center of the United States," declared Daniel Elazar, "crossed by the great waves of migration that spread settlements across the country in the late eighteenth and nineteenth centuries from the middle states, the South, and New England, reinforced by the great migrational streams from Europe in the nineteenth century and of African Americans, Latinos, and Asians in the twentieth."[27]

The diversity of Illinois is real and deep. For example, the classic "southern" movie *In the Heat of the Night*, featuring Sidney Poitier and Rod Steiger, was filmed almost entirely in the Illinois towns of Sparta and Chester because the moviemakers wanted a southern feel in an area that was close to a major airport, that in St. Louis. And Sparta and Chester are not even in deep southern Illinois!

At the other end of the state, on the Chicago Transit Authority train to O'Hare Airport a rider often hears more Spanish and Polish than English spoken by the passengers in this great entrepôt city for immigrants.

If politics in Illinois is a business, votes are the currency, and since its earliest days Illinois politics has been shaped by the demographics of the voting public. In 1858, senatorial candidate Abraham Lincoln gave most of his campaign speeches in central Illinois (and only one in Chicago), from Danville in the east to Carthage and Dallas City in the west. This made sense because nearly half of the state's population lived in the central third of the state.[28] The sympathies of voters in northern Illinois were clearly with the new Republican Party, and those of voters in southern Illinois were strongly with the Democrats. Central Illinois was mixed, and either party could win elections. Today, statewide candidates devote great effort to garnering coverage by the television stations based in Chicago, which reach two-thirds of all the households in Illinois. Candidates spend little, if any, time in Danville, Carthage, or Dallas City.

The demographic profile of Illinois has been shifting, often dramatically, since the 1840s, when immigrants fleeing famine or turmoil in Ireland, Germany, and the Scandinavian countries began to reach the state. For the whole of the nineteenth century, Germans made up the largest immigrant group in St. Louis as well as in Chicago and Illinois as a whole. By 1860, one-half of Chicago's burgeoning population was foreign-born, and by 1890, 79 percent of Chicagoans were born abroad or were children of immigrants.[29]

A decade later, the sources of immigration had shifted to Italy and Eastern Europe; people from those areas came in great numbers until quotas went into effect in the 1920s. Poles began pouring into Chicago around the turn of the century, and by 1920 they numbered almost five hundred thousand.[30] In 2020, it was estimated more than one million people of Polish descent were living in the city's metropolitan area, more than in Krakow, Poland's second largest city.[31]

The first Blacks were brought to the Illinois Territory as slaves. The state's first six governors were all slave owners at one time, and several had registered Black servants while in office.[32] The Northwest Ordinance of 1787 had banned slavery, but it had failed to ban its surrogate, registered servitude. The white folks in southern Illinois generally favored slavery and forced a compromise in the 1818 constitution that maintained the status quo for French slaves and indentured servants brought in during the territorial period.[33] Any future introduction of slavery was prohibited, with the exception that slaves could be used to mine salt at the salt springs near Shawneetown until 1825. The adoption in 1824 of a "Black code" effectively prevented free Blacks from settling in the state.[34]

Major settlement by Blacks did not begin until after the Civil War, and even then it grew slowly. In 1871, Chicago's Black neighborhood was three blocks wide and fifteen blocks long, with about twenty-five hundred residents.[35] But when, during World War I, severe labor shortages hampered production in Chicago factories, a large-scale migration from the South began. Between 1910 and 1920, about fifty thousand Blacks rode north on the Illinois Central Railroad and crowded into the expanding Black Belt, triggering the first of many waves of white flight. (Segregation was not limited to Chicago; even after World War II, Black state legislators were denied access to restaurants and hotel rooms, including rooms—supreme irony—at the Abraham Lincoln Hotel, in Lincoln's hometown of Springfield.) The expansion of the South Side Black Belt and, after another surge of migration during World War II, the growth of the West Side Black community proved politically important; the concentrated voting power resulted in the 1928 election of a Republican Black congressman, former Chicago alderman Oscar DePriest, and, by 1983, the election of Harold Washington as Chicago's first Black mayor.

Slow Growth Masks Increased Diversity

The population of Illinois has grown to an estimated 12,812,508 in 2020, although growth has been slow in recent decades.[36] (Since the release of the 2020 census, a May 2022 report from the U.S. Census Bureau on the Post-Enumeration Survey revealed that Illinois's population had actually been undercounted by 1.97 percent;[37] however, in 2022, the Census Bureau estimated that Illinois's population had dropped back to the 12.8 million range, so we stick with the 2020 official census.) Between 1970 and 2020, Illinois grew by 14 percent, while the population of the United States grew by 38 percent.[38] Figure 1.2 plots the relative population growth of our state and nation since 1970, confirming this slower growth by Illinois, and even showing that Illinois lost population between 2010 and 2020. This slow growth cannot be attributed to a lack of migration into the state, especially by Latino and other foreign-born immigrants, which has been substantial. As figure 1.4 shows, persons of Latino heritage tripled in number

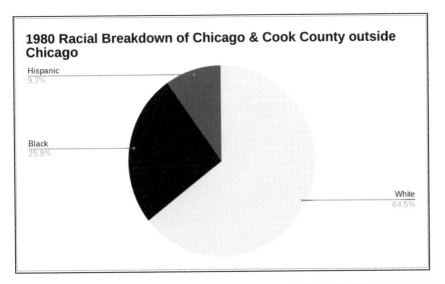

1980 Racial Breakdown of Chicago & Cook County outside Chicago

Hispanic
9.7%

Black
25.9%

White
64.5%

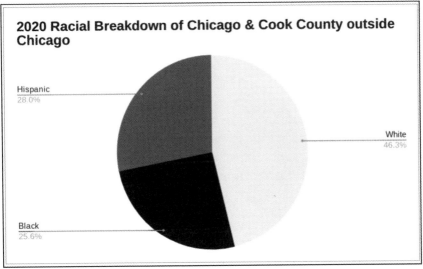

2020 Racial Breakdown of Chicago & Cook County outside Chicago

Hispanic
28.0%

White
46.3%

Black
25.6%

Figure 1.4. 1980 and 2020 Racial Breakdown Comparisons. Sources: "U.S. Hispanic Population by County, 1980," Pew Research Center; "Population Change, 1970 to 1980, by Race and Spanish Origin for the Chicago Metropolitan Statistical Area: Counties, Political Townships, Incorporated Places, and Community Areas in the City of Chicago," The Chicago Area Geographic Information Study, University of Illinois at Chicago Circle, June 1981; "Fact Sheet: Black Population Loss in Chicago," Great Cities Institute, University of Illinois at Chicago, July, 2019; U.S. Census Bureau, 1980 decennial census; "Our Changing Population: Kendall County, Illinois, 1980 and 2020," USA Facts, last updated 2022; "Shifting Population Trends in Chicago and Chicago Metro Area," Report for the MacArthur Foundation by William Scarborough, Amanda E. Lewis, and Ivan Arenas, Institute for Research on Race and Public Policy, University of Chicago, June 2022. Not included in Illinois population numbers are "other races," most of whom were counted as Asian & Pacific Islander in 1980, totaling 172,213. According to the U.S. Census Bureau, the U.S. population was undercounted by 1.2 percent in 1980. (continues)

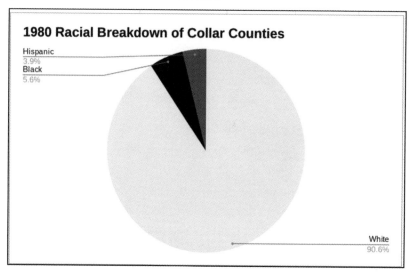

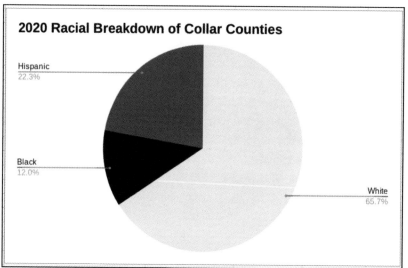

Figure 1.4. Continued

in Illinois between 1980 and 2020 from 636,000 to more than 2,242,000, going from 5.6 percent to 17.5 percent of the total population of the state.[39] Asians showed even faster growth rates, more than quintupling their numbers from 1980 to 2020, to more than 780,000.[40]

Instead, the growth has been slowed by a significant net outmigration of non-Hispanic whites in recent decades. For example, an estimated net outmigration of 700,000–900,000 whites occurred in the 1970s alone, and this outmigration continues.[41] (*Net migration* is the difference between the total number moving into a state and the total number moving out in the same period.) Indeed, over the past half century, Illinois has been importing residents from other countries and exporting them to other states, primarily to southern and Sunbelt states. In 1970, Illinois had 9.6 million whites, or 86 percent of the total population; as of 2020, that number had declined to 7.8 million, or 61 percent of the total population.[42]

In 1950, one in thirteen residents of the state belonged to so-called minority groups; by 2020, the ratio was more than one in three, with African Americans representing 14.7 percent, Latinos 18 percent, and Asians 6.1 percent.[43]

And the city of Chicago has been declining in actual population as well as its share of total state residents. In 1970, Chicago's population was 3,381,557, or 30 percent of the total state population; by 2020 that figure had declined to 2,746,388, or 21 percent of the total state population.[44]

Figure 1.4 shows significant rearrangement in population between 1970 and 2020 within the state's geopolitical regions: Chicago, the remainder of Cook County, the six suburban "collar counties," and the ninety-five "downstate" counties.

Between 1970 and 2020, the white share of population in Chicago declined from about two-thirds to one-third of the city's population, with Blacks and Latinos also each representing about one-third of the population. Cook County outside Chicago saw even more dramatic change in the period, from an almost all-white populace to one that is now only one-half white. The six suburban counties that ring Cook also saw major growth in Black and Latino populations.

Although the population of the remaining 95 of 102 counties, those known collectively as "downstate," has seen a slight increase since 1970, growing from 4,236,676 to 4,293,677 in 2020, growth has been slow compared with the rest of the state.[45] The white population downstate fell by more than half a million. Downstate has dropped from 38 percent to 34 percent of the total state population in fifty years.[46]

Generalizations and statistical trends tend to drain the color and texture from Illinois's rich mosaic of people from the world around. In the early 1970s, coauthor Nowlan was a state representative from a rural district in northwestern Illinois. He recalls enjoying *bagna cauda* ("hot bath") dipping sauce and *sumpanella* (a flat, tortilla-like bread) with the Italian Americans in Dalzell and Ladd, watching preparations for pigeon races at the Flemish-American Club in Kewanee, and enjoying late-night music at the Latino-Americano Club in Rock Falls.[47] Later, as a statewide candidate, he helped celebrate the birthday of Santa

Lucia (a Swedish holiday) in Galesburg in central Illinois, hoisted steins of beer with descendants of German immigrants in Belleville and Millstadt, east of St. Louis, watched bocce ball played by Italian Americans on the green along the commuter rail tracks in suburban Highwood (which in recent years has become heavily Latino), and marched with Blacks in the Bud Billiken Day parade on the South Side of Chicago.[48]

Diversity can be appreciated by looking at the languages spoken at home in Illinois. Figure 1.5 shows that in both Chicago-Cook County as well as in the surrounding collar counties, languages other than English are spoken in nearly one-third of all households.[49]

For ethnic whites in metropolitan Chicago, the melting pot metaphor applies fairly well. There are now more Irish, Italians, Germans, and Poles in the Chicago suburbs than in the city. Within the city, however, *mosaic*—with sharply etched lines separating the pieces—has often been a more apt term than *melting pot*.

Languages Spoken at Home in Chicago Collar Counties*, 2015–2019

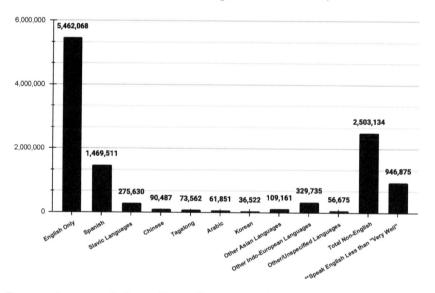

Figure 1.5. Languages Spoken at Home. Chart source: Chicago Metropolitan Agency for Planning (CMAP), Community Data Snapshot, Cook County, data drawn from 2015–2019 American Community Survey five-year estimates. Universe: Population five years and older. *Data drawn from CMAP region, which includes Cook, DuPage, Kane, Kendall, Lake, McHenry, and Will Counties. Note: For people who speak a language other than English at home, the ACS asks whether they speak English "very well," "well," "not well," or "not at all."

According to Gregory Squires and his coauthors, "In the city, race has come to be a far more significant characteristic for defining group membership and neighborhood residence than ethnicity."[50] As of 2020, seven of the city's poorest fifteen neighborhoods are at least 96 percent Black.[51] However, this is a decrease since 2006, when ten of the city's poorest fifteen neighborhoods were at least 94 percent Black. Since 2000, these Chicago neighborhoods have seen a significant decrease in their Black population, with a 15.4 percent decline in Humboldt Park, for example, which is now largely Latino.[52] Blacks now represent 29.2 percent of the population of Chicago—down from 37 percent in 2000—while Latinos comprise 28.6 percent of the city.[53]

Five-year estimates of median household property values in Chicago, 2015–2019, illustrate that the median worth of Black and Latino homes is significantly less than white homes. The median Black-owned home in 2019 was valued at $150,000; that for Latinos, $200,000; and for whites, $320,000.[54]

Population and Politics in Illinois's Three Regions

Caesar divided Gaul into three provinces, the better to govern it. Illinois political observers have traditionally divided the state into three regions, the better to understand it—Chicago, the suburban collar around the city, and the ninety-five downstate counties. However, because of the significant migration of Chicago's Blacks and Latinos from Chicago into nearby Cook County suburbs in recent decades, the authors believe it makes sense now to reframe the central urban region of Illinois from "Chicago" to that of "Chicago-Cook County," with the suburban "collar" region to now be the six counties that ring Cook (see figure 1.6).

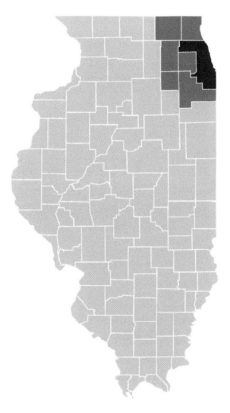

Figure 1.6. Geopolitical Regions of Illinois

Chicago-Cook County

Immigrant groups have brought different political needs and skills to Illinois. The Irish, the Poles, and the Italians brought less capital and education—and received less social acceptance—than did the English and the Germans who generally preceded them. The former three ethnic groups found, however, that democratic institutions offered opportunities for success and acceptance that were often denied them in business and the professions.

The Irish dominated Chicago politics from the Civil War, and especially since the time of the Kelly-Nash machine of the 1930s, until the election of African American mayor Harold Washington in 1983. They became skilled at sharing the rewards of power, and soon came to master Chicago politics after working their way up from jobs as canal diggers and policemen. They honed the art under Mayors Edward J. Kelly and Patrick Nash from 1933 to 1947, by sharing patronage first with other white ethnic groups and then with the city's growing Black population.

By 1940, Democratic ward committeeman William Dawson was the top Black political boss in the white-dominated Cook County Democratic Party. He was among those who urged the party to drop Mayor Martin J. Kennelly in 1955 and replace him with new party chairman Richard J. Daley. Dawson delivered five wards in the primary to put Daley over the top. Daley's majority of 125,000 votes over Democrat-turned-Republican Robert Merriam in the subsequent general election came largely from margins provided in Dawson's ward and four other Black wards.[55]

Daley became legendary following more than two decades as both chairman of the Cook County Democratic Central Committee (1953–76) and mayor (1955–76). He skillfully gathered immense political power over patronage, nominations for office, and policymaking in local, state, and federal government. Anyone who wanted one of the thirty thousand patronage jobs or hundreds of elective offices that he controlled had to go through the local Democratic ward committeeman and the mayor's office. In return, loyalty to the mayor and the Democratic Party was obligatory.

His son, Richard M. Daley (mayor 1987–2011), won his sixth four-year term as mayor of Chicago in 2007 with 71 percent of the vote and carried all fifty wards in a three-way race. He wielded political power almost as great as his father. Having eschewed the role of party leader, Daley drew power from the ability to award contracts for business with the city. Chicago's tax increment financing districts alone generate more than a half-billion dollars per year, and mayors direct the spending of that money with contractors who "appreciate" the mayors with large campaign contributions. Daley I tutored, and Daley II partnered with, former Illinois House Speaker Michael Madigan and Chicago alderman Edward Burke, both indicted for political corruption as this is written in 2023. Each served in office for more than half a century and together were undisputed primo leaders of the Chicago and statewide Democratic Party.

Always a distinct minority of the population in Illinois and in Chicago, Irish political leaders have been skilled at building coalitions, especially with Poles and Italians.[56] On arriving in Chicago, the Poles seemed to find boss-directed patronage organizations attractive. The political bosses welcomed immigrants and helped them. "Seemingly anyone could become a boss in America," writes Edward Kantowicz, in contrast to the feudal nobility caste in Poland to which peasants had no access. "Thus, American politics fulfilled economic, occupational, and psychological functions in 'Polonia' (Poland in America)."[57]

For many participants, Chicago politics has been a full-time profession rather than a part-time civic activity. During the years of machine politics, many hundreds of people did strictly political work (or no city work at all), although their city paycheck might have been for street-cleaning or an obscure desk job. Former U.S. judge Abner Mikva found this out when, as a college student in 1950, he called on the local Democratic ward committeeman: "I came in and said I wanted to help. Dead silence. 'Who sent you?' the committeeman said. I said, 'Nobody.' He said, 'We don't want nobody nobody sent.' Then he said, 'We ain't got no jobs.' I said, 'I don't want a job.' He said, 'We don't want nobody that don't want a job. Where are you from, anyway?' I said, 'University of Chicago.' He said, 'We don't want nobody from the University of Chicago.'"[58] Mikva would later learn that patronage and insider contracts were frequently used tools that created webs of fierce political loyalty and rigid hierarchical management.

Suburban Growth but Fragmented Power

Metropolitan Chicago as defined by the U.S. Census Bureau in 2020 was a 9.6-million-person megalopolis stretching from the business parks and hamlets of southern Wisconsin to the steel mills of Gary, Indiana. Since this book is about Illinois, we are limiting our admittedly blurry boundaries of metropolitan Chicagoland to the seven counties of Cook, Lake, McHenry, Kane, DuPage, Will, and Kendall. But as homes and businesses spiral outward, residents of the Rockford and Kankakee regions (to the northwest and south of Chicago, respectively) have begun to wonder when their open spaces will be absorbed by what we have termed the "metropolitan frontier."

The hallmarks of the expanding metro frontier are independence, space, a sense of security, lack of congestion, cleaner air, and a "back-to-the-land" appeal. For first-time home buyers, who make up half of the suburban market, the largest and most affordable lots are found on the fringe of the region.[59] The outward trek generally moves along the interstate highway corridors that radiate from Chicago almost as neatly as bicycle spokes: I-57, I-55, I-88, I-90, and I-94.

The formerly rural Huntley, located in McHenry County, has evolved from farm town to boom town. From a population of a little more than 2,000 in 1990, the community grew to 27,740 in 2020. Naperville, in the center of the region, had only 5,000 residents after World War II, yet expanded to 149,540 in 2020. Farther south in Will County, the quiet, attractive town of Frankfort saw its population double in the 1980s to 7,844 and reach 20,296 in 2020.[60]

While Chicago and Cook County experienced a decrease in their population by over 160,000 between 2000 and 2020, the other six suburban Illinois counties grew substantially in the period.[61] The population of Will County has increased 38.6 percent between 2000 and 2020, and Kendall County's jumped 141.8 percent in the same time frame. The six suburban counties (Lake, McHenry, DuPage, Kane, Will, and Kendall) have 3.3 million residents as of 2020, double the six-county population in 1970.[62]

Suburban Blacks and Latinos tend, however, to be concentrated, and somewhat separated by color and income. As suburbanites with the means to do so reach farther out on the collar to fulfill their dream of a single-family home with a spacious yard, Latinos often move behind them into the aging suburbs adjacent to Chicago and to older industrial cities farther out, such as Aurora and Elgin in Kane County. In 1990, Cicero, which abuts Chicago's West Side, was 37 percent Latino; in 2003, the figure had climbed to 77 percent; by 2020, 89 percent. In 1990, Aurora and Elgin had populations that were, respectively, 23 and 19 percent Latino. By 2020, they were each nearly half Latino, at 43 percent and 47 percent.[63]

Low-income suburban Blacks tend to be concentrated just south of Chicago in communities such as Calumet City (pop. 36,000), where they made up 77 percent of the residents in 2020; Dolton (pop. 20,705), 92 percent; and Harvey (pop. 15,793), 65 percent.[64] Nearly 50 percent of the total households in Dolton and Calumet City, and 65 percent of households in Harvey, have incomes of less than $50,000.

Meanwhile, many middle-class Black families have also been congregating in suburbs to the south of Chicago. Five of the top nine predominantly Black municipalities in the United States that have more than 80 percent Black home-ownership are located in the south suburbs. The five are Olympia Fields, South Holland, Flossmoor, Matteson, and Lynwood. Most of these suburbs had been majority white in 1990.[65] "Blacks are moving for the same reasons as white families—better schools, less crime, more space," according to the late political observer Paul Green. The suburban settlement appears to be perpetuating the same patterns of segregation that separated poor Blacks, middle-class Blacks, and whites in Chicago. "The south suburbs will become an extension of the old south side of Chicago," averred Green.[66] This concentration makes it easier for Democrats to craft suburban legislative districts in which their candidates, often minorities now, can win.

The suburbs appear to be even more diverse in religious terms than in racial terms. One major survey found that Catholics outnumber Protestants in the collar region.[67] Nineteen parishes in the suburbs offer masses in Polish.[68] There are nearly 300 Christian churches in DuPage County, in addition to 17 Hindu temples, 12 Muslim mosques, 10 Korean Christian churches, 13 Chinese Christian churches, 3 Vietnamese Christian churches, and at least 1 Taiwanese Christian church, 1 Quaker meetinghouse, and 1 Buddhist temple, among others.[69]

With the emergence of the suburbs and their demands for a fair share of resources, the politics of redistribution may dominate state politics in the coming years. John Foster and John Jackson of the Paul Simon Public Policy Institute at Southern Illinois University found, using 2013 data compiled by the Legislative Research Unit of the Illinois General Assembly, that for every dollar Cook County residents sent to the State of Illinois in various taxes, Cook received back about 90 cents in state services such as education and social services. The five collar counties (the analysis did not include Kendall County, as this book does elsewhere) received only about 53 cents back for every tax dollar contributed. The "big winners," we might say, were the ninety-six counties downstate, which received $1.69 for every dollar the region sent to the state.[70] This should be expected because there is more wealth per capita in the collar counties than in the other regions, and government policies tend to redistribute wealth from richer to poorer communities.

Erosion of Downstate

The first region of the state to rise to power historically is the weakest player on the field today. In the twenty-first century, much of the downstate region is struggling to regain economic and political health. Boasting only five cities of more than one hundred thousand people, downstate's checkerboard landscape is dotted with 1,456 mostly small towns such as South Beloit (population 7,932), on the Wisconsin line, and, four hundred miles to the south, Cairo (population 1,884), south of Paducah, Kentucky. Cairo has seen a 61 percent loss in population since 1990.[71] The poverty rate in Alexander County, home of Cairo, was 24.2 percent in 2019, higher than the 13 percent rate of Cook County and more than twice that of the state average of 11.4 percent.[72]

In between is the desperately poor, isolated Black community of East St. Louis. Cutting diagonally across rich farmland from the St. Louis area toward Chicago, along old Route 66, is a string of nearly all-white market towns, among them Litchfield, Lincoln, and Pontiac. Indeed, there is little sense of a single downstate, other than as a geographic identifier and for longstanding geopolitical policymaking and analysis.

The increasing concentrations of population, wealth, and media in Chicago and the collar counties have drained downstate of the influence and prominence it enjoyed in an earlier era. Even the state capital of Springfield is less visible. The center of gravity, politically, has shifted from downstate, which was dominant until World War I, to the metropolitan regions. Politicians must go to Chicago if they want major television coverage, because the Chicago stations do not staff the Capitol pressroom.

Meetings of statewide public commissions and advisory councils are more likely to take place in Chicago's Loop than in Springfield.[73] An example: from 2011 to 2014 coauthor Nowlan was a member, then chair, of the Illinois Executive Ethics Commission. The ethics panel held twelve meetings a year; eleven meetings were in Chicago and one was in Springfield. This is not unusual, given the population distribution in the state, and travel convenience. Members, including downstaters, often find it easier to gather in or near Chicago. Upon election in 2002, Governor Rod Blagojevich announced that he would continue to reside in Chicago, rather than occupy the executive mansion in Springfield, striking a psychological blow to the capital and to downstate generally. Since then, most governors have lived in Chicago rather than in Springfield.

Simply put, downstate has been "shrinking" relative to the collar county region, in population, political strength, economic wealth, and media visibility.

Regional Conflict

For all the variety within each region, and the policy values shared by the regions, there are important economic distinctions in the twenty-first century that provide powerful political justification for perceiving and acting on regional differences. The contrasts in wealth generate periodic calls from each one for its fair share of the state's largesse. This has become a serious issue that divides the regions.

The formula for allocating state aid to local schools provides a good illustration. Collar county legislators argue that their voters are already paying much more than other regions in state taxes and getting much less back. School politics pits the suburbs against the downstate schools, with many suburban lawmakers resisting an income tax-property tax swap because their suburbs would be net losers and downstate residents would be net gainers.[74] Downstate and Chicago legislators retort that their schoolchildren are getting less financial support per pupil from all sources than are the suburban children (true, generally speaking). At the heart of the problem is a school funding structure based heavily on local property taxes rather than on major state financial aid.

In 2017, the state enacted the Evidence-Based Funding Formula. It looks at dozens of factors such as the number of English language learners and special education teachers to come up with an "adequacy target" of how much the state believes a school should spend. The hope is that over time, the resource inequities between property tax-poor and property tax-rich districts will be reduced significantly through increased state funding for low-resource local schools.[75]

In the 1960s, when the University of Illinois created a major new campus in Chicago, downstate leaders insisted, successfully, on a new campus in Edwardsville for Southern Illinois University. More recently, in 2007, the Downstate Democratic Caucus in the Illinois legislature declared that there would be no state budget until rate relief was provided for Ameren electric utility customers (Ameren serves central and southern Illinois). And that's the way it worked out, with Ameren customers winning about $1 billion in rate relief. In 2009, Chicago Democratic state senators tried to reverse the historic road fund split of 55 percent for downstate and 45 percent for the Chicago region. "That split is closer to the collective heart of downstate politics than anything else," observed Rich Miller.[76] Downstate senators from both parties rebuffed the challenge to the split, but the issue will be back.

Single regions are, however, not always able to achieve their objectives. For example, in 2007–08, when Chicago and suburban leaders pushed for new taxation for regional mass transit, downstate lawmakers demanded, unsuccessfully, a highway and schools construction program intended largely for downstate.

In summary, regional political differences result largely from self-interest, differences in wealth, and strong perceptions that the other regions are out for themselves. And as is discussed in chapters 2 and 3 on political power and elections, as of 2023, downstate had become largely a Republican, minority party enclave and metropolitan Chicago a dominant, heavily Democratic super-region. Political struggle and conflict across the regions of Illinois will continue. In chapter 2, we explore this struggle and conflict, which are, after all, what politics and government are all about.

2

POWER AND INFLUENCE
IN ILLINOIS POLITICS

In the spring of 2020 the general consensus among practitioners and observers of Illinois politics was that the most powerful politician in the state was House Speaker Michael J. Madigan. Madigan entered politics under the sponsorship of legendary Chicago Mayor Richard J. Daley. He was elected a Chicago Democratic ward committeeman in 1969 and then a member of House of Representatives in 1970. In 1975 he became part of the Democrats' leadership team after they took control of the House. After Daley's death in 1976, Madigan began to build a power base in Springfield. The Democrats drew the legislative maps for the 1982 elections and Madigan became Speaker after they won a majority. He would hold that office for thirty-eight of the next forty years.

Madigan built his power by centralizing control over the legislative process and the administration of the House in the Speaker's office. As he increased his control in Springfield, he also developed the capacity to fund and run campaigns for his members out of his office by fundraising through a caucus committee. He also added legislative staff who provided political support for members during the session and took leaves of absence to work on campaigns during election time. In essence Madigan took on the functions of a political party for his members: recruiting candidates, raising money, and running campaigns and then controlling the process and setting the agenda when the legislature was in session. In 1998 he also became chair to the state Democratic party, adding to his political power and fundraising capacity.

His success in keeping the Democrats in the majority and his control over the flow of legislation attracted financial support from the major interest groups that supported the Democratic party, particularly private and public sector unions. Because of his power and the majorities he helped elect, he also received large contributions from business and professional associations and major corporations that wanted to maintain the status quo and have access to power.[1]

Going into the 2019–20 election cycle the future looked bright for the Speaker in spite of a number of ethical controversies involving his staff and Democratic legislators. But a revolt among some of his members against his tight control of the House gained support after he became a target of the U.S. Department of Justice in a major political corruption investigation during the summer of 2020. Late in the year it became clear that he would not be able to gain the support of a majority of the Democratic caucus to retain his office when the new General Assembly convened in January of 2021. In spite of retaining a supermajority in the House in the 2020 election, supporting a major progressive legislative package sponsored by the legislative Black caucus, and retaining the strong backing of his union supporters, he was forced to suspend his effort to be reelected Speaker. Early in the spring of 2021 he resigned from the legislature. Madigan's story illustrates how an individual can build and exercise political power successfully over time. It also shows the limits of power and how quickly it can slip away.[2]

Defining Power, Influence, and Authority

Political power, influence, and authority are exercised within the context of a governmental system. The United States is a representative democracy with a written constitution that establishes liberal democratic institutions (i.e., rule of law, individual rights, due process, fair and free elections, and orderly transfer of power). Federal and state governments operate in a federal system where the national government is constrained by both the U.S. Constitution and the separation of powers between the executive, legislative, and judicial branches. State governments are constrained by the rights guaranteed by the U.S. Constitution, federal laws under the supremacy clause of the U.S. Constitution, and limits and prohibitions within their own state constitutions.

In government, public policy is made by people with authority taking public actions. This is an interpersonal process where interactions allow for the exercise of power or influence to affect the actions taken by those with authority. Authority is the legal right to make a binding decision within the scope of a person's authority. Power is the ability to control the actions of others to your benefit. Influence is the ability to persuade a person to make a choice that is to your benefit.

Political authority is granted to public officials as a function of their holding an elected or appointed public office. This gives them constitutional or statutory authority to make specific decisions.

Political power is the ability to make a person act in ways that further your political and personal goals. Public officials, interest groups, political groups, corporate entities, and single individuals can acquire political power. But the exercise of power takes place through interactions between individuals. Power does not respect the hierarchy of authority. Elected officials can exercise power over interest groups, but the converse also happens. In a given situation power can reside with an elected or unelected official, a party official, an interest group, a corporation, or an individual. Political power in action means that elected and appointed political actors, interest groups, political party organizations, corporations, or private individuals do what you want when asked because they believe that you can help or hurt their ability to achieve their political goals or personal goals. Exercising political power to achieve outcomes leads to acquiring more of the attributes of power. Failure to successfully exercise power diminishes the power of the political actor.

Political influence is the ability to persuade a person or group to make a voluntary choice that favors your political goals. Both individuals and groups can exercise political influence. Like the exercise of political power, the exercise of political influence is personal and interactive. Political influence is acquired by aggregating the same kind of resources that are necessary to gain political power. These resources allow you to gain access to those you want to influence. Access creates opportunities for persuasion. Over time you can build credibility and trust. The key difference between power and influence is the element of choice in the influence relationship.

Political power and influence are acquired by aggregating resources such as:

- winning elections;
- holding positions of authority;
- support from political allies;
- support from interest groups;
- support of political party organization;
- the ability to make campaign contributions;
- control over the distribution of campaign contributions after they have been received;

- large numbers of organized supporters who are politically engaged;
- large numbers of unorganized supporters who can be mobilized;
- being able to direct any or all of the above to help candidates win elections; and
- credibility and trust.

The distinction between the exercise of power and the exercise of influence in politics lies in the perception of the individual or group who initiates the interaction and perception of the individual or group who is the object of the interaction. Influence interactions have some element of voluntary choice on the part of the individual or group who is going to take an action. Pure power interactions do not. In reality there is a great deal of ambiguity in most political interactions. Very few of them qualify as exercises of pure power or pure influence.

People and groups can exercise political influence but not have political power. The reform groups that were able to get contribution limits signed into law in 2009 achieved an outcome that went further than the Speaker of the House and Senate president wanted. The reform groups had influence, but no one would characterize them as powerful.

Conversely, referring to Michael Madigan as the influential Speaker of the House or Richard J. Daley as the influential mayor of Chicago hardly seems adequate. "Powerful" is a term usually reserved for the most successful political groups and actors over time. In that context, power and influence are instrumental concepts, related but distinct ways of achieving political goals.

Personal political power and influence change over time. They can be limited or enhanced by elections, circumstances, and time. The most remarkable thing about the power of Richard J. Daley and Michael Madigan may not be the amount of power they were able to acquire, but how long they were able to maintain it. It is incredibly rare for any public official to be the most important actor in a state political system for ten years, yet alone twenty or thirty years. Elected public officials in Illinois have to renew their power every two or four years. Daley and Madigan were never in danger of losing the public offices that provided the foundation of their power through an election. But the political party system that sustained Daley was breaking down at the time of his death. Only a shadow of that system still exists in Illinois. Corruption and ethical scandals in the legislature and the growing electoral independence of Chicago and suburban Democratic legislators in his caucus and their ties to ideological or racial/ethnic identity groups presented growing challenges to Madigan's control of the House before the criminal charges he faces became public. In light of this, as discussed earlier, he concluded that he could not win reelection as Speaker and abandoned his candidacy.

Political Authority, Power, and Influence

Government Officials

Elected and appointed public officials have governmental authority to take official actions by virtue of their office. People with governmental authority have the ability to act within the scope of their authority. Their authority is also a resource that can be used to build and exercise political influence and political power. Authority can be a source of influence or power if a specific grant of authority gives the public official discretion in their official actions. The clerk renewing your license plates, when presented with the proper documentation and payment, does not have a choice. Legislators have a choice in how or if they vote. A legislator can impact the behavior of another legislator, an interest group, or a governor by threatening to give or withhold a vote on an important roll call. Elected officials in the state executive and legislative branches have the most important authority and the most discretion in how they can act. This gives them the strongest opportunity to use their authority to exercise influence and power.

A note on judges: In Illinois elected public officials include trial court, appellate court, and Supreme Court judges. Judges have discretion in exercising their authority, but that exercise is not transactional in the same way it is for other elected officials. While it does occur, the transactional application of power or influence to affect a decision by a judge is contrary to the rule of law and antithetical to the role that judges play within a liberal democracy.

The formal authority granted to the governor under the state constitution in Illinois is considered one of the strongest of any state. Illinois governors have broad authority to manage the executive branch of government. They also have authority in the legislative process to sign or veto legislation. The governor has the greatest opportunity to build and exercise influence and power of any elected official in the state. It is hard not to exercise some amount of influence and power as an Illinois governor. Yet only two of the past eight governors completed two or more terms in office. Only former governors Richard B. Ogilvie, James R. Thompson, and Jim Edgar are widely regarded as strong, effective leaders. Being elected governor of the state of Illinois does not guarantee success at furthering one's agenda.

The authority of the other statewide elected officials (attorney general, comptroller, treasurer, and secretary of state) is much more limited in scope. They also have no authority within the legislative process. In the height of the patronage era statewide officers had jobs to distribute in addition to their official duties, but those days are gone or at least significantly diminished. Among the other four statewide offices, the attorney general's office offers the greatest opportunity to build and exercise influence and power. In addition to representing the state in legal matters, the attorney general can choose how they approach the office. Lisa Madigan was elected attorney general for the first time promising to be the "people's lawyer."

The Speaker of the House and the Senate president who lead the majority caucuses in each chamber are the key officials in the legislature. While their offices and procedures for their elections are set out in the state constitution, their authority to control the legislative process and set the agenda within their chambers is established by rules adopted at the beginning of each legislative session. Beginning in the early 1990s, legislative leaders have used their positions and political power to centralize control of the legislature in their offices and limit the ability of legislative committees, committee chairs, and rank-and-file members to acquire the resources necessary to independently exercise influence and power. Because of the one-party dominance by the Democrats in the legislature, leaders and members from the minority party are less relevant.

The mayors of large cities can be important actors locally. The same is true for county board chairs and some elected county officers such as states attorneys. At one time the mayor of Chicago in the person of Richard J. Daley was considered one of, if not the most, powerful politicians in Illinois, rivaling the governor. Part of Daley's power was rooted in his position as mayor, but the heart of his power came from his position as the chair of the Cook County Democratic party.[3] The mayor of Chicago and the president of the Cook County Board, as the leaders of by far the largest units of local government in Illinois, are significant figures in Illinois politics. But none of the recent holders of these offices has been able to consolidate control over the local government and political party organizations to the extent that Daley did at the height of his power.

Appointed agency officials at the state and local level generally exercise influence or power as an extension of the power of the governors, mayors, or county boards that appointed them. Agency directors can occasionally become significant political actors within a narrow sphere of influence because of their statutory authority and the importance of the mission of their agency or the size of the budgets they administer. During the height of the patronage era, the director of the Illinois Department of Transportation was the de facto patronage chief for the governor's political party and a player in his own right. But those days are over as parties have grown ever weaker and overt patronage has been largely eliminated.

Statutory authority is the foundation for building power. After the 2022 election, the governor and the other four statewide officers were all Democrats. The Democrats held supermajorities in the House and the Senate in the legislature. In addition, the mayor of Chicago, a supermajority on the Chicago city council, the president and a supermajority of the Cook County board were all Democrats. The Democrats also had majorities on the boards of the three collar counites that border on Cook County. In terms of governmental authority, Democrats are in a dominant position to build and exercise power and influence in Illinois politics.

Private Sector Interests—General Considerations

Private sector interests lack governmental authority. Individuals, groups, formal associations, and corporations that want to have an impact on political decisions have to convince or coerce people with authority to act in the ways they want. Private sector interests often organize formally into interest groups. These are private organizations with public identities, governance and decision-making structures, and memberships that exist over time to influence public policy on behalf of their members through interactions with legislators, governors, and other statewide elected officials. They form political action committees (PACs) to engage in election activities by raising money and making campaign contributions in pursuit of their policy interests. But they are not political parties, which are organized to win elected office and control governments. Nor do they have official status within the electoral system that parties have.

Many private interests exercise significant power and influence in Illinois politics. They are able to do so because they have some combination of the following factors, which applied strategically are resources that translate into power and influence:

- the ability to make large campaign contributions;
- the ability to maintain a year-round lobbying presence in Springfield;
- strong visible support from the governor or another statewide elected officials;
- strong visible support from legislative leaders or groups of legislators;
- large memberships that are politically active;
- members who are influential in the state or their communities;
- the capacity to communicate through the news media and social media to generate attention and support for the issues they are promoting or opposing;
- core issues that generate strong support among the public and generate wide spread media attention.

Interest groups, corporations, and individuals pursue a variety of strategies to achieve their political goals. An "inside" lobbying strategy focuses on lobbying legislators, the governor, and state agency personnel directly, seeking access and building relationships that create the opportunity to exercise influence. If a group has the resources, it may form a PAC to make campaign contributions. The act of forming a political action committee and raising funds to make contributions or to fund public relations activities is an indication of a group's strength and organization. Even modest contributions signal support or acknowledge past actions. Delivering a check at a fundraiser creates an opportunity to build a relationship.

A status quo–oriented contribution strategy focuses on contributions to incumbent legislators who are supportive. The objective is to reinforce inside direct lobbying by increasing access. The Associated Beer Distributors of Illinois is an example of a group that used a direct lobbying strategy combined with a status quo contribution strategy while keeping a very low public profile.

An aggressive election-oriented strategy is an "outside" strategy in contrast to an inside strategy of direct lobbying. The goal is to increase the number of supporters in the legislature or help put a supporter in the governor's office by actively engaging in contested elections. This takes the financial resources to make significant contributions to incumbents in contested primaries or general election contests and significant contributions to challengers in contested elections. If a group has a large active membership that is politically engaged, they will also work on campaigns directly with volunteers. Personal PAC, a group that advocates for reproductive rights, is an example of an interest group that uses campaign contributions and its ability to mobilize voters and influence elections as its primary lobbying strategy.

Private sector interests also pursue outside strategies that focus on shaping public opinion. They will work through the news media and social media to generate attention and support for their positions on issues. This can be a secondary strategy in support of established direct lobbying and contribution strategies. For groups without financial resources or large memberships, this is their primary strategy, which lays the foundation for direct contact lobbying. The goal is to attain visibility and credibility, which will translate into access, which will provide the opportunity to build relationships and exercise influence.

As will be described below, the Illinois Education Association (IEA) is an example of an interest group that uses inside direct lobbying combined with a status quo–oriented contribution strategy, an aggressive election strategy, and a strong media presence to maximize its influence. Political reform groups, also as will be described later in the chapter, used outside media strategies to build support and viability, which provided the access to legislators and the governor, which provided the opportunities to pursue inside direct lobbying in pursuit of the policy goal of contribution limits.

While there is overlap, a major distinction between types of private sector interests is a group that has an economic focus and represents established economic interests and one with a policy or ideological focus. Another important distinction is between interests that seek to maintain the status quo and operate in a defensive posture and groups that want to change the status quo and operate in an offensive posture. Economic interest groups are primarily status quo–oriented, while policy or ideological interest groups are primarily change-oriented.

Economic Interest Groups

The most powerful/influential interest groups in Illinois are those representing economic interests. The primary categories are labor unions, business associations and individual corporations, and professional associations and firms.

In 2023 the strongest interest group in Illinois politics was organized labor. It is not a monolith. There are policy differences between private and public sector unions, between trade unions and service employee unions, and between public safety employee unions and teachers unions. But on their core issues, labor is united around the right to organize and bargain collectively with their employers. They contribute the most money to Illinois politics of any of the private sector categories. Their lobbyists are present in Springfield full time. They have a large number of members and those members are very politically active. They are organized at the local level and at the state level. Historically strong, the relationship between labor unions and the state Democratic party has become even stronger since 2002, with the Democrats holding majorities in both chambers and electing three of last four governors.

The key trade unions are those for the operating engineers (IUOE), the laborers, the plumbers and pipefitters, the electrical workers (IBEW), and the carpenters. The key teachers' unions are the Illinois Education Association (IEA) and the Illinois Federation of Teachers (IFT) with its largest affiliate, the Chicago Teachers Union (CTU). The key service employee unions are the service employees (SEIU) and the food and commercial workers (UFCW). The key public employee unions are the state, county, and municipal employees (AFSCME) and the firefighters unions.

In the 2021–22 election cycle the operating engineers union contributed $18.6 million to legislative and statewide candidate committees or state, legislative, and local party committees, while the laborers contributed $16.5 million. In addition, six more unions contributed between $3.9 million and $6.3 million, while four more contributed between $1.0 million and $2.1 million.[4]

Business and professional interests exercise strong influence in Illinois politics. But compared to twenty years ago they are much more diversified and collectively much weaker in relation to labor unions. These changes are indicative of the changes in the Illinois economy. We have been moving toward a service-based economy and away from a manufacturing economy. The e-commerce revolution has diminished the traditional retail brick-and-mortar economy. The changing nature of healthcare delivery and financing decisions have elevated the importance of nursing homes, hospitals, and health insurance companies and diminished the importance of healthcare providers. Changes in communication technology have increased the importance of wireless providers and cable companies. Energy production has become more diversified while distribution is more consolidated.

The dominance of the Democrats in the legislature and statewide offices results in business groups and professional groups being more bipartisan in their contributions and lobbying efforts than would be the case if the situation were reversed. In recent election cycles contributions from business interests favored Democrats over Republicans. Much of this reflects the fact that these groups want access to power, and the Democrats have been in power.

In the 2021–22 election cycle the top contributing business or professional group was the Illinois Association of Realtors at $4.2 million, followed at $3.9 million by the Health Care Council of Illinois, which represents nursing homes. In addition, the Illinois Health and Hospital Association contributed $1.5 million, Ameren (an energy corporation) $1.1 million, and the Associated Beer Distributors of Illinois $1.1 million. Five additional business interests gave more than $500,000.

The leading general business groups are the Illinois Chamber of Commerce, the Chicagoland Chamber of Commerce, and the Illinois Retail Merchants Association. The leading manufacturing groups are the Illinois Manufacturers Association and the Pharmaceutical Research and Manufactures of America. In communications, the key actors are AT&T and Comcast, a cable communication company. In finance the key groups are the Illinois Bankers Association and the Credit Union Association. Before 2020, Commonwealth Edison was a key contributor in the energy sector. It has taken a very low profile since it was named in political corruption indictments linked to Speaker Madigan; the company later signed a deferred prosecution agreement with the U.S. Attorney's office.

In terms of interest groups representing professionals, one stands out: the Illinois Trial Lawyers Association, along with a group of major trial lawyer law firms. They exercise enormous influence within their areas of interest because of their campaign contributions ($4.5 million) and their close association with Democratic legislative leaders and members. The Illinois State Medical Society is no longer a top-twenty group in terms of campaign contributions, but it still exercises major influence in areas of medical practice. Other prominent health professional groups represent dentists, nurses, and optometrists. In the finance sector, the most prominent professional associations are insurance agent/financial advisor groups and the Illinois CPA Society.

Policy Interest Groups

Policy interest groups can promote a single policy issue such as reproductive rights (Personal PAC) or charter schools (Illinois Network of Charter Schools, INCS). They can have a common set of related policy interests such as political ethics, campaign finance, and redistricting reform (Illinois Campaign for Political Reform and CHANGE Illinois). They also can have an overarching ideological focus such as economic liberty or social conservative values (Liberty Principles PAC). A signature characteristic of these types of groups are highly visible and often contentious efforts to promote or oppose major changes in the status quo.

Since the adoption of contributions limits in 2010 some policy interest groups have chosen to form independent expenditure committees as the way they use money to influence policy. The now defunct Liberty Principals PAC provides an example of this kind of strategy. It promoted economic liberty/social conservative ideology by recruiting and funding candidates, primarily for the legislature, sometimes working with Republican party and legislative leaders and sometimes against them. Primarily funded by billionaire Richard Uihlein, Liberty Principles began backing legislative candidates for the 2014 election through its independent expenditure committee and were very active in the 2016 and 2018 election cycles. Overall, the group spent more than $25 million. After a number of election failures Uihlein closed the committee in early 2019.

Policy interest groups also function as policy think tanks producing data and analysis in support of policy proposals and as public watchdogs monitoring public spending and political corruption. The Illinois Policy Institute or the Center for Tax and Budget Accountability (CTBA) are examples of the former, while the Better Government Association (BGA) is an example of the latter.

Policy interest groups are often engaged in direct conflict with other policy groups or with economic interest groups. INCS is primarily funded by a small number of wealthy donors. It has made $1.6 million in campaign contributions and independent expenditures in the 2021–22 election cycle promoting policies that would expand charter schools. The IEA and the IFT/CTU, its main opposition, contributed $10.5 million over the same time period. While Governor Bruce Rauner was a proponent of school choice, Governor JB Pritzker is not. Both sides of the issue lobby the legislature and work on legislation as the school choice groups look to gain an advantage within the current law or increase the opportunity to create more charter schools.

Personal PAC is a pro-reproductive rights group that pursues an aggressive election strategy. It made $2.5 million in campaign contributions over the past three election cycles toward legislative races. It also contributed $2.2 million to the Democratic candidates in two State Supreme Court races in 2022. Prolife groups rely on grassroots campaigns to influence elections and spend comparatively very little on direct contributions. Both groups focus on electing supporters and defeating opponents rather than lobbying undecided legislators, if there are any.

There are currently active policy interest groups in a number of areas. They generally exist in tandem around a policy conflict. There are policy interest groups promoting gun rights and gun control, LGBTQ rights and social conservative values, and prolife and prochoice groups. Some policy interest groups are in conflict with economic interest groups. Environmental groups are often in conflict with energy groups promoting oil, coal, and natural gas.

Interest Group Power and Influence: The IEA

For as long as there have been comprehensive digital records (seventeen election cycles beginning in 1989) the political action committee for the Illinois Education Association (IEA) has never been ranked outside the top ten groups in contributions to legislative elections, often ranking number one. In recent years combined contributions from trade unions have outpaced those from teacher unions, while contributions from the Illinois Federation of Teachers (IFT) and the Chicago Teachers Union (CTU), its largest affiliate, have reached parity with those from the IEA. Still, the IEA stands out as a model for how an interest group can successfully influence elections and policy to achieve its political goals over time.

Although the organization dates back to the 1850s, the modern IEA took shape in 1970 when it was reorganized to put teachers rather than administrators in control of the organization. Shortly thereafter the IEA organized a political action fund to raise money for political activity in elections and lobbying. The IEA has a large membership, representing 135,000 members. Those members are broadly distributed throughout downstate Illinois and the northeastern suburbs.

A majority of all legislative districts contain active IEA organizations. The IEA has a long history of endorsing legislative candidates who take pro-education positions and then actively working in their campaigns. While most of its endorsed candidates are Democrats, the IEA endorses candidates that it considers pro-education regardless of party. The IEA raises huge sums of money from its members and makes direct contributions to legislative candidates. In the 2021–22 election cycle those contributions totaled $5.3 million. Having legislators elected with IEA support strengthens the IEA's ability to lobby the legislature for policy legislation and funding. The IEA also has a presence in statewide races, ballot initiatives, and local elections for school boards and other offices.

In Springfield, the IEA funds a large professional lobbying organization with a year-round presence. Its staff brings policy expertise and political experience to their efforts. The IEA also uses its local members back in the districts to lobby legislators when the legislature is not in session. The IEA teams with the IFT/CTU on education policy and education funding issues. It has a long history of working with broad coalitions of labor organizations. In 1984 the IEA was a key partner in the effort to enact laws establishing collective bargaining rights for public employees and for teachers. In 2013 it joined with other teacher and public employee unions in the fight to protect the public pension benefits of retirees and current employees. The combination of campaign contributions, election volunteers, lobbying in the district and lobbying in Springfield, and working with effective lobbying coalitions makes the IEA a highly successful interest group with a very long record of advancing the interests of its members.

Lobbyists

People who are engaged in trying to influence the actions of government through direct, face-to-face contact are commonly referred to as lobbyists. In a generic sense, if you contact your legislator for a meeting to discuss a problem and a possible legislative solution you are is engaging in lobbying. You are trying to gain access to a political actor in order to provide information and to persuade the legislator to support a position or direct action that will help advance or kill a specific bill. Citizen lobbyists can be important at times in shaping public policy, but they are not what most people think of when they hear the word lobbyist. To most people, lobbyists are people who are *paid* to influence government decisions. Their targets are generally legislators and their staff, the governor and other constitutional officers and their staffs, or state agency directors and personnel, but the general public or the news media can also be targets of lobbying campaigns to influence government action.

Professional lobbyists fall into two broad categories. People who are directly employed by an interest group, association, or corporation and represent them before government by engaging in lobbying activities are commonly known as "inhouse lobbyists." Individuals or firms who are hired on contractual basis by individuals, interest groups, associations, and corporations to represent them before government by engaging in lobbying activities are commonly known as "contract lobbyists." Both types of lobbyist engage in core lobbying activities: gaining access, providing information, and engaging in persuasion.

Lobbying is personal, face-to-face, and interactive. Successful lobbying requires access to the person you are trying to persuade. You need phone calls and electronic messages returned, meetings set up, and invitations to your legislative receptions accepted. Representing an established interest group, a major corporation, or an important public official greatly facilitates access, allowing you to capitalize on the visibility, reputation, and influence of the group or individual you are representing.

Once you have access, you have to establish credibility and trust through your interactions. Providing accurate, relevant, unbiased, timely, and easily consumed information is key to persuasion and to building credibility and trust. This is true in terms of influencing someone who is uninformed about your issue or does not have a firm position. In the legislature it also enhances the effectiveness of your supporters when they are making your case to another legislator, during floor debates, or answering questions from the press. A well-written, concise fact sheet keeps everyone on the same page and on message.

Other keys to successful lobbying are a knowledge of legislative process or administrative process and experience in putting a plan into action. For groups with a stake in the budget, knowledge and experience in the budget process is another valuable asset. Finally, there is strength in numbers. You have to organize coalitions of interests to lobby for a bill or government action. The key is the ability to organize coalitions to negotiate agreements with firm commitments and then hold the coalition together.

Most lobbyists bring governmental experience to a lobbying career. They can be former legislators or legislative staff members, former governor's staff members or former agency directors and agency staff, former local government officials such as mayors, or former campaign staff, particularly those with marketing or public relations skills. Other lobbyists can be professionals who go to work for their professional associations, learning the political process from experience. Ultimately to be effective you need to understand the political process and issues for which you are advocating.

Contract lobbying groups can be stand-alone firms or specialized units of a law firm or governmental affairs/public relations firm. They can have a wide range of clients or specialize in a specific policy area. They can represent a few clients or dozens. They can have a partisan orientation or have members with strong relationships to both political parties. Some focus primarily on working legislation in Springfield from the inside. Others specialize in broad-based campaigns to shape public opinion and promote legislative action from the outside.

The influence of an inhouse lobbyist is a direct extension of the interest they represent. An effective lobbyist or lobbying team can enhance the influence of an association or group while an ineffective lobbyist or lobbying team can diminish the influence of an association or group, but only within limits.

Experienced contract lobbyists will build general influence and credibility relationships with legislative and executive branch actors over time that are independent of their clients. Having a reputation of integrity and policy expertise and making regular contributions to legislative leaders, committee chairs, and minority spokespersons and constitutional officers are ways lobbyist enhance access and promote good will. These contributions are separate from any contributions that lobbyists deliver on behalf of their clients. The total amount of contributions from lobbyists as individuals or from the corporate accounts of lobbying firms is relatively modest, averaging a little more than $2 million over the last three election cycles. In 2021–22 over 300 individuals and firms registered as lobbyists made contributions to the political committees of legislators, legislative caucuses, or political parties. Only five lobbying firms contributed more than $100,000 while another ten firms contributed more than $40,000. McGurieWoods, a national law firm, at $204,000 and Kasper & Nottage, an Illinois firm, at $166,000, were the two largest contributors.

Billionaire Donors and Wealthy Self-Funding Candidates

Wealthy individual donors and self-funding candidates have always been part of Illinois politics. Their role in the era of political machines and county and local party organizations was limited. The decline of political parties starting in the 1970s created more opportunities for wealthy donors and self-funding candidates to impact Illinois politics. At the same time, the continued concentration of wealth in American society means that there are many more billionaires in 2022 than there were twenty or thirty years ago. Some of them are running for office or getting involved in politics by supporting candidates, political parties, and ideological groups.

Bruce Rauner's decision in 2013 to run for governor as a Republican ushered in a sea change in the role of individual wealth in Illinois politics. In the 2014 and 2016 election cycles Rauner, a self-funding candidate for governor, and Ken Griffin and Richard Uihlein, two Illinois billionaires, contributed $100.9 million to Illinois politics. In 2018 they were joined by JB Pritzker, a self-funding Democratic candidate for governor. Rauner withdrew from Illinois politics after 2018. Still, the four of them contributed a total of $397 million in the 2018 and 2020 election cycles. In the 2021–22 election cycle Pritzker, Griffin, and Uihlein contributed an additional $264.1 million. All of this adds up to $762.8 million (more than three-quarters of a billion dollars) contributed to Illinois politics by four individuals over five election cycles. Calling this "the Billionaire Era" of Illinois politics is not an overstatement. It shifted the whole dynamic, with money from billionaires gaining a level of parity with contributions from traditional interest groups, legislative leaders, and political party organizations.

The dynamic involving Rauner, Griffin, Uihlein, and Pritzker is complicated. Rauner was a private equity investor who had been involved with Chicago school reform groups. He ran for governor and committed to self-funding because he felt his efforts to reform the Chicago public schools had been blocked by the Chicago Teachers Union and that economic growth in the state was being stifled by a bad business climate. His campaign did not stress any social conservative themes. His candidacy resonated with Griffin. He is a billionaire hedge manager who shared Rauner's concerns and agenda. Uihlein, the billionaire owner of the shipping and supply company, made a major financial commitment to Rauner's agenda after Rauner was elected governor. Uihlein is interested in promoting both fiscally conservative, probusiness policies and social conservative policies. He saw Rauner's election as a way to further part of his agenda. The support Rauner, Griffin, and Uihlein provided to Republican candidates and party committees in 2016 largely eliminated the large funding advantage from private sector economic interests that the Democrats had established in recent election cycles. The Republicans picked up two Senate seats and four House seats in 2016, ending the Democrats' supermajority in the House.

Governor Rauner attempted to use the state budget as leverage to force the Democrats in control of the legislature to pass a probusiness, anti-union policy agenda. His refusal to sign a state budget in 2015 and 2016 created a major budget crisis. The state's credit rating fell, its unpaid bills exceeded $16 billion, and state social services were severely damaged. The crisis ended in 2017 when Republican legislators in the House joined the Democrats to pass a budget and a tax increase. The legislature then overrode Governor Rauner's vetoes, ending the stalemate.

One of the fallouts from the 2017 budget and tax bill overrides and Rauner's support for a pro-reproductive rights bill in 2017 was a split between Uihlein and Rauner and the House Republicans. Uihlein provided major funding for a primary opponent against Rauner in 2018. He also supported a challenger to the House Republican legislative leader in the primary and backed candidates challenging House Republican candidates.

JB Pritzker is a businessman and billionaire heir to the Hyatt fortune. The impact that contributions from Rauner, Griffin, and Uihlein had on the 2014 and 2016 elections made Pritzker's bid for the Democratic nomination in 2018 attractive to Democratics and their major funders because he could self-fund his race. This would free up Democratic private sector money, particularly union money, to concentrate on legislative elections. Pritzker won the election for governor in 2018, defeating Governor Rauner 54 percent to 39 percent. The support his campaign provided to Democratic legislative and party committees help them pick up seven seats in the House and three in the Senate, establishing historic margins in 2018. After his defeat in 2018 Rauner withdrew from Illinois politics and moved out of Illinois.

In 2020 Uihlein largely withdrew from Illinois politics. Griffin also withdrew from trying to rebuild the Republican party but provided the vast majority of the funding to defeat a progressive tax amendment to the state constitution that was backed by Governor Pritzker. Griffin also provided most of the money used to defeat a Democratic State Supreme Court justice in a retention election.

In 2022 Griffin and Uihlein engaged in a battle in the Republican primary for governor by supporting rival candidates. Griffin recruited and provided $50 million of support for a suburban mayor, Richard Irvin, who tried to re-create Rauner's 2014 campaign strategy, stressing crime, political corruption, and fiscal responsibility. Uihlein backed a downstate social conservative, State Senator Darren Bailey, with $9 million in direct support and $7 million to an independent expenditure committee that attacked Irvin. Uihlein's candidate won the Republican primary with 57 percent of the vote, while Griffin's candidate finished third. Griffin also provided most of the funding for an independent expenditure committee that backed two losing Republican candidates for seats on the Illinois Supreme Court. In the face of all this Griffin publicly announced he was moving his residency and financial business to Florida and withdrawing from Illinois politics.

In the general election, Uihlein provided an additional $27.7 million for an independent expenditure committee that opposed Pritzker and an additional

$3 million to Bailey's campaign. He also provided $2.4 million for the Senate Republican legislative leader, $1.5 million for another independent expenditure committee supporting Republican legislative candidates, and $2.5 million for a committee opposing a workers' rights constitutional amendment backed by trade unions and the Democratic party.

Pritzker, who contributed $145 million to his candidate committee, defeated Bailey in the election for governor 54 percent to 36 percent. The Democrats also retained their supermajorities in the legislature and the union-backed workers' rights constitutional amendment was adopted. In spite of the results of the 2022 election, Uihlein may continue to engage in Illinois politics, supporting the Illinois Republican party, which has become narrowly focused on social and fiscal conservative policies and candidates. This would set up a battle between Pritzker and Uihlein for the next four years. But it is also possible that Uihlein will follow Rauner and Griffin in withdrawing from Illinois politics. That would leave Pritzker as the sole billionaire in Illinois politics for at least the next four years. Clearly the billionaire era in Illinois politics is not over yet.

Political Party Organizations

There are three political parties in Illinois that are officially recognized statewide under the Illinois election code: Democrat, Republican, and Libertarian. New parties can be formed by meeting a petition requirement and filing nomination papers for a full slate of candidates for statewide and federal elections. If the candidate for governor for the new party wins at least 5 percent of the statewide vote, the party is granted recognition and can organize and nominate candidates for partisan elective offices at the state, county, and local levels under the provisions of the Illinois election code. The party maintains that status as long as it continues to receive 5 percent of the vote for governor every four years. Historically Illinois has been a competitive two-party state—Democrats and Republicans. We do not have a history of successful third parties or independent candidates. Nor do our election laws facilitate ballot access for third parties or independent candidates.

Political parties are organized on a territorial basis. In Illinois, the members of the central committee of the state parties are elected from the state's seventeen congressional districts. The governing body of Cook County consists of thirty elected township committee members and fifty elected city ward committee members. In larger counties township committee members make up the parties' governing committees. In a smaller county like Sangamon County the precinct committee members constitute the electorate for the county party officers.

Historically, Illinois has been a state with strong county, township, and ward organizations. The state party organizations were controlled by local party organizations. The power was in the local party organizations. In addition to being territorial, political party organizations were centered on government patronage. Control over government jobs was dependent on winning elections. Political parties recruited candidates, raised money, organized campaigns, provided campaign workers, got out the vote, and ran government in a transactional way ("where's mine?") to the benefit of the party members. Mayor Daley's political machine was at the height of its power in the 1950s and 1960s. In the same era the county party organizations of deep southern Illinois gave rise to Paul Powell, the gray fox of Vienna, while the McBroom machine in Kankakee County gave rise to Governor George Ryan. All of this created a party-centered election process controlled by county party bosses.[5]

In the 1960s, 1970s, and into the 1980s the Cook County Democratic Party controlled nominations for statewide office for the Democrats through a slate-making process where candidates presented themselves to the county's central committee and the party bosses chose the candidate for the statewide ticket. The next step was the state party central committee, which would meet in Springfield and inevitably ratify the choices made the Cook County Democrats. The county party organizations would provide the votes at the local level to affirm the choices in the primary. This process broke down in the 1980s as parties became weaker and candidates had success running outside of the party organizations. The Republican party's process was less well organized and effective, but the power was still at the local level.

As campaigns became more candidate-centered and traditional patronage shrank due to changes in laws and collective bargaining for public employees in the 1980s and 1990s, political parties in Illinois became weaker. While the political process remained transactional and non-ideological (power and control rather than policy and public interest) elections became more candidate-centered and political parties became weaker.

Former governor Rauner and Governor Pritzker fit the candidate-centered election process profile of a self-recruited, self-funded candidate who builds his own campaign organizations outside of the existing party framework. Both provided support to build state and county parties instead of the traditional relationship of the party organizations supporting the candidate.

As far as contemporary political party organizations in Illinois have political power or influence, it is largely as an adjunct to a political leader. The Democratic Thirteenth Ward party organization was important because Michael Madigan was the ward committeeman, not the other way around. Madigan was chairman of the Democratic Party of Illinois (DPI) from 1998 to 2021. The DPI was not important because it was a policymaking body or because it endorsed candidates. It raised far more money from private sources than its Republican counterpart. But contributors were not giving money because it was the DPI. It was the fourth bucket that contributors subject to contributions limits could use to give money to Madigan after they have given the maximum to other three committees he controlled. Madigan raised money through his candidate committee and his caucus party committee and transferred it to the DPI. The DPI then functioned as an ATM to provide money to Democratic candidates without Madigan's name being attached to the contribution. After Madigan stepped down as chair, there was a fight over the chairmanship of the DPI between Pritzker and U.S. Senator Dick Durbin in 2021. Durbin's candidate won. Pritzker spent the next year recruiting and funding candidates for the positions on central committee that were on the primary ballot for 2022 after a new map was adopted through redistricting. This time Pritzker's candidate won. The DPI has value. Not so much in and of itself, but as an extension of the power and influence of the governor. The current weakness of the state Republican party (Illinois Republican Party) can be seen in its recent difficulties in recruiting and retaining a state party chairman.

News Media

Historically, the *Chicago Tribune* and the *Chicago Sun-Times*, the major daily statewide newspapers, and a small set of regional daily newspapers exercised influence in Illinois politics. One element was their role as the primary source of news for the citizens of Illinois. People became informed about the people and events of their community, region, and state by reading the newspaper. Another was through their editorial voice. Newspapers took positions on the issues of the day and endorsed candidates for office. If people had confidence in their judgment, objectivity, and credibility, then their opinions carried weight. Another source of influence was the role of newspapers as public watchdogs. Investigations and exposés both called public officials to account before the law and served as a warning that corrupt behavior could become public. Newspapers were not the only source of news. Radio and weekly newsmagazines were joined by network and then local TV news in the 1950s and 1960s as primary sources.

The current state of communications technology and the current configuration of news organizations delivering news and analysis to the public is vastly different from the 1970s. However, the foundational relationship between news media and the public has not changed. Information is being generated and disseminated by the new media and consumed by the public, which creates the opportunity to inform and influence public opinion. A unique aspect of the news media's relation to government is their right under the First Amendment to freedom of the press and free speech.

Newspapers, newsmagazines, TV networks, radio networks, internet networks, and satellite networks are also businesses. They organize into interest groups to influence government policies that affect their ability to be profitable. Associations of print media, broadcast media, and digital media all lobby to protect First Amendment rights as well as to advance their economic interests.

Since at least the early 1990s the influence of Illinois news media on state politics has steadily declined due to the downsizing of major daily newspapers in Chicago and other major cities along with the shrinking coverage of state and local politics from local newspapers, TV, and radio stations and ultimately the disappearance of many local news outlets. At the same time, the proliferation of ideologically driven news organizations (print, radio, TV, and online), and the explosive growth of social media as a vehicle for both providing political information and promoting partisan and ideological perspectives worked to make the news media more defused, polarized, and less professional.

Influence with Limited Resources: Enacting Campaign Finance Reform

In the spring of 2009, political reform and good government interest groups joined together in a coalition with the goal to enact limits on campaign contributions in Illinois.[6] The total membership and financial resources of these interest groups paled in comparison to those of groups like the IEA. What they did have was a long-time presence in Illinois working through the news media and with individual members to build support for strengthening ethics and campaign finance laws. They also had Illinois's long history of political corruption highlighted by the recent impeachment of Governor Rod Blagojevich as a symbol of the need for change. Following the impeachment, Pat Quinn, the new Democratic governor, and the Democratic legislative leaders made a public commitment to respond to political corruption by enacting ethics laws. While the focus of the response to the Blagojevich scandal centered on ethics laws creating inspector general offices within the executive and legislative branches, a campaign finance bill was part of the response.

The reform groups collaborated with supporters in the legislature to advance a bill that would limit both private money coming into the election process and the movement of money between political candidate committees and party committees once it was received. A comprehensive contribution limits bill had been a key goal of reform groups since the early 1990s. The Democratic legislative leaders advanced a much weaker bill. At the same time the Democratic leaders advanced a constitutional amendment favored by the governor that would allow for the recall of a governor through a citizen's initiative process. Both the recall constitutional amendment and the Democratic leaders' campaign finance bill passed at the end of the spring session. The governor announced his intention to sign the campaign finance bill.

During the summer, the reform groups mounted a lobbying campaign urging the legislature and the governor to start over and pass a stronger campaign finance bill. The lobbying campaign was directed at legislators and the governor through direct lobbying and a broad-based media campaign stressing the need for a stronger law to blunt the corrupting impact of money on Illinois politics. Ultimately, the public pressure generated by the efforts of the reform groups prevailed. The governor vetoed the bill passed in the spring and announced a commitment with the legislative leaders to pass a new bill. After negotiating during the fall, the reform groups agreed to back a bill that limited private money coming into the system but did not limit the movement of money between political party committees and candidate committees. In exchange the reform groups also got greatly expanded disclosure requirements for contributions and expenditures and greater enforcement powers for the State Board of Elections.

The reform groups were able to influence the governor and the legislative leaders to reconsider what they had passed in the spring but were only partially successful in achieving their goal of comprehensive contribution limits. The legislative leaders had the power to shape the final terms of the bill, backed by the threat of passing a weaker bill. By Illinois standards, the bill that became law was a major positive change. The reform groups had the choice to reject the compromise bill dictated by the legislative leaders. But doing so would have resulted in a much weaker bill or no bill at all. Passing contributions limits shows that groups without money or large numbers can exercise political influence in Illinois. It also shows that success in passing political reform in Illinois is always incremental and always a long time coming.

The Changing Nature of Political Power and Influence in Illinois

The politics of Illinois in 2023 are a product of the changing nature of who has power and influence within elections and governmental decision-making. Those changes shape the processes and policy outcomes that define who we are as a state. The timeline from the mid-1950s to the present tells a story of change in who and what influences our elections and policymaking.

The Old Model: Political Machines and Party Bosses Dominate—1955–1968

The old model of Illinois politics will always be identified with Mayor Richard J. Daley, the boss of the Chicago machine. He did not invent the politics of his era, but he did perfect it. While the start of a timeline is somewhat arbitrary, his election as chairman of the Central Committee of Cook County in 1953 and mayor of Chicago in 1955 is a logical point to begin an examination of what the old model looked like.

Illinois politics under the old model rested on the foundation of local political parties at the precinct, ward, and township level. These were the building blocks for county political party organizations. The county political party organization recruited the candidates, controlled the primaries, provided campaign workers for the primary and general elections, and delivered the votes on Election Day. Party members voted for party-endorsed candidates who, once in office, provided services for the citizens and jobs for the party members. The Republican state party was a coalition of strong downstate and northeastern county organizations. The Democratic state party was an adjunct of the Cook County Democratic party, which was controlled by Mayor Daley's political machine. Cook County's power was shared with strong downstate Democratic county party organizations.[7] Every four years the two state parties would endorse a regionally balanced slate of candidates who would win their respective primaries and face off in the general election.

Politics was personal and face to face, relying on relationships, trust, and loyalty. The energy, resources, and the material rewards of politics were all tied up in the transactions between voters and political parties. The party leaders controlled the party organization, which in turn controlled or were the elected officials. The party members provided the votes and the elected officials provided the local government jobs and services. The resulting politics was transactional and job-oriented—patronage and pork over principle, party over the public interest. The political culture of power, winning, and control facilitated and protected the culture of political corruption that has long been a distinguishing feature of the political identity of Illinois.

The regional model for statewide and legislative elections was Chicago versus downstate with downstate being anything beyond the Chicago city limits. Statewide elections were competitive between Republicans and Democrats during the period. The Republicans controlled the legislature for most of the period, particularly the Senate. The critical context is that the important political action was at the local level, not the state level. State government was weak, limited by antiquated, restricted governmental structures and limited sources of revenue. Mayor Daley was the dominant political figure of the era. He was more than happy to divide the state into two spheres of influence—Chicago, which he controlled, and the rest of the state, which he negotiated with to find mutual agreements.

Because of the partisan and regional balance in Illinois and the transactional nature of Illinois politics, public policy during this era was cautious, pragmatic, non-ideological, and above all else, status quo oriented. Unlike Wisconsin, our neighbor to the north, Illinois was not known for progressive ideas or innovations during this time period.

Because of the party-based nature of the political process, interest groups and wealthy contributors worked through political parties and elected leaders rather than trying to impact elections directly. Influential daily newspapers in Chicago, the northeast suburbs, and downstate cities had some impact on local and state politics, particularly through election endorsements and their role as public watchdogs.

Transition to the Modern Era: Governors and the Legislative Leaders Build State Government as Political Parties Grow Weaker—1969–2002

In 1968 Illinois voters elected Republican Richard Ogilvie governor and adopted a call for constitutional convention to consider revising the 1870 Illinois constitution. The next year Governor Ogilvie proposed that Illinois levy an income tax for the first time. The income tax passed the legislature with the support of Mayor Daley. The following year delegates to the constitutional convention drafted a new state constitution, which was approved in a special election in December of 1970 and took effect July 1, 1971. The new constitution removed a number of constraints on state government and increased the power of both the governor and the legislature. The combination of the new constitution and the income tax greatly enhanced the fiscal and policy power of Illinois state government. Over time Illinois state government would gain parity and then dominance over local political power.

While Ogilvie is credited with expanding and modernizing state government services during his term, the income tax proved to be unpopular. Dan Walker, a businessman who had never held public office, defeated the candidate slated by the state Democratic party in the primary and then narrowly defeated Ogilvie in the general election. The results of the election revealed an important shift in the regional model of Illinois elections. The growth of Republican election strength in the northeastern suburbs around Chicago had matched the Democratic vote in Chicago, while a competitive downstate provided the margin of victory for Walker. The new regional model for statewide and legislative elections had become a standoff between suburban Cook County and the surrounding suburban collar counties on one side, and Chicago on the other, with a competitive downstate holding the balance of power. Instead of a two-ring circus, regional politics in Illinois was now a three-ring circus.

Walker only served one term, losing in 1976 to Jim Thompson, a former U.S. attorney slated by the state Republican party. Walker's election over party-based politics was an aberration. But it foreshadowed a permanent change. Local and state political parties were beginning to lose strength as the power of patronage began to wane. A slow but steady shift from party-based elections to candidate-based elections was beginning to take place as candidates recruited themselves, raised money, created political organizations, and then ran whether or not they had the support of party organizations.

During this era power in Republican party was shared between the northeastern suburban counties around Chicago and downstate rural and suburban areas. Power in the Democratic party became more centered in Chicago and later in suburban Cook as the strength of downstate Democrats declined except in a few urban areas. Chicago political power fragmented with the death of Boss Daley in 1976 and the infighting that followed with the election and then untimely death of Harold Washington, Chicago's first Black mayor. The election of Richard M. Daley in 1989 brought stability, but with diminished influence in the face of growing state executive power and legislative power.

The competitive battle for partisan control of state government produced a pattern of Republican governors versus Democrats in the legislature. During the twenty-six consecutive years that Republican governors were in office, between 1976 and 2002, the Republicans controlled both chambers of the legislature for only two years.

At the same time the legislature was undergoing a transformation into a modern body that would function as a coequal branch of government. During this era, House Speaker Madigan (D-Chicago) began his climb to becoming the dominant player in Illinois politics. A protégé of Daley, he built a power base outside of Chicago by centralizing legislative power in the Speaker's office and funding and running legislative campaigns through his legislative office. He served as Speaker for eighteen of the twenty years in this transitional era. By the end of the 1980s, power in the legislature had been centralized in the offices of the four legislative leaders. During the Thompson administration negotiation over budget and policy were characterized in the press as summits between "Big Jim and the 4 Tops."

But as important as Madigan became, the most important politicians during this time were Governors Jim Thompson and Jim Edgar. During their twenty-two years in office, they oversaw a great expansion of the scope and power of state government, the slow demise of political party dominance, and the rise of executive power to match the growing power of the legislature. The content of public policy was more public-regarding and service-oriented, but the ideological thrust was still pragmatic, status quo–oriented, and cautious.

The importance of interest groups and their campaign contributions grew as the power of political parties decreased. The loss of patronage resources limited the ability of political parties to control primary elections or deliver votes in general elections with turnout driven by loyal party workers. Private sector money increasingly flowed toward candidates and legislative leaders.

In the 1970s and 1980s the major contributors to Illinois politics were business groups and professional associations followed by labor unions. The power of trade, teacher, and public employee unions grew in the 1990s and 2000s and reached parity with business and professional interests. Supreme Court elections in 2000 marked the beginning of hyper-expensive State Supreme Court races fueled by contributions from business groups, trial lawyers, labor unions, and state political parties.

Political corruption continued to be a constant theme of Illinois politics. A fitting end point of the period was Governor Ryan's decision not to seek reelection in 2002 in the face of a growing political scandal that would lead to his serving time in federal prison.

The importance of the traditional news media in state politics declined during this period due to the loss of print media outlets and readership and the growing diversification of electronic media on cable TV.

Modern Era: Madigan, Billionaire Politics, Growing Democratic Dominance, and the Advent of Progressive Politics—2003–Present

In 2002 Rod Blagojevich became the first Democrat elected governor in twenty-six years. Under the new legislative map drawn by the Democrats after they won the right in the redistricting commission tiebreaker, the Democrats regained control of the Senate after ten years of Republican control while continuing their control of the House.

In the preceding decade Chicago, suburban Cook County, and the suburban collar counties become more diverse with growing Hispanic and Asian populations. That trend would continue for the next decade and then slow during the next. The racial makeup of downstate remained largely unchanged with small percentages of racial minorities. The total population of the state grew slowly with the collar counties increasing their share of the total population while the relative shares of Chicago/suburban Cook County and downstate declined.

The regional electoral politics had also changed since Walker's election. Chicago became more Democratic and downstate became more Republican. Suburban Cook County flipped from leaning Republican to leaning Democratic by the end of 1990s. The collar counties become less Republican and more competitive through the past two decades. The new regional model for statewide and legislative elections that had emerged by 2002 was a standoff between Democratic Chicago and suburban Cook County on one side and Republican downstate on the other, with the competitive suburban collar counties holding the balance of power. This pattern has intensified over the past twenty years. The northeastern suburban counties around Cook County (primarily DuPage, Lake, and Will) are now the battleground that decides control of election and policy. It is still a three-ring circus, but the makeup of the rings has changed.

Chicago politics fragmented after Richard M. Daley retired in 2011. Internal racial, ethnic, and ideological conflicts and fiscal problems weakened Chicago's ability to influence state politics. After two terms in office marked by controversy and conflict, Mayor Rahm Emanuel chose not to run for reelection. In 2019 Lori Lightfoot was elected as Chicago's first Black female and first gay mayor. After four years of continued conflict and controversy she did not qualify for the runoff in the mayor's election in 2023, finishing third in the primary. Brendan Johnson, a progressive Cook County commissioner and former Chicago Teachers Union organizer backed by teacher and service employee unions was elected by a narrow margin over Paul Vallas, a former Chicago city and Chicago school district official backed by business and trade union interests. Chicago remains a divided city with serous political, social, and economic problems.

Control of state government has shifted more and more toward the Democrats since 2002. Democrats controlled the governor's office from 2003 through 2014. After four years of a Republican governor, a Democrat won the office in 2018 and was reelected in 2022. Democrats control the other four statewide offices. No Republican has been elected secretary of state since 1994 or attorney general since 1998. The election of Governor Rauner in 2014 clearly shows that there is a pathway for a Republican to win statewide office. But election results since then indicate that the pathway is narrowing. The victory of a socially conservative downstate Republican state senator backed by billionaire Richard Uihlein over a moderate suburban Republican mayor backed by billionaire Ken Griffin in 2022 illustrates the shift to the right in the Republican primary electorate. This makes it harder for Republicans to nominate candidates for statewide office who can appeal to moderate voters.

The Democrats drew the legislative maps for the 2002, 2012, and 2022 elections. They have controlled both chambers since 2002 with supermajorities every term except 2017–18 when they held only a simple majority in the House. Power in the legislature remained firmly in the hands of the Democratic legislative leaders. The current legislative maps will be in effect until the 2032 election.

A successful campaign to block the retention of a judge elected as a Democrat in 2020 funded by Ken Griffin and Richard Uihlein created a second competitive Supreme Court election in 2022 and potentially put Democratic control of the court at risk. This led to the Democrats in the legislature drawing a new judicial district map for the 2022 election that created districts more favorable to Democrats. The Democratic candidates won the two seats up for election in 2020 in districts located outside of Cook County, increasing their majority on the court to five to two. Those two judges will serve ten-year terms.

Private sector funding of Illinois politics has shifted in five significant ways since 2002. First, instead of going primarily to local political parties, contributions are now directed to candidates and legislative leaders or used to fund independent expenditures. Independent expenditures eliminate the control of candidates over the content and targeting of campaign messages from these groups. Second, the amount of private sector money that is contributed has increased dramatically, replacing the labor of the political party machines with hard dollar resources. Third, the sources of private sector money have changed. There has been a dramatic increase in trade union money and service employee union money as well as a significant increase in teacher union money. At the same time, some groups have dramatically reduced their contributions from the levels of a decade ago. In relative terms there is less manufacturing money and less retail trade money as Illinois has lost manufacturing companies and retail trade has shifted toward online marketing. The major source of healthcare-related contributions used to come from doctors and other health professionals. Now the dominant players are nursing homes, hospitals, other health facilities, and health insurance and third-party payers. Fourth, there has been a major increase in contributions from ideological groups and national dark money groups whose sources of funding remain hidden. Finally, the increased impact of groups like labor and the trial lawyers who have a strong partisan preference for Democratic candidates, the lack of competitiveness from Republican party organizations, and deterioration of the Republicans' private sector base have put the Republicans at a huge fundraising disadvantage, which limits their ability to compete in statewide and legislative elections.

Billionaire money was a major factor in Illinois elections from 2014 through 2022. Contributions from Griffin and Uihlein helped Rauner win the governor's office in 2014 and helped Republicans make gains in the legislature in 2016. Pritzker self-funded his campaign for governor and provided support for Democratic legislative leaders and legislative candidates who made historic gains in 2018 and for other Democratic candidates for statewide office. All the Democrats won. In 2020 Pritzker's contributions again gave the Democrats a major advantage in funding legislative races while Griffin and Uihlein largely ignored them. Griffin's contributions matched Pritzker's in the fight over an amendment to allow the legislature to levy a graduated income tax. The amendment failed. In 2022 Governor Pritzker self-funded his reelection campaign and provided support for legislative elections and party building. Uihlein focused his support on a conservative candidate for governor, who won the primary, but lost to Pritzker in the general by a wide margin. Griffin funded a more moderate candidate in the Republican primary for governor who finished third. Uihlein provided little support for other Republican candidates for statewide office. All of them lost after being massively outspent.

Illinois has become a reliable blue state in statewide and national elections, and the ideological center of its public policy has shifted. The core of the Democratic electorate has become more ideological and more progressive. The core of Republican electorate has become more ideological and more socially conservative. As a result, Illinois politics has become less transactional. At the same time, because the Democrats control the legislature, the governor's office, other constitutional offices, and the State Supreme Court, public policy in a number of areas has become more progressive. This is reflected in the following policy changes since 2011. Illinois abolished the death penalty in 2011, legalized gay marriage in 2013, strengthened reproductive rights in 2018 and 2021, legalized recreational cannabis and sports betting in 2019, enacted a major criminal justice bill in 2021 that included abolishing cash bail, passed a constitutional amendment in 2022 that protected workers' rights and prohibited right-to-work laws, and enacted an assault weapon ban in 2023. The only major policy defeat suffered by the Democrats was the failure of a constitutional amendment to allow the legislature to enact a graduated income tax in 2020. These major progressive policy victories both reflect and reinforce the influence of progressive legislators and policy groups.

The indictment of former governor George Ryan for political corruption and his conviction in 2006 could have marked the beginning of the end of Illinois's long history of political corruption. The arrest of his successor Rod Blagojevich on charges of political corruption in December of 2008 and his subsequent impeachment and removal from office in 2009 and the flurry of new ethics laws enacted the same year could have been another hopeful sign. But the latest round of federal criminal indictments and convictions of legislators and local officials followed by the indictment of former Speaker Michael Madigan and a number of his close associates and the plea agreements by Commonwealth Edison and AT&T admitting a conspiracy to bribe the Speaker cast doubt on how much progress has been made. Three lobbyists and a former CEO of Commonwealth Edison were convicted of bribery and conspiracy in late April of 2023. Speaker Madigan and one of the convicted lobbyists are scheduled to go on trial in March of 2024 for bribery and conspiracy. Will this be the time for real change in Illinois's political culture or just one more round of getting rid of the bad guys without questioning why this continues to happen?

The influence of Illinois's news media on state politics has continued to decline with the diminution of major daily newspapers in Chicago and other major cities, the loss of local newspapers, and the shrinking coverage of state and local politics from local newspapers and TV and radio stations. The proliferation of ideologically driven news organizations (print, radio, TV, and online) continues, along with explosive growth of social media as a vehicle for both providing political information and promoting partisan and ideological perspectives.

Illinois Politics in 2023

The basic geographic regions of the state have remained the same, but their population and political demographics have changed. The regional model for statewide and legislative elections is now a standoff between Democratic Chicago and suburban Cook County and Republican downstate, with the competitive northeastern suburban collar counties determining the outcome of statewide elections and control of the legislature.

Historically, political party organizations controlled candidates and elected officials; that relationship has largely been reversed. Elections are now candidate-centered rather than party-centered.

The power-oriented, transactional, and corruption-stained political culture of Illinois still persists, but the underlying dynamic of patronage has been replaced by a greater focus on policy and ideology. Whether the latest round of political corruption trials and convictions will result in fundamental change in the laws and the political culture of Illinois is unclear, given the state's long and largely unsuccessful struggle to reform its politics.

Democrats and Republicans still face off for control over the executive, legislative, and judicial branches, but the nature and identities of the two parties has changed. The Democrats have become more progressive, while the Republicans have become more conservative, particularly on social issues. Political conflict has become more polarized along partisan, ideological, and regional lines.

Recent election and campaign funding trends also indicate the partisan balance and competitiveness in our politics is disappearing as the Democrats have achieved a dominant position. Power in the legislature is still firmly held by the Democratic legislative leaders, but there is more parity between the House and the Senate with Speaker Madigan gone. This has increased the power and influence of Governor Pritzker relative to the legislature.

As political parties weaken and elections became more candidate-oriented, interest groups and individuals have become more influential in elections and policymaking. Between 2014 and 2022 big money from self-funding candidates and billionaire donors exceeded the impact of private sector money in statewide elections and heavily influenced legislative elections. With the withdrawal of former governor Rauner and billionaire Ken Griffin from Illinois politics it is not clear how long this will persist. Pritzker's current term will not end until the beginning of 2027. It is uncertain if Uihlein will continue to fund Republican politics at the level necessary to overcome Pritzker's money and the Democrats' advantage in contributions from private sector sources. With or without Uihlein, the prospects for Illinois Republicans are very bleak, while the power and influence of Governor Pritzker is clearly growing.

The capacity, influence, and financial viability of the traditional news media has been weakened by competition from an explosion of alternative and often highly partisan and ideological sources of information fueled by the digital communication revolution.

Illinois state government is no longer the sleepy backwater of the 1950s. It is a powerhouse that impacts every citizen's life. The Democrats did not achieve a position of political dominance because they solved all of the fiscal, economic, social, and service delivery problems that have plagued the state during the modern era. Those problems are still present. And the Democrats' current dominance of Illinois politics places the challenges and pitfalls of governing Illinois squarely on their shoulders.

3
ELECTIONS

Elections are important. The road to political power and policy change runs through elections. But elections are important for two broader, more fundamental reasons. Elections provide the vehicle through which citizens grant legitimacy to the political system. The authors of the Declaration of Independence characterized this transaction as the "consent of the governed." Regularly scheduled, free and fair elections and the peaceful transfer of power are the institutional bedrock of the legitimacy of the American political system.

Elections also provide the opportunity for representation. Ideally, when two-way communication exists between elected officials and their constituents, trust and understanding of both the wants and needs of the constituents and the limitations and trade-offs necessary for collective action by elected officials will contribute to a shared sense of trust and the legitimacy of the political process. Although the practice of government can fall woefully short of the ideal, it is essential to remain committed to the goals of the consent of the governed and representation by supporting and maintaining free and fair elections and the peaceful transfer of power.

Elections and Illinois Political Culture

In the era when political party organizations dominated Illinois politics, participation in elections through running for office and voting was strongly encouraged, not for the public in general, but for party members. The goal was to have dependable candidates and voters who were loyal to the party organization.

Participation in general was not valued as a public good. Rather, participation by loyal party members kept the party strong and in power. The election laws reflected this goal, discouraging independent candidates and third parties, allowing parties to register voters, and organizing party workers to encourage and monitor voting by those with connections and allegiances to the party organization. The precinct captain and the ward committeeman provided the nexus between the voter and the party organization through face-to-face contact. The linkages were based on jobs and services, not policies or ideas.

Before the law was changed in 1997, voters in general elections in Illinois had the option of voting for an entire slate of party candidates by selecting a single box of the ballot that would cast their vote for all the candidates of their chosen party. Straight party or straight ticket voting is now allowed in only six states. The practice made it easy for party loyalists to vote. It also created an incentive to vote quickly by punching a straight ticket so a voter would not raise the suspicions of the party's poll watchers that the voter was taking too long in the voting booth because they were being disloyal and giving some votes to the opposition party.

Illinois has historically held primaries in March. Bad weather often plagues March primary elections. The public's attention is far removed from thinking about general election campaigns and voting decisions that are eight months away. The rhythm and energy of a spring primary is far different from a late summer or fall primary. All of this favors the ability of the party organization to control candidate nominations. Party functionaries knew they could count on the party voters to get to the polls and vote the right way regardless of the weather or the issues of the day. The act of going to the polling place on Election Day in the primary and the general election provided public validation of the strength, not of democracy, but of the party organization.

Illinois has adopted laws over the past thirty years that made registering to vote and the act of voting much easier. These laws create the potential for greater participation. Some of the motivation for change came from a belief that political participation itself is a public good that benefits the individual and society. Good government groups have long supported increasing participation and implicitly, and sometimes explicitly, weakening traditional political party control over the mechanics of elections. But these changes also benefit candidates and interest groups who want to operate independently from political parties and have the resources to build campaigns around candidates and policy positions. Once you have energized someone to support your candidate or your cause, you want them to be able to participate as quickly and as easily as possible. You want to expand the electorate. Rules and processes that make voting difficult for those who have not previously voted or are not regular participants in the process work to the advantage of party organizations and voters who are strong partisans and have long records of participation. These kinds of rules and processes also work to maintain the status quo by making it harder for to build political support through elections for new candidates, parties, or ideas.

The Administration of Elections

The administration of elections within the American political system is highly decentralized.[1] Each of the fifty states has created a structure for registering voters and conducting elections. The long history of states administering elections has its roots in the U.S. Constitution, which gives each state legislature the power to prescribe the rules and manner for holding elections for U.S. senators and representatives. In Illinois, the rules governing state elections are contained within a state law, the Illinois Election Code. State laws cannot supersede the U.S. constitution or federal election laws, nor can they restrict the voting rights of citizens granted by the federal constitution as interpreted by the U.S. Supreme Court. But within those constraints, states have adopted a wide range of systems for conducting elections.

All states have a central election authority at the state level that sets rules and regulations for elections and coordinates the process of voter registration and the conduct of elections which take place at the local level. Thirty-three states elect the chief election official, and in thirty-one of those the secretary of state is the person who oversees elections. In six states the governor appoints the chief election official. In four states the legislature appoints the chief election official.

In seven states the chief election official is appointed by a state board. Illinois is one of those states. The 1970 Illinois state constitution created a state board of elections with the power of "general supervision over the registration and election laws of the state."[2] The size and manner of selection of board members is determined by law with the sole restriction that no political party have a majority. The Illinois State Board of Elections currently has eight members. Four are Democrats and four are Republicans. They serve staggered four-year terms. If a position becomes open that needs to be filled by a member of the governor's party, the governor makes the selection. If a position becomes open that needs to be filled by a member of a party opposite of the governor's party, the governor selects the person from a list of nominees submitted by the highest ranking official of the party opposite the governor's political party.

The governor's appointments must be approved by the State Senate. The State Board of Elections selects an executive director of the state board who becomes the chief elections officer for the state. The executive director of the Illinois State Board of Elections answers directly to the board, which makes policy decisions and final judgments on complaints of violations of Illinois's election law. The votes of five members of the board are required to sustain a complaint. In contrast, a chief elections officer who is a constitutional officer elected statewide, such as a secretary of state, has greater independence and control over the conduct of elections.

In thirty-four states the tasks of registering voters, maintaining voting rolls, and holding elections at the local level are conducted under the direction of a single individual or entity. In twenty-six of those states, elections are administered at the county level under the direction of a single individual, usually an elected county clerk. In eight states, the administration is managed within a county by a board. Sixteen states have mixed structures. Illinois is one of those states.

In Illinois, elections are conducted by 101 county clerks and 1 county election commission. In addition there are 6 municipal election authorities who conduct elections within the municipal boundaries and coordinate their county clerk(s). While the number of municipal election commissions that operate separately from the county clerk have been reduced significantly over the years due to concerns over efficiency and duplication of staff and effort, municipal election commissions still exist in Chicago, Bloomington, Danville, East St. Louis, Galesburg, and Rockford. Aurora abolished its election commission in 2018 and all election administration in Kane County was consolidated under the county clerk.[3]

The Structure and Calendar of Elections

Prior to 1982 the scheduling of elections in Illinois was both crowded and chaotic, particularly in the case of local government elections, which took place on different days of the week during different months of the year.[4] In 1982 the legislature created an election calendar that established partisan primaries and general elections in even-numbered years. Combined with the federal election calendar this law basically ratified the status quo of even-numbered presidential election years followed two years later by midterm election years. Illinois conducts federal elections for president and the U.S. House of Representatives and state elections for the legislature and selected county government officials in the presidential election years. In the midterm election years Illinois conducts federal elections for the House of Representatives and state elections for governor and the other five constitutional offices,[5] the state legislature, and selected county government officials. Federal elections for the U.S. Senate occur in both presidential and midterm election years. The timing comes from a staggering of the elections of the two senators from a state and a staggering of Senate elections between the states. U.S. Senate elections occur in Illinois twice every six years. Elections in even-numbered years have spring primaries (usually in March) where the political parties select their candidates for the general election and fall general elections in early November when the federal, state, and county elected officials are chosen.

Elections of Illinois judges at the circuit, appellate, and Supreme Court level occur irregularly in both presidential and midterm election years. Judges are initially elected on a partisan ballot. Once judges elected on a partisan ballot completes a first term, they can run for a second term and succeeding terms on a "retention ballot" in the general election, with retention requiring a 60 percent yes vote.

The 1982 law also established a structure for local government elections in the odd-numbered years between the presidential and midterm elections. The law established a consolidated primary in February with partisan ballots to select party candidates for township offices and partisan municipal elections. It also provides for nomination elections on the same day for nonpartisan municipal officials, which could eliminate the need for a later election if a candidate receives more than 50 percent of the vote.

Finally, the law created a consolidated election in April to elect township officials and mayors and city council members who were nominated in the primary. At the same time, nonpartisan elections are held to elect mayors, municipal officers, and city council members for municipalities that have chosen nonpartisan elections; and to elect nonpartisan officers for special districts (school boards, park districts, library districts, etc.). As a result, all of the odd-numbered year election activity was consolidated into two days in the spring, a Tuesday in February and a Tuesday in April.

Who Can Run for Public Office in Illinois?

The Illinois state constitution sets a basic set of qualifications for people running for state public office in Illinois.[6] Candidates for governor, lieutenant governor, attorney general, secretary of state, treasurer, and comptroller must be U.S. citizens, twenty-five years of age, and residents of the state for at least three years preceding the election. Candidates for the General Assembly must be U.S. citizens, twenty-one years old, and residents of the district they are to represent for at least two years. Candidates for judicial office must be U.S. citizens, licensed attorneys-at-law of the State of Illinois, and residents of the district to which they are elected. Statutory qualifications specified by law for elected local government offices such as a mayor, county board member, or school board member generally require that a person must be a citizen, a registered voter, and a resident of the jurisdiction they are elected from for a period of one to two years prior to being elected. Being eighteen years of age is implied by the requirement to be a registered voter.

The state constitution prohibits anyone convicted of a felony, bribery, perjury, or other infamous crime from holding a public office created by the state constitution. Eligibility may be restored as provided by law.

Who Can Vote in Illinois and How?

The state constitution provides that a U.S. citizen who is eighteen years of age and has been a permanent resident of the state for thirty days prior to an election shall have the right to vote in that election.[7] The General Assembly by law may establish registration requirements and require residency in an election district not to exceed thirty days. A person convicted of a felony or otherwise under sentence in a correctional institution or jail shall lose the right to vote, which right to vote shall be restored not later than the completion of the sentence.

To vote in Illinois elections, you must be registered to vote. Illinois has become one of the easiest states for people to register to vote. Illinois citizens have a number of options for registering to vote, and the requirements for becoming a registered voter are not difficult to meet.

In order to register to vote you must be a U.S. citizen, eighteen years of age prior to the next consolidated or general election, a resident of the precinct thirty days prior to the election, and submit two forms of identification.[8] One form of identification must have your name and address. The second must have your name. You are not required to submit proof of citizenship such as a birth certificate or a photo ID, although both are acceptable forms of identification. A utility bill that has your name and current address and a credit card that has your name would meet the identification requirement. When you sign your voter registration form you affirm that you are a citizen of the United States, eighteen years old or will be prior to the next general or consolidated election, and will have lived in the state of Illinois and at your current address thirty days prior to the next election. You also acknowledge that if you have provided false information on your application that you may be fined or imprisoned. In addition, you acknowledge that if you sign the application and are not a U.S. citizen you may be deported from the United States.

You can register in person, by mail, or online. There are deadlines for when you can register, depending on the method of registration, because the registration form needs to be processed and approved and the registration information transmitted to a polling place prior to Election Day.

In-person registration can be done at the office of the election authority for your voting jurisdiction, which is usually the county clerk's office. It can also be done by a designated representative of an established political party such as a precinct committee member or deputy registrar.

Registration by mail involves getting a registration form from your election authority, filling it out and mailing it back or delivering it to the election authority in person along with the required identification documents such as a driver's license. If you do not supply the necessary ID numbers on your form, you must vote in person (not by mail) the first time and supply the necessary documents at that time.

Online registration is done through the State Board of Elections website. It must be complete at least sixteen days prior to the election. Acceptable forms of identification for online registration are limited to the full Illinois driver's license or state identification card number and the date issued and the last four digits of your Social Security number. The online application software does not have the capability to handle documents such as utility bills or photocopies of credit cards.

A process for online registration is also available when an Illinois citizen interacts with certain state agencies, such as the secretary of state's office. The same information needed to get a driver's license or register a car can be used to support an application to register to vote. Citizens are offered the opportunity to register to vote while completing their business with the agency. Depending on the agency, citizens will be given a choice of opting in or opting out.

While Illinois does not have what is commonly referred to as same-day registration, it does allow for in-person registration or change of address during the period from the close of registration through Election Day. This period is called the grace period. Registration and changes of address can only be done at the election authority office or on Election Day at the polling place. Once this is completed the voter will be able to vote in person early or on Election Day depending on when the registration is completed.

Who Chooses to Vote?

Not everyone who is eligible to vote is registered to vote. Conservative estimates put the portion of eligible voters who are not registered at 20–25 percent. Absent reliable data, it is not clear if this represents a reservoir of people who, given sufficient information and opportunity, would participate. It may well be that the majority are uninterested, unengaged citizens who are unlikely to participate in voting under any circumstances.

Participation rates for those who are registered vary in a uniform pattern. They are highest in even-year elections that include a presidential election. They are lowest in odd-numbered years where only local government offices are being contested. Participations in elections in even-numbered years that do not include a presidential election (midterm elections) fall in between the highs and lows. Midterm elections that include the election of a governor and other statewide offices generate more participation than those that involve only congressional and state legislative elections.

The adoption of the 1970 Illinois constitution shifted the election of the governor and the other constitutional officers from a presidential election year to a midterm election year. The stated rationale was to increase the focus on state elections rather than sharing attention with the presidential election. The transition was accomplished by electing a governor and the other constitutional officers in 1976 for two-year terms and then reverting to four-year terms after the 1978 election.

The turnout rates for registered voters in Illinois in the last ten elections starting in 2004 averaged 71 percent for presidential elections and 51 percent for midterm elections. The rates for presidential elections were very stable, while the rates for the midterm elections dropped to 49 percent in 2014, rose to 57 percent in 2018, and dropped back to 51 percent in 2022. Rates for consolidated elections in odd-numbered years are generally much lower, with the exception of the elections for the mayor of Chicago. While not as high as the turnout delivered by the Daley machine, the ward organizations and the competition between ethnic and racial groups in Chicago generates greater participation than in most Illinois municipal elections.

The Process of Voting—Choices for Participating in Primary and General Elections

Illinois provides voters with a wide range of options for voting.[9] You can vote in person on Election Day, you can early vote by going in person to a central site designated by the local election authority, or you can vote by mail. Both early voting and voting by mail begin forty days before Election Day.

Illinois voters can choose to participate in the spring primary election in the even-numbered years where the official political parties nominate the candidates to run in the fall partisan elections. Regardless of how you choose to participate in a primary election (in person, early voting, vote by mail) you must choose which party primary to participate in. You do not have to *register* as Democrat, Republican, or third-party member prior to primary Election Day, but once at the polling place you must choose which party primary you want to vote in. This choice is a matter of public record, but it is not binding for future elections. In the fall general election you will receive a unified ballot that will have all the nominees for both parties. The same choice of what party primary you want to vote in has to be made for any consolidated primary election in an odd-numbered year partisan election.

Voters always have the choice to vote in person at a designated polling place on Election Day.

You can vote early in person before Election Day. The general election in 2022 Illinois provided for thirty-three days of early voting, twenty-seven weekdays, four Saturdays, two Sundays, and the Monday before the election. Early voting takes place at the offices of the election authority or other location designated by law or administrative action. Once your registration and address are confirmed you will receive the same ballot that you would have received if you had voted at your precinct on Election Day.

You can vote by mail by requesting an application for a vote-by-mail ballot. Prior to the general election in 2022 voters needed to request an application form from the election authority and submit it. Current law provides that the election authorities shall provide vote-by-mail application forms to all registered voters living in the election jurisdiction. Those forms include a checkoff line where, in addition to requesting a vote-by-mail ballot for the current election, you have the option to put your name on a permanent list to receive a general election ballot and a consolidated election ballot in all future general elections. You can also choose to receive a Democratic or Republican primary ballot in all future primary or consolidated primary elections.

Once the election authority receives and approves your request for a vote-by-mail ballot they will send you a ballot, a ballot security envelope for your ballot, and a mailing envelope for the ballot security envelope. You fill out the ballot, seal it in the ballot security envelope, fill out the required identification information on the ballot envelope, sign and date it, and then either return your ballot security envelope in person to the election authority or put the ballot security envelope in the mailing envelope and then either mail it to the election authority or drop it off in a drop-box provided by the election authority. Vote-by-mail ballots must be returned to the election authority or put in a drop-box before the polls close on Election Day or postmarked no later than Election Day to be counted.

Ballots postmarked no later than Election Day that are delivered after Election Day are treated as provisional ballots. They will be processed and, if authenticated, tabulated and added to the vote totals for each office. Election authorities have fourteen days to resolve issues with any provisional ballots (questions over name, addresses, etc.) before certifying the vote for the election jurisdiction.

You may have your mail-in ballot mailed or delivered by a close relative. You can ask someone other than a close relative to mail or deliver your mail-in ballot, but you and the person delivering your ballot must fill out and sign the form on the mailing envelope authorizing the transfer of your sealed mail in ballot to the third party. This process allows for a very restricted procedure for third-party involvement. Some states allow the unrestricted collection of mail in ballots. This is referred to as "ballot harvesting" and is controversial because of concerns over ballot security.

Even if you receive a vote-by-mail ballot for a primary or general election, you can still choose not to use it and vote in person either early or on Election Day by returning the vote-by-mail ballot to your election authority or voting precinct and then voting in person.

Regulating the Financing Elections in Illinois

In addition to providing a structure and regulations for who can run for office, who can vote, and how they can vote in Illinois, Illinois law also provides a structure and regulations for the financing of elections in Illinois. Those regulations govern state and local elections within the context of federal law and the constitutionally protected right of free speech. The financing of federal elections is governed by federal law within the context of the constitutionally protected right of free speech.

The modern framework for the constitutional regulation of campaign finance was established by the U.S. Supreme Court in 1976 in *Buckley v. Valeo*. This case established the principle that spending or contributing money to influence an election is protected free speech, which can only be limited in a very narrow framework. All the constitutional law established since then is rooted in *Buckley*. In the simplest terms, limits and regulation on spending money are not permissible because they keep people from engaging in political speech, which is protected speech under the First Amendment. Limits and regulations on contributing money are not permissible unless they are crafted to prohibit quid pro quo corruption or the appearance of quid pro quo corruption. Illinois can place reasonable limits on contributions to candidates, political parties, or PACs to limit the possibility of those contributions becoming bribes or extortion or if the size or source of the contributions might create the appearance of corruption. Illinois cannot limit contributions to an independent expenditure committee or the expenditures of that committee to benefit a candidate because, by definition, this activity is independent of the candidate because it is not coordinated. Since there is no interaction, there is no opportunity for corruption through a quid pro quo. The same logic applies to contributions from a political party to a candidate. They cannot be limited because, by this logic, a political party cannot corrupt a candidate. The Supreme Court's *Citizens United* decision allowing corporations to give and spend to influence elections as long the activity is not coordinated with a candidate follows directly from the underlying logic of *Buckley*.[10]

The foundation of regulating the financing of elections is providing transparency so that voters, the news media, and the opposing candidates and political parties know who is contributing to a campaign and how a campaign is spending the money it raises. Transparency has two key components. The first is reporting. The second is disclosure. The quality of the reporting and disclosure is a function of what information is reported and when, how quickly it is disclosed, and how accessible the data is. Illinois has an excellent system of reporting and disclosure. Candidates, political parties, and other groups that want to raise money and spend it to participate in politics are required to form a political committee, register with the State Board of Elections, and then file regular reports itemizing receipts and expenditures from their committees. The State Board of Elections then discloses the records from those reports to the public through an online, searchable database. Committees are required to file comprehensive reports electronically every three months. In addition, reports of contributions received of $1,000 or more and independent expenditures of $1,000 or more supporting or opposing a candidate must be reported within three to five days through electronic filings. All this data is automatically posted in a searchable database that can be accessed by anyone.

There is an argument for relying only on transparency to make a campaign finance system self-regulating. The proponents of this approach contend that "sunshine" alone can be sufficient. The assertion is that if you know that your opponent, the news media, and your family are watching, then you will not take money from a source or in amounts that will create bad publicity, concern over conflicts of interest, generate attention from law enforcement, or bring shame or public ridicule to you and your family. The logic is that given enough public scrutiny, the system will become self-policing. All of this presumes that the disclosure and reporting requirements will provide timely information that can be considered before an election. The same argument applies after a person takes office, that public knowledge of who made contributions to a candidate will constrain the officeholder from acting in ways that raise concerns that the public officials are voting to please a contributor rather than pursuing the best interests of their constituents, lest they be subject of unfavorable news coverage or investigations by law enforcement. Very few states rely on transparency alone to regulate the financing of campaigns.

The companion to transparency in regulating the role of money in elections is a system of limits and prohibitions that restrict the flow of private money into public elections. Examples are bans on contributions from companies or individuals with state contracts, prohibitions on direct contributions from corporations to candidates, limits on the amount of money different entities can give to candidates, and limits on the transfer of money between political committees once they have raised the money from private sources. The logic is that contributions from certain sources or large contributions would lead to corruption, which would damage the political system and harm citizens or lead to the appearance of corruption, which would reduce the public's support for the legitimacy of the political system. To pass constitutional scrutiny, contribution limits and source prohibitions must be narrowly tailored to address the threat of quid pro quo corruption or its appearance.

Prior to the mid-1990s Illinois had a very wide open, opaque, unregulated campaign finance system. As will be discussed in the next chapter on public corruption, a number of significant changes have been put in place to increase transparency and limit, restrict, or prohibit contributions that might increase the likelihood of corruption or the appearance of corruption. These changes almost always came in response to a highly visible, serious political corruption scandal. Contribution limits and increased transparency were added to the election code in 2009 following the impeachment and removal from office of Governor Rod Blagojevich.[11]

Campaign Finance Transparency and Anti-Corruption Regulations as of 2023

The Illinois election code requires candidates for public office to form a candidate committee once they meet a threshold of raising or spending a nominal amount of money. To do this they must register the committee with the State Board of Elections. Political party organizations are required to form political party committees and register them. Groups of individuals, entities, or organizations that join together to contribute directly to candidates for office are similarly required to form political action committees (PACs) and register them. The same requirements apply to groups formed to support or oppose ballot questions and constitutional amendments. Finally, the same organization and reporting rules apply to independent expenditure committees that spend money in support or opposition to candidates, but do not contribute directly to candidate committees or coordinate their activities with candidate committees.

All committees organized under the election code and registered with the State Board of Elections (candidate, political party, PAC, ballot, and independent expenditure) are required to file comprehensive reports of receipts and expenditures with the State Board of Elections every three months. While committees can organize and file initial reports on paper, they are required to file all reports electronically going forward. They must file quarterly until they officially discontinue operations. They are required to itemize receipts and expenditures with a cumulative value of $150 or more from or to a single source during a quarter. They are also required to provide occupation and employer information for individuals who contribute $500 dollars or more during a quarter. In addition, any contribution of $1,000 or more received during a quarter must be reported electronically to the State Board of Elections within three to five days. All quarterly reports and reports of contributions of $1,000 or more received since the last quarterly report are posted immediately on the State Board of Elections website as they are received. They become part of a searchable database and are accessible through a search engine on the website. Records and the results of searches can also be downloaded from the website.

An additional reporting requirement applies to independent expenditure committees. While these committees do not contribute directly to candidate committees, they make expenditures that benefit candidates by placing TV, radio, or social media ads or by distributing direct mail pieces that either support candidates or attack their opponents. These committees are required to report electronically any independent expenditures of $1,000 or more that they make in support of or opposition to a candidate for public office to the State Board of Elections within three to five days. The records from these reports are immediately posted in the State Board's database and are accessible through its website.

The combination of the quarterly reports and the reports of contribution received and independent expenditures made between the quarterly reports provides the public, the news media, and the participants in an election a close to "real time" picture of the total value of all the contributions and independent expenditures that have been made in support of a candidate at any point in a campaign. The same is true for the identity of those who have contributed or made independent expenditures in support that candidate. This picture allows the public to evaluate who is funding the campaign and evaluate the relationships that are being created between the candidates and those who support them. It also provides a picture of the scope and focus of private sector groups and individuals who are trying to influence the election through contributions or independent expenditures. The one part of the picture that is not complete in real time is the expenditures of a candidate committee. How much a candidate has spent and on what is only updated every three months by the quarterly reports.

While Illinois law provides a compete and timely record of the activities of committees that are organized and regulated under Illinois law, it cannot force organizations that raise money outside of the scope of Illinois law and then make contributions or expenditures to influence Illinois elections to reveal the sources of their funding. For example, the Democratic Governors Association and the Republican Governors Association are national groups that raise money from various companies, groups, and individuals and make contributions to multiple candidates in multiple states. They report the sources of their funding once a year to the IRS. These groups made large contributions to both Democratic and Republican candidates for governor in Illinois in recent election cycles. Even if you know who their funders are, once the money goes into a general fund, it becomes fungible and the identity of the source of the funds for a particular contribution is lost.

Nor can Illinois law force groups with the nonprofit status of a 501(c)4 to reveal the source of their funding when they make large political contributions to campaigns. These groups retain their nonprofit status as long as a majority of their activity is nonpartisan. For example, in 2022 the Government Accountability Alliance made a $1 million contribution to a ballot committee opposing a workers' rights amendment to the Illinois constitution and a $500,000 contribution to an independent expenditure committee that supported Republican candidates for the legislature. In spite of those contributions the group did not organize as a committee and register with the State Board of Elections or file quarterly reports with the State Board of Elections, claiming an exemption as a nonprofit corporation. As such there is no record of who contributed money to the Governmental Accountability Alliance. While not fatal to the overall effectiveness of a disclosure system, these contributions, often referred to as dark money, limit transparency in the system and therefore the effectiveness of Illinois campaign finance law.

In contrast to the transparency side of the Illinois campaign finance law, restrictions and prohibitions on the permissible sources of contributions are weak. The system of contribution limits adopted in 2009 applies only to the flow of private money into the process, and even that has limited effectiveness. It does not significantly impact the movement of money once it is within the system, leaving its flow between various committees largely unrestricted.

Under federal and most state laws, corporations are prohibited from contributing directly to candidates for public office. In contrast Illinois does not prohibit corporations from contributing directly to any type of political committee. Since 2009 Illinois has had a "pay to play" law that prohibits companies and the owners of companies from contributing to elected officials who approve or oversee contracts between a company and the state of Illinois that exceed $50,000. It also prohibits contributions from companies and the owner of companies who are bidding on state contracts with a value that exceeds $50,000 to elected officials who oversee the awarding of contracts.

Generally, Illinois does not prohibit specific businesses or individuals from contributing to candidates for public office. Contributions from individuals, companies, groups, and associations can create conflicts of interest, which can result in corruption or the appearance of corruption from undue influence when legislators cast votes on legislation in committee or on the floor of the House or Senate. An alternative to restricting contributions from particular sources is to pass and enforce conflict-of-interest prohibitions on legislators. While legislators are required to file annual statements of economic interest that can identify potential conflicts of interest, Illinois has no specific, enforceable conflict-of-interest laws that would prohibit legislators from voting on legislation that would benefit them financially or personally or benefit their contributors.

The Illinois contribution limits law places limits on contributions from private sources—individuals; corporations, labor organizations, and associations; and PACs—to candidate committees, political party committees, and other PACs. Because of the nature of independent expenditure committees and ballot committees these committees are not subject to limits on contributions from private sources. They do have to file quarterly reports and real-time reports of large contributions they receive as well as report any independent expenditures over $1,000 they make in support of or opposition to a candidate for public office. They are also prohibited from contributing directly to candidate, party, and PAC committees.

The law limits the transfer of funds from a candidate committee to another candidate committee. It does not limit the transfer of funds to political party committees from candidate committees or other political party committees.

Each of the four legislative leaders is authorized by law to have a legislative caucus committee that is classified as a political party committee. These legislative caucus committees can receive unlimited funds from candidate committees or other political party committees. This structure allows the legislative leaders to receive unlimited transfers into the legislative caucus committees they control from other candidate committees and the state political party as well as contributions from private sources. This allows the leaders to aggregate money and then distribute it to candidates from the legislative caucus committee or move it to the state party and then to a candidate committee.

State law also provides for a waiver from contribution limits when a candidate in a race self-funds at a certain level or when independent expenditures are made in an election above a certain level in a multicandidate race, regardless of which candidate is being supported or opposed. These provisions were put into law to protect candidates from wealthy self-funders or outside independent expenditure committees that are not subject to contribution limits. And they do function that way.

But waivers of limits can also be used to proactively remove limits and allow unlimited contributions that benefit those who already have a financial advantage. They are regularly used by the legislative leaders to raise unlimited funds through their candidate committees. The legislative leaders are rarely in competitive races, but they will either self-fund or have a friendly group do independent expenditures on their behalf in an amount that automatically waives the contribution limits on their campaign committees. They can then receive unlimited contributions in their candidate committees and transfer them to the legislative caucus party committees they control. Those caucus committees function as political party committees and can make unlimited transfers of funds to the candidate committees of the candidates leaders are supporting for election to the legislature.

Independent expenditures began in Illinois in 2010 after the contribution limits law took effect. The designation of independent expenditure committees allows for a clear distinction between expenditures made on behalf of a committee that are coordinated with the candidate (in-kind contributions) and contributions that are not coordinated with the campaign (independent expenditures). Independent expenditures were a major factor in legislative elections between 2013 and 2018, while much less a factor in 2020 and 2022. They were a major factor in state Supreme Court retentions elections in 2014 and 2020 and partisan state Supreme Court elections in 2022. In 2022 independent expenditures were a major factor in the Republican primary and the general election for governor. Darren Bailey, the losing Republican candidate for governor, spent about $13.5 million directly from his campaign committee while his major backer, a conservative billionaire, spent $34.7 million attacking one of Bailey's primary opponents and the incumbent Democratic governor through independent expenditure campaign aids.

The absence of contribution limits allows funders of independent expenditure committees to work outside of the contribution limits in the 2009 campaign finance law. While contribution limits are quickly lifted for the primary and the general elections for statewide office elections and many legislative elections through self-funding and friendly or unfriendly independent expenditures, interest groups and major donors still spend heavily using independent expenditures. They provide a level of independence and control that is not present when you make a lump-sum contribution to a candidate or a legislative leader. They also allow interest groups and major donors to operate outside of the funding system for legislative races developed by the legislative leaders to control the flow of money. Spending controlled and facilitated by the legislative leaders is still the dominant factor in legislative elections but spending by independent expenditure committees continues to play a significant role.

Running for Office in Illinois: Building a Campaign Organization and Raising Money

The dynamics of party-centered elections are deceptively simple: get the message to the faithful and get the faithful to the polls. Building and maintaining a patronage-based, transactional political organization, however, is not a simple task. But one of the fruits of that effort is a face-to-face election process where the party organization provides the information, the motivation, and the verification for participation by party members. Absent the party organization, a candidate has to fund and build a campaign organization, execute a campaign by identifying and communicating with potential supporters, and create a turnout operation to get supporters to the polls.

The increasing weakness of political party organizations makes raising money to fund campaigns critically important in the current era of Illinois politics. There are still functioning party organizations for at least one party in most counties in Illinois. If you are running for the nomination of the dominant party in the area in a legislative race, you do not have to start from scratch, even if you are a first-time candidate. For incumbent legislators, particularly those in areas with functional parties, the task is even easier. In statewide elections, first-time candidates often do start from scratch. Candidates who are incumbents or have previously held or run for statewide office have a clear advantage. Outside the larger counties, local political parties generally have little money and some organization. Statewide parties have some money, but only limited organizational structure to assist campaigns.

Role of State and Local Parties

In the era of party-centered politics in Illinois, local parties controlled nominations and elections in their city, ward, township, or county. The local party may have exercised one-party control or operated in a competitive environment against the other party in the general election, but within the partisan primaries, they exercised great power. At the same time, money to support campaigns flowed through the party organization, which provided the resources and the patronage workers to conduct the campaigns and get out the vote on Election Day.

At the state level powerful county party organizations controlled the state parties, which controlled the nominations for statewide office through a slate-making process where candidates who received the party endorsement became part of the party's statewide slate. The county party organizations then raised money, provided campaign resources and workers, and then worked in a coordinated way to deliver the votes for the party's local and statewide candidates. The Cook County Democrats dominated the state Democratic Party process while a combination of downstate and suburban counties dominated the state Republican Party process.

In the modern era, this process fell apart and disappeared. In 1976 Republican Party leaders recruited U.S. Attorney Jim Thompson to run for governor. He won and held the office for the next fourteen years. In 1982 he appointed State Representative Jim Edgar to fill a vacancy in the office of secretary of state and chose House Speaker George Ryan for his Republican lieutenant governor. In 1990 Edgar was elected governor and Ryan secretary of state. After Edger chose not to seek a third term, Ryan was elected governor in 1968. After Ryan chose not to run in the face of a growing political scandal, the state Republican Party had only limited influence on the ensuing primary for governor between three self-recruited candidates. The pattern of self-recruited candidates for statewide office has continued ever since.

The state Democratic Party process was much more formal. During the Daley era, the Cook County Democratic Party organization held a formal slate-making process where candidates presented themselves to be chosen. Once that process was complete, the state Democratic Party convened in a hotel in Springfield and inevitably endorsed the slate put forth by the Cook County Democrats. The process did not always work as planned and after Daley's death it began to fall apart. After a close election between Governor Thompson and former senator Adlai Stevenson III in 1982, a rematch was anticipated in 1986. Any chance of Stevenson's winning was crushed when the state and local party organizations, including Cook County, failed to push the party-endorsed candidates for lieutenant governor and secretary of state. Two followers of a right-wing political movement won the nominations. Stevenson was forced to form a third party to avoid running on the same ticket with them. He lost badly.

In 1990 Speaker Madigan orchestrated a takeover of the state party. He backed a successful challenge to the sitting chairman by his chief of staff. In 1998 he took over the position by securing enough votes to get himself elected chair. He proceeded to turn the party organization into an adjunct of his campaign and fundraising organization. He raised money directly through the state party's committee and also transferred money raised through his other committees into the state party's committee. That money would be transferred to candidate committees. Candidate committees would transfer campaign funds to the state party, which would then do mailings and other in-kind services for campaigns at a cheaper rate than they could obtain individually. A greatly weakened state Republican Party also provided in-kind services for campaign committees that transferred money to the committee. But the state Republican Party committee raised very little money directly from private sector sources compared to the state Democratic Party. Currently neither state party engages in trying to shape a statewide ticket for constitutional offices or U.S. Senate seats.

Whatever influence Madigan exercised over primary elections for nomination for statewide office during his twenty-four years as Democratic Party state chair was not the result of his party position, but his legislative one. Going forward, the role of both state party organizations is likely to remain one of direct fundraising and receiving transfers from candidate committees, followed by providing in-kind services to candidate committees. It is unlikely either organization will evolve into playing an independent political leadership or policymaking role in the state.

Interest Groups and Major Donors

The methods and technologies that allow candidates to build organizations and identify and communicate with potential voters are very expensive. You can substitute capital for labor in modern elections, but that requires having or acquiring a lot of capital. All of this makes interest groups and wealthy candidates and donors much more important now than in the era of party-centered elections.[12]

In the last twenty years Illinois statewide and legislative elections have become increasingly expensive, far outpacing the rate of inflation. In 2002 Rod Blagojevich and Jim Ryan combined spent $38 million running for governor. Governor Pat Quinn and Bill Brady spent $47 million contesting the office in 2010. Four years later Bruce Rauner and Governor Quinn spent $104 million at the beginning of the era of billionaire politics in Illinois. In 2018 Rauner, with support from Ken Griffin, spent almost $84 million while JB Pritzker self-funded more than $172 million in spending. Together they spent more than $256 million. In the 2022 election the losing Republican candidate Darren Bailey totaled $52.5 in direct spending and independent expenditure support, while Governor Pritzker spent $141.3 million directly out of his campaign fund for a combined total of $193.8 million. A candidate backed by Griffin spent $50 million in the Republican primary and finished third. Since 2014 the staggering increase in the cost of races for governor and a few other constitutional office races has been funded primarily by individual wealthy and billionaire contributors rather than private sector sources. While the 2018 race for attorney general exceeded $22 million, the races for the nongubinatorial constitutional offices in 2022 were not competitive due to the lack of funding for the Republican candidates. None of the losing Republican candidates was outspent by a ratio of less than 6 to 1.

Targeted legislative races are those where one or both candidates receive heavy support from the legislative leader. In 1992 the average combined spending in a targeted House race was $250,000, and $500,000 for the Senate. By 2006 the averages for a targeted House and a targeted Sente race were $1.00 million and $1.35 million, respectively. Spending on these races has continued to escalate. In 2022 they averaged $264,000 combined spending in the House and $4.55 million in the Senate. The number of targeted races has declined as a function of the Democratic maps, which are designed to minimize competitive districts, and the sharp decline in Republican fundraising. After the 2018 election House and Senate Republican caucuses have struggled to raise money from private sector sources to replace the decreased support from Griffin and Uihlein. Individual races continue to become more expensive. One targeted Senate race in 2022 had combined spending of $6.2 million while two others exceeded $5.1 million. In the House, spending in the most expensive race topped $3.9 million, while three other races reached $3.0 million.

Money from private sector sources has always been important in funding legislative races. Table 3.1 shows the top twenty-five private sector contributors to Illinois politics for the 1999–2000 election cycle. A teachers' union, the Illinois Education Association, is the top group, and another teachers' union is fourth, while the Illinois State Medical Society is second. Sixteen of the top twenty-five groups are business and professional associations or individual companies. Seven are labor unions: two teachers' unions, three trade unions, one public employee union, and one service employee union. The remaining top twenty-five organization is a policy advocacy group for reproductive rights.

Table 3.2 shows the top twenty-five private sector donors from 2021 to 2022. The contrast is dramatic. Not only are the totals much higher in 2022, but unions have taken over the top of the list. The top seven groups on the list are five trade unions followed by two teacher unions. Two government worker unions, two service worker unions, and two more trade unions bring the total to thirteen unions in the top twenty-five. There are six business or professional associations, five individual companies, and one policy advocacy group.

Business and professional groups have lost ground over the past two decades. The Illinois Medical Society was the second biggest private sector contributor in 2000. In the last twenty-two years its contributions have decreased by 50

Table 3.1. Top 25 Private Sector Contributors, 1999–2000 Election Cycle (Interest Group, Association, Policy Group, and Corporate Contributors to Statewide and Legislative Candidate Committees and Political Party and Legislative Caucus Party Committees)

$1,394,000	IL Education Assn
$1,026,000	IL State Medical Society
$1,000,000	IL trial lawyers ($567,000 from IL Trial Lawyers Assn PAC and top 5 trial lawyer firms)
$976,000	IL Federation of Teachers and Chicago Teachers Union
$881,000	IL Hospital/Health Systems Assn
$776,000	Assoc Beer Distributors of Illinois (ABDI)
$716,000	Manufacturers PAC
$650,000	IBEW Electrical Worker Union ($238,000 IBEW Ed Committee)
$600,000	Ameritech-SBC Com
$550,000	Laborers unions ($204,000 Construction and General Laborers Chicago Council)
$486,000	AFSCME Council #31
$473,000	Cable TV & Comm Assn of IL
$450,000	IUOE Operating Engineers ($300,000 IUOE Local 150)
$446,000	IL Realtors Assn RPAC
$434,000	Commonwealth Edison
$425,000	IL BANK PAC
$401,000	Illinois Chamber of Commerce/Chicagoland Chamber of Commerce
$349,000	Philip Morris Co
$327,000	Personal PAC (Prochoice PAC)
$326,000	United Distillers & Vintners UDV
$292,000	Mayer Brown & Platt
$280,000	ILN PAC IL Power
$270,000	Empress Casino
$252,000	Hotel & Restaurant Employee Union TIP

Source: Illinois State Board of Elections.

Table 3.2. Top 25 Private Sector Contributors 2021–22 Election Cycle (Interest Group, Association, Policy Group, and Corporate Contributions to Statewide and Legislative Candidate Committees and Political Party Committees)

$18,634,000	International Union of Operating Engineers IUOE ($9,874,000 Chicago Land Operators Joint Labor-Management Committee)
$16,554,000	Laborers unions ($10,500,000 LiUNA Chicago Laborers District Council)
$6,301,000	Pipe Trade & Plumbers Union ($3,140,000 Illinois Pipe Trades PAC)
$5,574,000	Carpenters unions ($5,015,000 Carpentry Advancement Fund PAC)
$5,554,000	IBEW unions ($4,227,000 IBEW Illinois PAC)
$5,338,000	IPACE Illinois Education Assn
$5,193,000	IL Federation of Teachers and Chicago Teachers Union ($3,006,000 Illinois Federation of Teachers)
$4,476,000	IL Trial Lawyers Association & top 10 trial lawyer firms ($963,000 IL Trial Lawyers Assn)
$4,195,000*	Illinois Realtors PAC & IE ($2,953,000 Realtor PAC)
$3,985,000	SEIU Unions ($1,950,000 SEIU Illinois Council PAC FUND)
$3,926,000	Health Care Council of Illinois (nursing homes)
$2,103,000	AFSCME unions ($1,489,000 AFSCME)
$1,717,000	UFCW unions ($850,000 UFCW Local 881)
$1,547,000*	INCS Illinois Network of Charter Schools PAC & IE ($1,442,000 INCS IE)
$1,493,000	IL Healthcare & Hospital Association & affiliated entities ($666,000 IHA PAC)
$1,468,000	Firefighters unions ($959,000 Associated Fire Fighters of Illinois)
$1,278,000	Teamsters unions ($390,000 Teamsters Volunteers in Politics)
$1,117,000	Assoc Beer Distributors of Illinois ABDI
$1,088,000	Ameren Illinois
$891,000	Affordable Assisted Living Coalition
$740,000	SMART unions (Sheet Metal Air Rail Transportation Workers ($685,000 SMART Local 265)
$664,000	Comcast Cable
$543,000	J&J Ventures Gaming
$525,000	Accel Entertainment Gaming
$504,000	AT&T

Source: Illinois State Board of Elections.
*Combined PAC contributions and IE expenditures that benefit a candidate, caucus, or party committee.

percent and it has fallen out of the top twenty-five list. In 2000 the Illinois Manufacturers Association ranked seventh and the Illinois Chamber of Commerce/Chicagoland Chamber of Commerce ranked eighteenth. Neither was in the top twenty-five in the 2022 election cycle. The highest-ranking five business and professional groups are those representing trial lawyers, realtors, hospitals, nursing homes, and the beer distributors. The highest-ranking corporation is an energy company.

Historically, business and professional interests contributed more to Illinois politics than unions and contributed more to Republicans than Democrats. Those ratios have been reversed. In 2000 labor unions contributed almost $9 million to statewide and legislative elections, of which 79 percent went to Democratic committees. Business and professional interests contributed almost $34 million, of which 66 percent went to Republican committees. In 2022, labor contributions had increased more than nine times to $75 million, of which 93 percent went to Democratic committees. Business and professional contributions had increased more than 50 percent to almost $58 million, but 62 percent went to Democratic committees. The magnitude of these shifts can be seen in table 3.3, which compares the size and the partisan distribution of private sector contributions in four sectors of economic activity in the 1999–2000 election cycle with those in the 2021–22 election cycle. Law firms and attorneys are listed separately from business and professional contributions in these tables because of the increasing role that trial lawyers and firms play in Illinois politics. Their contributions now go overwhelmingly to Democratic committees.

In 2000, the Republicans controlled the governor's office and the State Senate with a three-seat margin, while the Democrats controlled the House, also by three seats. The legislative majorities remained the same after the election. The Republicans received 55 percent of all the private sector contributions, which gave them an advantage of almost $5.4 million. The largest contribution

Table 3.3. Changes in the Partisan Distribution of Private Sector Contributions over Time (in millions)

1999–2000 Election Cycle—Private Sector Contributions Benefiting Candidate, Legislative Caucus, and Party Committees*

	Total	Democrats	Republicans
Labor	$8.699 m	$6.923 m	$1.776 m
Business & professional	$33.851 m	$11.529 m	$22.322 m
Law	$5.834 m	$3.285 m	$2.549 m
Lobbyist/gov. affairs	$0.921 m	$0.284 m	$0.637 m
Policy organizations	$0.910 m	$0.392m	$0.518 m
Totals	$50.215 m	$22.413 m	$27.802 m

Republican advantage = $5.389 million

2021–22 Election Cycle—Private Sector Contributions and Independent Expenditures Benefiting Candidate, Legislative Caucus, and Party Committees†

	Total	Democrats	Republicans
Labor	$75.116 m	$69.811 m	$5.305 m
Business & professional	$57.731 m	$36.032 m	$21.699 m
Policy organizations	$6.843 m	$2.599 m	$4.244 m
Law	$9.319 m	$8.798 m	$0.521 m
Lobbyist/gov. affairs	$2.712 m	$2.274 m	$0.438 m
Total	$151.721 m	$119.514 m	$32.207 m

Democratic advantage = $87.307 million

Source: Illinois State Board of Elections.
Note: Independent Expenditures classification system began in 2011. Previously these were reported as in-kind contributions.
* Legislative elections in 2000, no statewide elections. Excludes judicial ballot elections.
† Statewide and legislative elections in 2022. Excludes judicial ballot elections.

sector was the business and professional groups, with more than 65 percent of the total contributions.

By 2022 the total contributed from private sector sources had tripled, while the partisan distribution had shifted strongly in favor of the Democrats. They received 79 percent of the total private sector contributions, which translates into an $87 million advantage. In addition to the shift of contributions from business and professional groups to Democratic committees, the Democrats continued to receive strong support from labor groups and law firms and groups. Labor at 49 percent was the largest contributor. The only area where the Republicans has a majority of the contributions was from policy advocacy organizations.

In addition to labor unions (trade, service, teacher, and public employee unions) the rest of the core of the funding base for the Democrats consists of trial lawyers and health facilities (hospitals and nursing homes). These groups have increased the size of their contributions and their share of the total contributions over the last two decades. The core of the funding base for the Republicans in 2000 was manufacturing, business associations, health professionals, realtors, and financial associations. With the exception of the realtors, these groups are contributing less in relative and in some cases absolute terms compared to twenty years ago.

When we think of the influence of interest groups on elections, we usually think in terms of a goal to win elections and either change or reinforce the partisan distribution of power. However, many interest groups make contributions not to influence elections but to build good will and facilitate lobbying activity. Major contributors to Illinois politics who focus more on access than on partisan outcomes include major utilities (AT&T, Ameren, Commonwealth Edison, Comcast) and wholesale and retail trade (Associated Beer Distributors of Illinois, Walgreens, Illinois Retail Merchants Association). The same is true to a lesser extent for groups representing business professionals. As a result of this focus, a significant part of the money contributed to candidate and party committees is not directly interested in partisan outcomes. These contributions do, however, have an indirect impact on elections.

Interest groups seeking access make contributions to incumbent legislators, committee chairs, and the legislative leaders, particularly those leaders who control the chamber. The Democrats have controlled both chambers of the General Assembly since 2002 and governor's office every term since 2002 except for 2015 through 2018. Since 2012 they have had supermajorities in the legislature for all but one two-year period. They currently hold more than 65 percent of the seats in each chamber. The cumulative impact of groups contributing strategically to gain access to power benefits the majority party and its leaders and members in each chamber. Money flows to power, which reinforces the power of the majority and the status quo.

The same dynamic applies to contributions from lobbyists and governmental affairs firms. While some of them have definite partisan affiliations, the majority of their contributions are aimed at gaining access. As a whole these groups give more to Democrats by a 3-to-1 ratio, largely reflecting the current power differential in Springfield.

Looking at overall fundraising by the Republican and Democratic candidate and party committees, the most important takeaway from the twenty-two years ago to now is that the Democrats fundraising advantage over the Republicans in contributions from private sector sources has become staggering when you exclude contributions from billionaire donors. But the important caveat is that this picture does not include the dynamics of wealthy self-funding candidates and billionaire politics that Illinois has experienced since the 2014 election cycle.

The Role of Billionaires and Wealthy Self-Funders in Elections

Prior to the 2013–14 election cycle, wealthy self-funding candidates and mega-wealthy donors (a few of them billionaires) played an irregular and secondary role in Illinois elections. As candidates they were almost always unsuccessful. Even when they won they did not sustain their political careers over time. Mega-wealthy donors were either consistent contributors to the candidates of one party or supporters of specific causes. That all changed in 2014 when Bruce Rauner contributed an unprecedented $27 million of his own money to his successful campaign for governor. He attracted the support of Republican-leaning billionaires, the most notable of whom were Ken Griffin and Richard Uihlein. In 2018, billionaire JB Pritzker self-funded his campaign, winning the Democratic nomination for governor and then defeating Rauner in his bid for reelection.

The shock to the established patterns of Illinois politics from the engagement of two extremely wealthy self-funding governors (one a billionaire) and two additional billionaires since 2013 is hard to put into perspective. At the end of the 2022 election cycle these four individuals will have spent more than three-quarters of a billion dollars to influence Illinois politics. In ten years in elections at all levels Pritzker has spent $383 million, Griffin $177 million, Uihlein $90 million, and Rauner $112 million, a total of $763 million.

The impact of billionaire politics on gubernatorial elections in 2014 and 2018 has already been noted. It also impacted other statewide elections. The election to fill the remaining two years in the vacant comptroller's office in 2016 was an

$11 million contest between big labor contributions and funding from Rauner, Griffin, and Uihlein. The attorney general race in 2018 was the most expensive in Illinois history. Total spending was more than $22 million, with Rauner and Griffin battling Pritzker and big labor.

This new dynamic also had a direct impact on legislative elections. In 2016 Rauner, Griffin, and Uihlein contributed more than $41 million directly and indirectly to the two Republican legislative leaders and the Illinois Republican Party. The money was then directed to Republican candidates and local county party organizations for legislative races. This reduced the resource gap created by the Democrats in fundraising from private sector sources to a more manageable $22 million, and helped the Republicans pick up four House seats and two Senate seats. The dynamic changed back to favor the Democrats in 2018 when Pritzker gained the Democratic nomination for governor. In addition to funding his own race, he contributed $20 million from his campaign fund to the two Democratic legislative leaders and the Democratic Party of Illinois. That canceled out all but $10 million of the $22 million that Rauner and Griffin directed to the Republican legislative leaders and Republican State Party and the $11 million that Uihlein gave to Liberty Principles PAC to fund Republican legislative candidates. With a $72 million advantage in private sector contributions for the 2018 cycle, the Democratic Party had a significant funding advantage in legislative elections again. The Democrats more than made up for their losses in 2016, gaining seven seats in the House and two in the Senate. With Rauner gone and Griffin and Uihlein disengaged in 2020, the funding patterns for the legislative elections were back to a pre-2014 pattern of a significant advantage for the Democrats. The same was true for the 2022 legislative elections, with the Democrats picking up five seats in the House, while losing one seat in the Senate. This is not good news for the Republicans given the underlying changes in demographic and voting patterns that we will be considering later.

It is not clear how billionaire politics will continue to be a part of Illinois politics. After losing in 2014, Rauner moved his residence and his company to Florida. Griffin followed suit in the summer of 2022 after the candidate he backed for governor in the Republican primary with $50 million finished third. Uihlein's continued participation in Illinois politics may be in doubt after little success in electing Republican candidates despite his spending more than $60 million in 2022. With Pritzker reelected to another four-year term, the Democrats will continue to benefit from his support until at least the end of 2026.

The Role of Money from National Groups in Illinois Elections

National groups engage in state elections when they see opportunities or dangers in elections that can shift the balance of power in a state or in the House or Senate in the U.S. Congress. These are usually an election for a governor, a US senator, or a congressional representative. But state attorney general races or elections for members of a state supreme court can also attract attention. In the 2010 and 2014 Illinois gubernatorial elections, both the National Republican and the National Democratic Governors Associations contributed a combined total of more than $22 million. In both cases, national Republican groups saw an opening to win in a blue state and national Democratic groups were playing defense. The 2018 and 2022 gubernatorial elections saw no national money, a reflection of Illinois's emerging solid blue voting patterns. While some congressional districts in Illinois both the northeast suburbs and downstate attracted attention from national groups in 2020 and 2022, the trends in voting and demographics discussed below suggest it is unlikely that Illinois will present more than a few congressional election contests in the near future that would interest any national groups.

Evolving Voting Patterns in Illinois

The evolution of the regional demographic profile of Illinois, its relation to the state's political profile, and the emerging voting patterns of the state were presented in chapter 2. Voting patterns have followed suit.[13] Table 3.4 shows the population change by region in Illinois over the last four census periods.

The basic takeaway is that the northeastern collar county region around Cook County has been gaining population, suburban Cook has been stable, and both Chicago and downstate Illinois have been losing population. These are not dramatic changes. A deeper dive into the census data shows that the state has become more racially diverse since 1990 largely due to increases in the

Table 3.4. Population Breakout by Region of the State

	1990	2000	2010	2020
Chicago	24.4%	23.3%	21.0%	21.4%
Suburban Cook	20.3%	20.0%	19.5%	19.7%
Five collar counties	19.2%	22.3%	25.1%	24.7%
Downstate	36.1%	34.4%	34.3%	34.1%

Source: U.S. Census Bureau.

percentage of Hispanic and Asian populations, the African American population remaining stable as percentage of the population, and the non-Hispanic white population declining approximately 10 percent. The state's significant population gains between 1990 and 2010 came from increases in the Hispanic and Asian populations, which offset losses in the white population.

The major political significance of the large demographic changes between 1990 and 2010 is that they took place primarily in seven northeastern counties—Cook, DuPage, Kane, Kendal, Lake, McHenry, and Will. During that time period this area gained 1.3 million Hispanics and Asians. At the same time the area lost 300,000 white residents while the African American population remained flat. This increase in diversity significantly changed the nature of the region. Because of changes in national policies on legal immigration, this pattern slowed significantly in the last decade.[14]

As discussed in chapter 2, Illinois politics during the time that Chicago mayor Richard J. Daley was at the height of his power followed a two-region model—Chicago versus downstate. The term "downstate" masked a lot of economic, social, and cultural diversity. But the defining attribute was "not Chicago." Chicago was Chicago Democratic, not to be confused with the downstate Democrats and the downstate Republicans.

The end of the Daley era in 1976 also marked a political split between the interests and politics of the growing northeastern suburbs around Chicago and the mixture of rural agriculture and mining and manufacturing of the rest of what was more clearly defined as downstate.[15] These economic and cultural distinctions framed the states politics as a three-region dynamic—Chicago, the suburban 5½, and downstate. The suburban area consisted of a solidly Republican area in Cook County surrounding Chicago and the five counties surrounding Cook County—DuPage, Lake, Will, McHenry, and Kane. With Chicago and the suburbs often battling to a standoff over political and policy conflicts, the more politically competitive downstate region was the battleground for statewide elections and control of the legislature.

With the regional shift in population and the growing diversity of Chicago and the northeastern suburbs since 1990, Illinois is now in its third iteration of regional politics. By the end of the 1990s suburban Cook has shifted from a Republican to a competitive, Democratic-leaning area while the collar counties were still reliably Republican but showing signs of being competitive. Over the next twenty years those trends continued. Suburban Cook is now solidly Democratic. The collar counties lean Democratic in statewide races. The county boards of DuPage, Lake, and Will Counties all have Democratic majorities and in 2022 for the first time a Democrat was elected chair of the DuPage County

Table 3.5. Change in Vote Share

Regional Share of General Election Vote for Governor					
	1990	2014	2018	2022	Change since 1990
Chicago	20.8%	18.1%	19.5%	16.1%	-4.7%
Suburban Cook	19.4%	19.0%	19.1%	18.3%	-1.1%
Cook	40.2%	37.1%	38.6%	34.4%	-5.8%
Collar counties	17.2%	24.9%	35.2%	26.5%	+9.3%
Downstate	42.4%	38.3%	36.1%	39.0%	-3.4.3%

Partisan Preference of Regional Share of General Election Vote for Governor					
	1990	2014	2018	2022	Change since 1990
Chicago	65.5% D	77.3% D	81.3% D	81.6% D	+15.1% D
Suburban Cook	58.5% R	53.8% D	62.2% D	65.1% D	+23.6% D
Cook	53.6% D	64.7% D	71.9% D	73.6% D	+20.0% D
Collar counties	62.8% R	59.5% R	48.6% D	53.8% D	+16.6% D
Downstate	51.2% R	60.8% R	58.7% R*	59.3% R	+8.1% R

Source: Illinois State Board of Elections.
*Non-Pritzker vote includes independent candidate.

Board in a countywide election. Chicago has become even more Democratic. At the same time, downstate has become solidly Republican. The only Democratic legislators come primarily from six districts anchored in downstate's six largest urban areas.

Table 3.5 shows the shift in the regional share of the statewide general election vote between 1990 and 2022 and the shifts in the partisan preference of the votes within the key regional areas. These numbers reflect the continuing consolidation of these trends in the politics of the three political regions of the state. Chicago and suburban Cook are more Democratic, downstate is more Republican, while the collar counties are competitive but lean Democratic. Whichever candidates can win the collar counties while retaining their base are likely to win in a statewide election.

The Outcome of Statewide Elections: President, Governor and Other Constitutional Officers, and U.S. Senate

The last Republican presidential candidate to carry Illinois was George H. W. Bush in 1988. When Illinois voters look at politics through a national lens, the Democratic base overwhelms the Republican base. Presidential candidates may visit Illinois looking to raise money, but they do not come here looking for votes. The outcome of the election is never in doubt. In 2022 U.S. Senator Tammy Duckworth was easily reelected for a second six-year term. She defeated

Senator Mark Kirk in 2016. Since 1985, Illinois has elected only two Republicans to the U.S. Senate. Both served only one term. It is still possible for a Republican to be elected to statewide office in Illinois. It has only been eight years since a Republican was elected governor. However, the last Republican governor before Rauner left office twenty-four years ago after one failed term amid a growing political scandal that would send him to prison. The population and demographic trends and the changes in regional voting behavior continue to work in favor of the Democrats. The recent shift of the Republican primary electorate to the right and the continuing collapse of the private sector funding base of the Republican Party only add to the difficulties of the Republican Party in Illinois.

The 2022 election did not provide any reason for optimism for the Republicans as a party. The Democrats captured all of the constitutional offices in 2022, repeating their sweep in 2018. Aided by new congressional and state legislative maps, which they drew, they continued their overwhelming success in legislative elections.

The regional breakdown of Governor Pritzker's reelection victory in 2022 in table 3.6 shows the regional structure of the dominance of the Democrats in statewide elections.[16] Chicago, suburban Cook, and the collar counties contributed 61 percent of the total vote for governor in 2022. Pritzker won 64.6 percent of those votes. Downstate accounted for 39 percent of the total vote. Bailey won 59.3 percent of those votes.

A breakdown of the votes in Bruce Rauner's victory over incumbent governor Pat Quinn in 2014 (table 3.7) shows a path for a Republican to win statewide. But it takes the right combination of factors—a substantial funding advantage, an unpopular governor, and a campaign aimed at both suburban and downstate voters stressing economic issues and the failures of Democratic control of state

Table 3.6. 2022 Election for Governor

Pritzker (D)	Vote totals	% of vote for the region
Chicago margin	415,000	81.6
Suburban Cook margin	240,000	65.1
Cook County margin	655,000	73.6
Collar county margin	113,000	53.4
Total margin	768,000	
Bailey (R)	Vote totals	% of vote for the region
Downstate margin and total margin	346,000	59.3
Pritzker	768,000	54.4%
Bailey	346,000	42.8%
Final margin	422,000	

Source: Illinois State Board of Elections.

Table 3.7. 2014 Election for Governor

Quinn (D)	Vote totals	% of vote for region
Chicago margin	373,000	78%
Suburban Cook margin	51,000	54%
Total	424,000	
Rauner (R)	Vote totals	% of vote for region
Collar counties margin	196,000	61%
Downstate margin	370,000	64%
Total	566,000	
Rauner	566,000	50.3%
Quinn	424,000	46.4%
Final margin	142,000	

Source: Illinois Board of Elections.

government while downplaying or avoiding social issues. In 2014 Rauner won the collar counties, cut Quinn's margin in suburban Cook compared to his showing in 2010, and won downstate decisively.

In 2018 Pritzker won the collar countries by a narrow margin and won suburban Cook with 65 percent of the vote. Combined with his margin in Chicago, his lead going downstate was insurmountable. The results of the 2022 election show a further consolidation of Democratic strength in the collar counties to go with their dominance in suburban Cook and total dominance in Chicago. In 2022 Pritzker won Chicago and Cook County by 655,000 votes. He won the collar counties by 113,000 votes. Heading downstate the Pritzker margin stood at 768,000. Even through Bailey won Downstate by 342,000 votes he still lost the election by 422,000 votes (see table 3.6).

No Republican statewide candidate can run strong enough downstate to counter the current loss of Republican votes in the collar counties against a Democratic candidate who also produces the same margins coming out of Chicago and suburban Cook as in 2018 and 2022. The dilemma for the Republicans is how to nominate candidates who can win both suburban voters and downstate voters. Rauner was that candidate in 2014, but by 2018 he had lost suburban support because of his failures on the budget and governing and lost downstate support after a conservative challenge in the primary because he was seen as soft on social conservative issues like abortion. Current trends show that the downstate share of the statewide Republican primary vote is increasing while the collar county share is decreasing. This makes a repeat of the 2022 Republican primary more likely, when the candidate with the most appeal to suburban Republican moderates and independent voters in a general election ran third in the primary to a socially conservative downstate Republican state senator.

Legislative Redistricting—The Importance of Maps

All legislative bodies that elect members from districts, rather than at large, must redistrict every ten years following the decennial U.S. Census. This is in response to U.S. Supreme Court decisions that require the districts from which single members are elected to be substantially equal in population. This principle, commonly referred to as "One person, one vote," was established by the U.S. Supreme Court in a series of cases in the 1960s.[17] Before the Court got involved there were large discrepancies in the populations of legislative districts. It was not unusual for one legislator to represent twice as many voters as another legislator in another district. The court found such arrangements unconstitutional. An additional problem was that states and local government would go many years without changing the boundaries of districts. The one person, one vote ruling instituted a process of redistricting every ten years based on Census population data.

Legislative redistricting is not the same as congressional reapportionment. Current law provides for 435 members of Congress, with each state having at least one representative and the rest being divided among the states on the basis of population. This process takes place every ten years after the U.S. Census. States with growing populations gain seats while states with slow or no growth lose seats. In the latest reapportionment Illinois lost one congressional seat, dropping from eighteen to seventeen. Illinois then drew new congressional districts through the process of redistricting to ensure that the new districts complied with the one person, one vote criteria.

In addition to substantially equal populations, districts are also required to be compact and contiguous. Contiguous means that all the territory in a district must be connected. You cannot have a county board district that has one part in the northern end of a county and a second part of in the southern part of a county with no physical connection between the two parts. You could make the district contiguous by connecting it by a road that went through the two parts, but the shape of the district would not be compact. In addition, districts must comply with Supreme Court rulings and federal law (the 1965 Voting Right Act) to ensure that voting rights are protected. Maps that discriminate on the basis of race are unconstitutional, but it is unclear from recent decisions how the Supreme Court will apply the 1965 Voting Rights Act in specific cases going forward.

Federal constitutional protection does not extend to protection against maps that are drawn to create a partisan advantage. Such maps are called partisan gerrymanders. The U.S. Supreme Court in 2019 refused to invalidate maps explicitly drawn to create a partisan disadvantage as being a violation of individual voting rights in *Rucho v. Common Cause*.[18] Any action to address the inequities created by partisian gerrymanders will have to come from the states for the foreseeable future.

State and local bodies like city councils, county boards, and school boards must comply with federal and state laws and constitutional principles when redistricting, too. Laws and ordinances that create new legislative districts are subject to state and federal judicial review. States vary widely in the process and politics of redistricting. Some states have created appointed redistricting commissions outside of the legislative process that have the power to adopt binding redistricting plans. Most states, however, begin with a legislative process. District maps are temporary laws that set the boundaries for state legislative and congressional districts for a ten-year period. If one party controls the legislature and the governor's office, the potential exists for the majority party to draw a map without input from the minority party. If control of the legislative chamber is split or if the governor is of a different party than one or both chambers, the potential for a stalemate exists. States have various methods to resolve stalemates. Some rely on the state courts to resolve stalemates over state legislative maps and federal courts to resolve stalemates over congressional maps.

The basic population and political demographics of a state or a region provide a structure that is overlayed by a map. Where people are located and their voting tendencies are fixed in the short run. Mapmakers have to work with that structure. Downstate Illinois is strongly Republican. Its population is mostly spread out over large rural areas, but some of it is concentrated in a few urban areas. Those urban areas tend to be Democratic. Although you cannot redistribute the population or dramatically change voting behavior in the short term, you can join groups of voters together or split them apart. The same is true for the collar county suburban region and Chicago/suburban Cook.

Illinois Congressional Redistricting and Elections

The Illinois constitution is silent on the process for redistricting congressional districts. In recent history there have been three outcomes in Illinois. The legislative process either produces a partisan map that is signed into law, a compromise map that is signed into law, or a stalemate that is resolved by the federal courts considering alternative proposals.

The 2001 congressional map created for the 2002 election was a compromise map negotiated by sitting members of the Illinois congressional delegation. Illinois was losing one seat due to reapportionment. The new map was designed to eliminate the district of the newest member of the delegation (a downstate

Democrat) and then reelect the remaining ten Republican and nine Democratic incumbents. It worked as planned for two election cycles, but after the 2010 election there were eleven Republicans and eight Democrats elected.[19]

The Democrats won of all branches of state government in 2002 and retained supremacy through the decade. In 2011 the Democrats in the legislature passed a new congressional map, which was signed by the governor. The new map had eighteen districts after losing one through reapportionment. The map retained seven Chicago-based districts from the old map, reduced the suburban districts by one from six to five, and retained six downstate districts. Democrats held the seven Chicago-based districts through the five election cycles the map was in effect.

The intent in the suburbs was to create three Democratic-leaning districts and pack Republicans into two safe districts while eliminating one Republican district. The result would be a shift from four Republican districts and two Democratic districts in the suburbs to three Democratic districts and two Republican districts. The demographic and political shifts in the suburbs since 1990 made this reconfiguration possible. The maps worked as planned for the first three elections of the cycle. In 2018 the Democrats flipped the two remaining Republican districts in the suburbs and retained those seats in the 2020 election. These outcomes reflected the changing demographics and voting patterns in the suburbs that the 2011 Democratic map had underestimated.

The intent downstate was to create three Republican districts and three Democratic districts. One potential Democratic district was based in Rockford, the Quad Cities, and Peoria; one in the metro east; and a third was a north-south district in central Illinois. The central Illinois district failed to elect a Democratic during the life of the 2012 map, while the metro east district elected a Democrat in the 2012 election and then Republican in the next four elections. Instead of a 3–3 split, the Republican held a 5–1 advantage by the end of the cycle. This portion of the map underestimated the shift toward the Republicans downstate. Overall, the Democrats held a 13–5 majority after the 2020 election.[20]

In 2021 the Democratic legislature passed a new congressional map, which was signed by Democratic governor Pritzker. Illinois lost one district through the 2021 reapportionment, which reduced the number of congressional districts in Illinois from eighteen to seventeen. The intent of the new map is to maintain the seven Chicago-based districts and the five suburban districts that elected Democrats under the old map in 2020.

Downstate, the Democrats' intent was to reduce the number of districts from six to five by eliminating a district that had elected a Republican, which stretched from Wisconsin to Indiana along the border between downstate and the extended northeastern suburbs. All that territory was placed into the surrounding new districts. Next, they created a district designed to elect a Democrat that stretched from Champaign/Urbana through Springfield and then south all the way to East St. Louis in metro east. Then they expanded the one district that had elected a downstate Democrat under the old map to include more of the area around Rockford, the Quad Cities, and Peoria. If successful, this would change the downstate configuration from five Republicans and one Democrat to three Republicans and two Democrats. The new maps worked exactly as planned in the 2022 election: eliminating a Republican district through reapportionment, flipping a Republican seat to a Democratic seat, and holding the remaining districts that elected Democrats under the old map. The overall result was a fourteen-to-three majority for the Democrats in Illinois congressional delegation.[21]

Congressional elections are contested in districts within states, but they have national implications. Because of the competitiveness of the two downstate Democratic seats, both national parties will evaluate them every election cycle under the current maps and make judgments about whether a particular election cycle raises a threat to the Democrats or an opportunity for the Republicans. National political groups that are either highly ideologically or policy motivated will make the same calculations. This process of evaluation is critical, because contested congressional elections are very expensive and the funding is dominated by national party money and money from national groups.

If current demographic and political trends continue in the northeastern suburbs, the suburban districts that have generated national attention from Republican funders may generate less attention going forward than they did in the 2020 election under the old map and the 2022 election under the new map. The Democrats created a second district to elect a Hispanic member in the 2022, which resulted in two Democrats incumbents running against each other and less flexibility overall in creating stronger districts in the suburbs for the remaining incumbents. The fact that that all the Democrat's suburban incumbents ended up winning comfortably is a good sign for the viability of the map for the Democrats for the rest of the ten-year cycle in which the map will be in effect.

Like the map created for the 2012 election, the 2022 map represents an extreme partisan gerrymander that takes advantage of Democratic control of Cook County and growing Democratic strength in the northeastern suburbs while using creative mapmaking to link up pockets of Democratic strength downstate. The 2012 map did not work out as planned downstate. This new map is less ambitious and may be as effective as is possible in maximizing Democratic advantage in congressional races through partisan gerrymandering. In 2022 statewide Illinois elected a governor and the other constitutional offices with majorities that averaged 54 percent of the total vote. At the same time, Democrats won 82 percent of the congressional districts in Illinois.

Illinois State Legislative Elections: Demographics, Redistricting, and Money

The Illinois constitution provides an initial legislative process for redistricting the state legislature. If the legislature passed a new map and the governor signed the map before the first of July in the odd-numbered year after the U.S. Census, the new map becomes law. If a map is not signed into law before the deadline, a process involving an appointed redistricting commission is triggered. The redistricting commission initially has eight members, two appointed by each of the four legislative leaders. If they are unable to reach an agreement that receives five votes, a ninth member of the commission is chosen by lot from two names submitted by the longest-serving State Supreme Court justice elected as a Democrat and the longest-serving State Supreme Court justice elected as a Republican. Once a map is approved with five votes it becomes law.[22]

This mechanism was designed to promote compromise in the legislature and in the initial redistricting commission because going to the tiebreaker process risks putting one party in charge of the process regardless of who controls the legislature or the governor's office. The process worked as intended once, in 1971 when the eight-member redistricting commission reached a compromise. In 1981 the process broke down and the Democrats won by drawing a name out of a hat. In 1991 the process again went to a tiebreaker. This time the Republicans won the draw. The Democrats won the draw in 2001 when the process again went to a tiebreaker. In 2011 the Democrats had control of all of state government and passed a new map without going to the redistricting commission. The same was true in 2021. The Democrats have now drawn the last three state legislative maps.

Like congressional elections, legislative elections begin by overlaying district maps on top of the population and political demographic of the regions of the state. Given the underlying dynamic present in 2022, the redistricting strategies pursued by the Democrats were not surprising. They played defense with downstate districts that had elected Democrats, seeking to protect the seats of the few incumbent senators and representatives they had elected under the old map. In Chicago and most of suburban Cook, the Democrats had compete monopolies. Most of the internal conflict in the Democratic caucuses about maps for districts located primarily in Chicago or suburban Cook centered around disputes among Black, Hispanic, and Asian interests over how many districts they would control. In the growing, more diverse suburban areas the Democrats were aggressive, trying to create districts that would expand their caucuses in the House and the Senate. In the 2022 election, this strategy worked better for House districts than for Senate districts in the suburbs.

There are natural conflicts between the goals of the House members and the Senate members of the party that controls the map making. The Senate would like to create 59 districts that maximize the number of districts they can win and then split them into 118 House districts. The House would like to create 118 districts that maximize the number of districts they can win and then combine them into 59 Senate districts. On the margins, these divergent goals can create conflicts.

Overall, the Democrats won 78 of 118 House seats and 40 of 59 Senate seats in the 2022 election. This was a gain of five House seats and a loss of one Senate seat for the Democrats. As percentage of the total seats, the Democrats won 66 percent of the House seats and 68 percent of the Senate seats.[23]

The real action created by the 2022 map took place in contests for House seats in the northeastern suburbs. The Democrats were aggressive in constructing districts that put incumbent Republicans at a disadvantage and created opportunities to flip seats. The Democrats in the House already had thirty-four of the fifty House seats located primarily in suburban Cook and the collar counties. They added five more in 2022. At the same time, they retained the same number of House seats in Chicago and downstate that they held after the 2020 election. These gains in House seats in the suburbs are partially attributable to the changing population and political demographics of the area. But control of the map allowed the Democrats to take maximum advantage of these trends in elections for House seats.

At the same time, the Democrats in the Senate lost one downstate seat, while maintaining the same number of suburban and Chicago seats. This is consistent with past redistricting outcomes. Over the last five times the legislature has drawn new maps through the redistricting process, the party controlling the process has gained an average of almost six House seats. The gains in the Senate are slightly more than two seats. This is partially explained by the fact that House districts are easier to manipulate for partisan gain because both their populations and geographic size are smaller than Senate districts. In competitive

areas, getting enough voters in a Senate district to meet the population requirement may dilute the partisan strength of the district because of a lack of options about where to draw those voters. Creating a favorable House district is
not contingent on joining it with a district that would create a favorable Senate
district.

Another factor is the limit to how much partisan advantage you can gain
through a partisan gerrymander. In the case of congressional maps, as noted
above, the Democrats control 82 percent of the congressional seats, but only
enjoy a 54–46 percent advantage in statewide elections. After the 2020 election the Democrats controlled 62 percent of the House seats and 69 percent
of the Senate seats. The new map raised the Democrats share of House seats
to 66 percent, which is still slightly less than their share of Senate seats. An
alternative perspective on the 2022 outcome is that after drawing three maps
in a row the Democrats are reaching the maximum partisan advantage you can
wring out of a map for Senate districts, given the underlying demographics
and voting trends. From this perspective the House Democrats may have been
underperforming in the suburbs under the 2012 map, while the 2022 map created better opportunities in the northeastern suburbs for them to match the
gains they had already made in Senate districts.

While maps are important, they are only one of a number of factors that
explain the outcome of any legislative election. The one Senate seat the Democrats lost in 2022 illustrates their limitations. As downstate has become more
Republican, a familiar pattern emerged. Voters in areas represented by long-
term conservative Democratic legislators tended to reelect incumbents even
though they were voting Republican in national and statewide elections. When
these legislators retire, the Democrats nominate conservative Democrats to
replace them. Without the familiarity of incumbency, the voters looked at their
choices and said in essence, "If I am going to vote for a Republican, I might as
well vote for a real Republican."

While this pattern occurred first in rural areas, it is also occurring in downstate urban areas, where population and job losses have reduced the Democratic
base. Under the old map the Democrats initially elected two state senators and
four representatives in the metro east area. By 2020 the number of Democratic
representatives from the area had been reduced to three. The new map for the
2022 election tried to shore up the weaker of the two Senate districts by moving
some minority voters from the stronger district into the weaker district. Not
only did that fail, but a long-time Democratic representative from the stronger
Senate district also lost. While the Democrats may reclaim that House seat,

history suggests that the Senate seat will remain in Republican hands as the demographics and voting trends work against the Democrats.

In addition to the underlying demographics and a favorable map, the Democrats also had a huge advantage in money to spend on campaigns. As noted earlier, the private sector funding base for the Democrats is very strong and growing, while the funding base for the Republicans has been shrinking over the past twenty years. In 2022 the two Republican billionaires who had provided support to compensate for part of the Republicans' funding deficit focused their contributions on statewide offices rather than continuing their support for legislative elections. Griffin spent only $1 million on legislative races. Uihlein spent less than $3 million on state legislative races. In almost all the competitive legislative elections in 2022, the Democrat candidate had an overwhelming funding advantage.

The Nature of Legislative Elections: Two Worlds and the Critical Role of Legislative Leaders

In elections for the Illinois legislature, the length of the terms of legislators and the structure of the two chambers of the General Assembly set up by the 1970 state constitution create two different rhythms. With House members serving two-year terms, all 118 house seats are up every two years. Each House seat is contested within the state and national political context of that particular election cycle. In the Senate, all of the seats are up in a redistricting year (for example, 2022). Each district then fits into one of three patterns of length of terms for the next ten years: 4–4–2, 4–2–4, or 2–4–4. As a result, some senators will be initially elected for four-year terms and some will be elected for two-year terms. Following the 2022 redistricting election when all the House and Senate seats were up, only one-third of the Senate seats will be up for reelection in 2024 along with all the House. In the third and fourth elections held under the new map (2026 and 2028), two-thirds of the Senate seats will be up along with all of the House, and in the final election before decennial redistricting (2030), one-third of the Senate seats will be up along with all of the House.

When it comes to competition and campaign spending, there are two different worlds of legislative elections in Illinois.[24] In the first world, which constitutes the large majority of the legislative districts, one party has a distinct advantage in the district. These are "safe" districts. In the general elections, well-known, well-funded, usually incumbent majority party candidates easily defeat unknown, underfunded candidates representing the party that is in the political minority in the district. Competitive elections do occur occasionally in this world when an incumbent chooses not to run for reelection, but these competitive elections take place in the primary election, not the general. The majority's local party organizations in the counties, townships, and wards exercise great influence in the primary elections in these districts. Success breeds success. The party in the majority tends to control local political offices and hold power on a consistent basis because it is able to raise money and build organizational strength in ways the minority party in the district cannot match. Candidates in primaries in safe districts tend to be recruited by local party organizations or are self-recruited. Legislative leaders rarely get involved with primary elections in safe districts.

In the second world, a small number of contests that will determine control of the legislature are fought between two well-funded candidates backed by professional campaign staff. These hyper-expensive and usually very competitive races are known as targeted races. The name comes from the fact that they are being targeted by one or both of the legislative leaders in the House or the Senate. Initially, the number of potential targets may be 20 of 118 House seats and 5–10 of the one-third or two-thirds of the Senate seats that are up for election in a non-redistricting year. Ultimately, 8–10 House seats and 4–6 Senate seats will be the major targets for the election cycle.

Not all competitive districts become targets, and not all targeted districts become competitive. Regardless of the criteria for designating a district as competitive (for example, 55 percent to 45 percent or 52 percent to 48 percent), it is not possible to know in advance whether a district will be competitive. Legislative leaders and interest groups make reasoned judgments about which districts present the best opportunities or dangers for change and invest in those elections accordingly. After an election is over, a review of the election results and the money and effort spent by leaders on legislative races will show a number of targeted districts with competitive results. But there will also be districts targeted by one or both sides where the race was hugely expensive but not very competitive. Less frequently there will be districts where the outcomes were very close but where little or no money from leaders or organizational resources were directed at the race.

In 2022, there were 41 of the 118 House seats with only one candidate. This number was below average because the House Republicans tried to field as many candidates as possible through a recruitment effort. Of the remaining seventy-nine seats that were contested, the losing candidate received 40 percent or less in forty-six of them. Of the twenty-three that were at least mildly competitive, only ten had sufficient leadership funding to be considered a targeted race. In the Senate thirty-four of the fifty-nine seats were uncontested. There were five additional races where the losing candidate had 40 percent of less. Of the remaining twenty seats only five had sufficient leadership funding to be considered a targeted race.

The world of the targeted legislative elections in Illinois is dominated by the legislative leaders, who function as political parties. The leaders recruit candidates, raise money with their personal political committees or leadership political committees, and manage and fund the campaigns. When the legislature comes into session, the legislative leaders provide organization and structure by means of their caucuses. As is discussed in more detail in chapter 6, "The Legislature," in the past four decades power in the legislature has become extremely centralized in the legislative leaders. Their power comes from the interrelated dynamic of their ability to raise money and spend it on legislative campaigns, their dominance of the policy process in the legislature, and their monopoly control over the partisan legislative staffs.

Although the Speaker of the House and the Senate president are the most powerful actors in the legislature, each of the leaders in each chamber exercises power in the legislative process through control of political caucuses and partisan legislative staffs. Power in Springfield translates into the ability to raise money and influence legislative elections. It also translates into the ability to build campaign organizations using legislative staff members on leave from the legislature. The resulting strength in legislative elections builds power in Springfield. And the resulting increase in power in Springfield builds power in legislative elections.

As noted earlier, under Illinois campaign finance law, legislative leaders can manipulate the system of contributions limits through waivers to raise money through their candidate committees from private sector sources in unlimited amounts. Money can also be transferred from their candidate committee without limits to the legislative caucus committee they control or their state party committee. Because these legislative caucus committees are considered political party committees under Illinois law, they can transfer money without limit directly to the candidate committees of their members or direct money through the state party committee to a candidate committee. Although the mechanisms vary, over the past four decades legislative leaders of both parties in the House and the Senate have become more and more involved with raising money and using it to fund legislative campaigns.

The four legislative leaders operate independently in their election activities. There is usually very little coordination or cooperation between House and Senate Democrats or between House and Senate Republicans. Elections in House districts in 2022 were contested between House Speaker Welch's "political party" and House Minority Leader Durkin's "political party"; while elections in Senate districts were contested between Senate President Harmon's "political party" and Senate Minority Leader McConchie's "political party." Individual House members sometimes get involved in a Senate race, and vice versa, but it is not a regular pattern. For purposes of legislative elections, there is no unified Democratic or Republican Party in Illinois. This compartmentalization carries over into the legislative process, further complicating the task of solving public policy problems.

As the legislature comes into session in the spring after the fall general election, the next two-year election cycle has already begun. Each of the legislative leaders will look at the results of the past election and begin planning how to keep a majority or gain a majority. The legislative maps, political geography, and election results will drastically limit the number of districts where there may be a chance for a change in party control. In the Senate, the fact that only one-third or two-thirds of the seats may be up will further limit the available options for change. This election calculus is more compressed and complicated following a redistricting because the new districts may not be known until early fall of the first year of the cycle, and new district lines increase uncertainty about the outcome of elections. Each leader will begin with a list of districts where there is an opportunity to pick up a seat or the danger of losing a seat. Events such as an unexpected retirement or a personal scandal may alter that list. The leader will also make a judgment as to how favorable the political climate will be at the time of the general election. One leader may pursue an aggressive, offense-oriented strategy that focuses on potential gains; another may pursue a cautious, defense-oriented strategy that focuses on potential losses.

Leaders will become actively involved in candidate recruitment if the targeted district is without an incumbent or if the incumbent is from the other party. If possible, they will work with local parties and interest groups. If the leaders have a strong preference for a candidate in the primary, they will provide campaign support that can range from organizational support and candidate training to workers, funds, and expenditures on behalf of the candidate. The financial and organizational support will usually come directly from the leader's political committee rather than from the legislative chamber's political committee in order to avoid the appearance that the legislative party is taking sides in a local primary. If a leader is committed to a candidate, the expenditure of funds on building support for the candidate as a foundation for the fall election can be substantial.

Once the candidates are in place for the general election, the legislative leaders will make another assessment of their election strategy. Since campaigns are relational contests between two candidates, the strength or weakness of the opposition candidate may cause a district to rise or fall as a priority. Any movement beyond an initial level of support may be contingent on the candidate's ability to raise money locally, build an organization, or increase their polling numbers. Because the leader's goal is to win seats rather than elect a particular candidate, it is not unusual to see resources shifted from one district to another as the campaigns progress.

The keys to executing the leaders' election strategies are money and organization. The leaders may transfer money to a candidate directly or spend it on behalf of the candidate in the form of campaign staff, direct mail, or media advertising. The amount of money spent in targeted legislative races is staggering compared to the amount spent in nontargeted races. In 2022 one targeted Senate race exceeded $6 million in combined spending, while two others exceeded $5 million in combined spending. In the House four targeted races exceeded $3 million in combined spending.

As noted earlier, the dramatic increase in contributions from wealthy self-funding candidates and billionaire donors in 2014 combined with decrease in the traditional funding base of the Republican Party dramatically altered the dynamics of funding legislative elections for the Republicans. The impact of those changes on funding legislative elections can be seen in sidebar 3.1, which shows the funding of legislative races in 2016.

In 2016 Rauner, Griffin, and Uihlein on the Republican side were fully engaged. The Democrats had no billionaire supporters to counter them. The Republicans focused their efforts primarily on the House. The impact of the billionaire funding produced a slight advantage for the Republican in spending on targeted races. It also gave the House Republicans an almost 3 to 1 advantage over the House Democrats in fundraising for legislative leader and caucus committees. Committees controlled by the House Republican leader received $12 million from Rauner, $5 million from Griffin, and $10 million from the state Republican Party. The state Republican Party topped the Democratic Party of Illinois by a margin of more than 2 to 1. Rauner contributed $21 million from his candidate committee while the Munger campaign for comptroller transferred $3 million after receiving $8 million from Rauner, Griffin, and Uihlein. In the Senate, the Democrats retained an advantage in leadership fundraising and a slight advantage in spending. (See sidebar 3.1.)

The efforts of Rauner and Griffin to fund Republican candidates in 2016 produced a more level playing field, particularly in the House. The Democrats' advantage in fundraising from private sector sources was still substantial, but the Republicans were fighting on much better terms. They picked up two seats in the Senate and four seats in the House. The pickups in the House dropped

Sidebar 3.1. 2016 General Election:
Total Spending in Key Legislative Races

Senate: 7 key races, two-thirds of seats up → Republicans pick up 2 seats (D 37, R22)

Democrats	$13.69 million	$1.95 million per race (average legislative leader support 56%)
Republicans	$10.92 million	$1.56 million per race (average legislative leader support 71%)
Total	$24.61 million	$3.51 million per race

Senate leaders—total net resources available from leader and caucus committees

Democratic Senate president	$12.01 million
Republican Senate minority leader	$9.53 million (includes $5.91 million from state Republican Party)

House: 16 key races, all seats up → Republicans pick up 4 seats (D 67, R 51)

Democrats	$25.26 million	$1.58 million per race (average legislative leader support 57%)
Republicans	$26.68 million	$1.68 million per race (average legislative leader support 62%)
Total	$51.94 million	$3.26 million per race

House leaders—total net resources available from leader and caucus committees

Democratic House Speaker	$11.64 million
Republican House minority leader	$31.41 million (includes $12 million Rauner, $5 million Griffin, $10 million state Republican Party)

State political party net resources

Democratic Party of Illinois	$9.27 million
Illinois Republican Party	$25.13 million (Includes $21 million Rauner and $3 million Griffin/Rauner/Uihlein through Munger campaign)

Total private sector contributions to statewide, legislative, legislative caucus, and political party committees

Democrats	$93.23 million
Republicans	$30.26 million
Democrat advantage = $62.97 million	

Source: Illinois State Board of Elections.

the Democrats' majority below 60 percent, which meant that they no longer had a supermajority. For the next two years the Republicans were in a position to sustain vetoes issued by Governor Rauner.

The profile of the 2022 general election, shown in sidebar 3.2, contrasts significantly from the one from 2016. Rauner left the state in 2020. Uihlein stopped funding Liberty Principles PAC in 2019. In 2022 Griffin and Uihlein were focused on the Republican primary for governor. Griffin contributed $1 million the House Republican leader in the primary, but by the time the general election campaign had begun he had disengaged from Illinois politics except for funding in an independent expenditure committee for State Supreme Court

Sidebar 3.2. 2022 General Election:
Total Spending in Key Legislative Races

Senate: 5 key races, all seats up → Republicans pick up 1 seat (D 40, R 19)

Democrats	$15.65 million	$3.11 million per race (average legislative leader support 70%)
Republicans	$7.20 million	$1.44 million per race (average legislative leader support 75%)
Total	$19.7 million	$4.55 million per race

Senate leaders—total net resources available from leader and caucus committees

Democratic Senate president	$26.15 million (includes $3.0 million from Pritzker)
Republican Senate minority leader	$9.36 million (includes $2.6 million from Uihlein)

House: 10 key races, all seats up → Democrats pick up 5 seats (D 78, R 40)

Democrats	$19.78 million	$1.98 million per race (average legislative leader support 67%)
Republicans	$6.59 million	$0.66 million per race (average legislative leader support 50%)
Total	$26.37 million	$2.64 million per race

House leaders—total net resources from leader and caucus committees

Democratic House Speaker	$33.86 million (includes $8 million from Pritzker)
Republican House minority leader	$8.55 million (includes $1 million from Griffin)

State political parties net resources

Democratic Party of Illinois	$21.76 million (includes $4.4 million net from Governor Pritzker)
Illinois Republican Party	$7.40 million

Total private sector contributions to statewide, legislative, legislative caucus, and political party committees

Democrats	$119.51 million
Republicans	$32.21 million
Democrat advantage	$87.30 million

Source: Illinois State Board of Elections.

races. Uihlein was primarily engaged in supporting his candidate for governor. He contributed $2.6 million to the Republican Senate minority leader. He also contributed $1.5 million to an independent expenditure group making contributions in Republican candidates' House races. Governor Pritzker contributed $3 million to the Democratic Senate president and $8 million to the House Democratic Speaker, more than matching Griffin and Uihlein's support. He contributed a net $4.4 million to the Democratic Party of Illinois. The major advantage the Republicans had from contributions from billionaires in 2016 is gone, leaving the Democratic with more money, favorable demographic and voting history advantages, and favorable legislative district maps.

The fundraising and spending on legislative races in 2022 strongly reflected the Democrats' advantage in raising money from private sector sources for legislative elections. The House and Senate Democratic legislative leaders had an overwhelming advantage over the Republicans in the leadership and legislative caucus committees they use to support their candidates in targeted races. The Senate Democrats' advantage was almost 2 to1, while the House Democrats' advantage was almost 4 to 1. The same is true for the resources available for the two state political parties, with the Democratic Party of Illinois holding an almost 3 to 1 advantage. In terms of the targeted races, the spending advantage for Senate Democratic candidates was more than 2 to 1, while it was almost 3 to 1 for the House Democratic candidates. In overall contributions from private sector sources, the Democrats has an advantage of more the $87 million.

Looking at average spending per target race, the Senate Democrats increased $1.16 million per race over 2016, while the Senate Republicans decreased by $120,000. In House targeted races, the Democrats increased their average spending by $400,000 while spending for House Republican candidates decreased by over $1 million per race. Only one of the ten House Republican candidates spent more than $1 million, while four of the ten House Democratic candidates spent more than $1 million and five spent more than $3 million.

Historically in these targeted contests, the leaders were directly responsible for nearly one-half of the money spent by incumbents and nearly two-thirds of the money spent by challengers. The figures are higher for challengers because incumbents can raise money more easily than challengers. The leadership support figures understate the fiscal impact of the leaders on targeted races because interest groups who care which party controls the legislature will direct contributions to the candidates whom the leaders support. It is always interesting how a labor union from Chicago or a manufacturing company from Rockford will find candidates in a targeted race in deep southern Illinois. The leadership support for House Democratic candidates was 67 percent of the total spent, while leadership support for the House Republicans is significantly lower at 50 percent. This reflects a weakness of the candidate and party fundraising for the House Republicans spread out over ten candidates, while the Senate Republicans were engaged in only five targeted elections. The final result of the 2022 election saw the Democrats pick up five seats in the House while losing one seat in the Senate. The five pickups in the House came from the competitive northeastern suburbs, while the loss in the Senate was in a downstate urban area where control over the map and major leadership support could not save a seat that had been already slipping away under the old map.

As important as the money raised by legislative leaders is in winning targeted races, the organizational support that the leaders provide is just as important. Their control over partisan legislative staff in Springfield has allowed them to build large, professional campaign organizations. A great many people who work on legislative staffs go off the state payroll during election years to run or work on legislative campaigns. These organizations exist from election to election. They work for the leader, not for individual candidates. Many staff are experienced organizers or specialists in campaign media and communications. Their loyalty is to the leader, and their ultimate success is measured by the leader's political success. If the leader decides to pull staff from one race and move them to another, they will shift campaigns and candidates. This stands in sharp contrast to the loyalty of the personal campaign organization of a long-time incumbent congressperson in a safe district; that organization exists solely for the incumbent. The impact of legislative staff and leadership control is addressed in more detail in chapter 6 on the legislature.

Unless there are significant changes in the political culture, the redistricting process, the style of legislative leaders, and Illinois campaign finance laws, the two worlds of legislative elections will continue. One will be characterized by safe, one-party districts with noncompetitive elections, the other by targeted districts with extremely expensive, leadership-controlled elections.

The question going forward is how will the Republicans in the legislature aggregate enough money to take advantage of the weak candidates, political scandals, and governmental failures that will inevitably occur in the future to regain a competitive posture? The 2014 election demonstrates how a Republican can be elected governor in Illinois. The 2016 legislative elections show how Republicans with the right combination of sufficient funding and favorable issues can make gains in the legislature against a strong partisan map. However, after the 2022 elections the Republicans are now in a position where they need to pick up five Senate seats or seven House seats just to be able to overcome the supermajorities the Democrats hold in both chambers and be able to sustain a veto from a Republican governor.

State Supreme Court Judicial Elections

Judicial elections at the circuit and appellate level are usually low-profile, low-spending contests with the candidate who wins the nomination of the dominant local political party or parties prevailing in the elections. They are often uncontested. State and county bar associations evaluate judicial candidates and rate their level of qualification for judicial office. Up until 2000 Supreme Court elections were also generally low-profile contests with modest campaign spending, but since then Illinois has had a number of high-profile, hyper-expensive State Supreme Court elections.

Judges in Illinois are elected through partisan primaries and general elections at the circuit (trial) court level, the appellate court level, and the Supreme Court level. Circuit court judges serve four-year terms, appellate court judges serve six-year terms, and Supreme Court judges serve ten-year terms. After being elected as a Democrat or a Republican and completing their initial term, judges can run for a second term on a nonpartisan retention ballot. There is no limit to how many times a judge can run for retention. The State Supreme Court has seven members. The state constitution provides that three judges be elected at large from Cook County (the First District), while the other four judges are elected from single-member districts created by statute.[25]

In 2000 there were three high-profile Supreme Court elections and an important retention election. In the First Judicial District (Cook County), the contest for an open seat was notable for two candidates raising more than $1 million each. One of those candidates ran a series of negative ads against a respected judge that generated so much negative publicity that the Chicago Bar Association withdrew its qualified ranking and the candidate finished fourth. There also was an important retention election where the incumbent was opposed by the *Chicago Tribune*. The judge did win retention, but there was concern among leaders of the Democratic Party that the failure of the retention would result in an appointed judge holding the seat in 2002 when redistricting could be before the State Supreme Court.

In the Second Judicial District, which includes the northeastern suburbs and a string of counties over to the Iowa border to the west, an open seat was won by an appellate judge who was a former field goal kicker for the Chicago Bears and ran as prolife social conservative. He beat two other candidates who raised more than $1 million each. One of them self-funded with more than $1.46 million and was supported by a prochoice group.

There was also an open seat in the Third Judicial District, which ran from the Iowa border to the Indiana border across the northern edge of central Illinois. This district had never elected a Democrat but was competitive in statewide elections. The Republicans nominated a state senator, Carl Hawkinson. Fueled by fear that the retention election in Cook County would not go well, House Speaker and Democratic State Party Chairman Michael Madigan actively recruited an attorney, Thomas Kilbride, to run for the seat. He was unopposed in the primary. The majority of the $900,000 raised by Kilbride for the general election came from the state Democratic Party ($688,000) and labor unions ($137,000). Hawkinson raised $575,000 for the general election: $300,000 came from the state Republican Party and $125,000 from a committee associated with U.S. House Speaker Dennis Hastert. Neither candidate raised a significant amount from lawyers, although trial lawyers were major contributors to the state Democratic Party. The Republicans were slow to realize that the Democrats were making a serous push for the seat, The Democrats' aggressive campaign prevailed, with Kilbride wining with 52 percent of the vote. As a result, the Democrats gained a 5–2 majority on the State Supreme Court.

In 2004 an open seat in the Fifth Judicial District triggered a major fight between Illinois trial lawyers on one side and the U.S. Chamber of Commerce and tort reform groups on the other. It was also a fight between the state Democratic and Republican parties. The Republican Lloyd Karmeier raised $4.8 million while the Democrat Gordon Maag raised $4.6 million. At the time, the contest was the most expensive State Supreme Court race in U.S. history. Karmeier won with 55 percent of the vote, becoming the first Republican ever elected to the Fifth District seat on the State Supreme Court. His victory reduced the Democrats' majority on the State Supreme Court to 4–3. Republicans have continued to hold the Fifth District seat since 2004.

In 2010 Kilbride ran for retention in the Third District. An Illinois tort reform group organized a campaign to oppose his retention. Kilbride raised $2.7 million for his campaign with $1.5 million coming from the state Democratic Party and $1 million coming from labor groups. The two biggest contributors to the state Democratic Party are labor union and trial lawyers. The tort reform group opposing retention raised $800,000, with $455,000 coming from national tort reform groups and the U.S. Chamber of Commerce and $343,000 coming from business groups. Kilbride was retained with 66 percent of the vote, a low total compared to other retentions but comfortably above the 60 percent threshold.

In 2014 a group of Illinois trial lawyers put together a campaign to oppose Justice Karmeier's retention in the Fifth District. They raised $2 million through an independent expenditure committee. The committee was formed on October 20, 2014, and immediately reported spending $700,000 in opposition to Karmeier's retention. Ultimately they would spend $2 million in opposition to Karmeier. On October 29ʼ an existing independent expenditure committee reported receiving $950,000 from a national dark money group, the Republican State Leadership Committee. That committee began running ads to counter the antiretention campaign. The campaign was hard fought in the last three weeks before the election. Karmeier won retention with 60.8 percent of the vote. Without the rapid response of the national group Karmeier would have lost his retention election.

In 2020 Kilbride again ran for retention in the Third District. An opposition group, Citizens for Judicial Fairness, was formed to oppose his retention. Citizens for Judicial Fairness raised $6.2 million the 2020 election cycle and spent $4.3 million opposing Kilbride. Billionaire Ken Griffin contributed $4.5 million to the committee, billionaire Richard Uihlein contributed $1 million, and two dark money groups contributed $550,000. Kilbride's candidate committee raised $5.6 million with $2.3 million coming from labor unions and $2.3 million from trial law firms and lawyers. The opposition campaign focused on Kilbride's ties to House Speaker Madigan and Democratic corruption in Illinois. Kilbride lost the election, receiving only 56.5 percent. The loss triggered a temporary appointment to fill the seat until an election could be held in 2022 to fill the seat.

In 2022 two elections were held to fill openings in the Second and Third Districts. The opening in the Third District was created by Kilbride's not being retained in 2020. A resignation of a Republican judge in the Second District created an open seat in that district. Under the old map the Second District (which had a lot of rural territory in addition to the northeastern suburbs) would have elected another Republican. The Third District would have been very difficult for the Democrats, given the outcome of the Kilbride retention in 2020. Under the old map, which was created in 1964, if the Republicans could have won both open seats, the court would have flipped from a 4–3 Democrat majority to 4–3 Republican majority. Faced with this situation, the Democrats passed legislation that drew a new judicial map. The 1970 constitution gave the legislature the power to create the Supreme Court judicial districts. Governor Pritzker signed the new map into law. There were still two elections scheduled to fill two open seats but the districts would be new. The Second District leaned a little Democratic and the Third District was competitive. Both were mostly suburban with the rural counties from to old Second and Third Districts shifted into the Fourth District. The stakes were still the same. If the Republicans could win both, they would flip partisan control of the court.

Before the 2022 spring primary billionaire Ken Griffin contributed $6.2 million to the Citizens for Judicial Fairness, the same committee he used to block Justice Kilbride's retention in 2020. The Republican candidate who won the primary in the Third District was a strong candidate and had been appointed to fill the vacancy in the Second District in 2020. However, the preferred candidate of the local and state Republican Party organizations and Judicial Fairness lost the primary in the Second District to a former Lake County sheriff who was prolife conservative and had never been a judge. He won on the strength of the social conservative turnout generated in part by Darren Bailey's campaign in the primary election for governor.

Governor Pritzker contributed $500,000 to each Democratic candidate while teacher unions were big contributors to both as well. Abortion became a huge issue in both races and Personal PAC, a prochoice group that works campaigns and raises substantial amounts of money, was all in to keep the court in Democratic hands. It made more than $2.0 million in independent expenditures to support the Democratic candidates. Labor put in money and worked these Supreme Court elections because they were pushing a collective bargaining/anti-right to work constitutional amendment and unions did not want a Republican court interpreting the new workers' rights amendment if it passed and became part of the Illinois constitution. All of this helped offset the more than $5.3 million in independent expenditure that Judicial Fairness made to support the two Republican candidates.

Both Democratic candidates won. The margin was substantial in the Second District, 55 percent to 45 percent. The Democratic candidate in the Third District won a close race 51 percent to 49 percent. While the Democratic candidate in the Second District had a $5.0 million to $1.7 million spending advantage over the Republican, it appeared the Democrat in the Third District had won in spite of being outspent $5.8 million to $5.0 million. But the quarterly reports filed in October of 2022 and January of 2023 by an independent expenditure committee turned out to be inaccurate. The independent expenditure group, All for Justice, was initiated by the Senate Democratic leader and funded primarily by labor unions ($4.0 million), trial lawyers ($2.3 million), and legislative leader and candidate committees ($1.1 million). They had sent $7.3 million in independent expenditures during the general election to benefit the two Democratic candidates but had failed to report those expenditures as they occurred as required by law during the campaign and filed third and fourth quarter reports that did not identify their independent expenditures as such. There appears to be no serious consequences under the election code for having committed such an outrageous "error."[26]

The actual spending totals for the Second District race were $8.7 million for the Democrat and $1.7 for the Republican. For the Third District race the totals were $8.8 million for the Democrat and $5.8 from the Republican. In all, a total of $25 million was spent to elect two justices to the State Supreme Court.

The Democratic candidates' winning formula in 2022 was a base of a solid Democratic voters where these judicial districts are located, favorable maps, a large spending advantage, favorable issues to attract independent voters, and organized, effective interest groups. Abortion was on the ballot symbolically and a prolabor constitutional amendment was on the ballot literally. Both prochoice and labor groups worked the election, which helped turnout. Instead of the 4–3 Republican court that the Republicans had envisioned when they opposed Kilbride in 2020, the results of the election locked in a 5–2 Democratic majority for at least the next decade. Supreme Court Judges have ten-year terms and there is no limit on how many times they can run for retention. In the same election in the First District a Democratic justice was retained for another ten-year term. The First Judicial District has never elected a Republican to the State Supreme Court.

Elections to Ratify Constitutional Amendments

The Illinois election code authorized the formation of ballot committees to raise money supporting or opposing ballot questions, which can be put to votes in statewide and local elections. These committees can receive unlimited contributions, but they cannot transfer money to other political committees, including candidate committees. They must report contributions over $1,000 throughout the year and must file quarterly reports of receipts and expenditures with the State Board of Elections.

Ballot questions can be binding or advisory. The most important binding elections involving ballot questions are those that determine whether or not the Illinois constitution will be amended. To be approved, an amendment must receive 60 percent of the votes from those voting on the question or a majority of those voting in the election. There are two ways that a constitutional amendment can be placed on a general election ballot under the relevant provision of the state constitution.

The first way a constitutional amendment is placed on a general election ballot is through the legislative process. A proposed amendment must pass both the House and Senate with a three-fifths vote (60%).[27]

The most recent attempts to amend the state constitution through amendments placed on the ballot by the legislature involved high-profile, expensive media campaigns characteristic of modern political campaigns. In 2020, a proposal to eliminate the language in the state constitution that requires income taxes be levied at a flat rate was on the ballot. Three major proballot committees and four antiballot committees spent $122 million on the campaign. The primary funder of the opposition was Ken Griffin, a billionaire businessman who had been active in funding Republican candidates since 2014. He contributed

$53.8 million to the opposition. The primary funder of the pro-amendment side was Governor JB Pritzker. He contributed $58 million. The anti-amendment forces successfully portrayed the amendment as the first step in allowing the governor and the legislature unlimited power to raise income taxes in spite of the enactment of a specific law targeting high-income earners that would have taken effect if the constitutional amendment had passed. The amendment was rejected by 53 percent of those voting on the question.

In 2022, at the urging of labor unions, the legislature placed a workers' rights amendment on the ballot. The amendment prohibited the passage of right-to-work laws in Illinois, expanded the rights of workers, and codified collective bargaining principles into the state constitution. The pro-amendment campaign presented the amendment as protection for the basic rights of workers and the right to form unions and bargain collectively. Given a very pro-union governor and legislature and the huge power of organized labor in state politics, it is unlikely that any antiunion laws will be enacted in Illinois anytime soon. Labor groups saw the amendment, however, as a way to put language protecting their current position in Illinois into the constitution with expansive language that would be interpreted by a Democratic State Supreme Court. The pro-amendment side spent $16.4 million on their campaign. The vast majority of the money came from trade and service worker unions. The anti-amendment campaign spent $3.2 million in opposition. Billionaire businessman Richard Uihlein contributed $2.0 million and an Illinois-based conservative dark money group contributed $1.2 million to the opposition, accounting for all but $12,000 of the funding. Although the Illinois Chamber of Commerce and other business groups publicly opposed the amendment, they spent no money in opposition. While the supporters were able to frame and dominate the campaign, the amendment passed with only a narrow margin, failing to get 60 percent of the vote of those voting the amendment, but receiving 54 percent of the total votes cast, which met the second standard.

The second way an amendment can be put on the general election ballot is a limited citizens' initiative process, which allows the circulation of petitions to place a question on the ballot that alters the structure and procedures of the Illinois legislature as set out in the legislative article of the state constitution.[28] It has been used once, in 1980, to reduce the size of the House of Representatives from 177 to 118 and to eliminate cumulative voting for multimember House districts. The state constitution sets out the required number of signatures necessary and the timeline to circulate petitions, which are certified by the State Board of Elections. Whether a set of petitions meets the procedural requirements and whether the content of the amendment satisfies the limitations on the citizens' initiative power are ultimately decided by the Supreme Court. In 2016, a petition to alter the redistricting process that involved the state auditor general, which met the signature and process requirements, was disallowed by the State Supreme Court on the grounds that it exceeded the limitation that changes could only be made to the legislative article.[29]

The Role of Candidates, Issues, and Policy in Illinois Elections

Finally, in addition to demographics, legislative maps, and money, elections also involve choices between candidates and consideration of issues and policy. Each election has multiple factors that make predictions problematic. In 2022, one incumbent Senate Democrat won a close election with zero support from the Senate legislative leader or the state party. The member was under an ethical cloud for alleged personal behavior and the leadership chose not to contribute to his campaign. Two long-time House incumbents, one Democrat and one Republican, lost unexpectedly with neither race being on either party's radar. This is unusual, but not unique with a new legislative map. An incumbent running in a new district may have a partisan advantage based on the voting history, but the name recognition and good will built up over time does not transfer from old voters no longer in your district to new voters who are. The advantages of incumbency must be earned.

In 2022 the Democrats had a strong counter for the Republican campaign themes of crime and inflation. The Democratic campaign focused on abortion, Republican extremism, gun safety, and collective bargaining/workers' rights. Governor Pritzker spent more than $141 million out of his campaign fund on his campaign and helping other Democrats. His campaign stressed his accomplishments and the state's improved fiscal health while focusing on the extremism of his opponent and the rest of the Republican ticket.

The Democrats took advantage of three factors that increased enthusiasm and turnout among their base and swing voters. The overturning of *Roe v. Wade* generated a clear issue that energized Democratic voters and pro-reproductive rights groups. Labor unions worked through the legislature to put a constitutional amendment on the ballot that made collective bargaining a protected right. Their campaign for the amendment increased turnout and provided enthusiasm. Finally, control of the State Supreme Court, abortion, and workers' rights were all big issues in Supreme Court races in two largely suburban districts. All this increased attention and turnout by groups that generally leaned toward the Democrats. The election was focused on themes that resonated with Democratic voters and swing voters and reinforced the factors that had been driving Democratic gains in Illinois politics.

Having the money to conduct a campaign that focused on issues important to your base and resonated with the structural advantages of favorable legislative maps and favorable population and voting demographic trends produced a result in 2022 that makes it harder for Republicans to gain traction as they seek to make themselves competitive again in Illinois politics. But nothing is certain in politics, as the Democrats learned in 2014 by running a status quo election and gubernatorial candidate in an election where change resonated with voters and the Republicans had the resources and the candidate to take advantage of the opportunity.

4
POLITICAL CORRUPTION

Political corruption has become so normalized in Illinois that it is easy to become numb to how pervasive and deep it is and how much damage it has done to our politics and to the vital services and programs that state government provides to it citizens. Isolated incidences of corruption by a state or local public official now elicit little more than a "there they go again" response from the public. Shocking, egregious, systematic corruption inevitably invites comparisons to the major scandals of our past. The record is not pretty.

One measure of corruption is sheer numbers. The U.S. Department of Justice compiles statistics on the total number of criminal convictions for public corruption by judicial districts. According to an analysis of that data by the *Anti-Corruption Reports* issued by the University of Illinois at Chicago, Chicago is the most corrupt city in the nation, while Illinois ranks third in public corruption on a per capita basis.[1]

Quantity is important, but so is quality. Illinois has the distinction of having two consecutive governors (George Ryan and Rod Blagojevich) convicted and sentenced to prison for public corruption. Having a small-town city treasurer convicted of embezzling money is not a unique story. But when the city treasurer of Dixon, Illinois, was convicted in 2012 of stealing $53 million from the city treasury over a twenty-one-year period, it was national news.[2] A decade later the most powerful member of the Chicago City Council, Ed Burke, and Michael Madigan, the powerful, longtime Speaker of the House, have left office and are facing federal trials after being indicted for political corruption. Burke is charged with extortion, while Madigan is charged with influencing the passage of legislation in exchange for bribes and jobs from the state's two biggest public utilities. Both utilities have entered into deferred prosecution agreements with federal attorneys.[3]

Political corruption in Illinois is not a recent phenomenon. The Chicago political machine of Mayor Richard J. Daley of the 1950s, 1960s, and 1970s was built on a foundation of power brokers and corrupt political organizations stretching back to the early 1900s.[4] And it is not just a Chicago problem. Political corruption is deeply rooted in the politics and the politicians of every region of the state.[5]

It is hard to overstate how wide-open and unregulated politics in Illinois has always been. Or how glacial the pace of efforts to establish an ethical and legal structure to fight corruption has been. In 1967 Illinois enacted it first comprehensive ethics law, the Illinois Governmental Ethics Act. It contained a general code of conduct with no penalties or enforcement mechanisms. In 1972 that act was amended to require elected and appointed state officials to file statements of economic interest annually with the Illinois secretary of state. In 1974 Illinois adopted its first comprehensive campaign finance law, the Illinois Campaign Disclosure Act. It was a weak law requiring only annual disclosure reports with no effective dissemination provisions. The next systematic effort to address campaign finance and ethics laws would not take place for another twenty years.[6] While the last thirty years have seen ethics and campaign finance reforms enacted in response to steady parade of political corruption, those reforms have been scandal driven and defensive rather than the result of proactive efforts to improve the ethical culture of Illinois politics.

Types of Political Corruption

Political corruption falls into three broad areas of illegal or unethical activities. First, there is corruption that directly subverts the political process. Buying votes, trying to intimidate specific groups from voting, and partisan gerrymanders are examples. Second, there is corruption when public resources are used for political purposes. Examples are putting an unqualified political supporter on the public payroll, having public employees perform campaign work while on public time, or using government grants to reward or punish people represented by allies or enemies. Finally, there is corruption that results from using public authority for private gain. Public officials extorting money or taking bribes from private interests seeking government contracts or services or favorable action on legislation, or misappropriating public funds or campaign funds for personal use are examples.

Although illegal political activity is by definition also unethical, the opposite is not necessarily true. Political patronage has always been unethical in terms of the standards of fairness and honesty in the employment process. But it was not universally illegal until the U.S. Supreme Court held in two seminal cases (*Elrod v. Burns*, 1976 and *Rutan v. The Republican Party of Illinois*, 1990)[7] arising out of Illinois politics that firing, hiring, promoting, and transferring governmental employees primarily on the basis of political affiliation violated a person's right to freedom of speech and freedom of association. Lying about your voting record or your policy positions in the course of a campaign is unethical, but it is not illegal. The same is true for a lobbyist misrepresenting the intent or impact of a bill to a legislator. Unethical political behavior is corrosive to the political process and the public's support and engagement in the process. But our primary concern here is when the unethical crosses the line and becomes illegal.

The Cost of Political Corruption

One estimate from 2015 of the cost of political corruption to the citizens of Illinois set the mark at $500 million a year.[8] Even that staggering sum does not measure the total cost, which goes beyond monetary losses to the state and local governments and the citizens of Illinois. There are also social costs. The first is the loss of the legitimacy of the political process for the citizens of the state. Real corruption destroys public support for the political system. But the appearance of corruption can be just as corrosive to the legitimacy of the political system as actual corruption. If everyone believes Illinois politics is corrupt, there is no reason for the general public to accept the results of elections or the authority of public officials to make decisions.

The second social cost of political corruption is a loss of participation. Participation in politics should be part of a civic culture that develops and ennobles both individuals and society. Individuals and society are both better when there is widespread participation in the political process. When citizens share in the decision-making and have a vested interest in the outcomes, the foundations of the political system are strong. A corrupt political system does not encourage participation. Neither does one where politics is reserved for professional politicians. When there is a widespread perception that politics is corrupt or someone else's business, the pool of citizens who participate in elections or seek to influence policy grows smaller and creates a vacuum that entrenched interests are all too happy to fill. Both the state and individual citizens lose when a corrupt political system limits or discourages political participation.

The third social cost is a shrinking talent pool of people who are willing to run for public office or seek employment in state and local government. A corrupt political system does not encourage young people to engage in politics or make government a career. If there is a widespread perception that patronage hires and political interference make it difficult for talented people without political connections to get state jobs or to do a professional job of delivering services, then people will not seek to become involved in government. As a result, the pool of those who want to get involved with government as a career keeps diminishing in quantity and quality as a result of the reality and the perception that government in Illinois is corrupt.

The final social cost of political corruption is the deterioration of the quality of the public services provided by state and local government. Do-nothing, make-work jobs and inflated no-bid contracts take resources away from providing the essential services that citizens need from state and local government. A lack of highly qualified people and the diversion of public resources to political or private ends makes meeting the basic obligations of government in the areas such as education, health, public safety, transportation, and social services increasingly more difficult.

Political Corruption and Ethics Reform in Illinois—A Timeline 1980 to 2023

Political corruption flourished in Illinois prior to 1980. A few highlights:

In 1952 Orville Hodge was elected state auditor of public accounts. In 1956 he was indicted and convicted of embezzling more than $1.5 million in state funds by creating false warrants and nonexistent state contracts, falsifying expense reports, and receiving kickbacks from employee salaries.[9]

Richard J. Daley became chairman of the Cook County Democratic Party and mayor of Chicago in 1953. He would preside over the Chicago political machine as mayor until his death in 1976, in spite of the political corruption convictions of hundreds of members of his political organization.[10]

Otto Kerner was elected governor in 1960 and reelected in 1964. In 1966 he purchased stock in two racetracks at a greatly reduced price in exchange for helping the owner of the tracks receive favorable racing dates. In 1972 while a sitting U.S. appellate court judge, he was convicted on federal income tax evasion charges stemming from the transactions. He was sentenced to three years in prison and resigned from the federal bench.[11]

When Illinois Secretary of State Paul Powell died in 1970, he had been in the legislature for thirty years and was elected Speaker three times. A search of his Springfield hotel room after his death revealed over $500,000 in cash, some of it in shoeboxes and paper bags. A full accounting of his office at the State Capitol and his home in Vienna yielded another $300,000 in cash. Absent statements of economic interest and campaign finance reports, it is impossible to know where the $800,000 in cash came from. Although Powell never earned a state salary of more than $30,000 a year as a public official, his estate at the time of his death was valued at $3.1 million.[12]

William J. Scott was elected Illinois attorney general four times beginning in 1968. He was convicted in 1980 of using campaign contributions in 1972 through 1975 for personal use and not reporting the funds as income. His conviction resulted in the forfeiture of the last two years of his fourth term as attorney general.[13]

In 1972 a representative of a construction materials company engaged in a bribery scheme to help pass a bill in the state legislature to raise the weight limits on trucks hauling ready-mix cement on Illinois roads. A federal investigation and trial resulted in the conviction of four current and former legislators, including a former Speaker of the House, and a lobbyist. Two other legislators agreed to plead guilty and cooperate with the prosecution. The president of the construction company who paid the bribes testified under a grant of immunity. The only official response from the legislature to the convictions was to pass legislation barring the state from contracting with a company whose chief executive in open court admitted to bribing a public official.[14]

The only significant ethics reform that impacted Illinois politics in the time before 1980 came not from legislative or executive action, but from the U.S. Supreme Court. In 1976 the Court issued a decision in *Elrod v. Burns*.[15] The case began with a suit filed against then Cook County sheriff Richard Elrod after he fired all the employees of his office hired by the previous Republican sheriff and replaced them with Democrats. The Court held that using political affiliation as the primary grounds for firing a public employee violated the free speech and freedom of association rights of the employee. This was the first major constitutional blow to the use of political patronage as a mechanism for building and holding political power.

In Chicago, legal action rather than legislation or city ordinances addressed this issue prior to the *Elrod* decision. In 1972 a consent decree was entered into following a federal lawsuit. Commonly referred to as the Shakman decree, that agreement limited the ability of Chicago public officials to fire employees because of their political affiliations or activities. A subsequent agreement in 1983 dealt with limitations on political hiring and extended the agreement to cover Illinois state government. The long history of the Shakman decrees in trying to limit the impact of political patronage in Illinois and pushback from state and Chicago public officials speaks to the resilience of political corruption in Illinois government. The City of Chicago was released from the agreement in 2014 and the State of Illinois was released in 2022.[16]

Political Corruption 1980–1998: Federal Focus on Chicago and a Gift Ban for the State

Beginning in 1980, the U.S. Attorney's Office in northeastern Illinois initiated a series of investigations that has kept public corruption in Chicago and Cook County in the public eye for more than two decades.[17] The scandals were so numerous that you need a scorecard to keep track. Among the most notable:

- Operation Greylord (corruption in Cook County courts). A federal investigation of corruption in the Cook County court system exposed corruption, incompetence, and influence peddling. In all fifteen judges, forty-seven lawyers, and twenty-four police officers were convicted or pled guilty.
- Operation Silver Shovel (landfill permits). An undercover operation documented public officials accepting bribes to facilitate illegal dumping and siting of landfills. Among the fourteen public officials convicted were the former president of the Metropolitan Water Reclamation District and six Chicago aldermen.
- Operation Haunted Hall (ghost payrolling). Four aldermen, the Cook County treasurer, and an Illinois state senator were among the thirty-four public official and city employees convicted of schemes to place employees on the city payroll for jobs that required no work.

In response to the wave of scandals, the Chicago City Council adopted a Governmental Ethics Ordinance in 1987 that established standards of ethical conduct for all persons involved in and with city government: city employees, appointed and elected officials, and persons or businesses who represent, have, or are seeking city business or who wish to contribute to candidates for elected city office or elected officials. A board of ethics was created to administer and enforce the act with civil penalties. The act establishes limits on contributions to elected city officials and candidates for elected city office, city officials, or employees from people doing or seeking to do business with the city. The board also administers and enforces Chicago's lobbyist registration law, which requires registration and regular reports of activities. In 1989 the City of Chicago created the Office of Inspector General, replacing the Office of Municipal Investigations. The mayor appoints the OIG subject to approval by the council.[18]

In 1996 indictments were issued in what would become known as the MSI scandal. In separate federal trials in 1996 and 1997, the two owners of Management Services of Illinois (MSI), a private company with a contract with the Illinois Department of Public Aid, and several employees and supervisors within the department were convicted in a bribery and influence-peddling scheme to fix a state contract. The indictments and convictions were limited to individuals from the company and the agency. But the news accounts of the trial and the details of the indictments suggested a broader picture of widespread corruption in access and influence built through gifts and campaign contributions. The prosecutors alleged that MSI and its officials gained improper influence by donating $270,000 in cash and computer services to Governor Jim Edgar's campaign fund and showering employees of the Department of Public Aid with gifts, including cash, meals, and trips. Among those linked to the scandal by the indictments and the testimony in the trial were legislative leaders, legislative staff, and officials within the Office of the Governor. Edgar gave testimony in open court as a witness, a first for a sitting Illinois governor.[19]

In response to the MSI scandal, former U.S. senator Paul Simon, the director of the Simon Public Policy Institute at Southern Illinois University–Chicago, initiated discussions with the governor's office and the four legislative leaders that resulted in a working group being formed in 1998 consisting of four legislators representing the four legislative leaders and a representative of Governor Edgar. The group's goal was to produce a mutually acceptable ethics and campaign finance reform bill that could pass the legislature and be signed by the governor during the spring session.

The result was the Gift Ban Act, enacted in 1998. The act prohibited gifts of monetary value to public officials, government employees, and judges from individuals who had an interest in the outcome of any official action that might be taken by the recipient of the gift. By making the giving and accepting of gifts between public officials and those with an interest in the official actions of those officials illegal, transactions that would corrupt the process or appear to corrupt the process were prohibited by definition. The act also amended the state's Campaign Finance Law to prohibit the spending of campaign funds for personal use, prohibit making campaign contributions on state property, require electronic filing of reports of receipts and expenditures, and require those receipts and reports to be searchable online. It also provided for fines and enforcement action. All this reduced the temptation for candidates or public officials to use their campaign funds as a personal bank account.[20]

The most significant reform of this time period again came for a court decision rather than legislative action. In 1990 the U.S. Supreme Court issued their decision in *Rutan v. The Republican Party of Illinois*.[21] Following the logic of the 1976 *Elrod* decision, the Court held that the use of a person's partisan affiliation as a factor in the hiring, transfer, or promotion of a public employee violated that person's freedom of speech and association. Combined with the *Elrod* decision, the Court found that the centuries-old system of political patronage that that provided the foundation of political party power in Illinois and elsewhere was unconstitutional. There is a combination of irony and social justice that the two cases (*Rutan* and *Elrod*) that sounded the death knell for legal patronage in government employment decisions came from Illinois.

Political Corruption 1999–2009:
The Reform Response as Governors George Ryan
and Rod Blagojevich Go to Jail

In 2002 House Minority Leader Lee Daniels stepped down as House Republican leader after coming under investigation for involvement in the diverting of public funds to the campaigns of Republican candidates for the House. In 2005 his former chief of staff, Mike Tristano, was indicted on fraud, theft, and extortion conspiracy charges for directing state employees to work on political campaigns and steering $1.3 million in state funds to a real estate group who put a Republican candidate on its payroll. Tristano was convicted in 2006. A former legislator, Roger Stanley, also pled guilty to charges arising out of the case. Daniels was never charged in the case.[22] No ethics legislation was passed in response these convictions.

George Ryan was elected secretary of state in 1990 and 1994. In 1998 he was elected governor. Following a tragic automobile accident in 1994 involving a truck driver with a fraudulently obtained commercial driver's license (CDL), the U.S. Attorney's Office began an investigation into the Office of the Secretary of State with the code name Operation Safe Roads. The investigation found evidence of SOS employees taking bribes to issue CDLs. That led to more than seventy convictions and guilty pleas, including the conviction of the secretary of state's inspector general for obstructing the investigation. The investigation also found that some of bribery money was being funneled into George Ryan's campaign fund as SOS employees were pressured to contribute. This led to an investigation of Ryan's 1998 campaign for governor, which yielded evidence that secretary of state employees and resources were illegally used for Ryan's campaign.

Under an ethical cloud Ryan announced in 2020 that he would not run for reelection. Ryan's campaign fund, Citizens for Ryan, and Scott Fawell, Ryan's former SOS chief of staff and head of his gubernatorial campaign, were indicted on federal RICO charges in 2002 and convicted in 2003. Former governor Ryan was indicted in 2003, convicted in 2006, and sentenced to six-and-a-half years in prison.[23]

The fallout from the Safe Roads investigation and investigations into Ryan's campaign for governor provided momentum for a major anticorruption bill. The result was the State Officials and Employees Ethics Act, which became law in 2003. The law contained a series of major reforms:

- Ethics commissions for the executive and legislative branches.
- Five executive branch and one legislative branch inspectors general with subpoena powers. The structure and power of the legislative inspector general are weaker than the executive inspectors general.
- Mandatory ethics training for all state employees.
- Prohibitions on political activity on state time, strengthening the personal use ban, strengthening revolving-door prohibitions, and various other provisions.[24]

Governor Blagojevich ran in 2003 as an anticorruption reformer and was actively involved with the negotiation for the 2003 ethics bill. At the same time, the U.S. Attorney's Office was investigating insider deals, influence peddling, extortion, and kickbacks by friends of the governor and appointees he placed on various state boards (code name: Operation Board Games). These investigations led to indictments in 2006 and 2008 of fifteen key associates of Blagojevich including Tony Rezko, Chris Kelly, Stuart Levine, and William Cellini. The evidence generated by these investigations provided the foundation for the U.S. Attorney's Office to obtain a judge's order authorizing wiretaps of Blagojevich's home phone and phones is his campaign committee's offices.

As a result of the scandals involving the governor's appointees, the legislature in 2008 enacted a pay-to-play law by overriding the amendatory veto of Governor Blagojevich.[25] The law provided that:

- Companies with state contracts or companies with bids on state contracts that exceed an aggregate of more than $50,000 must register with the State Board of Elections.
- Covered bidders and contractors are prohibited from making contributions to the officials who oversee the contract or candidates for that office for the term of the office or the length of the contract plus two years.
- Violations of the law by contractors or bidders will result in voiding the contracts or suspension from bidding for three years.
- Candidates and committees that receive contributions in violation of the law would be fined an amount equal to the amount of the contribution.

The legislature's action to override Governor Blagojevich's veto of the pay-to-play bill took place on September 22, 2008. On December 9, Blagojevich was arrested on federal corruption changes. In a press conference following the arrest, Patrick Fitzgerald, U.S. Attorney for the Northern District of Illinois, stated that "Governor Blagojevich has been arrested in the middle of what we can only describe as a political corruption crime spree. We acted to stop that crime spree." Fitzgerald made it clear that the prospect of the pay-to-play law taking effect had resulted in renewed efforts by the governor and his associates to generate campaign contributions prior to January 1, 2009. Fitzgerald also highlighted that the wiretaps had revealed that Blagojevich was trying to use his power to appoint a replacement for a seat in the U.S. Senate formerly held by President-Elect Barak Obama for financial gain and to enhance his political status.[26]

Articles of impeachment for Blagojevich were filed in the Illinois House in December. After a select committee considered the case, the House voted to impeach the governor on January 14, 2009. While legislators relied heavily on the actions that precipitated his arrest, they also focused on a number of offenses involving abuse of power by the governor during his six years in office. Blagojevich was convicted on all counts of the impeachment articles and removed from office by the Illinois Senate on January 29. He and five associates were indicted in April of 2009. Blagojevich was charged with multiple felonies, including racketeering conspiracy, wire fraud, and extortion conspiracy. In 2011 he was convicted on seventeen counts and sentenced to fourteen years in prison.[27]

As a result of the Blagojevich scandal, changes were made in 2009 to the State Officials and Employee Ethics Act that clarified and strengthened the law's prohibitions and disclosure requirements.[28] The changes:

- Prohibited agency officers and employees from taking outside employment for a period of one year with a private entity if they were substantially involved in awarding or administering contracts over $25,000 or in licensing or regulating decisions with respect to a private entity with contracts of $25,000 or more
- Expanded the application of the Lobbyist Registration Act to include more people who are engaged in trying to influence legislative and executive actions
- Required annual ethics training for people registered under the act and expanded reporting of expenditures under the act
- Required electronic filing of lobbying and conflict-of-interest reports
- Increased the authority of executive and legislative inspectors general

Building on the momentum for reform sparked by the arrest and removal from office of the governor, political reform groups were finally able in 2009 to pass a law that placed limits on contributions to candidates running for state and local offices in Illinois. The changes:

- Put limits on contributions from private sources to candidate, political party, and political action committees;
- Limited transfers from candidate committees to other candidate's committees or political action committees, but it did not limit transfers from candidate committees to political party committees or from political party committees;
- Required quarterly reports rather than semi-annual reports of receipts and expenditures from all committees and required real time electronic reporting and disclosure of contributions of $1,000 or more and independent expenditures of $1,000 or more;
- Increased the penalties for violations and the enforcement power of the State Board of Elections.

These changes limited the flow of money from private sources into the election process, increased the information available to citizens and journalists prior to primary and general elections and about who was contributing to campaigns, and enhanced the enforcement power of the State Board of Elections. The limits did not apply to transfers from party committees to candidate committees.[29]

The focus on ethics laws spread beyond the direct fallout from the Blagojevich scandal. In 2009 major changes were made in the Freedom of Information Act (FOIA) for the first time since the act was created in 1984. The changes established public access coordinators within the Office of the Illinois Attorney General to administer the law and facilitate public access through FOIA and the Open Meetings Act. It also streamlined procedures and eliminated some exemptions to FOIA.[30]

Political Corruption 2010–2023: The Path to Indicting Alderman Burke and Speaker Madigan

The carryover from the Blagojevich convictions also reached the Chicago City Council. Widespread publicity following an investigative report in the *Chicago Sun-Times* into a Chicago program to hire private firms for hauling jobs resulted in a federal investigation in 2004 and numerous criminal convictions of city administrator and employees and trucking companies. The "Hired Truck" scandal did not immediately result in changes in the city's ethics law, but in 2011 the Chicago City Council passed the first overhaul of Chicago's ethics code in twenty-five years. The ordinance limited campaign contributions by lobbyists and contractors, revised revolving-door prohibitions, and lowered the threshold that triggers the prohibition of gifts to city officials and employees.[31] In spite of these changes, Barbara Byrd Bennett, the chief executive of the Chicago Public Schools (CPS), was indicted in 2015 for taking kickbacks from vendors to influence the awarding of contracts worth more than $20 million. In 2017 she pled guilty to the charges and was sentenced to four-and-a-half years in prison.

With the pervasive nature of corruption in Illinois, it seems another scandal was just around the corner. In 2012 Derrick Smith, a legislator from Chicago, was indicted in March after being caught on tape accepting a bribe. What elevated the story above run-of-the-mill political corruption was the fact that Smith was campaigning in the Democratic primary when he was arrested. He won the Democratic primary election shortly after being indicted. When Smith refused calls for him to withdraw from the ballot, the Illinois House of Representatives formed a special committee and initiated an investigation. That process culminated in Smith being expelled from the legislature in mid-August.

Only a felony conviction could keep him off the ballot in the fall. Despite being impeached, he was elected to his old seat in November 2012 while the charges were pending. He was sworn into office in 2013. Because the Illinois constitution prohibits the legislature from expelling a member more than once for the same offense, he continued in office in 2013 but became a lame duck in March of 2014 when he lost his primary bid for reelection. He finally came to trial in June and was convicted of bribery. At that point he was automatically removed from office because convicted felons are barred by the state constitution from holding elected office in Illinois. While some have joked that the ethical standard one must meet to run for public office in Illinois is "not currently under indictment," it appears even that is not always the case.

In 2014, a former deputy commissioner of the Chicago Department of Transportation was indicted and found guilty of taking bribes from Redflex Traffic Systems, in return for helping the company secure a $100 million contract with the City of Chicago for red-light camera systems. These systems provide a low-overhead way to both control traffic and generate revenue from traffic tickets for moving violations. Late in 2019 political corruption and red-light camera systems were back in the news.

After the FBI raided the office of State Senator Martin Sandoval, in early 2020, he pled guilty to bribery charges. He admitted he solicited financial benefits from an individual affiliated with SafeSpeed Inc., a Chicago-area red-light camera company, in return using his official position to block legislation harmful to the red-light-camera industry. He also admitted to engaging in corrupt activities with other public officials, accepting $250,000 from other individuals in return for using his official position to benefit those individuals and their business interests. Sandoval agreed to assist the government as part of a plea agreement. One of the targets of the subpoena from the 2019 raid was information about lobbying for Commonwealth Edison. Sandoval provided valuable information that laid the groundwork for multiple indictments, but died of COVID complications in December 2020 before he could testify.

FBI agents also raided the offices of McCook, Illinois, in 2019 as part of their ongoing red-light camera investigation. In September of 2020, Jeff Tobolski, a Cook County commissioner and former mayor of the village of McCook, pled guilty to extortion in a red-light camera case. A total of more than $250,000 in bribes was involved. Earlier Patrick Doherty, chief of staff to Tobolski and an employee of SafeSpeed, Inc., pled guilty to bribery and conspiracy charges. In separate cases, the mayors of Oak Park Terrace and Crestwood were also convicted on bribery charges related to contracts for red-light camera systems. Three years later State Senator Emil Jones III was indicted on federal bribery charges connected to a red-light camera company.

Faced with possible criminal indictments from an investigation going back to 2014, Alderman Danny Solis, then chair of the Chicago City Council's zoning committee, began cooperating with the U.S. Attorney's Office. Solis's cooperation included wearing a wire and recording conversations that help build corruption cases against Chicago City Council Finance Committee Chair Ed Burke and House Speaker Michael Madigan. In 2022 Solis was charged with a single count of bribery under his agreement.

In November of 2018, the FBI executed search warrants at both the ward office and City Council office of Alderman Ed Burke. At the time he was the City Council's longest serving member. In January of 2019 he was indicted on bribery and extortion charges involving steering business to his property tax appeals law firm. After his indictment he resigned his position as Finance Committee chair. In February he was reelected to his thirteenth four-year term as alderman from the Fourteenth Ward. In 2022 he announced he would not seek reelection.[32] Burke's trial began in the fall of 2023 and resulted in a conviction on multiple felony counts on December 21.

In 2019 State Representative Luis Arroyo was indicted for bribery in an attempt to advance gambling legislation. At the time of his indictment Arroyo was also registered as a lobbyist representing gambling interests before the City of Chicago. In 2022 Arroyo pled guilty to bribery and was sentenced to prison. State Senator Terry Link was indicted on tax evasion charges in August of 2020 and pled guilty in September of 2021. Link agreed to cooperate with federal investigation of public officials including Arroyo. In 2022 Arroyo was linked to the Madigan scandal for receiving a no-work contract from AT&T as part of the company's attempt to win favor for legislation before the General Assembly.

In May of 2019, the FBI searched the homes of lobbyist Michael McClain and Madigan political operative Kevin Quinn under grand jury subpoenas. The Chicago City Club offices of Jay Doherty, a consultant with Commonwealth Edison (ComEd), were also searched. In July of 2020 ComEd agreed to resolve a federal criminal investigation into a decade-long bribery scheme by paying a $200 million fine and entering into a deferred prosecution agreement with U.S. Attorney's office. The company admitted that "it arranged jobs, vendor subcontracts, and monetary payments associated with those jobs and subcontracts, for various associates of a high-level elected official for the state of Illinois, to influence and reward the official's efforts to assist ComEd with respect to legislation concerning ComEd and its business." The high-level elected official referred to as "Public Official A" was revealed in subsequent indictment to be House Speaker Michael Madigan.[33] In September ComEd VP Fidel Marquez pled guilty to a bribery conspiracy scheme to pay allies of Madigan in exchange for Speaker's support in Springfield.

In November long-time lobbyist Michael McClain, ex-ComEd CEO Anne Pramaggiore, ex-ComEd top lobbyist John Hooker, and ComEd political consultant Jay Doherty, the former president of the Chicago City Club, were indicted in a bribery scheme designed to curry favor with Speaker Michael Madigan. They were charged with funneling money through contracts and do-nothing jobs to Madigan's political allies in exchange for the Speaker's help with legislation that favored ComEd.[34]

In March of 2022 former Illinois House Speaker Madigan was indicted on federal racketeering charges alleging that his elected office and political operation were "a criminal enterprise whose purpose was to enhance Madigan's political power and financial well-being while also generating income for his political allies and associates." The indictment also charges that Madigan directed the activities of McClain and that McClain conducted illegal activities at Madigan's behest. While the focus of the indictment is the bribery scheme with ComEd, it is only one of multiple alleged schemes to unlawfully solicit benefits for businesses and other private parties to benefit Madigan, McClain, and their associates.[35]

In late October of 2022 AT&T Illinois entered into a deferred prosecution agreement with the U.S. Attorney's office, pleading guilty of trying to influence former Speaker Michael Madigan to support legislation by paying a bribe to a Madigan ally. The agreement alleges that Paul La Schiazza, a former president of AT&T, conspired with three of their lobbyists to funnel money to a legislator, identified as State Representative Louis Arroyo, through a fraudulent contract during 2017 and 2018 for work that was never performed. The company agreed to cooperate with the prosecution and pay a $23 million fine. The deferred prosecution agreement is similar to the one Commonwealth Edison entered into in July of 2020. La Schiazza was subsequently indicted, and a new superseding indictment of Madigan and McClain was issued adding the AT&T-related charges to the bribery and racketeering conspiracy charges brought against them in July of 2020.[36]

In response to the ongoing investigations and indictments from the Madigan/Commonwealth Edison and red-light camera corruption scandals, the Democratic legislative leaders and Governor Pritzker agreed to a broad ethics bill in 2021 that took effect January 1, 2022.[37] The new law:

- Prohibited lobbyists for public utilities from engaging in lobbying subcontracts;
- Prohibited legislators from lobbying other units of local government;
- Added a revolving-door provision that prohibited legislators from lobbying for six months after they leave office;
- Expanded lobbyist registration by requiring anyone who lobbies a unit of local government to register as a lobbyist with the Secretary of State's Office and comply with all the reporting provisions of the Lobbyist Registration Act;
- Expanded the definition of lobbying requiring registration to cover grassroots lobbying. It also required people who consult with lobbyists to register under the act.

To address transparency and conflict-of-interest concerns, the new law rewrote the statute requiring annual statements of economic interests by expanding the amount and type of information required to be submitted annually and redesigning the form. The law also removed the requirement that the legislative inspector general must have the authorization of the Legislative Ethics Commission before investigating a violation within their jurisdiction.

In 2022 the Chicago City Council passed an overhaul of the city's Governmental Ethics Ordinance.[38] The changes gave the city inspector general the authority to investigate aldermen and committees, increase the maximum fine for violating the ordinance from $5,000 to $20,000, banned members of the City Council from working as property tax attorneys, and required independent contractors who work for members of the City Council to file statements of financial interest and undergo ethics training.

The bribery trial of the ComEd 4 (the three lobbyists and the former ComEd CEO) began on March 15 and lasted six weeks. The prosecution's case, bolstered by tape recordings from wiretaps and cooperating witness, claimed that the company provided no-show jobs and lucrative contracts to associates of Speaker Madigan, working through the three lobbyists, in exchange for the Speaker's assistance in passing or killing legislation of interest to ComEd. This was a trial about bribery, not extortion. The defense countered by portraying the actions of the company and the lobbyists as routine political exchanges attempting to influence outcomes, and contending the prosecution was trying to "criminalize politics."[39] After deliberating twenty-seven hours over six days, the jury convicted all four defendants on all charges.[40] Madigan and McClain will be on trial in the spring of 2024.

Why Is Illinois Politics So Corrupt?

Since 1972 three Illinois governors, one constitutional officer, thirty members of the legislature, thirty-seven members of the Chicago City Council, and hundreds of other elected officials, appointed public officials, and lobbyists have been convicted on political corruption changes along with hundreds of officers and employees of private companies. The recent tidal wave of corruption beginning in 2014 has been stunning. But so were the seemingly endless scandals in Chicago and Cook County government in 1980s and 1990s, as were those surrounding George Ryan during his tenure as secretary of state and governor, and those surrounding his successor, Rod Blagojevich. Another round of reforms in 2021 followed the most recent surge in political corruption. Whether these will signal transformative change in Illinois politics or just another step forward that will be followed by another step back is not clear.

If the successful prosecutions of the ComED 4 and Alderman Burke are followed by the conviction of former Speaker Madigan, the cumulative impact could trigger an even more aggressive and comprehensive response to Illinois' political corruption problem. But it may be just as likely that the elimination of two of the "baddest" of the bad apples will drain away most of the concern and momentum for dealing with ethical faults of our political system that still exist.

Why is politics in Illinois so corrupt? Do we just have a lot of bad people? Do we have a political system that corrupts many of the people who get involved with politics? Or is it something in the water? The answer is all of the above. The basic political culture that every Illinoisan grows up with and experiences firsthand contributes to a climate of political corruption. Our political culture does little to attract good people to politics and even less to restrain the bad people who get into politics. Finally, the political system we have developed in Illinois reflects and reinforces the corruption in our political culture.

Commonly shared attitudes and beliefs shape what we expect from politics and politicians. Illinois has a political culture that emphasizes power, winning, control, and jobs over public interest or good public policy. Illinoisans tend to think of politics as primarily a business, a vocation people take up in order to pursue personal interests. Not only are we taught at our dinner tables, in our classrooms and churches, and through the news media that politics is a business; we also learn that it is a dirty business. We expect that politicians will cut corners in order to win and that they will place the interests of themselves and those who supported them above the interests of the general public. For those inside the process, politics is regarded as the province of professional politicians rather than concerned citizens. These attitudes translate into low expectations about politics, along with a tolerance for corruption, a lack of incentives for citizens to participate in the process, rules governing elections that favor entrenched interests and incumbent office holders, and an acceptance of patronage as a fact of life in hiring for government jobs and the awarding of government contracts. Political scientists call this type of political culture "individualistic." Illinois has long been the poster child for individualistic politics.[41] Our expectations and our standards for politics are very low and our politicians live up (or down) to them.

The political structures that have developed and the types of politicians that have dominated Illinois since statehood tend to favor the interests of the politicians and private interests over the interests of the general public. Prior to the modern era, Illinois election laws discouraged easy access and widespread participation in the process. Access to public documents was very limited and often discouraged by those who had the responsibility to administer the law. Prohibitions against economic relationships between public officials and private interests that might compromise public actions existed only in the broadest sense. Public disclosure of the official actions and private interests of public officials was limited in both content and access. Illinois missed the good government movement that impacted local and then state governments between 1890 and the 1920s. The contrast between Illinois and our neighbor Wisconsin to the north could not be starker. Illinois also missed most of the post-Watergate governmental reforms that were adopted elsewhere when state governments began to grow and modernize in the 1970s. While there were watchdog and reform groups active in Illinois going back to the early 1900s, the most recent organized political reform movement concerned with governmental ethics and campaign finance reform did not emerge until the mid-1990s.

There is not a lot to be gained from speculating about why Illinois historically developed a political culture that was different from a state like Wisconsin. At any given point in time, political culture is fixed, rooted in learned behavior and attitudes, and slow and difficult to change. The current political culture is an "is" that is the starting point for moving forward.

The Intransigence of the Illinois Political Culture

Transactional, individualistic political culture is very resistive to change because political actors have learned to be successful in a political system that has a set of rules and expectations that facilitate a politics of self-interest. Everyone knows and abides by the rules of the game. Political reform is about altering the rules of the game. Change can have direct negative impacts on those in power and there are always unintended consequences from change.

The essence of Illinois politics is power, winning, and control in the pursuit of individual self-interest. Historically it has been a largely non-ideological politics that recognizes no public interest beyond the aggregate of individual self-interest. Politics is the business of professionals, not amateurs. There is a mindset among public officials that campaign contribution records, lobbyist expenditure reports, and public documents "belong" to the political actors, not the general public. While not highly ideological, this kind of political culture is highly partisan with parties functioning as mechanisms of organization and control. The attitudes, opinions, and beliefs of political culture are learned. They are fixed in the short term. Achieving the goals of political reform, including strengthening the ethical foundations and guardrails of our political system, requires changing political culture, but that is a long-term process.

The resistance to making campaign finance records accessible to the general public that held sway from 1974 to 1997 was rooted in a belief that knowing who contributed to campaigns was the business of the politicians and the political parties, not citizens or the news media. When the State Board of Elections began publishing summary reports of contribution data in the early 1990s, officials from the office were challenged by lawmakers at a legislative budget hearing for exceeding their authority and mission. When laws were adopted in 1997 and 1998 to increase reporting and disclosure, the legislators did not embrace the change because it was the right thing to do or because it was in the public interest. They acquiesced and passed the changes in the face of the threat of greater reform—contribution limits. When the potential for mandatory electronic disclosure to increase the scrutiny of role of money in Illinois politics by citizens and the news media became clear, there were immediate attempts to make electronic filing optional rather than mandatory. Those efforts were unsuccessful but the response was predictable. Maximizing public access to campaign finance data was not the logical expression of Illinois political culture. The continuing resistance among public officials to granting maximum access to public documents through the Freedom of Information Act and the resulting compliance problems at all levels of the state government that persisted until 2010 were rooted in the same set of values and beliefs that resisted disclosure and reporting of campaign finance records. The FOIA reforms enacted in 2021 show that the battle is not over.

Enacting political reform through legislation is difficult because those who have power and benefit from the status quo must relent and change the basic rules of the game. Political reform always carries risks for those with power. It can upset a stable equilibrium and cause unforeseen consequences. It creates an uncertain future where the benefits of reform may or may not occur. It challenges the assumption that problems and shortcomings within the political system only come from the actions of bad individuals and the failure of institutional structures to work properly. Assertions that our political culture and the design of our political institutions attracts bad people to politics and corrupts good people are not received warmly by those who have achieved power and success under status quo. Neither are assertions that bad behavior and bad policy are not the result of the system breaking down but are the result of the political system working the way it was designed to work.

At its worst, Illinois political culture engenders a sense of entitlement among public officials. Public documents are "my documents." Lobbyists buying meals and drinks for legislators and legislators handing out legislative scholarships were seen as part of the natural order of things. In this mindset, government exists to serve the self-interests of those in power. Former governor Blagojevich was recorded on a federal wiretap giving voice to this sense of entitlement when he talked about what his official power to appoint a replacement to the U.S. Senate meant to him: "I mean, I've got this thing and it's f***ing golden. And I'm just not giving it up for f***ing nothing." If we are to address the corruption problems in Illinois politics from a strategic standpoint, it is imperative to recognize that the Illinois political culture provides a context that frames everything that takes place.

Changing the Political Culture

As noted earlier, culture is learned behavior. We learn values, attitudes, and beliefs about how the world works, what the rules are, what is acceptable and what is not, and what is important, fair, and just from our experiences. Cultural values are a very powerful force in human society. How do you minimize the number of bank robberies? You certainly make robbing banks a crime. You also install security systems and hire guards. You make every effort to apprehend and convict bank robbers and send them to prison. All of this will reduce bank robberies. But most people do not rob banks because it is challenging or because you could get caught. Most people do not rob banks because they believe it is wrong. Honesty is a basic cultural value. That does not mean that people will not rob banks or that we should not take every measure to keep them from doing so. But the best protection against bank robbery is a shared value of honesty.

The ultimate goal of eliminating political corruption from a cultural standpoint is to create a way of thinking about and behaving in politics that reflects ethical values and a commitment to democratic self-government. We need to ensure that our citizens and public officials internalize values of honesty and ethical behavior on behalf of the public good. This requires a number of initiatives. Investments in civic education and building a civic culture that promotes citizen engagement are critical. Bringing attention to corruption and conflicts of interest, prosecuting illegal behavior, and enacting new laws all work to modify political culture. The lessons need to be about the nature and values of the political system rather than just about bad people and institutional failures. The goal is change in a positive direction in contrast to a downward spiral of public disengagement fed by the corruption and cynicism that currently infects attitudes about Illinois politics.

The Limits of Scandal-Driven Ethics Reform in Illinois and the Road to Progress

One takeaway for looking at the history of political corruption and ethics reform in Illinois is that ethics reform tends to be episodic and scandal driven. There has never been a time when the political leadership of the state has come together absent the pressure of a recent, major political scandal and committed to a comprehensive effort to think about how a statutory and behavioral norm-driven regime could be developed to achieve a clear set of goals for open, transparent, ethical government. Even the arrest and impeachment of Governor Blagojevich was not sufficient. After the impeachment, the legislative leaders formed a joint commission to craft a response. Their initial agenda focused on "fixing" what was wrong with ethics in the executive branch to the exclusion of examining the legislature or campaign finance, let alone a more general look at Illinois political culture. A citizen commission formed at the behest of the new governor Pat Quinn offered a wide range of proposals that did not gain traction.

The Role of Scandal and the Limits of Scandal as a Way to Reform

While political scandals are useful opportunities, they have two limitations as a vehicle for facilitating systematic, comprehensive ethics reform. First, scandals are high-profile events that involve good guys and bad guys. They fit into a narrative that the system is sound except for the occasional bad apple. This mindset makes it difficult to get beyond the bad behavior to the factors that facilitate or directly cause the corrupt behavior. Was Blagojevich just a corrupt individual or was he the logical conclusion of a political system that values self-interest and power over the public good and the public interest? The answer is both, but assuming that corruption is a random occurrence makes it unnecessary to ask if there are systemic problems that produce corruption. Second, scandals do not occur on a regular basis and may not involve the most critical issues that need to be addressed in order to reduce political corruption. Scandal-based reform is by definition reactive and episodic. It is not a substitute for building a strong institutional capacity and a proactive agenda.

Ethics Reform as Policy Change

There are similarities between proposing a new ethics law and proposing a new fee on cable providers. Both require a strategy for moving them through the legislative process. What is the message? What is the public policy argument? Do you engage legislative leaders, fight them, or try to work around them? Does it help or hurt to have the issue perceived as partisan? Can you build general good will in the legislature over the long term that will facilitate achieving a short-term specific goal? Do you engage in public activities to bring outside pressure on the legislature or do you work on the inside, as far away from press scrutiny as possible? Most of these questions are universal.

However, there is a fundamental difference between ethics reform and a fee for a private industry. A fee for a private industry is a change in a portion of a policy status quo. Ethics reform requires changes in the rules of the game under which elected officials, interest groups, and political parties operate. Any change in the rules of the game poses a threat, or at least uncertainty, to those who hold power and those who benefit from all of the policy biases that are part of the status quo. Negative reactions can be based on the specifics of a particular proposal or a general fear of unintended consequences. Good government and watchdog groups are often taken aback by the lack of enthusiasm, indifference, and sometimes outright hostility that is generated by what appears to those groups to be greatly needed, commonsense improvements in the political process.

To enact a new ethics law or strengthen an existing one, you must have a realistic understanding of the concerns that reform proposals create. It is a mistake to underestimate the legitimate concerns that changes in the rules of the game generate for those who are part of the political process. It is a mistake to assume that any opposition or reluctance is rooted in evil motives. It is also a mistake to underestimate the resistance and resolve of those in power to changes that threaten their power.

The resistance by the legislative leaders who were in the majority to a system of comprehensive contribution limits that would fundamentally challenge their power over elections and policymaking has been constant and unwavering since the issue was publicly raised by the report of the Simon-Stratton commission in 1993. At the end of the 2009 battle over the campaign finance bill, that position was as nonnegotiable as it was in 1993. All of the changes in political culture, all of the reform victories, and all of the political scandals had not altered the dynamic enough to make an achievable goal comprehensive limits on how legislative leaders could use the money they had raised.

Ethics Reform as Politics

You cannot enact new ethics laws without engaging in politics. The framers of the U.S. Constitution designed the American political system to operate in a very messy, time-consuming, difficult process. They trusted in majority rule and a democratic process to prevail over the tyranny of the minority. They tried to protect basic rights through the Bill of Rights. But faced with the prospect of tyranny by the majority—the fact that majorities can do bad things—they created a governmental system where the fragmentation of power and the sharing of power makes it is difficult to get things done quickly, if at all, unless you have overwhelming consensus or are willing to compromise. Reformers who do not like politics and are offended by the process are rarely successful and continually frustrated. "Playing politics" has a very negative connotation. But that negativity comes from how politics is being played, not from the nature of politics itself. Engaging (playing) in politics is the essence of democratic self-government. Most successful participants understand and respect the political process. It probably helps if you actually like politics. An outcome that is not legitimately achieved does not have to be respected. But having a political process with integrity and the opportunity to participate does not guarantee "good" outcomes. Sometimes you lose. If the fight was fair, then the only recourse you have is to figure out what went wrong and how to do better in the future. When reformers fail, they fail at politics. They do not fail because of politics.

What Needs to Be Done?

Since 1972 Illinois has adopted or significantly strengthened the following ethics laws to fight political corruption:

- Required statements of economic interest from elected and appointed officials at the state and local level;
- Enacted campaign finance disclosure laws with online and real-time disclosure;
- Put limits on contributions from private sources and banned personal use of campaign funds;
- Strengthened the Freedom of Information Act (FOIA);
- Required lobbyist registration, regulation, restrictions, and reporting at the state and local level;
- Enacted a gift ban;
- Created a Chicago Governmental Ethics Ordinance with Ethics Commission and Office of Inspector General;
- Enacted the State Officials and Employee Ethics Act with State Executive and Legislative Ethics Commissions and inspectors general;
- Required annual ethics training of all state employees and officials;
- Enacted a pay-to-play law;
- Established and strengthened revolving-door prohibitions.

In light of these successes, do we really need more laws? And even more fundamentally, do laws really matter? Won't bad people do bad things in spite of the law? On one level, the solution lies in identifying the bad people and enforcing existing laws. Stealing public funds, engaging in fraud, taking bribes, and using public office to extort money has always been illegal in Illinois and everywhere else in the country.

Having said that, the fact remains that laws do matter and new laws can make a difference. Laws define what is legal and illegal. They set the tone for what society considers acceptable behavior and allows us to draw a line in the sand. However, there can be a lot of gray area around that line with far too many viewing the law as a ceiling rather than a floor on acceptable behavior. For example, look at the way the gift ban law was constructed in 1998. In general, a gift ban prohibits people who could benefit from the actions of a public official from giving anything of value to those officials. These kinds of exchanges invite both real corruption (bribery and extortion) and the appearance of corruption (by creating conflicts of interest). Rather than police these exchanges on a case-by-case basis, a gift ban prohibits them. The original gift ban law had a blanket exemption for "food and beverages consumed on the premises." In plain language, lobbyists could spend an unlimited amount of money on "wining and dining" legislators. A limit of $75 per day was added by the 2003 changes to the law. But the fact remains that a lobbyist can legally buy $75 worth of food and beverages for a legislator in a restaurant, but the lobbyist cannot legally buy the same food and beverages at a grocery store and drop it off at the legislator's home. The message the law sends to participants and to the general public about political ethics is far from clear.

Historically in Wisconsin, a lobbyist cannot buy so much as a cup of coffee for a legislator. There is a bright-line, zero-tolerance policy. The assumption is that, just as there is no such thing as being a little bit pregnant, there is no such thing as being a little bit corrupt. Unlike Illinois, the ethical message of the Wisconsin law is clear.

There are actions beyond throwing the bad people in jail that would result in major improvements to the ethical climate in Illinois politics. Key changes in the laws that govern Illinois politics would significantly reduce both actual corruption and the appearance of corruption. In general, these involve hardening the target, prohibiting actions and relationships that invite corruption and the appearance of corruption, making governmental actions and information more transparent, making it more difficult for individuals and groups to concentrate power, regulating and limiting the roles that money plays in elections and policymaking, and raising the ethical standards and expectations of public officials and the general public in Illinois.

Hardening the target means making it more difficult and riskier for individuals to engage in political corruption by increasing transparency and strengthening oversight and penalties. Prohibiting relationships and actions that invite corruption and the appearance of corruption means pay-to-play laws, conflict-of-interest laws, and revolving-door prohibitions. Transparency means making political actions and processes and information about government and political actors more open and accessible and corruption more visible. Regulating and limiting the role of money in elections and policymaking means enacting better disclosure, prohibitions on contributions from corporate entities, comprehensive limits on contributions, and enacting public finance and small donor systems. Making it more difficult for individuals and groups to concentrate power means placing term limits on legislative leaders and opening up the legislative process. Raising expectations means convincing the public and politicians that standards of ethics need to be higher in politics and government than in any other sphere of human activity because politics and government, ultimately, are the people's business.

An Anticorruption Agenda—What Else Could Be Done?

The following ideas would strengthen Illinois political culture and reduce political corruption and the appearance of corruption:

- Adopt conflict-of-interest rules that require public disclosure of conflicts prior to roll calls and in some cases prohibitions on legislators voting on certain bills.
- Increase the length and scope of revolving-door bans for both legislative and executive officials and staff.
- Increase the independence of the legislative inspector general.
- Limit the expenditure of funds contributed to candidate committees to election activities as specified by law and prohibit their use for non-election activities.
- Require current and former elected officials with active candidate committees to file compliance audits every two years with the State Board of Elections and post them online.
- Significantly increase the fines and penalties the State Board of Elections can levy for violations of filing requirements.
- Place term limits on legislative leaders.
- Reduce or eliminate the partisan gerrymandering of legislative districts.
- Give the state attorney general the power to impanel grand juries to investigate political corruption.
- Expand the information required to be disclosed on statements of economic interests and lobbyist registration and expenditure reports.
- Require statements of economic interest, lobbyist registrations forms, and lobbyist expenditure records to be filed electronically with the secretary of state and disclosed through a searchable database.

All these measures would increase transparency or directly make it more difficult for public officials to engage in corrupt activity. None of them would be a silver bullet. To be effective they would have to be part of a proactive, systematic effort to change Illinois political culture. That can only come through the combination of a pull from leaders at the top of the political system and a push from broad citizen engagement at the grassroots. Illinois cannot change its history of political corruption, but it does not have to constantly repeat it.

PART II
INSTITUTIONS

5
CONSTITUTIONS

For inspiration, the drafters of the Constitution of the United States drew heavily upon the charters of colonial Virginia and Massachusetts. Colonial and then state constitutions provide the dimensions of the ballpark in which the game of politics is played. The charters provide the structure of government and enumerate elective offices to be filled. Equally important, constitutions grant powers and impose limitations on government in general and on the legislative, executive, and judicial branches in particular. Unlike the federal government, which has had only one Constitution since the Articles of Confederation, Illinois has had four constitutions since its admission to the Union in 1818.

The number may be misleading, though, because the first "frontier" constitution was written hurriedly. Drafted, debated, and passed in three weeks, it was a rough document in a state with little sense of its future. Twice in the following fifty-two years, as the state evolved and Chicago emerged as its largest city, the constitution was rewritten, but the versions of 1848 and 1870, like the first constitution, often created new problems while trying to resolve earlier ones.

Constitutions are designed to serve as the bedrock on which a government's structure is built. This is a risky engineering feat in almost any case, and it certainly was in early Illinois, where the framers were unsure what kind of building was to be erected on their foundation. Still, they made use of a major concept that appears in all state constitutions except that of Delaware: it must be harder to change than a simple state statute; the constitution can only be amended with the voters' approval in addition to the legislative action.

As evidenced by the United States Constitution, this primary set of rules need not be long, and many argue that it should not be. Rather than being filled with provisions detailing exactly how government should be structured and what offices should be filled at what salary, a short-form constitution is little more than a framework of rights and responsibilities. Idealists say that a constitution should contain fundamentals (although there is disagreement about what is fundamental) and that nonfundamentals should be placed in legislation, that is, statutory law enacted by the legislature and executive branches. For instance, idealists would say the basic organization of state government into three branches is fundamental, but that creation of a specific state agency (for example, the state board of elections created by the 1970 constitution in Illinois) is not fundamental. Another point of contention is how restrictive a state constitution should be. A "negative" constitution is one that contains many restrictions on state and local governments. Illinois's second constitution had a number of such negatives, many intended to rein in the power of the legislature. One of them limited legislators' pay to a penurious two dollars per day; this backfired in that it spurred creation of a system of "fees," paid by private interests for introduction of bills.[1]

When Illinois's constitution is compared to California's, for example, the former looks quite basic. The current Illinois document does not include many negatives and nonfundamentals, whereas the California constitution is very lengthy and full of details. The other major difference is that the latter provides for the "general initiative," by which voters can propose constitutional amendments by citizen petition (rather than through the legislature). It is common for voters to face twenty constitutional and other initiatives and referenda at a primary or general election. Although this system provides far more avenues for debate about constitutional issues, it also turns constitution writing into a highly politicized undertaking in which advertising and financial backing play major roles. A general initiative for Illinois was discussed by the 1970 Constitutional Convention but was not given serious consideration because delegates took California as a cautionary example.[2]

Although important in establishing general rules for a state's government, state constitutions and their construction do not often attract the public's attention. The exception is when a controversial amendment is proposed or, as happened in the 1960s in Illinois, a complete rewrite is contemplated. This indifference is the case even though, in accordance with Illinois law, high school students and some college students must pass a test concerning the contents of the state's constitution.

Constitutional Compromise in 1818

The first Illinois constitution was adopted in 1818 as a condition of statehood. One issue that received much attention—and had national implications—was the question of slavery. The original draft language, borrowed from Ohio, prohibited both slavery and involuntary servitude, and although indentured servants were to be allowed, the indenture had to be voluntary and for no longer than one year. Proslavery delegates argued, however, that use of enslaved persons would bring economic benefits to Illinois and would continue generating revenue from the salt springs in Gallatin County. They were smart enough to avoid advocating full slavery, knowing that such a provision could doom the constitution's review by the U.S. Congress and president. But they inserted language that protected existing property rights, including the holding of indentured servants, and that allowed continued "renting" of the enslaved from Tennessee and Kentucky to perform the backbreaking work in the salt mines.

The final constitution also omitted a provision that had been included in the Ohio and Indiana constitutions that expressly prohibited an amendment to allow the introduction of slavery. The phrase's absence sparked debate when the U.S. Congress reviewed the document, but opposition from northern states was insufficient to prevent passage. On December 3, 1818, Illinois became a state.

That this omission was intentional was later confirmed when proslavery forces pushed for a constitutional convention in 1824. They succeeded in both houses of the legislature but were defeated at the subsequent election, after a vigorous antislavery campaign by several of the state's leaders.[3]

The first constitution gave the legislature so much power and the governor so little that the system was ripe for abuse. The constitution enacted in 1848 contained some improvements. It reduced the legislature's ability to control the judiciary through appointments, provided legislative authority to create corporations or associations with banking powers, and eliminated the option of using a "viva voce" system of voting in elections (in which the voter calls out his vote and thus must publicly show his preference) in favor of the written ballot.

The product of the 1870 convention was longer and more detailed than earlier documents, signifying the growth in complexity of the state's needs and problems. The convention delegates, according to the historian Robert Howard, "cured most of the faults of the 1848 constitution. They drafted a new basic law that was voluminous in detail and in time would be criticized as being a straitjacket on progress. Nevertheless, the new constitution endured for a century as

Illinois kept abreast of its sister states, while advancing from a predominantly rural civilization into the atomic age."[4]

One of the most controversial side issues put to the voters in 1870 provided a new method of electing members to the House of Representatives. The cumulative voting method was devised to reduce regional tensions by means of a controversial system of "minority representation." The system allowed each voter to cast three votes for representatives, splitting the votes or giving them all to one candidate. Because many voters took advantage of the three-in-one "bullet" vote, a Republican could often be elected in a predominantly Democratic district and vice versa. Cumulative voting was eliminated by constitutional amendment in 1980, as part of a constitutional amendment package that also included a popular reduction in the size of the state House of Representatives.

The 1870 constitution proved to be very difficult to amend "because the leaders of the state's important interests were afraid to upset the balance of forces established by the compromises," according to Daniel Elazar.[5] The charter presented many problems for state officials, especially in regard to financial matters. For example, because of strict limitations on the debt of any one local government, a large number of special districts, which overlapped other local governments, were created, each with its own authority to incur debt. In addition to the limitations and extensive detail, narrow court interpretations of the constitution made it difficult for elective officials to govern. For example, in 1932 the State Supreme Court ruled that the constitution did not permit the state to levy an income tax, a funding source that might have provided for a broader, more responsive revenue mix during difficult times such as the Great Depression.[6]

Samuel Witwer's Long Road to Reform

For one hundred years between the 1870 vote and the approval in 1970 of the current constitution, the state moved forward in spite of the 1870 constitution's restraints; leaders tried again and again to rewrite or amend the state framework but failed each time. They were victims not only of the restrictions written into the constitution they hoped to improve but also of poor preparation, a leaning toward partisanship, and opposition from special interests.

After World War II, a coalition that included the League of Women Voters and the Chicago Bar Association decided to push for a convention. They appointed a Committee on Constitutional Revision and asked a respected Chicago attorney, Samuel W. Witwer, to be chair. "As Witwer recalls it," write Elmer Gertz and Joseph P. Pisciotte, "'in a weak moment,' he agreed to do so, being assured by them that the committee would have its work done in a matter of only a few years."[7] In fact, it would take the next twenty-five years of his life.

Witwer recruited a blue-ribbon committee to help him plan the campaign but found to his dismay that there was almost no written scholarship about the weaknesses of the 1870 constitution. So, he set out to become an expert on the subject and was well prepared in 1947 when he appeared before a Senate committee to lay out the need for change. The senators, it turned out, "had no real desire to hear from the Witwer committee,"[8] and some hardly listened to the presentation. Witwer was infuriated and became more determined than ever.

Constitutional reform gained momentum when Adlai E. Stevenson became governor in 1949. Stevenson presented a constitutional convention package to the legislature that year. Handling the matter for Stevenson was Richard J. Daley, who at the time was Stevenson's director of revenue. The proposition lost on a close vote in the House of Representatives.

The Republicans in the legislature offered an alternative to Stevenson's constitutional convention package—the Gateway Amendment. It eased the ratification requirement for constitutional amendments by providing that an amendment could be adopted by a favorable vote of two-thirds of those voting on the amendment itself, loosening the prior requirement of a majority of all those voting in the election. It also provided that three amendments instead of one could be submitted in each general election. The legislature, with Stevenson's support, approved the Gateway Amendment, which was then enacted by the voters.

Many felt at the time that constitutional revision by amendment was more desirable than a constitutional convention. Enthusiasm for this approach soon diminished. From 1950 to 1966, only two far-reaching amendments were approved—on reapportionment in 1954 and judicial reform in 1962. Three amendments to revise the revenue article, which restricted government powers of taxation, were defeated.

In 1965, the legislature created a Constitution Study Commission. After two years, this panel concluded that "a Constitutional Convention is the best and most timely way to achieve a revised Constitution."[9] The call for a convention was placed on the November 1968 ballot and approved by the voters.

Convention Success at Last

Delegates were elected in the fall of 1969 on a nonpartisan basis, two from each of the fifty-eight State Senate districts. Con-Con, as everyone called the convention, included a mix of civic, business, and labor leaders from across the state, many of whom had never before run for office, as well as a delegation from the powerful Cook County Democratic Party, the organization headed by Chicago mayor Richard J. Daley.

During a nine-month period, under the skilled and energetic leadership of longtime constitutional advocate Samuel W. Witwer, they overhauled the law of the land and engineered a political alliance to gain voter support for ratification.

Witwer, who had been quietly building trust and alliances during the previous two decades, was elected convention president. The delegates set to work in a collegial atmosphere with a small army of clerks, lawyers, writers, researchers, and committee aides. For nine months in 1969, the delegates worked to create a more streamlined document that would allow state and local governments in Illinois to function effectively. All the while, they realized that without ultimate voter approval their work would be for naught, and that approval probably required the support of the Daley vote-production machine.

Thus, the document ultimately presented to the voters in 1970 would accord major new powers to the governor, clarify and strengthen the role of the legislature, and grant independence of action for major municipalities, including of course Chicago.

In addition to the complete and line-item vetoes in the 1870 charter, the governor would also have the power by veto to reduce spending lines in the budget and even amend legislation enacted by the legislature. Before 1970 the governor had the complete bill veto as well as the capacity to veto specific line items within bills, and he used them frequently. Added in 1970 were the reduction veto, used within appropriations (spending) bills, and the amendatory veto. These powers changed the calculus of lawmakers during legislative sessions as to how to craft their bills, mindful of the varied veto actions that a governor could impose on bills of theirs that might be fortunate enough to reach his or her desk. (See chapter 7 for a discussion of gubernatorial use of these expansive veto powers.)

The 1970 constitution also made changes in offices elected statewide. The governor and the lieutenant governor were to run as a team in the general election and had to be of the same political party. A new State Board of Elections was created and the previously elected superintendent of public instruction was replaced by a State Board of Education, which appoints the superintendent of education.

The delegates gave the legislative leaders the power to call themselves into special session, a power hitherto held by the governor alone. The lieutenant governor was removed as the presiding officer of the Senate, and the office of auditor general was made a constitutional office, appointed by the legislature.

The grant of home rule to cities and counties became arguably the most important new element of the proposed constitution. Before 1970, Illinois had been a "Dillon's Rule state," which meant that local governments had only the powers granted to them by the legislature. Home rule reversed this relationship by providing that, with certain limitations, local governments had all the powers not *denied* them by the legislature. In practice over the past half century, home rule has created a kind of federalism within the state, that is, a division of powers between the state and its cities as well as in the counties that have adopted home rule by a vote of their respective citizens.

The home-rule provision proved instrumental in the later political alliance that helped pass the final document; it was one of four items on Mayor Daley's "must" list. The others were classification of property taxes in Cook County, an elective judiciary, and continuation of cumulative voting. Home rule and property tax classification were put in the main document; the other two were advanced as side issues. With all four of his "must list" in the document that went to voters, Daley endorsed the proposed constitution and swung his political machine behind it, which helped pave the way to adoption.

The 1970 convention submitted a main document and a "package" of four side issues, to avoid burdening the main document with possibly unpopular provisions that could cause the whole document to fail. These side issues provided for lowering the voting age to eighteen, abolishing the death penalty, choosing between appointive and elective selection of judges, and continuing cumulative voting for state representatives.

On finishing their business in an atmosphere of tired jubilation, the convention delegates decided to submit the proposed constitution to the voters at a special election on December 15, 1970. An Illinois Citizens for the New Constitution advocacy group was established at the urging of Governor Richard B. Ogilvie. Special campaign groups were organized to support or oppose certain issues such as an appointive judiciary.

The new constitution passed statewide with bipartisan support by a 56 percent favorable vote. As for the side issues, the death penalty was retained; cumulative voting was chosen over single-vote districts; the elective judiciary was retained; and the option of reducing the voting age to eighteen was rejected.

The vote was more favorable in Cook County than in downstate Illinois. Only 30 of the state's 102 counties supported the document, but they represented three-fourths of Illinois's population. Sixty-five percent of Cook County's voters supported the main document, as opposed to 45 percent of downstate voters. Voting followed historic geographical patterns set by constitutional amendments (1950–66) and the call for the 1969–70 Constitutional Convention:

northern counties generally voted favorably on constitutional questions and southern areas consistently voted negatively.

Academics such as the late Samuel K. Gove considered adoption a remarkable achievement in a large, divided industrial and partisan state, and in a state not known for reform.[10] Elazar said the new constitution was "one of the most advanced in the country."[11] It was a compromise between the political and managerial approaches to governance.[12]

Standing Up over Time or Showing Its Age?

The authors of this volume consider the 1970 constitution a distinct improvement over the 1870 charter. Hammered out by a mix of experienced politicians and "good government" delegates, both young and senior, the document does not totally satisfy either the politicians or the reformers. For example, the 1970 constitution continues the election of officials to a number of state offices that are filled by appointment in other states. The election of judges continues as well, which some observers consider a possible factor in the extensive corruption and favoritism in the courts, discussed in chapter 4. One national observer, Neal Peirce, wrote in his book *The Megastates of America* that the 1970 constitution was "not a terribly distinguished piece of work."[13]

The test of time has shown, however, that the package approved in 1970 seems to be working for the people as well as the special interests of Illinois. Drawing on a suggestion of Thomas Jefferson that constitutions should be revised every twenty years, the delegates to the 1969 Con-Con included a provision that every twenty years voters should be asked if they wished to call a new constitutional convention.

In both 1988 and 2008, voters said "no" resoundingly. At the first twenty-year period since the call of a convention in 1968, there was broad interest group opposition to another convention from groups ranging from the Illinois Chamber of Commerce to the AFL-CIO and the League of Women Voters. Some felt that new controversial issues, such as abortion rights, would be brought up in a convention. Further, the business community wanted to maintain the flat-rate, 8:5 ratio between corporate and individual income taxes, which tends to limit corporate taxation.

There was some vocal support for another convention, to consider merit-based selection of judges, the initiative and referendum system used in California, and a revised tax system with more progressive taxes. The *Chicago Tribune*, which reached a large statewide readership, strongly recommended a "no" vote on the proposal for a state constitutional convention:

Illinois already has a modern, workable Constitution, a model for other states. Delegates to the 1969–70 Convention that wrote it thought voters should have an opportunity at 20-year intervals to decide whether it needed an overhaul. They underestimated the excellence of their work. The Constitution they drafted is still a fine fit for Illinois, dealing only with the basics: the scope and authority of state government, the powers of local government, the mechanics of amendment and the guarantee of individual rights. It keeps its nose out of other matters, and that is one of its great strengths.[14]

Seventy-five percent of the 3.6 million voters agreed with the editorial and in 1988 soundly defeated the call.

The question of calling a constitutional convention was on the ballot again in 2008. And once again, a coalition of business, labor, and civic groups came out in opposition. Operating as the Alliance to Protect the Illinois Constitution, the coalition raised $1.6 million and ran radio and internet ads featuring popular former governor Jim Edgar.

Some opponents privately feared that a new convention might affect provisions dear to them. For example, labor interests worried about elimination of the pension guarantee for public employees, and business interests opposed changing the income tax from a flat rate to a graduated rate. Progressives among the opponents feared that a new convention called in a time of large state budget deficits and general economic distress might saddle the state with unworkable constraints on budgeting, such as a limit on appropriations increases and a requirement of a supermajority to adopt annual state budgets. In other words, the present we know is better than a future we don't.

Proponents welcomed the idea of opening the constitution to change. Lieutenant Governor Pat Quinn and others favored, again, the adoption of the initiative, referendum, and recall available in California. Conservatives wanted to change the constitution to rein in state spending. But proponents lacked adequate funding to get their message out. This time they did have the support of the *Chicago Tribune,* which stated in an editorial that a Con-Con might be able to address what it considered the dysfunctional and corrupt state political and governmental system.

Following a campaign that was mostly invisible to the electorate, the opponents of a Con-Con carried the election, but this time by a lesser majority of 58 to 42 percent. Only 60 percent of those voting in this presidential election year bothered to vote on the question of a constitutional convention; constitutions are of much less interest to voters than taxes, roads, and education.

The Illinois constitution is a living document. There have been twenty-five attempts to amend the charter, of which fourteen have been approved.

Amendment requires a three-fifths vote by each house of the legislature, plus a vote of either three-fifths of these voters voting on the issue, or half of those voting in the election. In addition, the legislative article alone may be amended by an initiative of the voters, by petition, followed by referendum at a general election.

Indeed, arguably the most important amendment enacted thus far was put on the ballot by voter initiative in 1980, when cumulative voting was replaced by single-member districts and the House of Representatives was reduced in size from 177 to 118 members. In order to pass, the amendment needed 60 percent of those voting on the measure or 50 percent of total votes. In this case, the total of all votes on the measure was almost 69 percent—enough to pass.

In 2022, organized labor persuaded the Democratic-controlled legislature to put on the ballot a proposal to enhance collective bargaining rights and prohibit right-to-work legislation. "Right to work" means that employees in a collective bargaining workplace would have the right not to join the union that represents workers. The amendment did not hit the 60 percent threshold, but garnered more than 50 percent of all voters and was narrowly approved. The new constitutional provision is expected to generate significant litigation before an Illinois Supreme Court that has generally been sympathetic to organized labor. Issues that may come before the court include the breadth of collective bargaining for the purpose of negotiating wages, hours, and working conditions, "and to protect their [workers] economic welfare and safety at work."[15]

The Illinois constitution also "lives" by virtue of how its provisos have been interpreted by the courts and adhered to, or not, by the legislative and executive branches. For example, during the Governor Rod Blagojevich administration (2001–09), the governor and House Speaker Michael Madigan battled over the governor's expansive interpretation of the breadth of the amendatory veto.

The amendatory veto was generally thought to be an instrument for correcting technical flaws in legislation so as to avoid the necessity of starting a bill anew to make the corrections. The Illinois Supreme Court has ruled on the one hand that the amendatory veto may not be used for the substitution of completely new bills (*Klinger v. Howlett*, 1972). On the other hand, the state high court has ruled that it is to be more than "a proofreading device" (*Continental Illinois National Bank & Trust v. Zagel*, 1979), and that the amendatory veto "was intended to improve the bill in material ways, yet not alter its essential purpose and intent" (*City of Canton v. Crouch*, 1980).[16]

Blagojevich used the prerogative extensively. In a series of amendatory vetoes in 2008, characterized by the former governor as "Rewrite to Do Right," the governor took, for example, a tax increment finance bill for a small community and changed it by amendatory veto to a bill that eliminated property taxes for disabled veterans.

Under the leadership of Speaker Madigan, the House simply refused to consider amendatory vetoes. This killed the bills, and required both lawmakers and governor to start over, if the objectives of the original bills were important.

Neither the governor nor the legislature has followed the constitutional requirement that the annual budget and spending "shall not exceed funds estimated to be available" in a fiscal year; annual state spending has often exceeded revenues for the year. Nor have these two branches adhered to the requirement that "the state has the primary responsibility for financing the system of public education," as the local property tax has fulfilled that responsibility.

As citizens look ahead in 2028 to the automatic ballot question of whether to call a new constitutional convention, a number of provisos in the document—as well as those not in it—will come under scrutiny, such as possibly clarifying the amendatory veto.

Other hot-button issues will include, but certainly not be limited to, the following:

Redistricting (art. 4, sec. 3). This section has not worked as expected by the 1970 convention delegates. As written, if the legislature and governor fail to enact a redistricting plan by June 30 following each decennial census, the task is turned over to an eight-member commission of four Democrats and four Republicans. If that panel fails to agree to a plan by August 10, the Illinois secretary of state draws a "tiebreaking" ninth member name from a hat (once a hat purportedly worn by Abraham Lincoln); one name is a Republican, the second a Democrat.

The game-theory thinking was that the importance of redistricting to the political parties would induce them to compromise and agree before facing the 50–50 uncertainty of losing the draw from the hat. However, in 1981, 1991, and 2001, the process went to the tiebreaker, with Democrats winning twice and Republicans once. Strong public criticism of "government by lottery" followed each use of the tiebreaker process. Further, there were two efforts, in 2010 and 2016, to use the legislative initiative process to put on the ballot a proposal to create an independent commission to redistrict the state legislative districts. Both efforts were rejected by Illinois courts as failing to meet the criteria required by the language of article 4, section 3.

Election versus appointment of judges (art. 6, sec. 12). Circuit, appellate, and Supreme Court judges are elected in partisan primaries and subsequent general elections. Illinois is one of the few states that elects judges on a partisan basis. Many states use an appointive process. State Supreme Court election campaigns have become multimillion-dollar contests.

Expansion of the initiative process (art. 14, sec. 3) and authorization of the recall of public officials (art. 3, sec. 7). During the campaigns in 1988 and 2008 over whether to call a constitutional convention, some proponents of calling a convention identified the initiative and recall as provisions they would advocate in a convention. This advocacy can be expected in future, automatic campaigns for the call of conventions.

Limitations on income taxation (art. 9, sec. 3). This section requires that a tax on income shall be at a nongraduated, or flat, rate. In 2019, Governor JB Pritzker led a ballot effort to authorize graduated rates, that is, higher rates of taxation for higher incomes. Following an expensive campaign in which the governor spent $56.5 million of his own money, voters rejected the proposal soundly.

Pension and retirement rights (art. 13, sec. 5). This section of the 1970 constitution guarantees state and local pension benefits as "an enforceable contractual relationship," but does not attendantly require adequate funding of the pension systems. The five Illinois public pension systems (state employees, public university, teachers, judges, and legislators) as well as many local government systems have been inadequately funded by Illinois state and local governments. Retirees worry about whether there will be money to pay their benefits; many citizens worry that taxes will have to be raised significantly to pay benefits.

Abortion, the prohibition thereof, or the protection of abortion rights. The 1970 constitution is silent on this topic. The 2022 *Dobbs v. Jackson* decision of the U.S. Supreme Court to overturn the 1973 *Roe v. Wade* decision, which allowed abortion nationwide, will almost certainly engender debate over this topic at any future Illinois constitutional convention.

The arguments for and against holding a Con-Con in 2028 will probably, once again, include a preference for the known over the fear of the unknown, as well strength of the perceived need at the time to redress various imbalances in the processes and policies of Illinois government and politics.

Ann Lousin, professor of law at the University of Illinois at Chicago College of Law, is the author of the *Illinois State Constitution: A Reference Guide*.[17] Lousin also served as a key staff researcher at the 1970 Illinois Con-Con. In her book, Lousin looked back, and ahead:

Anyone attempting to predict the future of constitutional revision in Illinois should remember that Illinois constitutional revision is a microcosm of the history of Illinois. Each of the six constitutional conventions focused upon the key issues of that time, and each of the four constitutions attempted to address those concerns. For example, each convention struggled with the status of minority groups in Illinois, with suffrage and elections, with the powers of governmental officers, and with raising state and local revenue. Each solution offered, however imperfect in modern eyes, was a solution that reflected the times. One can expect that Illinois constitutional revision in the twenty-first century will continue this tradition. For the time being, however, it seems that Illinoisans want few changes in their constitution.[18]

6
THE LEGISLATURE

In the spring of 2022, an unlikely candidate emerged in the near western suburban Twenty-first House District to challenge the incumbent in the Democratic primary. Abdelnasser Rashid, the son of Palestinian immigrants, a Harvard graduate, and previous field director for Jesus "Chuy" Garcia's run for Chicago mayor, had gotten a late start. In what would become a foreshadowing of the work ethic of his campaign, Rashid got double the required number of signatures to get his name on the ballot in less than two weeks. Immediately after turning in the signatures he started knocking on doors, for hours every day, no matter the weather. While he believed he had a chance of victory, he knew primarying the chair of the Budget and Finance Committee would be a lot of work.

This perhaps caught the incumbent, Representative Mike Zalewski (D-Riverside), by surprise. Zalewski had never been primaried, nor had he even faced a Republican challenger since he was first elected in 2008. Zalewski ran after the retirement of Robert Molaro (D-Chicago), a heavy hitter who was also Chicago's Twelfth Ward committeeman. But Zalewski was no novice: he is the son of Michael R. Zalewski, longtime alderman of Chicago's Twenty-third Ward and prominent Daley ally.

In 2018 the elder Zalewski was implicated (but not charged) in a scandal with former House Speaker Mike Madigan, alleging Madigan used ComEd as a patronage source in exchange for favorable legislation.[1] When ComEd admitted wrongdoing and later appeared before the Illinois Commerce Commission to defend its plan for ethics reform, it was the younger Zalewski's wife, Carrie

Zalewski, who was the chairperson. Carrie had been appointed the year before by Governor JB Pritzker.

When Rashid began canvassing, the ComEd scandal and conflicts of interest would have been enough for most residents to seek change, especially after Madigan was indicted. But a United States Supreme Court leak that the landmark abortion decision, *Roe v. Wade*, was about to be overturned proved to be the most divisive.

Zalewski was not anti-abortion; he had voted yes on important abortion legislation, including that which would keep it legal in Illinois should *Roe v. Wade* be overturned. But in the veto session the previous fall, Zalewski joined Republicans as the only Democrat to vote not to overturn the state's 1995 Parental Notification of Abortion (PNA) Act. The PNA had required sixteen- and seventeen-year-old women to notify their parents before seeking an abortion. This vote allowed Rashid to paint Zalewski as a candidate who was not a friend of choice at a time when abortion rights were on the line. Both candidates flooded mailboxes and airwaves claiming they were the one most poised to protect a woman's right to choose in Illinois.

The ground game mattered, of course, and new to this district was a large swath of Berwyn and a corner of Cicero. Part of Berwyn was already in Zalewski's district, and some people were happy with him. Yet others felt ignored. And in much of the new territory, due to corrupt local machines that ran their city governments, there was skepticism among those that Madigan-allied Zalewski would be any different. Many in the district also saw a bona fide reformer in Rashid, now endorsed by progressive and local hero Chuy Garcia, United States representative from the Fourth District. At the doors the conversations were about business as usual or a new politics. On election night in June, residents opted for the latter: Rashid defeated Zalewski by a vote of 52.3 percent to 47.7 percent.[2] Rashid went on to win the general election overwhelmingly against his Republican opponent. It was the beginning of a new era for the district.

The General Assembly Today

Rashid's win was not the only history-making race in 2023. He will join newly elected Nabeela Syed in the Fifty-first House District as the first Muslim members of the General Assembly. Syed, who is twenty-three years old, will also become the first Generation Z member elected to the legislature. Sharon Chung won in the Ninety-first House District, the first Korean American, and in the Thirteenth House District Hoan Huynh will be the first Vietnamese American.[3]

An ILLinois LegisLator, As Seen By...

A Chicagoan...   ...A DownStater

Figure 6.1. "An Illinois Legislator." Cartoon by Bill Campbell.

The new legislature that convenes in January 2023 will be the most representative Illinois has ever seen.

Today's Illinois General Assembly is a full-time, professional branch of state government. Whereas short hours and low pay marked the early legislatures, today lawmaking is a full-time endeavor for many, and good pay and generous pension benefits have lured many to make a career as a legislator.[4] Voters elect two House members and one senator from within each of fifty-nine State Senate districts. Many of these describe themselves as full-time legislators. Many others generate all or a significant part of their income from legislative salaries that range from at least $85,000 to well over $100,000, with the higher amounts going to the four-fifths of the lawmakers who serve as chairs or minority spokespersons for the scores of legislative committees.[5]

The Illinois legislature spends about $94 million per year and employs hundreds of people as partisan staff for leaders, members, and committees and as nonpartisan staff for support agencies such as the bill drafting and research units.[6]

The legislature is, like the state, highly diverse. Among the 177 members of the House and Senate in the current 103rd General Assembly (2023–24) were

73 women, 33 African Americans, 18 Latinos, 8 Asian Americans, and 1 Arab American. For the first time, 2 members are Muslim. It is the most diverse General Assembly in Illinois history. However, the diversity is almost exclusively on the Democratic side: Republicans are all white except for John Cabello (R-Machesney Park) who identifies as Hispanic.

Lawyers represent almost one-fifth of total membership; nine have had some military service, five members are farmers, and three are schoolteachers. The roll call also includes a former NFL linebacker, a minister, a funeral director, an optometrist, a firefighter, and a former reporter.

These legislators are real people with needs, ambitions, doubts, and anxieties. It takes great motivation to raise $1 million or more for a targeted reelection campaign and devote endless evenings to running for a position that may grind down one's nonpolitical career. People are spurred to candidacy for various reasons, including a sense of civic responsibility; a need to prove oneself; the challenge of the competition; professional advancement, especially for Chicago Democrats for whom politics is often a lifelong career; the salary and attractive pension benefits; and opportunities to get involved with well-known figures and to work on important issues. Many legislators, especially those from downstate, see the General Assembly as the culmination of their public service. Others see it as a stepping-stone to higher office.

Legislators want to feel good about what they are doing. They want to feel that their work is important and to take pride in having contributed to a better hometown and state. For all these reasons, legislators enter the General Assembly with high hopes. Sometimes these hopes go unfulfilled. Each lawmaker is but one in an unwieldy group of 177. Moreover, a legislator's direct participation in most issues often is limited to a final passage vote on policies largely shaped without their actual involvement.

Alas, as we discuss in this chapter, legislative leaders, the governor, and their unelected staffs often seem to be the ones in overall control of the legislative process. Nowadays that perception is more real than rank-and-file legislators care to admit.

Life in the Political Trenches

This does not mean that there is little to do for ordinary legislators. Usually there is more to do than time permits. Legislators must shepherd bills of their sponsorship along the winding legislative path; help process legislation in committees and on the floor; respond to hundreds of phone calls, letters, and emails weekly; and host visiting constituents. They also must read until the pages blur—bills, staff analyses, interest group position papers, letters, newspapers, and research reports. They must return endless phone calls from lobbyists, constituents, and reporters.

Back home, legislators serve as advocates for their constituents, dealing, for example, with the secretary of state for driver licensing matters, the Department of Transportation for road improvements, the Department of Revenue concerning tax matters, the Department of Professional Regulation for occupational licenses, the Department of Natural Resources for park improvements, the Department of Public Aid for social services, and the Department of Public Health regarding nursing home care. This is the bread-and-butter work of a career politician. Constituents appreciate a legislator who takes care of a problem by guiding them through the bureaucracy of state or local government agencies, and they often show their appreciation on Election Day and, perhaps, at fundraising events.

In order to build visibility with voters, lawmakers maintain from one to three offices in their districts. Some downstate legislators do regular "circuit-riding" to meet constituents at courthouses throughout the district, and their constituents and the weekly newspapers and local radio and television stations often treat them as celebrities. Meanwhile, legislators in Chicago and the surrounding suburbs rarely enjoy media coverage. Instead, they struggle to achieve name recognition by mass-mailing glossy, picture-laden "after-session reports" to their constituents and greeting riders on CTA elevated platforms and Metra train stations near Election Day. Several host cable television shows or write columns for local newspapers, and many attend countless community events. Most have turned to email, texting, and social media to help get their names in front of constituents. If any time and energy remain, lawmakers look after what might remain of their law practices or businesses.

As a result, lawmakers must establish priorities. The most important goal for nearly all is reelection. They often regard all other activity as a means to this end. Many legislators specialize. For the sake of simplicity, they usually fit in one of four categories: the issues advocate, the district advocate, the committee specialist, and the broker. The issues-oriented lawmaker might be a committed conservative, populist, antitax, or gay rights advocate who sponsors legislation that supports his or her ideological commitment. The district advocate focuses more on issues of specific benefit to his or her constituents such as highway and park projects, the location and staffing of a new prison, or funding for university campuses. All legislators sit on committees, but some sit on the same one for many years and become experts in the specific policy issues covered by that committee. Finally, there is the broker, a pragmatic legislator who enjoys getting things done by means of the bruising work of stitching together bipartisan, regional, and other majority coalitions for or against controversial bills.

Despite cultural and regional differences among lawmakers, the legislature is a close-knit political club in which a degree of camaraderie develops. Liberals and conservatives may disagree about issues just as downstate farmers and Chicago corporate lawyers enjoy different cuisine, but they also have a great deal in common. All have run for office; raised campaign funds; and endured potshots from opponents, disgruntled groups, and the media. The voters elected all of them; those who want to stay will have to go through the process again. All must respond to constituent inquiries, meet visiting school groups, listen to lobbyists, and typically spend more than eighty nights a year in Springfield, eating and drinking in the same few places.

For this reason, patterns of mutually useful behavior have developed. Legislators generally treat their colleagues with trust and respect and engage in good-faith negotiations. Thus, they generally avoid becoming personal in the heat of debate, keep their word and commitments, reciprocate favors done, and help one another whenever possible. These patterns help explain what would otherwise be paradoxical behavior. For example, legislators will often help a colleague from the other party to get his or her bill out of committee. If the committee vote looks close, a committee member might change his vote with language such as the following: "so that my respected colleague can get his bill reported to the floor for the full debate it deserves, even though I may have to vote against it at that time." This helps the colleague get a little favorable publicity in the home district; regrettably, it also clogs the legislative process with bills that legislators must consider later on the chamber floor even if they are unlikely to enact them.

Conflict and Resolution:
How the General Assembly Works

Legislators typically find themselves in a pressure tank where conflict, accommodation, and interdependence characterize relations among themselves, the governor, and interest groups. Conflict between lawmakers and governors is natural, for there is an inherent clash of perspectives. Lawmakers mainly focus on the people in their districts, whereas the governor must think about the whole state. Legislators go about their business in a piecemeal fashion, each developing bills based on individual interests and special knowledge, whereas the governor has to be comprehensive in his or her annual state of the state and budget messages. The legislator's job has a short-term focus because about seven of ten Illinois lawmakers are up for election every two years.[7] The voters elect a governor every four years, and they expect him or her to take a long-term view, to present a vision for the future.

As a result, each branch frustrates and exasperates the other. They contend on fairly even terms. The governor has greater formal powers, information resources, stature, and visibility; as a single actor, the chief executive can be decisive. Nevertheless, the legislature has its own strengths: strong leadership in the four caucuses, sophisticated staffs, nearly full-time commitments by most legislators, and the political will to live up to its billing as a coequal branch.

The legislative cycle lasts two years in Illinois, with each year known as a biennial session; the biennium in 2021–22 was the 102nd General Assembly. State representatives serve two-year terms, and state senators serve a four- or two-year term, depending on the cycle (see chapter 3 on elections).

The legislature convenes each year on the second Wednesday in January and continues to meet, with periodic recesses, during the two-year period. Typically, the legislative leaders divide each year into three phases: the regular spring session, the interim summer period, and the fall veto session.

Figure 6.2. "Proposed Legislation." Cartoon by Bill Campbell.

The spring session generally begins slowly in January and traditionally ends with a roar in late May or early June. In 2022, legislators voted to end the spring session on April 8 to accommodate the primary elections, usually held in March, that were pushed to June 28 that year. The reason for the primary change was redistricting after the 2020 U.S. Census: delays in data from the Census Bureau, due largely to the COVID pandemic, meant the required redistricting of legislative districts was also delayed.

Legislators enact laws by means of bills only, and bills may originate in either house with the sponsorship of one or more members. The Illinois constitution confines bills, except bills for appropriations and for the codification, revision, or rearrangement of laws, to one subject, and limits appropriation bills to the subject of appropriations. Typically, all legislators combined introduce between 5,000 and 7,000 bills during the biennium, most during the spring of the first year, hundreds of these during the first week. The president of the Senate and the Speaker of the House assign bills to the Senate Assignment and House Rules committees, which assign the bills to standing committees. The Speaker and the president, who are the leaders of the majority party in each body, control the rules committees and therefore control which bills advance or languish in committee.

In contrast to the U.S. Congress, where committees control bills, legislative sponsors steer their bills through the Illinois legislative process. Tradition dictates that the committee chairperson schedule a hearing date for a bill in order to accommodate the sponsor, if possible. Timing is important because a sponsor must gather support and count votes in committee as well as at the passage stage. Each bill receives three formal readings by title on the floor of each house on three separate days. The first reading occurs at introduction; the second takes place after committee action, when the bill returns to the chamber floor; and the final reading occurs when the members of the chamber vote to either approve or reject the bill.[8] The Illinois legislature records all votes electronically at the stage of final bill passage.

Even with the imposition of successive deadlines, a logjam of unfinished bills typically develops as the spring session approaches its scheduled adjournment date. This is understandable because the pressure of a deadline is a critical component that keeps the legislative process running and induces brokering and compromise among lawmakers. Bills must receive a majority of the votes of all those elected, sixty in the House and thirty in the Senate, rather than simply a majority of those voting.

Drafters of the 1870 and 1970 Illinois constitutions sought to encourage negotiation and final legislative action by June 30 (now May 31) of each year and to avoid having sessions go into overtime. As a result, all bills passed after that date could not take effect until the following July unless they were passed by three-fifths of those elected. Attaining an extraordinary majority generally requires cooperation from the minority party in each house, so the constitution's framers assumed that the presiding officers in the General Assembly would do their best to get the job done before or very close to the deadline.

Nevertheless, whenever the two parties divided control between the governorship and at least one house of the legislature, the three-fifths proviso occasionally discouraged on-time adjournment. In overtime session, votes from both parties would be required in order to adopt the annual budget and controversial or unpopular legislation. Thus, the governor and legislative leaders tended to delay serious negotiations until the three-fifths proviso imposed the political necessity for compromise and shared responsibility. For example, the governor and the legislature could then enact budget cuts and increase cigarette taxes only with bipartisan support. In 1991, with a new governor, legislators could not reach an agreement before the spring session ended on June 30. That forced the legislature into overtime session, and they finally reached an agreement on July 18. In 1993 the overtime spring session lasted until July 13.

As a result, in 1994, the legislature considered a constitutional amendment to move the deadline from June 30 to May 31, the date after which an overtime session starts and a three-fifths majority is required in order to pass bills with an immediate effective date. Both houses enacted the amendment unanimously; in November 1994 the voters ratified it.[9] The deadline change reflected the reality of the political dynamic at the time of divided state government. In 2017, during the final year of the Illinois "Budget Impasse," lawmakers were called into special session in June after adjourning in May with no budget. They worked for five weeks and eventually passed a budget with the necessary three-fifths vote.[10]

The second phase of the legislative process occurs after the spring session adjourns and the legislators depart Springfield for the summer. During this interim period, the governor's staff, the Governor's Office of Management and Budget (GOMB, formerly the Bureau of the Budget), and agency managers face the task of reviewing the thousand or so bills passed by the legislature in a typical spring session. The constitution requires that the governor receive a bill from the legislature within thirty days of passage. Then the governor has sixty days to sign the bill or impose one of several types of vetoes. Legislators commonly refer to this as the bill's "drop" date. In the rare event that a bill is neither signed nor vetoed within sixty calendar days after it is presented to the governor, it becomes law.

Legislative staff members are busy during this interim period compiling summaries of the spring session and analyzing gubernatorial actions on bills. Other legislative staff prepare for and attend public hearings of legislative subcommittees, special committees, or task forces to gather testimony and other evidence and make recommendations about how to resolve certain public policy issues.

In the third and final phase of the legislative process, the lawmakers reconvene in the fall for a veto session that allows further debate and action on bills vetoed by the governor. In odd-numbered years, the fall veto session generally opens in October; in even-numbered years, lawmakers reconvene in mid-November following the general elections. The fall session typically lasts six to twelve days. A vetoed bill returns to the house where it originated, and the members have fifteen calendar days in which to act. If the legislature overrides a veto in one house, then the bill moves to the second house, where the same fifteen-day deadline applies.[11]

The expanded veto power given the governor in the 1970 constitution has an unintended consequence. The delegates institutionalized the fall veto session as a countervailing legislative power that ensured that the legislature had an opportunity to override vetoes. Delegates intended to prevent a pocket veto, which the U.S. Constitution permits; however, the legislature often takes up not only vetoes but also postponed or new legislative initiatives during the fall session.[12] It gives legislators another bite at the apple and affects their strategy with regard to matters that might be too hot to handle during the spring session, especially in even-numbered election years—items such as tax increases and pay raises. It also allows legislators to amend previously passed legislation before controversial provisions take effect.

Because of retirements and defeats in even-year elections, numerous lame-duck lawmakers may feel less responsive to caucus leaders' demands and constituency pressures during a fall veto session. Some will even reverse themselves and become proponents of certain parts of the governor's program because the governor can provide a job with good pension benefits in addition to salary. In other words, all bets are off during even-year fall sessions.

Role of Committees

Much of the work of committees is routine and has little effect on the policies embedded in a bill because even if a bill dies, legislators may resurrect the main idea later. Committees are almost meaningless because bad bills often get out so easily.

Regular committee members feel the influence of caucus leadership strongly. Under Speaker Michael Madigan, House Democratic leaders regularly circulated bill lists with arrows that pointed up or down to indicate the position of the leadership. Because of the strong party discipline, lobbyists often considered a bill dead if it had "down arrows" from the Speaker's office. Thus they lobbied hard with the Speaker, his staff, and assistant leaders to get the arrows reversed or at least removed to indicate a neutral position. When Republican Lee Daniels was briefly Speaker (89th General Assembly, 1995–96), he attempted to impose a similar rigid type of arrow system on the House Republican caucus. Owing to stiff resistance among the caucus members, the arrows soon became merely leadership "recommendations." In the Senate, where marching orders regarding legislation are typically more informal and less routine, leaders tend to limit their coercive influence over committee members to major or controversial bills.

Under Speaker Chris Welch, who was elected Speaker in 2021, this has changed somewhat. He relies more on committees to vet bills, and especially his committee chairs. Unlike Madigan, who some lawmakers described as a "heat shield" of sorts because of his ability to absorb criticism, Speaker Welch lets sponsors defend and shepherd their bills. This has resulted in an increase in the number of bills that the House considers.

In the House, leaders also have authority to replace committee members with others from their party's legislative caucus. The House rules state, "A member may be temporarily replaced on a committee due to illness or if the member is otherwise unavailable."[13] House leaders routinely interpret the phrase "otherwise unavailable" broadly. When considering an important bill, a House caucus leader can replace for that day a committee member who refuses to follow leadership's position on the bill with another member who will. Senate leaders interpret a similar rule narrowly, and they seldom invoke its authority to replace a member.

The number of standing committees in both chambers has significantly increased since the 90th General Assembly (1997–98), when the House had twenty-eight standing committees and the Senate had sixteen. In the 102nd General Assembly (2021–22), the standing committees in the House numbered forty-seven and those in the Senate thirty-one. As the number of standing committees increases, so does the number of legislators who serve as committee chairs and minority spokespersons and receive a stipend of $10,327 in addition to their base salary.[14] The leaders make all committee appointments, and so this arrangement gives the leaders an opportunity to reward or punish, which they can use to enforce caucus discipline.

Moreover, with more bills in the legislative process, more committees will meet and hold hearings that consume more of members' scarce time. Leaders can exploit this opportunity to exercise further control over members by manipulating the committee meeting schedules and the assignment of bills to the committees. Busy members have less free time to act on their own or in combination against the leaders' wishes. In order to cope with the demands of ever-increasing committee workloads, regular members must heavily rely on the professional staffs, who work for the leaders. A member who acts in opposition to the leadership's agenda in committee might have to do so unassisted by staff.

Working the System: Staff Professionals

Forty-five years ago, there would have been very little to write about legislative staff because there were so few, but today staff members outnumber legislators and have a significant effect on the dynamics of the legislative process.

There are four staffing categories: those who report directly to the leaders or their assistants; those who provide analysis and staff the committees; those who provide clerical or administrative assistance for individual legislators in their Springfield offices; and those who work for the legislature's various support agencies, including the bill-drafting reference bureau, research unit, committee on administrative rules, and information service. Legislative leaders hire and assign those in the first three groups on a strictly partisan basis, and their work assignments continue at the sole discretion of the leaders. Those who work for the support agencies do so for the most part on a bipartisan basis. It is common for a legislative agency director to be affiliated with one party and the assistant to be affiliated with the other.

Regular legislators hire their own district office staff using their district office allowance, which is about $70,000 annually for every member.[15] Normally, the allowance is enough for basic clerical staff, office space rental, and the cost of supplies, though adequacy varies depending on the location of the district office and the regional cost differences. In addition, the leaders might provide extra district office staff for selected members, generally those whom the leaders predict might be targeted for serious challenge in the next election cycle. This incumbency protection stratagem bolsters the selected members' constituent services and presumably their reelectability. This is yet another example of calculated member dependence on leaders and their resources.

Legislative staffers are typically in their twenties and are working on or already have master's or law degrees. Lawmakers are dependent on them to manage not just the office but information as well. As social media and the internet especially have allowed unprecedented access to legislators, staff can serve an important gate-keeping function.

Like the legislators for whom they work, staff members have ambitions, priorities, and frustrations. Some see staff work as a stepping-stone. United States Senator Richard Durbin and former governor Jim Edgar are among scores of former staffers who have subsequently served as elected officials, agency heads, gubernatorial aides, and lobbyists.

In the shorter term, however, what most staff members want is to see their ideas, bill drafts, amendments, and budget recommendations become law and implemented as public policy. Those who work and negotiate with staff, including lobbyists, appreciate the objective of having one's idea adopted by a respected legislative staffer, which is often an important initial step in the legislative process. Staff members also want recognition for the work they have done, in spite of the hard-and-fast institutional requirement that all credit go to the boss. They appreciate people who thank them for their contributions to the process. Finally, staff members are usually open to bipartisan cooperation, even within the context of partisan assignments. Committee staff from both parties often share information while their bosses publicly engage in partisan debate about the same issues.

Each committee has at least two staff analysts, one for each party. Before each committee hearing, staff members prepare analyses of each bill. Typically, an analysis includes a synopsis that outlines the proposed change in the law; current law and descriptions of possible problems to be resolved; discussion of the positions of the caucus, affected agencies, interest groups, and the governor's office or affected state or local government agencies; and suggestions for member's questions at the hearing. In most cases, the analysts will have contacted the pertinent government agencies and other interested parties to generate information for their detailed analysis of the proposed change in statutory law. This detailed groundwork provides the foundation on which lawmakers build legislation and public policy.

How Legislators Make Decisions

A legislator makes thousands of decisions each year, from the insignificant to the momentous, in committee, on second reading, at passage stage, and in response to lobbyists, constituents, and reporters. The lawmaker must apply a split-second calculus to many of these decisions. Should they help a colleague get a dubious bill out of committee (an easy affirmative decision for most)? How should they vote on possibly career-threatening tax increases or abortion legislation? A legislator cannot blithely abstain from voting, allowing those who know more about an issue to make the decision. The Illinois constitution requires that bills receive a majority vote of all those elected, so failure to vote or a formal present vote operates in the same way as a no vote. There is no easy way out.

Barack Obama, a former Illinois state senator, discovered this when he ran for president in 2008. During the contentious Democratic primary elections, Hillary Clinton attacked Obama for voting "present on 129 bills and 11 personnel appointments out of roughly 4,000 votes cast during his nearly eight years in Springfield."[16] Few states allow a present vote, and Obama discovered that it is difficult to explain this quaint Illinois practice to a national audience. One explanation given was that it is an appropriate vote for legislators who have a conflict of interest that prevents them from voting yes or no on a bill. Regarding some of the votes, Obama, a law school instructor, explained he was for some parts of a bill and voted present because he believed other parts unconstitutional. Yet some critics charged that the present vote was a cagy way of avoiding a difficult no vote, while having achieved the same result.

An Illinois lawmaker's political party affiliation and the position of their caucus leaders' positions provide the most apparent guides to decision making. For routine and noncontroversial matters, the party line is a good guide to the way a legislator will vote, but with difficult or unpopular issues, leaders impose positions on their members only to the extent necessary to achieve their objectives. Leaders take into account that the attitudes of voters in a legislator's district may be at odds with a caucus's partisan position, particularly for members facing a targeted race. In those cases, the leaders try to structure majority roll calls without demanding support from those who would have to vote against their constituents' wishes.

Voters' attitudes as reflected in mail and personal contacts also provide indispensable cues for lawmakers, especially for those in competitive or targeted districts. Most voters, especially those in large urban or suburban districts, have little or no idea how their legislators are voting, let alone who they are. Legislators understand this, so one might conclude that lawmakers could act without concern for constituents' attitudes. This is generally not the case, because careerist lawmakers view their political world in terms of actions that might increase or decrease their electoral base. Endorsement by large membership organizations of realtors, farmers, and labor unions can add scores or hundreds of votes to one's base of support, as can support from advocates of gun ownership or the prolife and prochoice causes. This is why small but intense groups often wield more influence than their numbers would seem to represent.

The institution has developed approaches to reducing conflict in decision making, especially concerning the many issues that lack strong partisan, constituent, or regional considerations. One of these is "going along," that is, voting for legislation unless there is visible opposition. In committee, as members try to wrap up a long hearing, one often hears a legislator ask, "Is there any opposition to this bill? If not, I move the attendance [or partisan] roll call." Legislators generally give their colleagues' bills the benefit of the doubt.

Reciprocity is another consideration. It makes more sense to help a colleague than to stand in the way, for their assistance may be useful another day. Reciprocity often takes place in committees; it is one reason so many bad bills get out of committee to clog floor action later. Passing a problem along seems to simplify decision making: "Let the other chamber clean up the problems" or "Let's send it to the governor, and let him resolve the conflict."

Making commitments early reduces conflict as well. Keeping one's commitment has been a hallowed norm, though it seems to have been breached more frequently in recent years. An early commitment to a colleague or lobbyist regarding a controversial bill that is going to plague the legislature all session effectively takes the committed lawmaker out of the lobbyists' crosshairs.

Not all conflict, of course, can be resolved, pushed along, or reduced. For the scores of decisions that involve conflict, the lawmaker complements their own values and knowledge with cues provided by the leadership, staff, colleagues, lobbyists, the governor's office, the press, and constituents.

Information is an important factor. Legislators have more information available than they can digest, and the amount they do absorb is impressive. Nevertheless, with regard to any one decision, the information is likely to be incomplete. Thus, the credibility of the information or of the person who delivered it becomes critical. The best cues tend to come from expert colleagues, veteran lobbyists, senior legislative staff, and longtime state agency experts.

A former legislator recalls one use he made of informational cues on the House floor: "I respected my seatmates to my left, right, and in front of me. One was on the judiciary committee, another on local government and agriculture, the third on revenue. I was on appropriations and education. We had most of the committees covered among us. So, on third reading as each bill came up we would ask who had it in committee, what he remembered, and how he was going to vote. While we didn't always agree, it was an invaluable set of cues."[17]

A Sometimes Long and Winding Road: How Laws Are Made

Some bills will work their way, step by procedural step, toward passage without major incident, but a likely fate for major appropriations bills and controversial pieces of substantive legislation is a long and winding road. Thus, a bill might seem irretrievably lost before its essence suddenly reappears in another bill, making a frantic dash for final passage before a scheduled deadline or adjournment.

Persuasion of fellow legislators is stock-in-trade in the legislative arena, but subtler techniques such as timing and personal knowledge of other legislators are often just as effective. A legislator shepherding their bill through a committee hearing tries to match the timing to the moods of the committee. For example, the lawmaker may have arranged for testimony on a bill by interest group representatives and other experts. Some of these people may have come hundreds of miles for the hearing and will want to have their full say in the matter. But if other bills have consumed a great deal of time, and if tired committee members are fidgeting in their chairs, the bill's sponsor may well size up the chances of a favorable vote and, if the count looks promising, curtail or eliminate his team's testimony to request a well-timed vote.

Most committee work is more hard-headed, especially when money is involved. The governor must make his budget recommendations to the legislature by the first Wednesday in March. The GOMB prepares individual appropriations bills for about sixty agencies; together these bills represent the governor's budget, which in fiscal 2023 totaled about $112.5 billion. Although the executive branch develops its budget over an eight-month period, the legislature must react, evaluate, and authorize the budget in the three-month period from March through the conventional late May adjournment. Each house conducts this work in appropriations committees.

Since the mid-1990s, the legislative leaders have designated the "budgeteer" for the caucus, usually one of the appropriations committee chairpersons. The budgeteer and appropriations committee staffs have then altered the governor's proposed budgets outside the hearings without the active participation of committee members. Strong, experienced, and knowledgeable budgeteers and staff budget directors have also shifted spending authority from a governor's objectives to those that reflect the preferences of the legislative caucus leaders.

Appropriations bills provide a good example of how the professionalized legislature with its full-time, partisan staff fully counterbalances the executive branch. In the case of appropriations, however, they do this at the expense of the active participation of regular committee members in the process. The appropriations bill for each agency proposes dollar amounts for line items such as personnel, contractual services, equipment, travel, and telecommunications. Appropriations committee staffers require agency responses to detailed questions to justify what the amount allocated for each line item would buy. Because staff analysts specialize in different areas, their questions cannot be derailed easily. Analysts from one or both parties will meet with the agency's fiscal officer and sometimes the agency head to discuss the proposed budget, laying groundwork for future legislative floor debate or actually brokering a deal outside of the committee hearing. During the public committee hearing, members play the role of receiving hours of agency testimony about the governor's budget proposals and may even make the news by grilling hapless agency officials, but the committee members rarely join in the actual process of negotiations and drafting of the budget bills.

Other technical and little-known tools used by leaders to various degrees for crafting compromises on controversial issues include conference committees, "shell bills," and "agreed bills." A conference committee reconciles differences between the House and Senate versions of a bill. Five members are appointed from each chamber, three by the presiding officer and two by the minority leader. Generally, they appoint the bill's sponsor and committee members who are specialists on the bill's subject matter.

These short-lived committees were traditionally not required to meet publicly or to meet at all. Often a legislator or staffer would simply circulate a conference committee report based on agreement between two or more key conferees, with approval of the leadership, seeking the six signatures needed to file the revised bill with the two chambers. For important bills, staffers for the governor and legislative leaders and key lobbyists routinely hold quick meetings in a corridor off the Senate or House floor or in the privacy of a leader's office.

Such a system allowed bills to be changed significantly or completely rewritten by conference committees. During the sometimes chaotic windup of the spring session, a score of conference committees were in existence simultaneously.

Skilled legislators and staff often manipulate this esoteric process. In 1989, for example, Senate Republicans under the leadership of minority leader James "Pate" Philip forced a change in Senate rules on the pretext of curbing the abuse of conference committee reports. The new rules required that a conference committee report lie on senators' desks for one day before a vote can be taken, that sponsors of bills be appointed to conference committees that will deal with their bill, and that all amendments adopted in conference committees be germane, that is, pertinent to the subject matter of the original bill.

After a decade of having the Democratic majority outmaneuver them, Philip and the Senate Republicans in 1993 took advantage of their new majority status and adopted rules that require the Senate Rules Committee to approve a conference committee report before the Senate can consider it. These rules, which remain in effect, considerably reduce the ability of a few people to make changes in legislation without the knowledge of other members and out of public view.[18]

While ostensibly preventing abuse of process, the leaders had designed such rule changes as part of the overall tightening of leadership control in the legislative process, which over time has resulted in a dramatic shift of power away from the regular membership to the leaders. Since the mid-1990s, the leaders of the majority caucuses of both parties consolidated their power through ever-tightened rules designed to enable them to manipulate the legislative process at the expense of regular members, and they did so under the disingenuous guise of reform and with the acquiescence of the regular membership. Former Speaker Madigan refused to allow the use of conference committee reports, and shell bills have been used instead.

The shell bill is another tightly controlled vehicle used by legislative leaders to revive dashed hopes. It allows leaders to introduce, late in a session, new proposals as well as compromises hammered out among leaders and the governor in closed meetings. Because new bills cannot be introduced after a certain date set by rule each session, the party leaders introduce early in the process a number of innocuous shell bills, empty of substantive content, that later can contain new or revived legislation or amendments. Leaders cannot use just any bill because amendments must deal with the same chapter of the state statutes as the bill they would amend. Thus, dozens of shell bills are moving along at any given time, available at strategic moments to carry forward late-developing compromises or to resurrect ideas seemingly killed earlier.

Legislative leaders in years past used the agreed bill process when their caucus members felt caught uncomfortably in the middle of intense conflicts between major interest groups on subjects about which the lawmakers have less expertise than the groups. For example, proposed changes in workers' compensation for injuries divide labor unions and management. Legislative committees sometimes direct the interest groups to try to iron out their differences outside the legislative chambers and then come back with an agreed bill, which the legislators would probably ratify. The agreed bill process sometimes works, especially if the interest groups think the legislative solution might be worse than their agreement.

Also checking a bill's fate is the governor with powers of veto in addition to the total veto of bills and, since the 1970 constitution, the line-item veto. These include the reduction veto for appropriations bills, which allows for the reduction in appropriated amounts, and the amendatory veto, which permits gubernatorial changes to substantive bills enacted by the legislature.

If the legislature disagrees with a governor's total, amendatory, or line-item vetoes, they can override them by a vote of three-fifths of the members elected to each chamber. Restoration of an appropriation reduced by the governor requires only a majority of the members elected to each chamber. Thus, after 1970 it became easier for the legislature to override a governor's vetoes by reducing the required majority to three-fifths from the previously almost insurmountable two-thirds.[19]

Four Tops—and the Governor

Legislation is a complex business in which byzantine procedures and layers of committees and staff are among the many barriers to turning a bill into a law. Its complexity ensures that a core of leaders will develop to guide the regular membership. The structure and political makeup of the General Assembly has led to the institution of a four-leader system that includes the majority and minority leaders of both chambers, known since the 1980s as the "Four Tops." They have generally shared control of the legislative process with the governor, who by the stroke of his veto pen has the discretionary power to undo years of legislative labor.[20]

The power of legislative leaders had begun to grow in the early 1980s, when leaders centralized selection and management of the partisan staffing for committees. Staffers are now loyal to the leadership and not to the committee chairpersons, who once had a say in the selection. Many of these staff assistants have also become skilled at campaign management and take leaves of absence during campaigns to help direct reelection efforts of members with difficult races, further tying them into the political apparatus of the legislative leaders.

The Four Tops bring significant legislative experience to their roles. Although experience and longevity explain their success in part, the rest of the story consists of their near monopolies on campaign fundraising and professional legislative staff and of the acquiescence to their caucus leaders' agenda by increasingly dependent regular members.[21]

Because of their powers, the leaders have become aggressive and successful at raising campaign funds that, along with campaign management services, they allocate to their members. Each of the four leaders directs a caucus political action committee and their own leader's fund. During the 2022 campaign cycle, fundraising among the leaders ranged from over $15 million by

Senate President Don Harmon (D-Oak Park) to $2.2 million by House Minority Leader Jim Durkin (R-Western Springs). Most contributions from big interest groups flow not to individual members' campaign accounts but to the leader-controlled funds. During the 2022 campaign Democrats for the Illinois House raised close to $18 million and Senate Democrats raised almost $13.2 million.[22]

The leadership of each party targets a small number of legislative districts for special effort based on the potential for gaining a seat by defeating primary challengers and the other party's candidates in the next election. For instance, in 2022, the Forty-eighth Senate District was targeted. Senator Doris Turner (D-Springfield), who was elected in 2021, received over $2.7 million from the Illinois Senate Defense fund in her race against Ninety-ninth House District Representative Sandy Hamilton (R-Springfield).[23] The Republican Senate Victory Fund donated close to $1 million to Hamilton. The race was close, but Turner won.

The leadership also protects members whom the other caucus has targeted by assigning committee staff to assist them in drafting and sponsoring popular bills and getting the bills through the legislature. The press staff publicizes the targeted members' legislative achievements in Springfield and in hometown news media. Members targeted in tough reelection contests sometimes vote the way the opposition might vote, with the tacit approval of their leadership, to avoid becoming vulnerable to attack by the other caucus's candidate. Veteran members know by hard experience that in a heated reelection campaign, a political attack launched by an opponent in a press release might cost a candidate tens of thousands of dollars in campaign funds because it forces him or her to buy expensive media advertising or mailers to explain or defend a controversial vote. Indeed, legislators who are in somewhat safer districts often vote with the targeted members. As a result, leaders designate a member to be the caucus whip, whose job it is to keep caucus discipline and see to it that caucus members in nontargeted districts vote as the party leadership demands.

Leadership powers are not without limits. Each caucus's membership is diverse, with varying ideologies, personalities, ambitions, and rivalries. Perfect discipline is impossible, and a lawmaker may be more loyal to their district interests than to a leader. Moreover, leaders depend on their members for support to win and retain their positions. As a result, leaders who run roughshod over members risk losing their position. Instead, they generally try to apply their powers in ways designed to generate credits among members, and leaders can draw on that political capital as needed.

THE END OF ANOTHER LONG, HOT, DUSTY DAY IN THE SADDLE.

Figure 6.3. "Long, Hot, Dusty Day." Cartoon by Bill Campbell.

Power: Sometimes the Luck of the Draw

Reapportionment represents the essential trench warfare of politics, for after a mighty struggle, new battle lines are set for a full decade.[24] The process begins following the decennial census and is intended to be a bipartisan effort of the legislature. Nevertheless, since candidates win or lose elections depending on where the lines are drawn, the redistricting processes of 1980, 1990, and 2000 became deadlocked in the legislature. The constitution requires that the new map be drawn by a commission of legislators and nonlegislators that comprises four Democrats and four Republicans selected by the legislative leaders. Because these commissions could not reach agreement by August of the redistricting year, a ninth member was chosen to break the tie, as provided by the state constitution. The State Supreme Court submits the names of one Democrat and one Republican, and the secretary of state randomly selects one of them.[25]

After the 1990 census, the Republicans won the draw; the following decade, the Democrats did. Not coincidentally, the Republicans controlled the Senate from 1992 to 2002, but after the 2000 census and remapping, the Democrats took over. In 2010 and 2020 Democrats had enough of a majority in both houses that the maps were passed and signed by the governor without having to go to commission.

Districts should be equal in population, compact, contiguous, and nondiscriminatory. Within those rules, the players draw boundaries that favor the party in control of redistricting. Computers are at the heart of the procedure, processing census information on a precinct-level basis so that legislators can tell instantaneously how moving a district line by one city block will change the population, political, racial, economic, age, and other dimensions of the proposed district.

The basic techniques for achieving partisan advantage are to pack your opponents and their voting strength into as few districts as possible or dilute your opponents' strength. Districts that are equal in population and acceptably compact and contiguous can be drawn to benefit either party.

To illustrate, consider Champaign and Urbana, which are contiguous central Illinois cities located in the heart of Champaign County. Put simplistically, the twin cities form a doughnut hole in which the two major parties are competitive, while the rest of the county is predominantly Republican. Over the years, depending on which party is in control after each new census, so goes the legislative map. In 1981 the Democrats were in control, and using the urban doughnut hole they drew a map with a solid Democratic House seat and divided the rest of the county among several Republican districts. After the next census, Republicans drew the map, and they split up the twin cities to produce House districts that Republicans won every year except 1992. In 2001, 2011, and 2021 Democrats drew the maps, which reunited Champaign-Urbana into a single safe House district easily won by a Democrat and divided the rest of the county into three Republican House districts.

Conflict is inherent. Although party leaders want to increase their respective total membership numbers, individual lawmakers are more interested in "safer" districts from which they can easily win reelection. Leaders of African American, Latino, downstate, collar county, and Chicago interests want safer districts and more of them.

The rise of the Latino Caucus is an interesting example. In 1987 a strong independent leader who got his start in Chicago politics as a community advocate became the first Latino senator in Illinois history. Senator Miguel del Valle swiftly moved up through the ranks to become an assistant majority leader. By 1994, as the number of Latinos in Illinois surpassed nine hundred thousand, their political and economic power began to be felt.[26] Because of more favorably drawn district maps, four Latino legislators served in the General Assembly and often worked together with the Black Caucus.

By 2003, as Democrats came back to power as the majority in both houses, the number of Latinos serving as legislators nearly doubled, and they formed a separate Latino Caucus and began to push for political change.[27] When the 102nd General Assembly (2021–22) convened, because of rapid Latino population growth in the Chicagoland area and favorably drawn district maps, the Latino Caucus included six senators and nine representatives, all of whom were Democrats. This, and the rapid population growth, has significantly increased the political influence of the Latino Caucus. So much so that in 2022 State Representative Lisa Hernandez (D-Cicero) was elected chair of the Illinois Democratic Party.

Madigan and the Best Mapmaker of All

The best mapmaker of them all was not coincidentally the most powerful of all the Four Tops in state history: former Speaker of the House Mike Madigan, who served for a combined total of thirty-six years in that role. He was not just the longest serving Speaker in Illinois, but of any state legislature in all of the United States.

Madigan was originally elected to the statehouse in 1970. As stated in chapter 2, Madigan grew up in the southwest side's Thirteenth Ward and honed his craft under Mayor Richard J. Daley. Because of Daley's support, Madigan rose through the ranks quickly. After working for the City of Chicago and serving three terms in the House, in 1976 he became the House Democratic majority leader. But Daley suddenly died, and Madigan would have to make it on his own. He did this through mapmaking.

In 1981, after census figures were released and mapmaking commenced, Democrats feared that the increase in suburbanization would translate into losses for the city and ultimately losses for Democrats. As a result, the legislature was unable to agree on a map by the required date. The commission that followed gave Democrats—and ultimately Mike Madigan because of his leadership position—control of the map.[28] The new population patterns should have resulted in about fifteen Senate and thirty-one House seats for Chicago, but instead the city was rewarded with nineteen and thirty-seven, respectively.[29]

Additionally, this was the year the "Cutback Amendment" to the Illinois constitution went into effect, shrinking the size of the House from 177 to 118. Madigan's artistry ensured over 40 of these 59 lost seats were Republican.[30] All this hard work finally paid off in 1983 when Democrats gained the majority and Madigan was voted Speaker.

The Cutback Amendment of 1981 had other implications that helped Madigan as well. Prior to it, three legislators were elected from a district in a system of cumulative voting, but there had to be at least one member of each party. This meant that in areas controlled by one party, the opposite party always won a seat because the dominant party could not hold all three. It gave minority party winners a degree of freedom, and its elimination meant that rank-and-file members would be less dependent on leadership.[31]

Republicans won the lottery in 1991, resulting in a brief interlude where Republicans controlled the House and Lee Daniels (R-Elmhurst) was Speaker (1993–94). This was a lesson that Madigan took harshly and would not forget. In 2001 when Democrats won the lottery, he drew a map that produced Democratic majorities so large that in 2011 and 2021 the legislature had the required vote to pass it (and Democratic governors to sign it).

Madigan used his power in three ways: to control legislation in the House, to amass a campaign fortune that could make or break candidates, and to dole out old-fashioned patronage.

Madigan's role as Speaker made him the chair of the Rules Committee, meaning he determined which legislation would be advanced. He used this power ruthlessly over the years to reward or punish members on both sides of the aisle. According to Ray Long, "At the Illinois Capitol, the question loomed over every major issue. The question came in over the phone, got whispered in the hallway, popped up at a committee hearing and rolled out in a press conference. It is a simple query, of course, expected to be asked in statehouses all across America. In Illinois, though, the answer carried far greater weight."[32] The question was, "What does the Speaker think?"

Lawmakers disagree today about the power of the Rules Committee. Some say that Madigan was a savant of sorts, with the ability to read every page of every bill and be familiar with intimate details of so many. They would characterize Madigan as someone who knew how to triage legislation, and insist he gave deference to those trusted and put in power over the committees. Others would say his ability to triage was abused.

Madigan's control over the General Assembly meant that donors lined up to fill his campaign coffers to ensure their legislation was passed. Madigan always stayed true to the working-class roots of his district, so it is no surprise that his biggest donors over time were unions. Over the past decade and a half, Madigan's personal campaign fund (Friends of Michael J. Madigan) has received close to $25 million from construction, labor, engineering, carpentry, teaching and public employee unions.[33] He has shared much of this cash with the Democratic Party of Illinois and the House Democratic Majority PAC, both of which he controlled and raised tens of millions for over the course of his tenure. This money was then distributed to candidates in need.

In a state that recorded some of the highest federal corruption conviction statistics, Madigan seemed to stay above the fray. While he drew the ire of Republicans and Democrats alike for his iron grip on power, he seemed almost invincible. Perhaps owing to his prowess, perhaps to his never using technology, perhaps, his supporters say, to the fact he was totally clean. That was until several scandals broke out that caused his image and brand to take a severe hit and paved the way for detractors to change the narrative.

In 2014 an exposé in the *Chicago Tribune* detailed how Madigan used his clout to get friends hired and promoted at Metra, the Chicago metropolitan area's local rail carrier. Investigations cleared Madigan of wrongdoing.[34] In 2018, former staffer Alaina Hampton reported being sexually harassed by Kevin Quinn, a top Madigan aide.[35] Hampton alleged a coverup ensued, and as a result she was retaliated against. She filed suit in federal court, which led to Quinn's ouster, and the case was settled in 2019.

During the course of the investigation, it came to light that Quinn was paid $30,000 by Madigan after his departure, but not directly: through lobbyists for public utility giant Commonwealth Edison (ComEd). This led to more questions from federal investigators, and by 2020 they had cracked wide open one of the biggest scandals in state government since Blagojevich: a massive scheme in which Madigan was trading favorable legislation in return for jobs and contracts in an old-fashioned patronage scheme. From 2011 to 2019 specifically, many of these contracts meant little to no work for Madigan allies at a time when Illinoisans saw $2.3 billion in rate hikes over the course of ten years to subsidize nuclear plants that were going bust.[36]

In July of 2020, a group of mostly female legislators came forward and demanded Madigan resign, but he refused. The calls grew louder, and so did the dissension. By January of 2021 it was clear that Madigan would not have the votes for a nineteenth term as Speaker, and he withdrew his name from consideration. A month after that, he resigned. And so ended the reign of one of the most powerful state legislators in the history of the nation. In April 2022, Madigan was indicted on twenty-two counts of racketeering and bribery related to these charges. The federal government also alleges Madigan pressured at least one contractor to use his law firm for a tax appeal in exchange for a zoning change.[37] As he awaits trial, he maintains his innocence.

The Future of the Illinois General Assembly

Many of the institutional pieces of the legislature have remained remarkably similar throughout the years. Politically, however, Illinois has undergone a potentially seismic shift with the resignation of Mike Madigan and the election of Speaker Chris Welch. Welch doesn't just represent the beginning of a new era; he is also the first Black Speaker that Illinois has ever had. And for the first time in thirty years, the Speaker is suburban. Welch's district contains very different communities, with rich and homogeneous River Forest; majority Black working-class communities of Broadview, Bellwood, and Maywood; and his diverse hometown of Hillside. Surely all of this will have an impact on his leadership style. Welch was able to out-fundraise Madigan and help more Democrats than ever get elected to the House in 2022. As a result, House Minority Leader Jim Durkin has recently announced he will resign his party post, citing the necessity for new leadership in the Republican Party.

Despite this, some lawmakers still lament Madigan's absence. But they admit that more bills are able to reach the floor for debate and passage. Some observers say this is a matter of quality versus quantity, but for those who are finally able to get bills passed it means the ability to deliver for their constituents and show real results. Speaker Welch, as noted above, is said to rely on his committees and chairs more as well, spreading things out. It is too early to judge Welch's leadership, but the legislature as a whole remains Democratic controlled with some of the largest majorities, something the 2020 remap will likely ensure for another decade.

7
THE EXECUTIVE

On March 12, 2020, Governor JB Pritzker issued a disaster proclamation for the State of Illinois, the state-level equivalent to a state of emergency, in response to COVID-19, the day after the World Health Organization had declared it a worldwide pandemic. Governor Pritzker issued executive orders that closed public schools, restaurants, and bars, required face coverings in public spaces, required insurance companies to cover telehealth services, halted evictions, suspended the expiration of vehicle registrations, and restricted the number of people who could gather publicly. He also issued several executive orders that required people to stay at home except for essential activities that eventually extended to May 29, 2020. The purpose of these executive orders was to prevent the spread of COVID-19 by restricting physical human contact.

Only a year into his governorship, the COVID-19 response would come to dominate his first term. Pritzker went on television daily during the stay-at-home period to update residents, and many waited daily for the briefings to understand how the pandemic was affecting the state and to hear any glimmer of hope that restrictions would be eased early. Eventually Pritzker's team issued a five-phase reopen plan called Restore Illinois. This plan divided Illinois into regions based on population, and listed five tiers of restrictions based on the rate of infection and hospital admissions in the region. This way, regions could ease or tighten restrictions based on local metrics so that hospitals could meet demand. The last phase of Restore Illinois occurred when vaccines were widely available to the public, which wasn't until the summer of 2021.

When Pritzker issued his disaster declaration, the federal government under then-President Donald Trump had not issued its own state of emergency. As governor of the fifth largest state, Pritzker had a responsibility to act. Moreover, Illinois had been affected sooner than other states. Home to O'Hare International Airport, the fifth busiest airport in the world, Illinois was the site of the very first U.S. COVID-19 case in January 2020 when a woman reported symptoms after traveling to Wuhan, China.[1] The sheer size of the metropolitan area meant that Pritzker had to act fast—and the numbers coming out of New York City were telling. Although they had their first confirmed case much later, in March, by May the New Yorkers were dying so fast that morgues could not keep up and hundreds of refrigerated trailers had to be brought in.[2]

By fall, however, infection numbers were falling and the population was growing restless with restrictions. Pritzker reopened schools provided masking, distancing, and other safety guidelines as outlined by the Illinois Department of Public Health (IDPH) and Illinois State Board of Education (ISBE) were followed.[3] Bars, restaurants, and other places of entertainment were allowed to reopen with these precautions. However, most other restrictions remained in place and per Restore Illinois, when infection rates climbed in certain regions, restrictions were tightened. As the weather was getting colder and people were spending more time indoors, transmission was easier and infection rates began climbing, causing more regions to experience higher levels of hospitalization and deaths.

Throughout the pandemic, Pritzker defended his decisions by saying he was "following the science." Guiding his decisions for each executive order, mitigation, and decision to move to a new phase was what the COVID-19 disease was doing. His director of the IDPH, Dr. Ngozi Ezike, was instrumental in helping him formulate his decisions. Many people waited for her to speak in the daily briefings, especially because her commitment to access meant that she delivered them fully in English and Spanish. Dr. Ezike had spent her entire career serving public health, first at a health center on Chicago's west side and then for the Cook County Public Health Department. This made her especially poised to be instrumental in aiding Pritzker in what was essentially unchartered territory. Of the early days she stated, "I try to just stick with what's the right thing to do. . . . No one is positive of the exact right course—we're building the plane as we're trying to fly it."[4]

Pritzker would need her counsel because his leadership would be tested early. Then State Representative Darren Bailey (R-Xenia) sued Pritzker in state court over the stay-at-home extensions and won a restraining order. By the time of the verdict the orders had expired, but this was important foreshadowing for the next year and a half. In the fall parents would challenge the masking orders at school, and businesses would challenge the capacity restrictions. When the vaccine was ready and the strategy changed to mandatory testing and vaccination, that too was tested in court.

By spring of 2022, Illinois was fully open and unmasked. Vaccines were widely available as well as boosters, even for children as young as five. Mandates went away, and the state transitioned to a mutating virus with variants that were "endemic" instead of a "pandemic." The plane was flying and more easily managed.

During the Spanish flu of 1918, mitigations were also made at the local level. Chicago's health commissioner Dr. John Dill Robertson led the charge, issuing recommendations for hygiene and distancing and later closing dance halls and theaters.[5] But Pritzker had what Dr. Robertson and then-Governor Frank O. Lowden did not—and that is mountains of data and statistics compiled daily that were sorted by county, municipality, and treating facility. This allowed a more targeted and informed response than doctors and elected officials in 1918 could dream of.

But Pritzker's following the science and relying on data was not without its detractors—that too was politicized and challenged. The strain of individualism that runs through Illinois is strong and some said that these decisions on mitigations should be individual, not collective. In fact, this was the biggest challenge for Pritzker: how could he protect all Illinoisans while respecting the rights of each one individually?

Approaches to Leading Illinois

Since Shadrach Bond first took on the job in 1818, twenty-one Republicans and twenty-two Democrats have served in the state's top post. Each brought his (all men so far) own approach to the job of governing. As the late Robert P. Howard explained in *Mostly Good and Competent Men*, several of the chief executives left lasting imprints as managers, builders, or social reformers.[6]

Thomas Ford (1842–46) was one of the managers. He inherited a huge debt from an overly ambitious internal improvements scheme to build railroads, canals, and plank roads throughout Illinois. Ford determined that, painful as it would be, the state must pay the principal and interest so as to restore the state's integrity as a place to invest. He sold government land and passed a permanent tax to pay off the debt, and he arranged new mortgage terms for completion of a canal between Lake Michigan and the Illinois River that would link the Great Lakes to the Gulf of Mexico. In so doing, Ford "made possible the future solvency and prosperity of Illinois."[7]

Another manager was Republican Frank O. Lowden (1917–21), who reorganized 125 boards and commissions, many of which operated as political fiefdoms, into nine executive departments. He also centralized the state's budgeting and accounting systems and became a leading candidate for president at the 1920 GOP convention. But after nine ballots in which Lowden was deadlocked with General Leonard Wood and Senator Hiram Johnson of California, the convention turned to Warren G. Harding.

Richard B. Ogilvie (1969–73) was a manager-governor who created the executive Bureau of the Budget (now the Governor's Office of Management and Budget) and staffed it with bright young professionals. Ogilvie established a strong Environmental Protection Agency before the federal government did. He also imposed the state's first income tax and shared part of the revenues with local governments.

Jim Edgar was perhaps the state's last manager. A skilled administrator, he created an agenda for two terms during his first campaign and stuck to it. He successfully handled one of the worst floods in the state's history, secured a permanent income tax increase, capped property taxes while still increasing spending for early childhood education, schools, and higher education. He also created a new Department of Human Services to handle streamlining social service spending.[8]

Governors who were builders measured the success of their tenure by the amount of concrete poured and steel erected. Helped by a bond issue and planning initiated by his predecessor, Governor Len Small (1921–29) took Illinois out of the mud and onto seven thousand miles of concrete pavement. Year after year he set new national records as a road builder. He rejected road bids of $40,000 per mile, threatened to have the state rather than contractors do the work, and ultimately reduced the costs to $27,000 per mile. Small also put state aid to schools on an equalization basis designed to help fiscally weaker districts.

William G. Stratton (1953–61) widened U.S. Route 66 to four lanes and by the end of his eight years in office took credit for 7,057 miles of new roadways and 638 bridges. Stratton imposed tolls to finance a network of superhighways for the burgeoning metropolitan Chicago region. He sponsored major bond issues that won approval in referendums and financed creation of new university campuses and a network of mental health centers. In addition, Stratton reformed the state court system and revised the state's malapportioned legislative districts for the first time in half a century.

Jim Thompson (1976–90) thought of himself as a builder.[9] In Chicago he constructed the State of Illinois Center, later to be named for him. It resembles a huge, glimmering, ungainly spaceship, plopped awkwardly in the heart of the city's Loop. He embarked on what appeared to be a major infrastructure renovation program called Build Illinois, which evolved instead into a potpourri of projects awarded in large measure to the districts of favored lawmakers or to those whose support was needed.

Illinois went through a tough economic transformation on Thompson's watch. Hundreds of thousands of well-paid manufacturing jobs were wrung out of the state's economy and replaced by comparable increases in jobs in a rapidly developing service sector that ranged from fast-food restaurants to financial services and information technologies. Illinois suffered a deep recession in the early 1980s and uneven economic growth thereafter, with economic improvement in the collar counties but weaknesses in rural areas and Chicago.

Thompson responded to the economic woes as did governors in other struggling states. He expanded the state's economic development agency, infused it with money for job retraining, and created incentives for industry. He established more state offices overseas (eleven by 1990 to woo trade and investment) than any other state. He became the state's chief salesman abroad.

Lastly are the social reformers who were perhaps the least easy to fit in the mold of individualistic Illinois politics. Edward Coles (1822–26) was an idealistic aristocrat from Virginia who freed the slaves he inherited. Robert Howard credited Coles with preventing Illinois from becoming a slave state: "Coles reacted quickly when the legislature's pro-slavery majority ordered an 1824 referendum on the calling of a constitutional convention that would have legalized the de facto human bondage that existed in early Illinois. Lacking power to veto the resolution, he assumed leadership in defining the issue, raised money for publicizing his views, and mobilized public sentiment against the pro-slavery movement. In what seemed to be a hopeless campaign. Because of him the cause of freedom triumphed 6,640 to 4,972."[10]

John Peter Altgeld (1893–97) became one of the heroes of American liberalism. Altgeld spent surpluses built up by his predecessor to open teachers' colleges at DeKalb and Charleston and insane asylums at East Moline and Bartonville; he increased appropriations for the University of Illinois and encouraged its expansion in graduate programs and medicine. Altgeld made his mark, however, in social reform. He appointed Florence Kelley, a protégé of Jane Addams, to enforce a new factory inspection law; the law also limited employment of women to eight hours per day and strengthened an earlier child labor statute.

According to Howard, the turning point in Altgeld's career was his eighteen-thousand-word justification for pardoning three anarchists who had been convicted on flimsy evidence of a bombing at the famous Haymarket Square labor rally in 1886 in Chicago. "This courageous but belligerent action made him the most hated man in Illinois and wiped out any prospect of his being elected to another office. Thereafter he devoted his multiple talents to the protection of the poor and downtrodden and to the enactment of progressive legislation."[11]

It is easier to leave a lasting imprint when financial resources are available to build lasting infrastructure, as was true of several of the governors whose careers are sketched above. Henry Horner (1933–40), the state's first Jewish governor, presided during the depths of the Great Depression. He financed unemployment relief by shifting the state's major tax burden from property to sales and worked effectively with fellow Democrats from the New Deal administration of President Franklin D. Roosevelt. "By background and performance, he was ideally suited to serve as Depression governor," according to Howard, who considered Horner among the state's best governors.[12]

George Ryan, the Tragic Dealmaker

After serving as chair of the Kankakee County Board, Speaker of the Illinois House, lieutenant governor (two terms), and secretary of state (two terms), George Ryan entered the governor's mansion in 1999. Ryan had all the political skills to be a builder in the fashion of Jim Thompson as well as an effective, favor-vending dealmaker. Because of some of his deal-making, a federal jury found Ryan guilty in 2006 on twenty-two counts of trading governmental favors for personal gain. He was sentenced to six and a half years in federal prison.

The Republican Ryan accomplished much in his single four-year term.[13] He raised license plate fees and liquor taxes to finance $12 billion in a program of highway and school construction known as Illinois First. He ended decades of political deadlock over rebuilding the lakefront home of the Chicago Bears by doing a deal involving the team, the City of Chicago, and the legislature. Ryan broke with Republican suburban mayors and agreed with Democratic Chicago mayor Richard M. Daley to expand O'Hare Airport.

Ryan loved to play a part in making big deals happen, and he disdained the details. He once told James D. Nowlan, with a note of pride, that in his decade as a state legislator (1973–83) he "never read a bill." He left the details to aides, some of whom took advantage of his trust.

Definitely a hands-off manager, Ryan generated an immense stock of credit with legislators and others over the years, based on favors that ranged from special license plates to pension-boosting jobs in his offices for legislators, to myriad favors as Speaker of the House in moving legislation along or blocking it.

In 2003 Ryan gained international notice, most of it favorable, when he commuted to life terms the death sentences of all 167 convicts on Illinois's death row.[14] Because of this he was even nominated multiple times for the Nobel Peace Prize.

Blagojevich and the Chicago Way

Rod Blagojevich was an accidental candidate who started his career as a state representative in the Thirty-third House District with the help of his influential father-in-law, Chicago alderman Dick Mell. Mell, who needed a reliable candidate to unseat incumbent Democrat Myron Kulas in 1992, knew Blagojevich had a good enough resumé after working for Alderman Ed Vrdolyak and the Daley administration. When Dan Rostenkowski lost the Fifth U.S. Congressional seat to a Republican after pleading guilty to federal corruption charges, Blagojevich (and Mell) saw this as his chance to get to higher office in 1996. In 2002, Mell helped his son-in-law win the governorship with massive fundraising and a winnable downstate strategy.[15]

Blagojevich was quite successful with his first-term legislative initiatives—hiking the minimum wage, passing ethics legislation, and, after decades of failed attempts, passing gay rights legislation.[16] Expanded healthcare and improved children's services were, however, the hallmarks of the Blagojevich administration. In his first term he created the All Kids plan, which sought to offer health coverage to all Illinois children, and a program of universal preschool for three- and four-year-olds.[17]

Blagojevich might well be characterized as an unpopular populist who early in his governorship adopted populist themes of taking on the political system, helping the disadvantaged through expanded healthcare, and protecting the little guy from an increase in income or sales taxes. But in the governor's second term (2007–09), things began to fall apart as he became more combative. He surprised lawmakers with massive proposals to provide health coverage for nearly everyone in the state and a $7 billion gross receipts tax on business to pay for the new program. Both were summarily rejected by the legislature, but the governor proceeded to expand his health program, called Illinois Covered, prompting lawsuits from Republicans that charged him with an unconstitutional usurpation of the legislature's authority to appropriate funds.

The challenge in all of the Blagojevich healthcare initiatives was to find the money to pay for the expensive programs. Indeed, the governor went deeper into deficit spending in each year to pay for regular programs. Adhering to his campaign promise of not increasing general sales or income taxes, he turned to other revenue initiatives: the $7 billion business tax, mentioned above, lease of the state lottery to generate a reported $12 billion up-front, massive increases in gambling, and long-term borrowing of $12 billion on the premise that the cost of borrowing money would be less than the interest income earned.

These proposals were repeatedly rejected by the legislature. The governor and Speaker Madigan checkmated one another. The governor declared he would veto any general tax increase, which dampened any interest among lawmakers in casting tough tax increase votes that would come to naught. At the same time, Madigan blocked all the revenue initiatives proposed by the governor. In addition, personal acrimony developed among the state's three top policymakers: Madigan and Blagojevich disliked one another, and then Senate president Emil Jones, who was originally aligned with the governor, lost trust in him, which is so critical in politics.

Further, in the summer of 2007 Blagojevich called sixteen special sessions of the legislature, generally without providing lawmakers with proposed legislation, and with the special sessions coming on successive days. In addition, the governor filed two suits against the legislature in 2007. The first asked Speaker of the House Michael Madigan to hold special sessions on the days and at the times the governor wished to force representatives to show up for sessions. The second asked a judge to order the House clerk to record the governor's budget veto message on a specific date, rather than some later date, as part of political maneuvering over possible veto overrides. As long-time capital reporter and analyst Charles Wheeler put it: "In the surreal world of here-and-now Illinois politics, the suits are among the latest signs of the toxic environment infusing government under the control of the state's dysfunctional Democratic leaders (governor, Speaker of the House, and President of the Senate)."[18]

Then federal agents arrested Blagojevich in December 2008 for trying to sell the appointment of a successor to the U.S. Senate seat previously held by President Barack Obama. This became an international news story. Exasperation with the governor's confrontational tactics had been building among legislators since at least the beginning of his second term. Failure to consult with the legislature on major new initiatives in healthcare and then proceeding to implement the healthcare expansion without legislative appropriation or approval were fundamental factors in lawmakers' anger toward the governor. In 2009 Blagojevich was impeached, convicted, and removed from office by the Illinois General Assembly for misuse of his governmental authority and for his corruption. The authors doubt, however, that Blagojevich would have been removed from office absent his arrest for allegedly trying to sell the U.S. Senate seat.

Nonetheless, "Gov. Blagojevich shattered the ethos, the set of values by which we have operated," observed veteran lobbyist Jim Fletcher. "We believed in getting out on time, protecting old programs, budgeting incrementally, and not proposing big new programs until the base spending was assured."[19] To make matters worse, the state had not seen a major capital investment program of building and maintenance for highways, mass transit, universities, colleges, schools, and state agencies since Jim Edgar was governor.

Pat Quinn, the Reformer

Pat Quinn became the forty-first governor of Illinois as almost an exact opposite of Blagojevich. Quinn started his career as founder of the Center for Political Honesty and is known for being instrumental in creating the Citizen's Utility Board, a group that advocates for utility customers. When the legislature passed a pay raise for themselves and the governor under Jim Thompson, Quinn organized sending tea bags in protest. He led a campaign to cut the size of the Illinois legislature, and when he campaigned for state treasurer, advocated no-frills checking for poor people and lower check-cashing fees.[20]

Unlike Blagojevich, Quinn was a workaholic. His only marriage was brief due to his preoccupations. He was not a social climber.[21] By this point that sort of image was welcome, but Blagojevich left Quinn a mess to fix. In the March 2008 report "Grading the States," *Governing* magazine and the Pew Center on the States awarded an overall grade of C to Illinois, whereas other states overall received a B minus grade.[22] In twenty categories concerning the state's handling of money, people, infrastructure, and information, Illinois was graded weak in nine: long-term outlook, budget process, structural balance (revenues keeping up with spending), workforce planning, training and development, managing employee performance, capital planning, maintenance, and budgeting for performance. Only in the category of online services and information did Illinois rate better than mid-level.

Quinn made getting the state's finances in order a top priority for his administration. His budgets included cuts to all departments, including millions from Medicaid, and a 67 percent personal income tax increase.[23] At the time, the state had an unfunded pension liability of close to $100 billion in its five funds, the worst in the nation.[24] In 2013 he signed a historic bipartisan bill aimed at erasing that debt in thirty years by raising the retirement age and reducing cost-of-living increases for current retirees. All of these were necessary reforms to shape up the state, but a national recession was already hurting Illinoisians. Because of past mistakes and the recession, Quinn still had the nation's worst gubernatorial approval ratings. His path to victory in 2014 seemed very steep after this.

Pat Quinn will, however, be remembered as the governor who abolished the death penalty in Illinois and commuted the sentences of the remaining death row inmates. A decade and a half after George Ryan put a moratorium on executions due to the staggering number of death row inmates who were ultimately found to be innocent, Quinn ended the practice forever.

Rauner, the Other Reformer

The lessons learned from Blagojevich's confrontational politics and later Quinn's attempted historic pension reform are that (1) success in major public policy initiatives requires the active support of both the executive and legislative branches; and (2) significant preconditioning of lawmakers and legislative leaders is needed before they are willing to consider taking on expensive, major new programs and revenue initiatives. But Bruce Rauner was not interested in these things when he ran for office. His plan was to "turn around" state government and end corruption.

Bruce Rauner was not a politician. Instead, he was a businessman who chaired a private equity firm after graduating from Harvard. He advertised himself as a successful CEO who would run the state similarly, but appeared on television ads in flannel shirts and jeans to show he was also a "man of the people." Tired of being on all the "worst" lists and looking for change, Illinoisans elected Rauner in 2014. And he did not disappoint, getting to work on day one by instituting a hiring freeze, halting discretionary spending, and ordering the sale of surplus property.[25] But it would be the Budget Impasse that would make the biggest impact on his tenure.

When Rauner took office in January of 2015, he inherited Quinn's FY2015 budget and immediately began preparing a FY2016 budget that he sent to lawmakers a month later. As will be discussed more in detail in chapter 10, "Budgeting, Taxing, and Spending in Illinois," spending cuts to various agencies, pension reform, education reform, and a property tax freeze were major parts of the governor's wish list. However, major clashes with the state's Democratic leaders, especially Speaker of the House Mike Madigan, led to no agreement. The General Assembly sent a revised budget bill back to the governor and he vetoed it, and the legislature did not have the votes to override.

In January of 2016, the governor sent another budget, and the General Assembly sent its own revisions. The disagreement resulted in deadlock until June of 2016, when a stopgap bill was passed that fully funded education and allowed the state to remain open.[26] That still left some $8 billion in backlogged bills and only got the state through the end of the year. In January of 2018, it was the same routine—a budget from Rauner to the General Assembly that they then changed drastically and sent back only to have him veto it. Only that summer, things were different. Democrats were able to convince enough Republicans to cross the aisle and override the governor's veto. After 793 days, the State of Illinois finally had a budget.

The Budget Impasse and the havoc it wreaked on the state will arguably be Rauner's lasting legacy, despite the role of the legislature in the budget failures. The impasse led to state's credit rating being downgraded to nearly junk bond status, an annual deficit that reached $6.2 billion, a backlog of bills of $14.7 billion, road construction shutting down, and state universities facing losing their accreditation.[27] However, Rauner's tenure also saw historic changes in the way the state funds public schools. He signed bills that expanded access to abortion, expanded immigration rights, and provided protections for transgender persons.

Pritzker and the Battle of Millionaires

When JB Pritzker announced his candidacy for governor against Bruce Rauner in 2018, news outlets decried this as the potentially the most expensive race in the history of gubernatorial races. Bruce Rauner's net worth was estimated to be in the hundreds of millions, and as heir to the Hyatt Hotel fortune, Pritzker's was over a billion. And journalists were right: when all was said and done, the candidates raised a combined total of $267 million, with Pritzker spending over $171 million of his own money and Rauner $70 million of his. California had previously held the record at $255 million. "It is very hard for the average person to be able to run effectively," said UIC political science professor Dick Simpson.[28]

By the summer of 2022, Pritzker had donated $125 million to himself for this reelection bid. Pritzker also tried to affect the results of the Republican primary by donating $24 million to the Democratic Governors Association (DGA). The money was for the DGA to run ads and encourage Republican voters to select the more conservative State Senator Darren Bailey (R-Xenia) over the more liberal mayor of Aurora, Richard Irvin. Pritzker believed he would have a much easier time in the general election against Bailey, a conservative from downstate who was backed by Donald Trump, than he would against Irvin, a Black mayor of Illinois's second largest city in the metropolitan area.[29] Irvin received $50 million from Chicago-based hedge fund manager Ken Griffin who believed he could beat Pritzker. It had all the makings of another 2018 rematch. However, Bailey won the primary, ostensibly because he did a better job campaigning, but it was not enough to win the general election in November.

All of this, along with COVID, obscures what is a true feat for JB Pritzker: he is the first two-term governor since Jim Edgar. In the twenty-first century, Illinois was the only state not to have accomplished multiterm governorship. Why was Pritzker different? As *Chicago Magazine* puts it, "Pritzker is neither corrupt nor incompetent. Those sound like obvious qualifications for a governor, but in modern-day Illinois, they're almost as rare as unicorn sightings."[30]

Pritzker also has accomplishments. In four years, Illinois has reduced its backlog of unpaid bills to one-sixth of what it was when Pritzker took office. Extra money has been added to the required pension payments, and the bond rating has been upgraded six times. Legalizing marijuana and adding gaming venues has generated new revenue. The state has benefitted from federal COVID relief funds. And Rebuild Illinois, a bipartisan infrastructure plan, was passed, paving the way for the largest upgrade to roads, bridges, rail, broadband, and schools in the state's history.

While Pritzker won with almost 55 percent of the vote, 43 percent still voted for Darren Bailey. The challenge for Pritzker in the coming four years will be taking this competency and uniting the state. The budget battles, COVID, and Bailey's candidacy have shown that the divide between the metropolitan areas and the rural parts of the state persists, especially as the former gets bluer and the latter gets redder.

A Sprawling Executive Branch

Like the Chicago suburbs, the executive branch of government in Illinois is a huge and sprawling operation, with 125,000 employees. Of these, about three-fifths work directly for the governor and another 40,000 are employed by state universities. If the estimated state revenues for 2022 of about $45.4 billion were equated with corporate revenue, Illinois would rank in the top 50 on the Fortune 500 list of leading American corporations.

The executive branch is both complex and highly diversified. It delivers healthcare each year to 2.9 million of Illinois's 12.7 million residents, most of them low-income workers, children, and the elderly. A small Department of

Financial and Professional Regulation examines, licenses, investigates, and sometimes disciplines about eight hundred thousand persons across forty-one occupations, from physicians and architects to boxers and wrestlers. The sprawling Department of Human Services spends $6 billion per year on community services, residential facilities, and hospitals for the mentally ill, the developmentally disabled, the addicted, the blind, and youth and children, among others. The Department of Corrections houses 45,000 inmates in twenty-eight correctional facilities.

The organization of the Illinois state government is as complex as the state is diverse. By the third decade of the twentieth century, the bureaucracy has grown into a sprawling, unmanageable collection of entities that Governor Frank O. Lowden had cut down to nine executive departments in 1917. Since then, the number of departments has expanded to twenty. In addition, twenty-seven major boards and commissions were created, each linked to the governor on the organization chart through members that he appoints. The executive branch had become so layered, in fact, that cabinet meetings in the Thompson administration had to be held in the ballroom of the executive mansion.

Governor Rod Blagojevich used his executive reorganization powers to consolidate several agencies into a huge Department of Human Services and a consolidated Department of Financial and Professional Regulation.

The first problem a chief executive faces in Illinois is that the executive branch is not theirs alone. The executive powers are divided by the Illinois constitution among five independently elected officials: the governor, the secretary of state, the attorney general, the treasurer, and the comptroller (see figure 7.1). This contrasts with the executive branch of the U.S. government, in which the president appoints all other constitutional officers.

Independently elected officers often use their offices as springboards to the governorship, as in the cases of Republican secretaries of state Jim Edgar and George Ryan who successful used the position to run for governor. In 1990 Edgar faced Democratic attorney general Neil Hartigan in the race for governor. Seeking to move up the ladder, the other three executive officers that year ran for the posts being vacated by the gubernatorial candidates.

The statewide officials also often make life difficult for their fellow executives. In 1994 the comptroller, Dawn Clark Netsch, frequently criticized Governor Edgar's management of his budget and ran against him in the 1994 election. In 2006 Republican treasurer Judy Baar Topinka ran unsuccessfully for governor against Blagojevich. By 2007 all executive officers were Democrats. That did not, however, stop Attorney General Lisa Madigan from investigating allegations of wrongdoing in the office of Governor Blagojevich.   .

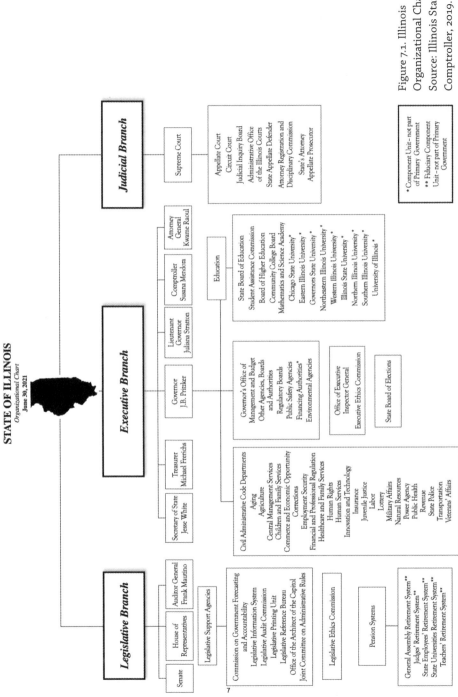

STATE OF ILLINOIS
Organizational Chart
June 30, 2021

Legislative Branch

Senate

House of Representatives

Auditor General
Frank Mautino

Legislative Support Agencies

Commission on Government Forecasting and Accountability
Legislative Information System
Legislative Audit Commission
Legislative Printing Unit
Legislative Reference Bureau
Office of the Architect of the Capitol
Joint Committee on Administrative Rules

Legislative Ethics Commission

Pension Systems

General Assembly Retirement System**
Judges' Retirement System**
State Employees' Retirement System**
State Universities Retirement System**
Teachers' Retirement System**

Executive Branch

Secretary of State
Jesse White

Treasurer
Michael Frerichs

Governor
J.B. Pritzker

Lieutenant Governor
Juliana Stratton

Comptroller
Susana Mendoza

Attorney General
Kwame Raoul

Civil Administrative Code Departments

Aging
Agriculture
Central Management Services
Children and Family Services
Commerce and Economic Opportunity
Corrections
Employment Security
Financial and Professional Regulation
Healthcare and Family Services
Human Rights
Human Services
Innovation and Technology
Insurance
Juvenile Justice
Labor
Lottery
Military Affairs
Natural Resources
Power Agency
Public Health
Revenue
State Police
Transportation
Veterans' Affairs

Governor's Office of
Management and Budget
Other Agencies, Boards
and Authorities
Regulatory Boards
Public Safety Agencies
Financing Authorities*
Environmental Agencies

Office of Executive Inspector General
Executive Ethics Commission

State Board of Elections

Education

State Board of Education
Student Assistance Commission
Board of Higher Education
Community College Board
Mathematics and Science Academy
Chicago State University *
Eastern Illinois University *
Governors State University *
Northeastern Illinois University *
Western Illinois University *
Illinois State University *
Northern Illinois University *
Southern Illinois University *
University of Illinois *

Judicial Branch

Supreme Court

Appellate Court
Circuit Court
Judicial Inquiry Board
Administrative Office of the Illinois Courts
State Appellate Defender
Attorney Registration and Disciplinary Commission
State's Attorney
Appellate Prosecutor

*Component Unit – not part of Primary Government
** Fiduciary Component Unit – not part of Primary Government

Figure 7.1. Illinois Organizational Chart. Source: Illinois State Comptroller, 2019.

7

Attorney General. The attorney general is the chief legal officer for the state. As such, the attorney general is responsible for representing Illinois in several ways. First, when Illinois is party to a lawsuit, the attorney general represents the people of Illinois. When laws inside of Illinois are broken, the attorney general is responsible for working with local state's attorneys to ensure the perpetrators are prosecuted. Third, the attorney general must defend other state officers if there are actions brought against them in their official capacity.

The attorney general and their staff also provide advisory opinions for state and local officials and represent in court more than three hundred boards, departments, and commissions of state government (though the governor retains legal counsel for his office and for most of his agencies). The attorney general also collects monies owed the state and works with county-level state's attorneys to prosecute certain criminal cases.[31] For instance, Attorney General Kwame Raoul (elected in 2018) has aggressively pursued drug manufacturers in the wake of the opioid crisis, leading a lawsuit against them that eventually meant a $760 million settlement for the state.[32]

Secretary of State. While the secretary of state is best known for administering motor vehicle registration and drivers' licensing, it actually has twenty-one departments. Driver's Services is the most well known because it affects more than just drivers: it also issues official state identification for those who do not have a driver's license. Adjacent to Driver's Services is the Breath Alcohol Ignition Interlock Device (BAIID) program, which allows certain qualifying drivers who have been convicted of driving under the influence to drive again, so long as they use a device designed to impair the vehicle if it detects alcohol on the driver's breath.

The secretary of state is the chief archivist for the state overseeing the state archives and the state library in Springfield. They are also responsible for the registration of corporations in Illinois, along with receiving their annual reporting and issuing certification of such.

The secretary of state also oversees the organ and tissue donation program known as Life Goes On. This program, started by former Secretary of State Jesse White in 1992, allows Illinoisans to register their wishes to be organ or tissue donors with the state so that their final wishes can be honored when they die. It also provides for education and awareness to expand outreach and increase the number of people on the registry. It is now administered by current Secretary of State Alexi Giannoulias, elected in 2022.

Because of these many duties and how diverse and far-reaching they are, the secretary of state has far more employees (about four thousand) than does any other state-level elected official except the governor.

Comptroller. The comptroller keeps the state's "checkbook" and pays all the state's bills. This office also prepares the comprehensive annual financial report (CAFR) for the state, which gives a picture of the financial state of the state. The comptroller also prepares a number of other reports on expenditures and revenues such as the state of the pension systems, Medicaid, and education. The comptroller also has a local government division, which assists local governments in fulfilling their required fiscal responsibilities to their own taxpayers.

Comptrollers have used the information at their disposal to evaluate and comment on the financial condition of the state.

Treasurer. The treasurer is responsible for receiving, investing, safeguarding, and disbursing (on the order of the comptroller) all monies paid to the state. This includes collecting income and sales taxes, pension payments, and fees for services to the state.

Some have suggested that the offices of comptroller and treasurer be combined into one office as they are in many states. The offices do work together, as seen in the state's Budget Stabilization Fund, colloquially known as the rainy-day fund, created in 2000 as a way for the state to put aside money and reduce the need for short-term borrowing. The fund is part of the state treasury, but the comptroller has also been a big advocate for it.

The fund has experienced some turmoil, mostly as a result of budget impasses that have resulted in its depletion. After the 2016–17 impasse, the fund had less than $70,000 after it was used to pay bills.[33] Due to deposits over the past few years, the balance will reach almost $2 billion by the end of 2023; however, current Comptroller Susana Mendoza is calling for legislation that would increase that amount.[34]

Although these thumbnail sketches fail to describe all that the governor's fellow elected executives do, their offices remain, when compared with the office of the governor, narrow and generally ministerial. For this reason, these officials have worked over the years to broaden the scope and visibility of their offices by enacting statutes that assign them responsibilities beyond the few set forth in the constitution and added by personal initiative.

For example, the lieutenant governor has no constitutional duties other than to take over the office of governor when it is vacated. Yet the report on that office in the *Illinois Blue Book* (2020–21) has sections about the lieutenant governor's activities as chair of various groups such as the governor's Rural Affairs, Broadband Deployment, and Main Street Councils, among others, and about her work as an advocate for taxpayers and consumers. As Juliana Stratton is the first Black woman to hold this office, it also details her work in advocacy and equity.

Likewise, recent attorneys general have been active in environmental protection and in concerns for senior citizens and consumer affairs. Similarly, when he was secretary of state, Governor Edgar expanded his motor vehicle responsibilities to crack down on drunk driving and used his role as state librarian to champion adult literacy programs.

These activities make political sense because these offices are often used as launching pads to higher offices.

Powers of the Governor

The governor has strong formal and informal powers, thanks in part to the enhanced veto and management powers provided by the 1970 constitution. Illinois governors need all these powers because they are expected to fill several roles beyond those of administering the state's business and managing their own bureaucracy.

By virtue of the governor's constitutional responsibilities to give formal state of the state and budget messages to the legislature each year, the chief executive is expected by legislators to propose comprehensive policies and a detailed budget, to which the legislature will react. In addition, their political party expects the governor to wear the mantle of state party leader. They are also expected to be the state's chief negotiator, the one who brings legislative, business, union, and civic leaders to the executive mansion or to the state offices in Chicago to resolve prickly conflicts such as school strikes in Chicago or legislative impasses that pit labor against management. In other words, there are great expectations for Illinois governors.

Because the state economy struggled during the 1980s, Governor Jim Thompson took on the role of chief salesman, or economic developer. He set up economic development offices in eleven overseas cities, including Moscow, São Paolo, Kyoto, Tokyo, Warsaw, and Budapest. He took two or more trips overseas each year to trumpet Illinois products and business opportunities. Governors since have continued with at least a few international outposts; Pritzker has six (Japan, Canada, Mexico, China, Belgium, and Israel).

In order to carry out their tasks effectively, governors need powers to do things *for* people, especially for lawmakers, and powers to do or threaten to do things *to* people. They have significant powers, though not always enough to accomplish their objectives. Among their fundamental powers are the ability to veto bills passed by the legislature; initiate comprehensive legislative programs and annual budgets; dispense patronage jobs, appointments, and contracts; and administer sprawling executive agencies.

The governor has the advantage of being a single decisionmaker who confronts a two-house legislature characterized by sometimes divided party majorities, scores of committees, and as many points of view as there are members. The governor also benefits from the stature, authority, and perquisites of the office.

The president of the United States, who can sign or veto a bill only in its entirety, would undoubtedly be envious of the additional veto powers granted the governor of Illinois, powers among the most extensive in the fifty states. In addition to the whole bill veto, the governor has the authority to make substantive changes in enacted legislation (the amendatory veto), to reduce the amount of money in appropriations bills (the reduction veto), and to eliminate specific line items from these spending bills (the line-item veto).

Since 1970 governors have used these powers frequently. Governor Dan Walker (1973–76) had difficult relations with the legislature. So, he vetoed 468 bills in their entirety during his single four-year term, more than 14 percent of all bills passed. The legislature was able to override only one in fourteen of his vetoes because an override requires a three-fifths majority vote in each house.[35]

Thompson used the amendatory veto more extensively than have other Illinois chief executives. In 1989–90, he applied amendatory language to 140 enacted bills. The legislature was able to override, or strip away, his changes on only 8 bills.[36] In the 1991–92 biennium, the legislature enacted 1,528 bills. Governor Edgar applied one of his four veto powers to almost one-fifth (290) of them. His vetoes were overridden just 16 times.

In his first year in office in 2003, Rod Blagojevich applied 115 vetoes of various kinds and was overridden 21 times by the legislature. Bruce Rauner used the veto less frequently; however, he vetoed the General Assembly's budget bill three years in a row. Pritzker has vetoed only a handful of times in each legislative session, mostly because his party has controlled both houses of the legislature, so conflicts have been less frequent.

The governor's ability to award jobs and contracts and make appointments represents another kind of negotiating power. In the 1980s just about every vacancy that occurred under Thompson's jurisdiction was scrutinized to see whether a lawmaker or political party leader had a qualified candidate. If so, that patron had a good chance of seeing his candidate selected. If the patron had a candidate who was not yet qualified by examination, the position was often held open for months while the candidate tried to become qualified.

Legislators sometimes sponsor themselves for job appointments in anticipation of voluntary or involuntary retirement from their elected posts. In addition to continuing their careers in government, they can add handsomely to their legislative pension benefits by holding such jobs. Of course, this interest in a postlegislative career can persuade a lawmaker to cast difficult votes on behalf of the governor's program.

The governor also fills by appointment nearly 2,100 positions on more than 282 boards and commissions plus 19 interstate compacts. Most are unpaid, yet many of these appointments are prestigious, such as those to the University of Illinois Board of Trustees and the Illinois Arts Council. Others are highly prized for the recognition they bring within a profession, such as the forty-one boards that oversee licensure for engineers, architects, physicians, real estate agents, and other regulated occupations.

Finally, there is the award of so-called pork barrel projects and the construction contracts that go with them. In Governor Pritzker's $45 billion Rebuild Illinois package, he told each state rep to designate over $2.5 million for their districts and each state senator $5 million for theirs.[37]

Each project provides contracts that benefit contractors, financiers, and law firms. Beneficiaries are expected to show their appreciation with large campaign contributions. In addition to financing reelection campaigns, campaign funds are used to help legislative candidates and to provide birthday, anniversary, and holiday gifts for friends and politicos.

Because of these powers, a legislator will frequently seek a governor's support and assistance. Years ago, during a closed conference of Republican members of the house, several GOP lawmakers were loudly criticizing the governor (Ogilvie, also of their party). Finally, a sage veteran silenced the bickering with this remark: "Okay, so the governor is an SOB. But just remember and appreciate this—he's *our* SOB!"[38]

The governor of Illinois has more latitude than do many governors in other states in administering the executive branch. Although the executive is divided, the lion's share of state government functions and personnel are within the governor's domain. Governors appoint all department heads and has statutory authority to terminate without cause several hundred senior civil service executives at the end of their four-year appointments.

The 1970 constitution grants governors the power to reorganize state agencies by executive order, subject to rejection by the legislature. In 1995 Governor Edgar used this power to merge the Departments of Conservation, Mines and Minerals, and Energy and Natural Resources and units of other agencies into a single Department of Natural Resources. As noted above, Blagojevich used the powers to consolidate several social service agencies into the Department of Human Services and consolidate a number of agencies into the Department of Financial and Professional Regulation.

A Peer of Corporate Executives

The most important informal power of the governor lies in the stature of the office itself and the perquisites that come with the job. The governor can become, by virtue of the office, a peer of top corporate chief executives. They will return phone calls when an executive needs their counsel or assistance. Their comments are often on the front page and on evening television, whereas those of most legislators are relegated to the back pages, if covered at all. The presence of top executives generates interest and increased participation in fundraising events for legislators and charities.

In Springfield, governors have at their disposal a handsome executive mansion for entertaining. Just down the street from the mansion is an even more impressive building, an expansive, restored manse designed by Frank Lloyd Wright and owned by the state. Governors also have a small fleet of aircraft and, in Chicago, impressive offices currently atop the James R. Thompson Center in the heart of the central business district.

Although this stature and the resources of the office are real, the personal style of the governor determines how effectively they will be put to use. Richard Ogilvie (1969–72), Dan Walker (1973–76), Jim Edgar (1991–98), Pat Quinn (2009–14), and Bruce Rauner (2015–18) lacked the expansive, outgoing personalities of Thompson, Ryan, Blagojevich, and Pritzker. The first five used the stature and resources of office less, and less effectively, than did Thompson and Ryan, who genuinely enjoyed entertaining and rubbing elbows with legislators, lobbyists, the media, and business leaders. Thompson used the mansion and funds from his campaign chest for annual as well as spur-of-the-moment parties and dinners. A Protestant, Thompson regularly celebrated certain Jewish holy days with Jewish lawmakers and friends. At the adjournment of each legislative session—often beginning at 2 a.m. or later—Thompson and later Ryan hosted legislators, staffers, lobbyists, and journalists for a lively predawn party on the lawn of the executive mansion.

Alan Rosenthal observes that to be effective with legislators, a governor generally needs several traits. One is to "stand tall," that is, to have a strong personality and presence and be willing to use that personality to "get tough" from time to time. The chief executive also needs to be willing to rub elbows with the lawmakers, consult with them, massage their egos, and "talk turkey," that is, be willing to use the powers of the office in making deals on legislation.[39]

If governors are selective in their proposals, makes use of blue-ribbon commissions to generate consensus, takes their case to the people (which Thompson and Blagojevich did with enthusiasm in whirlwind fly-around press conferences throughout the state), and works the legislature from the inside, they can achieve considerable success in getting programs enacted.[40] Thompson did all these things with gusto. As a result, he had generally good, though not always successful, relations with the legislature. Blagojevich had a more confrontational style with the legislature, referring to them as a "bunch of drunken sailors" in their spending habits.

Governors need all the powers and skills they can muster, for powerful constraints are imposed on them. In addition to sharing authority with other executive officers, a governor confronts a legislature that is often controlled by the opposition party. The legislature tries to live up to its textbook billing as an independent, coequal branch of government. During the four years Bruce Rauner was governor (2014–18), Democrats controlled the legislature with sometimes supermajorities, which led to epic battles over the budget and other issues.

The role of the federal government in state government also limits and frustrates a governor. Many of the laws enacted in Washington are designed to be administered by the states and paid for with a combination of state and federal funds. Prime examples include air and water pollution programs, the Medicaid program for the poor, Every Student Succeeds Act (ESSA), vocational rehabilitation, and transportation. Federal funds account for about one-quarter of the Illinois budget; the U.S. Congress and federal bureaucrats leverage that funding to direct the way major state programs are run and what they end up costing the state.

State and federal courts also tell a governor how to do their job. During the early months of the pandemic when Governor Pritzker was extending stay-at-home orders, the state courts said he overstepped his authority under current law, which only allowed him thirty days to require these restrictions. The courts again stepped in two years after the pandemic began when they ruled that decisions on masking inside of schools belonged to the individual district, and not the State of Illinois.

Inside the Governor's Office

Of the governor's several roles, management of state government occupies less time and attention than might be imagined. As Thompson put it: "Governors really, especially in the latter part of their service, don't manage the state. If they're still managing the state after their first term, they ought not to be governor."[41] Most governors derive greater personal satisfaction and political rewards from the pursuit of other functions such as formulating policy, steering programs through the legislature, building popularity and support among the public, and helping develop the state's economy. The bureaucrats run the day-to-day operations.

JB Pritzker operated with a governor's office staff of 105 persons in 2021.[42] This staff helps the governor make decisions—for instance, what legislation to propose, how to resolve a policy dispute between two agencies, whom to appoint as an agency director, how to satisfy the demands of an interest group, and which speaking invitations to accept.[43] In performing this role, the staff provides two important and related services: it manages the flow of information to the governor and serves as a surrogate with the groups that want the governor's attention.

Information flows in a variety of ways: memos, email, audio-video hookups between Chicago and Springfield, discussions with staff or agency personnel, staff debates within the office, contact with outside advisors, newspaper and media interviews, and meetings with interest groups or legislators. Because it is impossible for the governor to attend to all who seek favor, a staff member acting in the governor's stead can make a strong contribution to their boss's positive or negative image.

The use of staff as a go-between has obvious advantages. It tends to preserve flexibility on issues because the governor can always disavow the position taken by a subordinate. The surrogate also can sometimes say no for the governor, insulating them from that unpleasant duty.

Governors typically delegate the coordination of their staff to a deputy who has been called chief of staff, deputy governor, or chief of governmental operations. The deputy governor's job is a bit like being a secretary-general of the United Nations because the governor's office is at times not so much an organization as an alliance among nations. The reason is twofold. First, the organization of the office reflects the conflicts that are a fundamental part of state politics. Differences among staff members mirror the conflicting interests of the state's various political viewpoints. Second, it is difficult for a governor to delegate power. A governor draws legitimacy from being the person elected to do the job. The authority of anyone acting in the governor's place can be easily undercut or become suspect unless continually supported by the governor directly. Because power is personal and not hierarchical, the notion of organization can be misleading.

Ideally, the deputy governor runs the office to accommodate the decision-making style of the governor. That style may involve open debate among staff; preparation of detailed decision memos, acted on without much discussion; advice from people outside government, or a combination of approaches. Thompson's style encouraged staff at various levels to have direct communication with him in policy deliberations. Edgar operated a more traditional hierarchical office, with policy recommendations flowing up to the chief of staff through a "super cabinet" of seven executive assistants, each with functional areas of responsibility. A hands-off manager, Blagojevich delegated extensive responsibility to deputy governors, a chief financial officer, and the director of the Governor's Office of Management and Budget (GOMB). Pritzker has been described as a consensus-builder, someone who as a businessman his entire life is inclined to bring parties together to make deals, but who is also decisive when a decision is needed.

This chief of staff is part of the executive office of the governor, yet generally operates somewhat apart from the rest of the governor's staff. And some other officers have some independence as well. For instance, the budget process gives the work of the GOMB a much more structured focus than other staff activities. Budget analysts are hired by senior GOMB staff, and there is less major staff turnover with a change in governors. For these reasons and the technical nature of the work, the office tends to have an institutional life of its own.

During the budget process, conflict sometimes arises between the GOMB, which sees its role as to constrain agency spending, and agencies, which typically want increased spending authority. Some disagreements can only be resolved by the governor. Influential interest groups also have a stake in the process. Most groups want more spent on their constituents. All must be dealt with, and often the governor must take the lead and has the final word on the overall budget.

The GOMB plays a significant role in the governor's office because mistakes in budgeting can cost the governor dearly. There are tremendous political pressures to spend more tax dollars or to give tax relief and virtually no pressure to control that spending. Yet the constitution requires a balanced operating budget, at least in cash terms, and a governor who allows spending to get out of control runs the risk of severe embarrassment. Thus, the GOMB must carefully monitor both revenues and agency spending.

Links to Agencies and the Legislature

Executive assistants based in Chicago and Springfield provide the governor with primary day-to-day linkages with more than sixty state agencies, including many not under the governor's direct control, such as the state boards of education and higher education. The executive assistants are also the chief executive's eyes, ears, and voices in relations with interest groups, the legislature, and citizens. Each has an area of policy and management responsibility such as education, human services, or economic development.

Executive assistants try to increase cooperation among agencies and often have to mediate disputes among them. Agencies often have narrow responsibilities that overlap with those of others. Children's services, for instance, are delivered by several agencies, including the Departments of Children and Family Services, Healthcare and Family Services, and Human Services and the State Board of Education. Regulation of drinking water is shared by EPA and the Department of Public Health. Public Health shares responsibility for inspecting and certifying nursing homes with the Departments of Labor, Financial and Professional Regulation, Healthcare and Family Services, and Human Services, along with the State Fire Marshal.

Governors and their staff face even stiffer challenges in maintaining effective relationships with the General Assembly. The legislature must enact substantive legislation—much of it proposed by governors and their agencies—and pass the annual budget. The legislature also oversees the executive branch through committee hearings, biennial audits by the auditor general, and review of agency rulemaking by the Joint Committee on Administrative Rules. The legislature thus maintains a presence in virtually every area of executive branch activity, which makes good relations with lawmakers crucial to the success of a governor's tenure.

It is not surprising that a governor will often select a former lawmaker or legislative staff member to supervise the legislative office. For example, Tiffany Newbern-Johnson, Pritzker's deputy chief of staff for legislative affairs, held the same office for the City of Chicago. Prior to that she was assistant counsel to former Speaker of the House Mike Madigan. Familiarity with the members of each house, their personalities, and the politics of their districts is essential if the head of legislative affairs is to be an effective strategist for the governor.

Generally, the legislative office lobbies for passage of the governor's budget and other initiatives and works against bills that would be politically embarrassing for the governor to sign or veto. The legislative office channels information about legislative developments back to the governor and other members of the governor's staff, serves as a contact point for legislators who wish to deal with the governor or an agency, and provides legislative advice to other gubernatorial staff and agencies.

In order to be effective, the office must develop a close working relationship with the leaders of the governor's party in each house of the legislature. The staff must work through the leadership in selecting sponsors for administration bills, communicating the governor's position with regard to major legislation, scheduling legislative activity, and developing overall legislative strategies. Because much legislative work is done in committee, the staff must also work closely with the committee chairs and the minority spokespersons.

Governors maintain a traditional lawyer-client relationship with the lawyers on their staff. They advise governors about the extent of their statutory and constitutional authority and explore with them the legal implications of individual decisions. Usually governors appoint a chief counsel who supervises several lawyers. In addition to providing assistance with specific issues, the legal staff spends a considerable amount of time working with agency lawyers on litigation—particularly cases that are politically sensitive, involve large judgments against the state, or could commit the state to new and recurring program expenditures. The attorney general is designated by the constitution as "the legal officer of the state," but with the exception of environmental issues, the bulk of the governor's legal work is conducted by agency lawyers with the attorney general's concurrence.

The legal staff also engages in more routine activities. The constitution allows the governor to "grant reprieves, commutations and pardons" to convicted criminals. Four times each year the Prisoner Review Board refers fifty or so requests for commutation from prisoners to the governor's office. The legal staff reviews each one and makes a recommendation to the governor. The lawyers also draft executive orders, which must be limited in scope to operations within the executive branch, and review all legislation passed by the General Assembly for adherence to the constitution and for legal consistency. The latter activity keeps the lawyers well occupied from July to September.

Agencies Try for a Low Profile

Although the governor and the governor's staff are not involved in day-to-day management of the twenty departments under the chief executive's jurisdiction, the governor's performance is often judged on how well these agencies function. This can be problematic, because even here the governor does not have unfettered discretion. The major interest groups expect to have some influence over who is selected to run the programs that affect their members or constituents. The unions, for example, expect to have a say in who heads the Department of Labor; at the Department of Agriculture, it is the Illinois Farm Bureau; and so it goes throughout the organization chart. Groups that object strongly to a gubernatorial appointment can attempt to stall or prevent required confirmation by the Senate.

Once appointed and confirmed, directors gradually become part of a bureaucracy, with concerns and interests that often differ from those of a governor. Agencies and their subdivisions have longstanding relationships with local and federal bureaucracies, old ties to legislators and legislative committees, and strong commitments to existing procedures. The directors may owe their appointments to the governor, but they are quickly exposed to new claims on their loyalties.

For these reasons, subtle tensions often develop between the governor's office and an agency director and her staff. A former social services director observes:

> The biggest burden in running an agency is that created by many people who have their fingers in our pie. For example, you have: the governor's liaison with this agency; the governor's liaison to the rate review board [which sets purchase of service rates paid by the state]; the patronage director; the legislative liaison office. And the Governor's Office of Management and Budget, which is "knee deep in what we can and can't do"; the appropriations staffs in both houses, as well as between parties . . . ; several key legislators who have an interest in the agency; Art Quern and Paula Wolff in the governor's office [former chief of staff and program office director], and the interest groups. All of which makes for a great number of people telling you how to do your job. However, the buck stops with the director. These other people are not accountable and indeed often back away very quickly when something goes wrong.[44]

Government agencies are not run like a business, nor can they be. There are no profit-and-loss measures of accountability, and, indeed, state agencies feel a strong need to spend all their money by the end of the fiscal year or their budgets might be cut the following year. On-the-job performance is also difficult to assess. The quality of foster care provided to thousands of children is more difficult to evaluate than is the production rate of zero-defect earthmovers or cellular phones.

The lack of a clear bottom line allows a governor and agency directors to slip into fuzzy measures of success. Thus "no news is good news" is a byword for how well a director is doing. If the director keeps bad news about an agency from popping up on the evening news, then presumably everything is going well. Other techniques are to prevent problems from reaching the governor's desk, stay within the budget, and keep the lid on situations that could become volatile.

That sounds simple enough, but it has been a Herculean task for the directors of complex, demanding agencies such as the Department of Corrections, the Department of Human Services, and the Department of Children and Family Services. Each of these agencies has been given responsibilities and public expectations that cannot be met with the funding provided, if at all. Skilled agency directors and senior staff are crucial teammates of effective governors. Without them, the chief executives become reactive, defensive administrators and have little opportunity to become mentioned in the history books among the strong managers, great builders, or social reformers who have now and then made their mark in Illinois.

8

THE COURTS AND
CRIMINAL JUSTICE POLICY

The entangling of the courts with politics should come as no surprise to anyone in a state that elects its judges. Illinois voters nominate judges in partisan primaries and elect them to the bench in general elections. It is easy to see that in cases tried or appealed in the courts there will always be winners or losers. In any case, court decisions resolve conflicts, enforce community norms, stigmatize people, apply statutes or determine their constitutionality, and legitimize or reject decisions made elsewhere in state or local government. Clearly, litigants have the opportunity to wield power through the courts for political purposes.

A big battle is shaping up between the legislature and the courts in the wake of new criminal justice legislation. In January of 2023, another part of the Illinois Safety, Accountability, Fairness, and Equity-Today (or Safe-T) Act was set to go into effect. Known as the Pretrial Fairness Act, it has received a considerable amount of attention because it ends cash bail in the state of Illinois.

The genesis of the Safe-T Act was the murder of George Floyd by Minneapolis police in the May of 2020. That summer saw protests around the nation and a demand from citizens for reform in all aspects of criminal justice. The Legislative Black Caucus in the Illinois General Assembly took this opportunity to harness that energy and to work on legislation that would address several areas; the bulk of the legislation actually deals with police reforms. Among those are: tightening regulations on use of force, prohibiting deadly force against a fleeing person, requiring officers to intervene if a colleague is using unauthorized force, tightening no-knock search warrant rules, and requiring all officers to have body cameras by 2025. This legislation also creates a task force on qualified immunity and enacts new minimum standards. Decertification of officers has been expanded to include things like domestic battery, and law enforcement misconduct is now a punishable offense.[1]

What garnered the most attention during the 2022 election season, however, was the ending of cash bail. Cash bail is the exchange of money for the promise that a defendant will show up for a court appearance. Bail amounts are usually set for each offense, and defendants must pay 10 percent of that amount. If they do not show up, they forfeit the money. This section of the Safe-T Act is aimed at reducing the number of persons being held prior to trial and conviction.

About 90 percent of the jail population in Illinois is awaiting trial, and the vast majority are there because they do not have the resources to pay the bond.[2] The bonds can be as little as $100 for such low-level offenses as possession. Black and brown defendants are twice as likely to be jailed because they do not have the funds. Furthermore, being locked up makes someone 2.5 times less likely to be employed a year later, and any incarceration correlates to a 40 percent decrease in earnings.[3] Lake County public defender Keith Grant stated, "We find that when defendants are detained even for as little as, research shows, three days, they can become destabilized to the point of lacking all of the social netting resources that they would have otherwise had. . . . Keeping people in custody when they don't need to be actually creates a risk of harm to the community."[4]

While the Safe-T Act does away with cash bail, defendants awaiting trial can be subject to conditions like curfew or house arrest. Pretrial detention is still allowed for certain qualifying offenses or those who are found to be a risk. The law states, "Detention only shall be imposed when it is determined that the defendant poses a specific, real and present threat to a person, or has a high likelihood of willful flight."[5] The intent of abolishing bail is to prevent defendants in nonviolent cases from languishing in jail and give judges discretion in other cases. Governor JB Pritzker put it this way: "What we want to make sure doesn't happen is that someone who's wealthy and commits a terrible violent crime—it could be, by the way, a wealthy drug dealer—doesn't have an easy time getting bail compared to somebody who maybe commits shoplifting and for a couple hundred dollars is stuck in jail."[6]

This is not the first time bail reform has been tried in Illinois. In 2015, at the direction of the Illinois Supreme Court, Cook County began using a "Public Safety Assessment-Court" (PSA-Court) tool that scored defendants on their risk. At the time, Cook County jail had almost 10,000 inmates and was severely overcrowded. It was also costing taxpayers close to $150 per day per inmate.[7] But the new scoring helped bring the inmate population down to around 8,000, a significant reduction.[8]

In 2017 Cook County Circuit Court Chief Justice Timothy Evans issued a directive that similarly reduced the bail for detainees in Cook County jails. Cook County Jail is America's second largest jail and has an average daily population of 9,000 (including home monitoring) and cycles through about 100,000 prisoners annually according to its website. Evans's directive was simple: issue the lowest possible bail without jeopardizing public safety.[9] This meant no bail for low-level offenses, and more at-home monitoring for others. In 2020, Loyola University Chicago published a study that showed crime did not increase as a result.[10] Other studies, however, were not so sure. And as crime has ticked upward over the past two years, Chicago Mayor Lori Lightfoot has asked that Evans stop this practice at least in part for violent offenses.[11]

At issue with the Safe-T Act are so-called "non-detainable" offenses, or a category of offenses for which a person cannot be held in jail for while awaiting trial. While there is no such "non-detainable" category, the language of the law does exclude from possible detention offenses in which the defendant is eligible for probation. These can include drug-trafficking, arson, robbery, and second-degree murder. In the fall of 2022 during the election season, memes and other misinformation made the rounds on social media and partisan newspapers decrying nothing less than a real-life version of the movie *The Purge*. Supporters say all the prosecutor has to do is show that the defendant is a risk to the community or to a specific individual. But critics say judges do not have discretion in cases where the defendant does not have a prior record or does not pose an immediate or imminent flight risk, so the bar is set too high. Critics also say the bill is not exact enough. Said DuPage County State's Attorney Bob Berlin, "We believe judges are in the best position to make decisions about who should be detained or not."[12] He thinks there are advantages to ending cash bail for low-level offenses; however, the complete removal of judicial discretion goes too far.

The court has created the Pretrial Implementation Task Force, chaired by retired Judge Robbin Stuckert, with the responsibility to sort out these gray areas ahead of January 2023. According to Kane County Chief Judge Clint Hull, a task force member, if an arresting officer sees a defendant as a risk the officer will still have the authority to detain the individual.[13] If the individual is detained, they must have a hearing, at which time it will be determined what type of risk is posed to the community. These hearings will be more in depth, and the defendant will have the right to have an attorney present. During the fall 2022 veto session, some of the language was clarified; however, the vast majority of the bill remained intact.

Still, it is controversial because it is so complicated and because the same set of numbers can tell two very different stories. Had this portion of the law been in effect in 2020 and 2021, an estimated 56 percent of defendants would not have been detained. For some, that is good news. For others, it is dangerous.

Specifically, in December 2022 state's attorneys in Will, Kane, and Kankakee Counties sued in state court, stating ending cash bail was unconstitutional. On December 29, just four days before the law was to go into effect, a Kankakee judge agreed with them.[14] The law was put on hold until the Illinois State Supreme Court could decide it; oral arguments were heard March 14.[15] Eventually, the State Supreme court ruled and upheld the law.

The Courts Today

The judicial branch of the Illinois state government handled almost 4.9 million cases in 2021.[16] On a day-to-day basis, the courts hand down decisions rooted in constitutional, statutory, and common law in civil and criminal cases. At trial, the trier of fact—either a jury or a judge without a jury (in a bench trial)—will weigh the evidence adduced at trial, and based on the findings of fact the judge will then render a decision and enter a final judgment on the merits of the case. Subject to the rules of the Supreme Court, the parties in the case may have a judgment or order reviewed on appeal.

Litigation falls into two general categories: civil and criminal. In civil cases a complaint typically involves disputes about divorce, child custody, contracts, mortgage foreclosure, personal injury, or property damage. Civil cases usually pit individuals or businesses against each other, and both sides usually pay private attorneys to represent them while they litigate the cases in court. The court may enter judgments for money damages or orders that declare the rights of the parties to a case or controversy, or it may issue injunctions.

In contrast, a criminal case directly implicates the government's fundamental responsibility to preserve public safety and order. A state's attorney, on behalf of the people of the State of Illinois, prosecutes a defendant individual or business for violations of the criminal code. On a finding of guilt, the court may enter judgment that sentences a criminal defendant to penalties that range from monetary restitution to victims to imprisonment in a county jail or state prison, to, in capital cases, a life sentence.

Given the tremendous power vested in the courts, the question often arises whether the people should elect judges. Should we replace elections with an appointment process that selects judges based on their legal qualifications? Should the people depend on the judges to police themselves and protect the public from judicial corruption or abuse? What should the process be to remove corrupt judges from the bench? What is the appropriate balance of power among the coequal branches of state government? How far can the legislative and executive branches of government go in telling the courts how to sentence criminal defendants? How far should the courts go in interpreting statutes, rules, or procedures, in determining their constitutionality, or in resolving conflicts between the executive and legislative branches of government?

Unified System with Three Levels

In contrast to many states, Illinois has a court system that is neat and orderly in structure. Under the current unified system, there are only three layers of courts statewide with no overlapping jurisdictions: the circuit courts, the appellate courts, and the Supreme Court, which oversees the administration of the entire system (see figure 8.1).

State government pays for the salaries and benefits of the judges on all three levels. County governments provide office and courtroom space and support

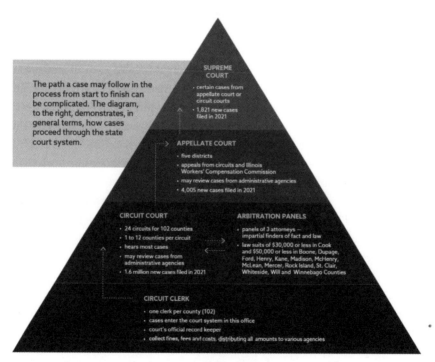

Figure 8.1. Illinois Court System. Source: Illinois Supreme Court, 2022.

staff to assist the circuit judges, primarily through the county-level office of clerk of the circuit court.[17]

Trial Courts. The trial courts of general jurisdiction are the circuit courts. These are the courts of original jurisdiction; in other words, they are the first step for any case in Illinois. The state is divided into twenty-three judicial circuits. Cook, DuPage, Lake, Kane, McHenry, and Will Counties each consist of a single circuit. The legislature determines the number of judges in the other circuits, which depends on the circuit's size and amount of business; the minimum number is three judges. In 2021 there were 476 circuit judges in Illinois, 241 of whom were in Cook County.[18] The term of the circuit judges is six years, and the retention ballot can be used.

Legislators in the General Assembly often try to increase the number of judges in their districts. Each circuit has at least three judges. Each county also has at least one resident circuit judge, who is elected from that county alone, bringing the total number of downstate circuit judges to more than two hundred. The constitution also provides for the appointment of associate judges who have limited jurisdiction. The elected circuit court judges appoint the associate judges to four-year terms and, like elected judges, they must be licensed attorneys. In 2021 there were about four hundred associate judges in Illinois.

The circuit courts themselves are organized by division. Each area is assigned a presiding judge who hears cases in only that area. This makes that division more efficient and knowledgeable about its area. The Circuit Court of Cook County is much larger than downstate circuit courts; indeed, it is the largest court in the world (see figure 8.2). As a result, its structure is more complex. It has much more specialization than do the twenty-two downstate circuits. Cook County has a separate section for mechanics' liens and a whole division for domestic relations, for example, and it uses "holiday" (weekend) and evening narcotics courts to keep the wheels of justice moving seven days a week.

Appellate Courts. The intermediate courts are the appellate courts. If a litigant believes there to be an error in the final judgment of the circuit court, the litigant may appeal to the appellate court except in certain cases where the law provides a direct appeal to the Supreme Court.[19] In certain circumstances, if there are multiple things to be decided in a case, those that have orders entered may be appealed prior to the entire case being resolved. Illinois also allows, again in certain circumstances by statute, for an interlocutory appeal.[20] This is an appeal over something procedural that may happen during a circuit court case prior to the final judgment.

Figure 8.2. Illinois Judicial Districts Maps. Source: Illinois Supreme Court, 2022. (*continues*)

Litigants must appeal to the appellate court in which their circuit is located. For instance, Adams County and the Eighth Judicial Circuit are part of the Fourth Appellate District, so any appeal would go to that court located in Springfield. The judges sitting in these courts also serve ten-year terms and are subject to a retention vote. An appellate court is located in each of the five judicial districts. In 2022 there were twenty-four appellate judges in the First District (Cook County), nine judges in the Second District, seven in the Third District, seven in the Fourth, and seven in the Fifth, for a total of fifty-four appellate judges.[21]

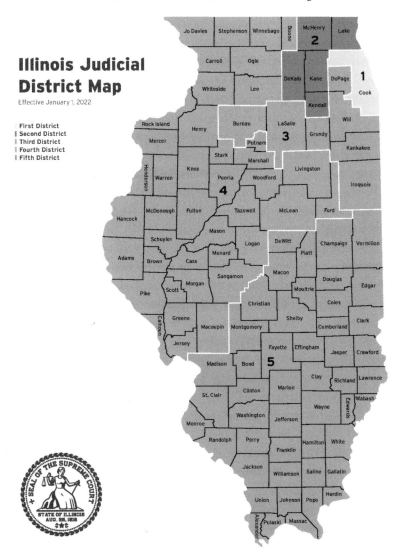

Illinois Judicial District Map

Effective January 1, 2022

First District
Second District
Third District
Fourth District
Fifth District

Figure 8.2. Continued

Supreme Court. The highest and final court is the Illinois Supreme Court, which has original and appellate jurisdiction. It has original jurisdiction in matters of revenue, mandamus, prohibition, or habeas corpus. For appeals cases, the Illinois Supreme Court may hear the case if, during the appellate case, a question of constitutionality (U.S. or Illinois) arises, or if the appeals judges themselves deem it of such importance. For cases requested by litigants that either were heard by the appeals court or had a matter that allowed it to go directly to the Supreme Court, the Supreme Court may make its own rules for accepting cases.

The Illinois constitution places administrative authority for the entire system in the Supreme Court; it is exercised by the chief justice.[22] The current chief justice is Mary Jane Theis, who took over after the retirement of Anne Burke. The Supreme Court submits the annual judicial budget to the General Assembly. It also appoints certain support staff headed by an administrative director, makes temporary assignments of judges, appoints judges to vacancies, and creates rules to provide for the orderly flow of judicial business.

The Supreme Court has seven members elected from five judicial districts; the larger First District (Cook County) elects three judges. The voters elect justices on a partisan ballot for a ten-year term. If a judge decides to serve a second (or additional) term, they are placed on a retention ballot. The judges are nominated in party primaries. In 2022 the Democrats picked up a seat to create a five-to-two majority on the Illinois Supreme Court.

In 2021, and effective for the 2022 races, the boundaries for the Supreme Court of Illinois were redrawn by the Illinois General Assembly (see figure 8.2). The reason given for this was due to population shifts—in 1964 when the boundaries were initially drawn the collar counties were far less populous than they are today.[23] However, many court observers also believe the retention loss of Thomas Kilbride created special impetus for the redistricting of the Supreme Court, so that a race this tight will never happen again. Cook County all but guarantees three Democrats, and in the past Kilbride's third did deliver. But as ex-urban areas remain red and rural areas get redder, the old boundaries would not do. The new third is now closer to the metropolitan area, and includes DuPage County, the state's second most populous county, which is now reliably Democratic. The Third District once again has the Democratic edge.

The justices have historically been white males, but following developments elsewhere in the electoral process, the first African American was elected to the court in 1990 and the first woman in 1992. In 2022 when Justice Rita B. Garman retired, Lisa Holder White, the first Black woman ever, was appointed to the high court. She is also a Republican, making her potentially the only Black female Republican state supreme court justice in the nation. In September 2022, Chief Justice Ann Burke announced her retirement, paving the way for the second Black female, Joy Cunningham (a Democrat).[24] The new court sat in December 2022 had one Black man and two Black women, and a total of five women altogether. While Illinois stands to have the most female and Black representation in the nation, no Latinos or Asians have ever been elected to the high court.

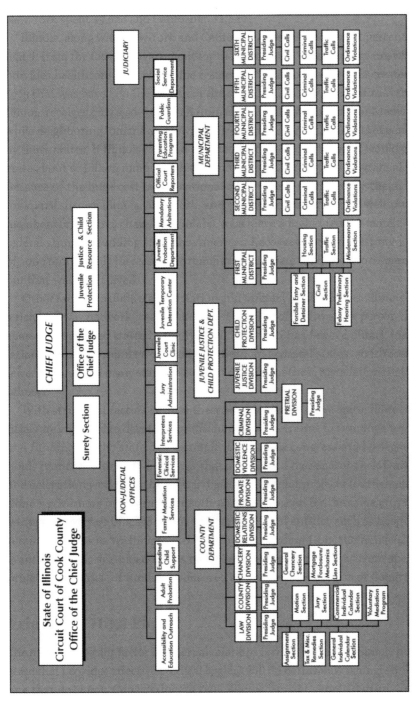

Figure 8.3. Cook County Court System. Source: Cook County Courts 2022.

Selection of Better Judges

In the 1980s and early 1990s, federal (not state or county) prosecutions resulted in the sentencing of sixteen judges for crimes including racketeering, bribery, mail fraud, and perjury. The judges were part of a deep-seated case-fixing network that involved crooked lawyers, bagmen, Chicago alderman Fred Roti, and Illinois state senator John A. D'Arco. In the two separate investigations known as Operation Greylord and Operation Gambat, fifty-seven attorneys were also convicted along with twenty-six criminal justice employees, including court clerks, deputy sheriffs, and police officers.[25]

The corruption issue drives the question of whether there is a better way to select judges. Voters in Illinois have elected trial, appellate, and Supreme Court judges since 1848. A 1962 amendment to the constitution reaffirmed the election of judges and provided a new method for voters to evaluate judges in office. Judges who seek another term notify the secretary of state of their desire. A question is placed on the ballot that asks whether the judge should be retained in office for another term. There is no party designation on the ballot. The 1970 constitution requires a three-fifths majority vote for retention.[26]

Supporters of election of judges tend to be populists of the Andrew Jackson school of thought. They believe that the people should pick their own judges just as they elect officials to the executive and legislative branches. Election, they argue, provides accountability by allowing voters to remove judges who have failed to maintain standards of judicial conduct or who have become incapacitated. In the 1970 vote on a new state constitution, voters decided to retain the election of judges in a side issue to the main document.

The argument for appointment of judges, often termed a "merit" system, is that it will bring better qualified attorneys to the bench and provide a more independent judiciary. Elections, some argue, involve judges in political matters that might later affect their independence on the bench, leading to the type of corrupt practices uncovered by Operation Greylord.

Proponents of the appointive system and their allies in the legislature have tried since 1970 to get the issue on the ballot as a constitutional amendment. No proposal has passed both legislative chambers yet. One reason is that subsidiary issues have divided the proponents. Some want local options, with each circuit or county deciding whether to have an appointive system. Others say appointments should be limited to the Supreme and appellate courts. Most proponents, including the bar associations, have argued that the governor should make the appointments after receiving nominations from a screening committee.[27]

In what may be a boost to proponents of judicial merit selection systems in the future, the U.S. Supreme Court has ruled that federal due process required disqualification of a state court judge from participating in the decision of a case in which a litigant had contributed $3 million or more to the judge's campaign for election. The court reasoned that the appearance of impropriety required the recusal of the judge.[28] The decision seems to add weight to the argument that the way to avoid undue influence in the courts is to replace judicial elections with merit selection systems.

Choosing from a Field of Unknowns

One enduring criticism of the elective system is that voters usually have little or no knowledge of the candidates on the ballot. The bar associations over the years have issued evaluations of candidates for the judiciary, as have the state's major newspapers, but these endorsements attract little attention among voters.[29] In the 1986 Cook County spring primary, three judicial candidates endorsed by Chicago mayor Harold Washington won despite being rated "unqualified" by the Chicago Bar Association. The *Chicago Sun-Times* in 1994 acknowledged the ineffectiveness of the primary system when it editorialized: "Once again, unqualified candidates in abundance are guaranteed subcircuit judgeships by merely surviving a crowded and confusing primary election."[30]

In June of 2022, ShawnTe Raines Welch ran for the Democratic nomination in the Fourth judicial subcircuit (Cook County) and was rated "not qualified" by the Illinois State Bar Association (ISBA).[31] Despite this, she bested her three opponents, two of whom were found qualified. Part of the reason could be her very well-known husband, Speaker of the Illinois House Emanuel "Chris" Welch, believed in her candidacy despite the rating. He campaigned for her, even though some called it a conflict of interest, helping her to raise $200,000.[32] Raines Welch defended her record, however, and also suggested that the ISBA might somehow be biased because one of her competitors was on the board. Further, she earned the endorsements and qualified ratings of many other bar associations, including those of Chicago and Cook County.

The bar associations do frequently disagree, making it even harder for residents to make a decision. During the June 2022 primaries, the Chicago Bar Association found all appellate candidates qualified. The Illinois State Bar Association, by contrast, found that in the First District races for the Shelvin Louise Marie Hall vacancy, Dominique Ross was not, and in the race for the Sheldon A. Harris vacancy, Devlin Schloop was not.[33] A group oriented around information and the Illinois judicial system, Injustice Watch, has begun to issue its own information on judicial elections both on the web and in print form so voters can bring information to the polls. They pull together recommendations from all thirteen bar associations in Illinois, along with biographies of the justices for voters. In the end, neither Ross nor Schloop won their elections, but with so many other electoral factors, it's hard to say why.

Another factor in the election of judges, particularly in Cook County, is the large number of candidates on the ballot. In 2022, sixty candidates ran for retention in Cook County alone. The Chicago Bar Association found that all but three were qualified. On Election Day, the voters looked over the excruciatingly long list of judges and retained them all.

Even the conscientious voter who consults newspaper editorials and advertisements of the bar association ratings is likely to be overwhelmed by such a list. In practice, unless it is a sensational race such as those described in chapter 3 on elections, many voters work down the list with no real knowledge of the candidates or skip the judicial part of the ballot entirely.

The Judiciary and State Government

As a coequal branch of state government, the judiciary has many interactions with the executive and legislative branches as it vigilantly struggles to uphold its independence. In 1992, after the Greylord and Gambat scandals, the Supreme Court formed the Illinois Supreme Court Special Commission on the Administration of Justice. In its final report, known as the *Solovy Report* after chairperson and attorney Jerold S. Solovy, the commission declared, "Judicial independence is an essential feature of democracy. Yet the principle of judicial independence is seriously eroded when elected officials or other political figures are able to manipulate judicial cases and the selection of associate judges. Enhancing judicial independence by insulating the judiciary from the political system remains an urgent need."[34]

It would be very difficult if not impossible to completely extricate the courts from the entanglement of politics. With regard to some issues the judiciary has the final word, but with others, it simply does not. An obvious example is that, though the Supreme Court prepares and submits its own budget, it depends on review by the legislature, passage by both houses, and the approval of the governor for the enactment of appropriations bills that include the court's budget.

Illinois has a strong separation of powers clause that states: "The legislative, executive, and judicial branches are separate. No branch shall exercise powers properly belonging to another."[35] Separation of the courts from the legislative branch was tested in a ten-year running controversy between the Supreme Court and the auditor general, a constitutional officer appointed by the legislature.[36] The main issue was whether the auditor general could audit the funds of two judicial agencies administered by the court: the Attorney Registration and Disciplinary Commission and the Board of Law Examiners. These two funds are not appropriated by the legislature; rather, the court collects fees from lawyers and candidates for the bar for the respective funds.

The auditor general nonetheless ruled that these were public funds, but the Supreme Court claimed that the commission and the board are not state agencies under article 8 of the constitution. The media generally were on the side of the auditor general, as were the delegates to the 1970 Constitutional Convention when they reconvened unofficially in 1987. They passed a nonbinding resolution saying it had been their intent to give the auditor general the power and duty to audit these two agencies. Even so, the Supreme Court considered its refusal to permit the audit a matter of constitutional principle: "The independence of the Judicial Branch of State Government is a fundamental precept of government which is grounded on the constitution's separation of powers clause and the inherent power of courts to safeguard their authority. The branches of government must cooperate with each other but such cooperation is subordinate to the doctrine of separation of power."[37]

As it turned out, personalities may have had as much to do with the battle as constitutional rights. In 1990, after the legislature appointed a new auditor general, the court made overtures to heal the division and requested that the new official audit the very same judicial agencies.

In 1997 yet another clash between the legislature and the courts took place. The Illinois House launched impeachment proceedings against the chief justice of the Illinois Supreme Court, James D. Heiple, to remove him from the bench. The controversy erupted from his alleged misconduct during a series of traffic stops in which the judge was accused of disobeying police and abusing his position to avoid speeding tickets. A special House investigative committee, on a vote of 8–2, issued a report that concluded that Heiple "was 'imperious,' 'arrogant' and discourteous to his colleagues, but that those shortcomings still did not amount to an impeachable offense."[38] The two dissenters were also the only two who were not attorneys. Heiple, who was the first Illinois judge threatened with impeachment by the legislature since 1833, retired when his term on the court ended on December 3, 2000.[39]

Another lesson concerning separation of powers unfolded in the process involving the fiscal 2003 budget. Thirteen years earlier, the Compensation Review Board had determined that judges' salaries should include cost of living adjustments (COLAs), adjusted annually. The legislature suspended the COLAs, however, including those for judges. The legislature later acknowledged that this violated the constitution, which read in part, "Judges shall receive salaries provided by law which shall not be diminished to take effect during their terms of office."[40] Accordingly, to remedy the situation, legislature included payment of the fiscal 2003 COLAs in the budget for fiscal 2004.

When the fiscal 2004 budget bill reached Governor Rod Blagojevich's desk, he vetoed the judicial COLAs. The Supreme Court issued an order—without any pending complaint or petition before it—to State Comptroller Dan Hynes and ordered him to pay the COLAs, but he refused to obey. Circuit court judges then filed a class action suit demanding payment of the COLAs for judges, and the trial court found that their elimination was unconstitutional and ordered payment. On appeal, the Supreme Court found that the COLAs had fully vested in 1990 and that efforts to block their payment violated the constitution. Moreover, the court ruled that a defense of legislative immunity was inapplicable and that the judiciary had authority to compel payment without a specific appropriation.[41] Thus the skirmish ended, and the state paid the judges' COLAs.

Blanket Clemency and Justice

In 1977 Governor James Thompson signed legislation reinstating the death penalty. The first execution was held on September 12, 1990. The second, in May 1994, was that of serial killer John Wayne Gacy. By that time, there were 154 others awaiting execution on Illinois's death row.

In 1999, when George Ryan took office, executions were halted. Only five years after the first execution, it was evident that there were serious doubts about the death penalty—the courts had overturned several murder convictions because of insufficient evidence. In response to this, Ryan appointed a commission to study the death penalty. In the meantime, the governor, with the cooperation of Attorney General Jim Ryan, declared a moratorium on executions. At the time, no death row inmates had completed all of the necessary appeals, which meant that there was no case ready that would require the attorney general to petition the Supreme Court for a final execution order, which was necessary before an execution could occur. As a matter of law, a governor has no authority unilaterally to suspend a final execution order; rather, the constitution gives a governor the power to grant reprieves, commutations, and pardons. In reality, the governor's moratorium was based upon the tacit agreement by the attorney general not to seek any final execution orders from the Supreme Court in the event that any death row inmate completed all appeals.

Meanwhile, the governor's commission reviewed all cases of death row inmates and heard testimony from prosecutors, private defense attorneys and public defenders, and other interested groups and individuals. The commission recommended extensive changes in the law and procedures involved in the investigation and trial of capital cases. Legislation was introduced that incorporated the commission's recommendations, but the legislature did not enact it before Governor Ryan left office in January 2003.

In the final months of his administration, Governor Ryan had concluded that he could not trust the justice system in all death penalty cases. During his last year in office, all inmates on death row either had filed a clemency petition or had one filed without their consent by a third-party advocate. In January 2003 the governor announced a "blanket clemency" for all inmates whom the courts had sentenced to death. Thus, he chose to give full pardons to 4 inmates and commuted the death sentences of the remaining 167 death row inmates to life without parole.

Death penalty opponents praised this action, but Attorney General Lisa Madigan filed a writ of mandamus in the Illinois Supreme Court that challenged the action on several grounds. *Mandamus* is a Latin word that means "we command." A writ of mandamus is a court order that requires another court, government official, public body, corporation, or individual to perform a certain act. The attorney general asked the court to command the director of Department of Corrections and the wardens of Pontiac and Menard state prisons to refuse to record commutation orders by Governor Ryan or expunge the orders if they had already recorded them. The court denied the petition.

Madigan alleged that a governor lacked authority to commute sentences for inmates who failed or refused to consent to their clemency petitions. The court acknowledged that the Illinois constitution grants authority to the legislature to regulate the clemency application process, and in fact the statutes enacted required an inmate's consent.[42] Nonetheless, this did not restrict the governor's constitutional authority to act on such terms as he thought proper. Rather, the Illinois constitution granted a governor unlimited power to issue as many pardons or commutations as he wished to whomever he wanted, even if an inmate had not requested it.[43] Nor did the governor's action create a separation of powers issue, because he had not exercised any power of the judiciary when he granted the blanket clemency. However, the court's opinion concluded with this admonition to future governors:

> As a final matter, we note that clemency is the historic remedy employed to prevent a miscarriage of justice where the judicial process has been exhausted.

We believe that this is the purpose for which the framers gave the Governor this power in the Illinois Constitution. The grant of this essentially unreviewable power carries with it the responsibility to exercise it in the manner intended. Our hope is that Governors will use the clemency power in its intended manner—to prevent miscarriages of justice in individual cases.[44]

When Governor Blagojevich took office in January 2003, he ostensibly continued the moratorium, though Ryan had obviously rendered the issue moot when he emptied death row. On the other hand, in Blagojevich's first term, the legislature did pass most of the reforms recommended by Governor Ryan's commission on the death penalty, which Blagojevich signed into law. From 2003 until 2010, homicide convictions resulted in about fifteen death sentences. In 2010 when Pat Quinn was elected, he worked with the General Assembly to abolish the death penalty, and those sentences were permanently commuted.

Judicial Review and the Age of Statutes

Today most law is of the statutory kind, and the statutes enacted by the legislature are the primary source of the state's public policy. Before the mid-nineteenth century, however, the judiciary in Illinois typically made public policy using the common law. This differed from statutes enacted by the legislature since it was comprised of legal principles and rules of action that relate to governance and security of persons and property, the authority of which was based solely on traditional usages and customs. Another source of common law came from the judgments and decrees of the courts recognizing, affirming, and enforcing such usages and customs, particularly the ancient unwritten law of England.

The early nineteenth-century common-law courts assumed that judges were better suited to discover the law as it existed and apply it to fit the needs and circumstances of a given case or controversy before the court. Conversely, they viewed the legislature's function as merely to codify common-law precedents and correct any technical deficiencies.

The rise of legislation in Illinois, and elsewhere among the states, began around the mid-nineteenth century, and the reaction of the common-law courts to the surge of legislative policymaking accounts for an inherent tension that naturally exists to this day between these coequal branches of government. Initially, the courts reacted with hostility and protected common-law principles from legislative encroachment by narrowly interpreting new statutes. The balance of power between the legislature and the judiciary has since evolved into the modern doctrine of separation of powers. With the shift from common-law courts as the source of public policy to the modern age of statutes as the primary source of law, the courts have embraced their role of interpreting and applying statutes to the facts or circumstances of a case before the court or determining the constitutionality of a statute, a function known as judicial review.

In *Kunkel v. Walton*, the Supreme Court in 1997 noted that the

> cardinal rule of statutory construction, to which all other canons and rules are subordinate, is to ascertain and give effect to the true intent and meaning of the legislature. *Solich v. George & Anna Portes Cancer Prevention Center of Chicago, Inc.*, 158 Ill. 2d 76, 81, 196 Ill. Dec. 655, 630 N.E.2d 820 (1994). In doing so the court should look first to the statutory language, which is the best indication of the legislature's intent. *Solich*, 158 Ill. 2d at 81. Where the meaning of an enactment is unclear from the statutory language itself, the court may look beyond the language employed and consider the purpose behind the law and the evils the law was designed to remedy. *Solich*, 158 Ill. 2d at 81. Where statutory language is ambiguous, it is appropriate to examine the legislative history. *People v. Hickman*, 163 Ill. 2d 250, 261, 206 Ill. Dec. 94, 644 N.E.2d 1147 (1994). However, when the language is clear, it will be given effect without resort to other aids for construction. *Hickman*, 163 Ill. 2d at 261; *Solich*, 158 Ill. 2d at 81.[45]

The plain meaning of the statute in the *Kunkel* case required that personal injury plaintiffs give written and signed medical release forms, but it was silent about judicial safeguards against abuse. The statute as written and enacted by the legislature required unlimited disclosure of medical information, and the court declared that as a matter of statutory construction it was "not at liberty to depart from the plain language of a statute by reading into it exceptions, limitations or conditions that the legislature did not express."[46] Yet the court then reviewed the constitutionality of the statute and declared that it violated the constitution.

Another example of judicial review is another 1997 case in which the Illinois Supreme Court invalidated the state's sex offender notification statute because it violated the state constitutional requirement that bills be confined to a single subject.[47] According to the high court, "What the Framers sought to do was avoid legislation being passed which, standing alone, could not muster the necessary votes for passage."[48] Prior to the *Johnson v. Edgar* case, the court had construed single-subject challenges liberally. So long as the various parts of the bill in question related to the overriding subject of the bill, then the court deemed the single-subject proviso to have been met. As an illustration, consider a bill whose subject was transportation or schools, and all the elements of the bill related to those subjects, respectively; that bill fulfills the single-subject requirement.[49] In *Johnson*, however, the court departed from its precedent and instead examined whether each part related to the others, rather than each part to the bill's overall purpose or subject. Consequently, legislation that the court once would have deemed properly drafted had become vulnerable to constitutional challenge.[50]

The bill under challenge in *Johnson* amended twenty-three existing statutes, most with provisos that were in some way related to criminal law or criminal procedure. But the bill also created an Environmental Impact Fee Law, which imposed a fee on refiners and manufacturers of fuel. Proposed earlier in the legislative session as an independent bill, the impact fee had failed. The Cook County Circuit Court, which had been the trial court in the case, declared the many-faceted bill "a textbook case of the situation that Article IV of the Illinois Constitution was enacted to prevent, that is, attaching an unpopular bill to a popular one to circumvent legislative input or scrutiny."[51] The Supreme Court affirmed the trial court ruling that the legislation was unconstitutional.

Subsequent single-subject decisions by the state high court have reinforced the *Johnson v. Edgar* decision.[52] Because of the sudden turnabout in the court's interpretation of the single-subject proviso, Michael J. Kasper, a former top aide to former House Speaker Michael Madigan, asserted that "the Supreme Court has greatly limited the legislature's flexibility in combining even tangentially related matters during the legislative process."[53]

Interest groups also turn to the courts to seek judicial review. In the *State Chamber of Commerce v. Filan*, an Illinois business trade group sought in 2005 to invalidate higher fees imposed by the governor on employers who utilized the Industrial Commission, which adjudicates claims of injury under the Workers' Compensation Act.[54] The chamber of commerce contended that the increased fees bore no relation to the cost of operating the commission; therefore, the increase violated various provisions of the state constitution. Although the Supreme Court declined to decide whether increasing fees to balance the state budget violated the constitution, it returned the case to the Cook County trial court for further proceedings.[55] The consequences of a decision that is favorable to the state chamber would be significant because the decision would call into question similar fee increases in about three hundred different programs and funds of state government that total several hundred million dollars annually.

Conclusion

Illinois courts play an integral part in the state's government and politics. And in 2023, the fate of the SAFE-T Act will challenge its relationship both with the governor and the legislative branch. Longstanding issues, however, such as the selection of better judges to root out political influence and corruption, remain. And, as we have seen with redistricting, the state's expanding suburban population will play an even larger role in determining the future.

9
LOCAL GOVERNMENT AND THE INTERGOVERNMENTAL WEB

In our federal system, powers are formally divided between the national government and state governments. Local governments are, in contrast, creatures of
their respective state's constitutions and laws. In the real world, however, the
federal government heavily influences and even controls many state-administered programs because of superior revenues and aggressive policy making
by Congress, the president, and the federal bureaucracy. Even governments at
the local level exert strong pressures on state government through organized
lobbies and local political power. This chapter provides an overview of Illinois
local governments and the relationships among the federal, state, and local
levels of government.

To begin with, it is important to recognize that Illinois has more units of
government than any other state. In 2021 the Illinois Civic Federation issued
a report that found a total of 8,923, far more than the figure of 7,000 that is
regularly cited.[1] Changing the methodology of calculation, the Civic Federation
drew on information not just from the U.S. Census Bureau's Census of Governments (the traditional source), but also the Illinois state comptroller's registry
of local government and information from the Illinois Department of Revenue.
New governments had not been formed, we just had not been counting all of
them, according to the Civic Federation.

And this is important—the number 7,000 that is usually used refers to governments that have taxing authority. The Civic Federation, however, included
any entity that possessed any governmental authority. For instance, the Chicago

Metropolitan Agency for Planning (CMAP), a regional planning organization for Cook and six collar counties, is counted as a government in the Civic Federation report. CMAP cannot tax; however, it does receive funds from the state and federal government and allocates and spends those monies in a governmental fashion. The Cook County Forest Preserve is counted as a separate government even though the board members are the same as the county's, because it levies a separate tax and has separate duties.[2]

Illinois is the only state to have *more* than 5,000 units of local government except Texas, which has 5,343 units. Texas, however, has more than double the population of Illinois. Several factors contributed to the growth of local governments in Illinois. First, as noted in chapter 1, Illinois platted townships as part of the Northwest Ordinances of 1785 and 1787. Township governments continue to function in Illinois, primarily to maintain rural roads. Most states outside the Midwest operate without township government.[3]

Second, the 1870 constitution limited the debt each local government could incur to 5 percent of assessed property valuation. Local civic leaders, therefore, simply created special district local governments, with their own debt capacity, to overlay on the cities, townships, and counties in order to raise funds to pay for government functions and to be able to issue bonds for long-term investments.

Third, Illinois has always had a large number of school districts, though the 852 districts that existed as of 2023 represent a continuing decline from the 12,000 districts, most of them one-room districts, that existed prior to World War II (see table 9.1).

This bewildering array of governments gives Illinois and metropolitan Chicago the distinction of being the nation's largest experiment in decentralized government.[4] The maze of overlapping jurisdictions is so thick that most Illinois residents live under the jurisdiction of eight or more local governments. Fairly typical are residents of Urbana, who could, if they had the time and energy, become active in the nine governments they purportedly control: the city, county, township, school, Urbana park, and community college jurisdictions and the Champaign-Urbana sanitary, public health, and mass transit districts. The first six of these have elected boards, and the last three have appointed boards. Residents pay property taxes to all of them.

Each of these 8,923 local governments is either a general- or special-purpose government. General-purpose governments number 2,826 and include municipalities (1,298), counties (102), and townships (1,426). Townships are controversial, and their elimination has been frequently proposed because,

Table 9.1. Units of Local Government

Type of District		1996	2000	2005	2019
Counties		102	102	102	102
Townships*		1,433	1,433	1,433	1,426
Road districts†		92	92	77	79
Cities, villages & incorporated towns		1,286	1,287	1,292	1,298
School districts	Elementary	389	383	377	368
	Unit	407	408	397	386
	High	105	102	101	96
	Non-High	1	1	1	2
	Community college	40	39	39	39
	Total school districts	942	933	915	891
Special districts	Fire protection	826	830	836	849
	Park	351	359	362	369
	Multi-twp. assessment	345	345	331	334
	Library	312	328	337	389
	Sanitary	144	142	127	119
	Cemetery	32	35	33	74
	Airport authority	28	28	28	28
	Street lighting	25	26	26	26
	Mosquito abatement	21	21	21	21
	Hospital	20	18	18	19
	Water authority	17	17	16	17
	River conservancy	14	14	14	17
	Forest preserve	13	13	13	14
	Mass transit	11	11	6	21
	Other	39	39	42	2,829
	Total special districts	2,197	2,225	2,220	5,127
Total—all types		6,052	6,071	6,039	8,923

Source: Illinois Department of Revenue, *Detailed Annual Report of Revenues and Expenditures*, 2006, https://illinoiscomptroller.gov/__media/sites/comptroller/Detailed%20Annual%202006.pdfIllinois; Civic Federation, "An Inventory of Local Government in Illinois," 2021.
*For 1996–2005, townships included road and bridge districts.
†Commission counties only.

with their generally narrow functions, they are considered by many reformers to be an unnecessary layer of government. Seventeen counties, mostly in southern Illinois, have historically operated without townships under the commission form of county government, which elects three commissioners to conduct their business, including functions that are otherwise the purview of townships.

This leaves a whopping 6,097 special- or limited-purpose governments. These governments provide a particular service to a particular geographic area; they include school, fire protection, mosquito abatement, and sewer districts, as well as authorities organized to operate exposition halls, convention centers, airports, ports, and mass transit systems. In Illinois we also have 14 port districts,

74 cemetery districts, 970 drainage districts, 1,391 road and bridge districts among the special districts.[5]

The large number of government units in Illinois, some argue, provides an opportunity for more people to participate in democracy. Indeed, by one estimate there are sixty-five thousand elected and appointed local officials in Illinois.[6] Because power and decision-making are broken down into small and distinct areas, the argument goes, citizens have more "public choice" and "local option" in the type of government they want and can pick and choose which functions their area needs or desires.

Although this may be so, the multiplicity of governments also provides a shield for weak performance, uncoordinated regional planning, and lack of accountability to citizens. The same functions that are managed in unified fashion in other states or regions are often fragmented and duplicative in Illinois. Instead of one bureaucracy, there are many; instead of one or two arenas of power, there are five or seven or ten. The extreme case is the seven-county metropolitan Chicago area, which comprises 1,450 governments with taxing powers. Here, region-wide problems of transportation, land-use planning, and flooding are solved piecemeal or not at all.

The Tangled Web Suburban Governments Weave

The problem of the intergovernmental web could not be clearer than in the suburbs of Chicago. Suburban Cook County and the collar counties contain over 280 municipalities but thousands of other special governments.

Take west suburban Oak Park, for example. Oak Park borders the city of Chicago along Austin Boulevard, and was incorporated as a village in 1902 to prevent it from being annexed by the City of Chicago. Proving it could do things by itself, its governments slowly multiplied, and property owners now pay taxes to sixteen different governments: a mosquito abatement district, metropolitan water reclamation district, park district, three school districts (community college, high school, grammar school), a library fund, the Village of Oak Park home rule tax, the Oak Park Mental Health District, General Assistance, township, and five Cook County units of government (forest preserve, elections, County Home Rule, public safety, and health facilities).

Simply paying a lot of taxes is one headache, and potentially costs more, but accessing services is a more serious problem. Residents of Oak Park must be very knowledgeable with what they want and need. And getting answers isn't always that easy or practical. Who has time to get reports from the mosquito abatement district?

Residents in Oak Park's southern neighbor, Berwyn, also pay taxes to sixteen governments, two of them park districts: the North Berwyn Park District and Berwyn Park District. This is in addition to the city's Recreation Department, which provides similar programming. All collect taxes, all have budgets and staff, all have governmental authority. Why not consolidate? It's not as easy as one might think, although it should be.

Oak Park and Berwyn's neighbor to the north, River Forest, tried this. River Forest has something in common with Oak Park and Berwyn, which is that its township is coterminous with its municipality. That is, the borders of the municipality and the township are exactly the same. That got some people in River Forest thinking, do we even need a township? Why not dissolve the township, and hand over the functions to the municipality, and save the taxpayers money? And it didn't seem like it would be that hard—at the time the township provided minimal services to youth and seniors and actually contracted them out to Oak Park Township.

For Village President Catherine Aducci, a former businesswoman, dissolving the township just made fiscal sense. But in order to do so, she needed an act of the state legislature, so she called on the village's state representative, Chris Welch, who agreed. In 2013, he introduced a bill that would put introduce a binding referendum to River Forest residents. The question would be simple—should the township stay or should it go?[7]

But River Forest was a rich community, with an average home value that approaches seven figures, and a few more dollars on a property tax bill could go unnoticed. Additionally, the township trustees and supervisor built a constituency by going door-to-door campaigning, making a case for why their services and structure should remain. Residents who never thought much of the township all of a sudden were in favor of it.[8] Pushback and lobbying from the township eventually led to Representative Welch's pulling the bill, and the township survives to this day.[9]

Cook County's neighbor, DuPage County, has also had its share of overlapping governments. DuPage County is divided into nine townships, which are about thirty-six square miles each and span several of the county's almost thirty municipalities. Naperville, located in southwestern DuPage County, lies in a township that bears the same name. The township manages only twenty miles of road, sixteen of which are wholly located in the municipality of Naperville, yet it has a road manager that makes $81,000 per year.[10] When the City of Naperville offered to take over repairing roads as it had all the resources necessary, the township balked, saying it did the work for less.

When the dust settled, the city did not get control of the roads. Instead, a deal was struck between Naperville Township and neighboring Lisle Township: Lisle would handle all of Naperville's twenty miles of road for a fee and then absorb the roads as part of its own government by 2021.[11] A binding referendum passed in 2016. In 2018, however, residents had a change of heart and tried to stop the consolidation. Instead, in 2019 voters overwhelmingly voted to abolish the Naperville Road district entirely by 2021 and merge its functions with Naperville Township itself, which has yet to actually occur. However, due to the reduced job functions of the Naperville highway commissioner, the township has voted to cut his salary by more than half.

Examples like these show why it is easy to say, "We have too many governments! Just abolish!" Behind every one of them are real people, and real interests, and of course, real paychecks. At the end of the day, these are people's jobs, and they aren't willing to lose them. And sometimes, people simply don't want to absorb their neighbor's problems, especially if their unit of government is running smoothly.

Some conjecture that, especially in the case of township offices and school boards, these offices are "farm teams" from which candidates for higher office are selected. And in DuPage County there is truth to this. While DuPage County was reliably red for many decades until about 2010, it was the slow takeover of the township governments by Democrats that created a crop of candidates to run for county offices and staff the DuPage County Democratic organization.

Still, there are some stories of successful government mergers. In 2014, north suburban Evanston voted to abolish its township and hand over all its functions to the city. Evanston, like River Forest, Oak Park, and Berwyn, had a township that was coterminous with its municipality.[12] Two years later, the city of Belleville, just outside of St. Louis, also with a coterminous township, voted to do the same.[13]

Ethics Issues

With so many governments, and thus so many elected officials and governmental employees, public oversight is necessarily limited. Lines of authority between one local government and another are blurred. As a result, featherbedding, patronage hiring, favoritism in contract awards, and other forms of corruption have surfaced repeatedly among local governments. As far back as 1928, officials at the Chicago-area Metropolitan Sanitary District "looted the public till through payroll padding, phony expense accounts, nepotism, mismanagement, and improper favors, among other malpractices," writes the historian Robert P.

Howard.[14] Similar stories have emerged from forest preserve districts, park districts, school districts, and other subunits of Illinois government.

The current SafeSpeed red-light camera scandal illustrates this well. SafeSpeed is a company that provides cameras to municipalities that take photos of vehicles that either drove through traffic lights when they were red or turned right when the traffic lights were red. The company issues a ticket for the suburban government for a $100 fine. Partners in the SafeSpeed company have admitted to bribing elected officials in multiple communities to get cameras adopted for their suburb and to get them up quicker. Former Cook County commissioner and mayor of McCook Jeff Tobolski, former mayor of Oakbrook Terrace Tony Ragucci, and former mayor of Crestwood Louis Presta all pled guilty for their roles in taking thousands in bribes. The sting also netted a state senator.[15]

The FBI also found during the course of its investigation that these individuals had been using their positions to shakedown constituents at every level. Tobolski, for example, as mayor, was also liquor commissioner. Along with his police chief, he was charged with extortion for shaking down business owners for liquor licenses. In one instance, a business owner accused Tobolski and the police chief of demanding $1,500 in exchange for the granting of the liquor license.[16]

Tobolski is a good example of another problem of multiple governments and that is, one person holding multiple governmental positions. In Illinois, it is possible to be elected to multiple offices at the same time. When State Senator Steven Landek was first elected, he was also mayor of Lyons and a Lyons Township trustee. And this is not just Cook County—when State Representative Deanne Mazzochi was elected to her seat, she was chair of the College of DuPage board of trustees and refused to resign for months. Illinois law allows this; it just disallows a second paycheck.

It does not disallow a second (or third) paycheck for unelected government employees, however. And this is where the multiplicity of governments becomes more nefarious. Recall the multiplicity of park districts, for example. The City of Berwyn, which is less than four square miles, has two park districts in addition to the city's Recreation Department. The North Berwyn Park District is responsible for the northern half of the territory. Its current executive director, Joe Vallez, makes over $145,000 per year. But he is also the executive director for Bensenville, a DuPage County suburb with a park district of over 5.5 square miles, making a salary of over $91,000. And until 2018 he was also working part-time in administration for the Justice Park District.[17]

Why are Berwyn taxpayers essentially paying double? How can one man work two full-time jobs and a third job part-time? Objectively, these are beautiful park districts and no doubt because staff has made them so. But there is more. The taxpayers are also on the hook for Vallez's pension. And in Illinois, it is legal to collect multiple pensions. Vallez stands to collect two very large pensions from two separate government entities. A clever reader would say, "so what?" If it was not Vallez, it would just be two different people. But a cleverer reader would say the redundancy of park districts in Berwyn means there is no need for his North Berwyn Park District position in the first place.

The pension crisis, which we discuss in chapter 10 on budgeting, has tainted what used to be a citizen's argument in support of the state's multiplicity of governments, on the basis of the low ratio of government employees to overall population. Although it is counterintuitive to most observers, the Illinois governments rank among the lowest of all the states in number of employees per unit of population. Illinois had about 616,00 state and local government full-time equivalent (FTE) employees in 2018, or 484 per 10,000 residents, making Illinois forty-fifth in the nation. The national average is about 509 FTE employees per 10,000 residents, so Illinois indeed has comparatively few government employees per citizen.

Elections and Leadership

What can be done about this? Good local leadership can help cut through the tangle of local governments, but even conscientious citizens have trouble keeping track of candidates at the local elections, which in Illinois are a strange mixture of partisan and nonpartisan races. In nonpartisan elections, there are no party labels on the ballot. In partisan elections, the national party labels (Republican and Democrat) or local party labels (for example, Peoples and Citizens) appear on the ballot. The local parties in some places are fronts for the national parties; in other places they represent local groupings of citizens concerned with one or more issues. In still other places, local party labels are simply devices for getting candidates' names on the ballot. There is no consistency to this approach. In one of Illinois's twin cities, Champaign, the elections are nonpartisan, but in Urbana candidates run with national party labels.

Some people would argue that all local elections should be partisan. Such a system would create political bonds between neighboring or overlapping governments, possibly improving cooperation across regions and boosting the strength of local and, over time, state parties as well. The "good government" supporters, however, argue for nonpartisan local elections because "there is no Republican or Democratic way to clean the streets." With no agreement forthcoming, the strange mixture of elections continues, possibly discouraging cooperation among governments and frequently confusing local voters.[18]

Another problem is fielding candidates for all of these elected positions. In Illinois, municipal elections occur in odd years after the national and state elections—precisely when everyone is exhausted. Petitions begin circulation in September, when the national and state elections are still red hot, making it hard to get excited or to get volunteers to help. Luckily, however, the number of petition signatures needed is usually low. However, candidates running for local office even in small municipalities still have to begin raising money (in wards in the City of Chicago aldermanic races routinely cost more than $250,000). Petitions are due in December, meaning campaign season is in icy January and February when it is difficult to go door-to-door to meet the voters and explain what these local elections are all about.

In municipalities with primaries, the big election is in February. For many Cook County suburbs controlled by the Democratic Party, this is the big contest. For the City of Chicago, which holds its elections in February and run-offs April, this is also the big contest. For all, this could not be a more terrible timeline for holding elections. For election officials, however, the thinking was that by taking local elections out of the national and state election cycle, it will remove them from corrupting elements. It has, instead, meant far lower participation rates than for either presidential or midterm elections. After record turnout in the 2018 and 2020 midterm and presidential races, the municipal elections of 2019 and 2021 saw voter turnout in some counties of 15 percent or less.[19]

Around the state the story is the same. In southern Jefferson County turnout in 2021 was 13.72 percent, in central Sangamon County it was 11.32 percent, and in western Rock Island County was just over 14 percent.[20] Factoring in eligible voters who aren't registered, this means that as few as 5–10 percent of the registered voters elect their local government.

Even where turnout was slightly higher, like DuPage County at almost 16.6 percent, the contests are questionable (see table 9.2). There are 38 communities that are wholly or mostly in DuPage County, and April 6, 2021, elections were held in offices for 123 cities and villages, 43 townships, 103 park, fire, and library boards, and 63 school boards. Because most of these were boards with multiple offices, this amounted to 596 seats that were up for grabs that night.[21] However, the actual numbers tell a different story.

In roughly half of the contests for cities and villages, there was no contest. But drilling further down into the data reveals that not one city or village clerk faced a challenger in DuPage County.[22] And this is an important position—this person is the one who keeps the official records and handles Freedom of Information requests for the municipality. A third of the township positions also went

Table 9.2. DuPage County Election Results

	Contested candidates	Uncontested candidate	Not enough	No
Cities and villages	58	63	2	
Townships	28	15		
Park, fire, and library	23	67	8	5
School	34	19	6	

Source: DuPage County Clerk.

unchallenged, although this was not as bad as park, fire, and library candidates, which only saw about a quarter of its boards contested. What's worse is for five of the park, fire, and library contests there was absolutely no candidate, and for eight there were not enough for the board. For the school district, there were not enough candidates six times. When no one runs for a seat, the board may, by state law, appoint someone to fill this seat. This of course leads to a government choosing itself, rather than the people choosing the government. With so many hidden governments in Illinois, this is not a rare occurrence.

What kind of leadership do we get when with low participation and uncontested elections? The abysmal 2021 data for DuPage actually represents improvement over 2017: in that year contests were about 25 percent fewer.[23] Political science literature differs on the importance of participation and contested elections for our democracy. Some say it is okay if only the most informed, concerned citizens turn out and participate, because what matters most is we elect the best people and informed voters do that for the rest of us. Others say that without all voices, we will never be able to accurately reflect the needs of all in society and without that, we will never be able to sustain a democracy.

Forms of Local Government

In Illinois, a municipality may take several forms: Aldermanic-City, Trustee-Village, Strong Mayor City, and Commission Government. All of these refer to the power-sharing arrangement between the executive and the legislative branches of the municipal government.

Aldermanic-City, Trustee-Village, and Strong Mayor all elect one chief executive at large. In the Aldermanic-City and Strong Mayor form of government they call this person the mayor, in the Trustee-Village governments they call this person the village president. All three also elect legislative boards either from districts or at large, depending on their charters (the larger the municipality the more likely that districts or wards are created). In the Aldermanic-City and

Strong Mayor format they call these a city or town council, in the Trustee-Village format they call this a board of trustees.

Running things a little bit differently are commission-style governments, which are better suited for smaller populations. A mayor and four other commissioners are elected at large from the entire municipality. At the first meeting they designate who will be the member in charge of each department, including the town clerk and treasurer.

An adaptation to these various forms of governments is the addition of a manager or administrator. About 200 communities and counties in Illinois have opted for this.[24] This person is usually appointed by the mayor or village president and confirmed by the council or board of trustees. The idea is that this appointed official acts like the CEO—the mayor/village president and council/board of trustees can handle the policy and the manager/administrator can handle the day-to-day running of the government. Contracts for garbage, snow removal, permitting for construction, water lines, and the like are best handled by professionals, they argue.

North suburban Waukegan, a community of 87,000, is one of the largest communities in Illinois not to have a professional city manager or administrator. Their current debate sums up the argument well. Said one alderman, "We need a professionally educated manager to run our city. . . . Our elected mayors are not educated to run or manage a city. We need professionalism, and this is one way of doing that."[25] Another alderman had a different take. "Having an elected mayor is more effective. . . . My constituents vote for the mayor on [his or her] ability, and the mayor has to work to pave the way to do what they want."[26]

Finally, local governments are not audited by any state agency. They are required to file either annual financial reports or audits with the Illinois comptroller, but that office lacks the staff to review the reports and the authority to force a local government to change its financial practices. The comptroller does provide a summary financial document about each type of government—municipalities, counties, townships, and special districts. (The state board of education performs this function for school districts and has tighter control.)

The value of the reports filed with the comptroller has been questioned. A study by the Taxpayers' Federation of Illinois concluded, "As it is currently constituted, the annual financial reporting requirement set forth in Illinois law is a useless exercise because the data collected is inadequate to satisfy basic research. The reports appear to be relatively worthless for comparative tax purposes."[27] Obtaining them is another story. Today most are posted on the municipal websites for at least the most current year, but for a substantial minority of towns they lack the resources to do so. Thus if someone wanted to read one of these reports they would have to go in person and either stay in the office or make a copy of a document that is hundreds of pages. And that is assuming they know how to read and understand them.

For Bigger Players, Home Rule

Even with all this choice, true to the individualistic culture of the state, Chicago and many smaller cities had bristled under the state's authority since the nineteenth century. They wanted home rule—the ability to make their own decisions, raise their own revenues, and in general be able to make decisions without first asking the state for permission. They got what they wanted when the 1970 constitution went into effect on July 1, 1971.

The constitution established home rule for Cook County and all municipalities with more than twenty-five thousand residents. Unlike other states, where voters have to approve a charter in a local referendum to receive such powers, the grant of home rule was automatic in Illinois. Municipalities with fewer than twenty-five thousand residents can also secure home rule by a vote of the people, and larger cities can vote out home rule by the same referendum process.

Home-rule units in Illinois "may exercise any power and perform any function pertaining to its government and affairs including, but not limited to, the power to regulate for the protection of the public health, safety, morals and welfare; to license; to tax; and to incur debt." Some limitations are spelled out in the constitution, but the courts are admonished that the "powers and functions of home rule shall be construed liberally."[28]

The 1970 constitution also provided that county governments with an elected chief executive automatically became home-rule units. Cook County was the only county to qualify for this power, and though other counties can qualify by adopting the chief executive office by referendum, all such referenda have failed. The state's second-largest county, DuPage, debated whether it qualified for home rule. The full-time chair of the DuPage County Board is elected on an at-large basis. The issue was whether he is a chief executive officer as prescribed in the constitution. The *Chicago Tribune* supported the move in an editorial in 1990: "Jack Knuepfer [the board chair] committed political suicide when he insisted on the eve of the March [1990] primary that the county, like Cook, had 'home rule' power—the right to govern itself." The editorial concluded: "With home rule authority, DuPage would have the power to manage its own affairs and chart its own future. Knuepfer understands that. Someday, the voters of

DuPage may understand that, too. For now, they at least should appreciate that someone with nothing more to lose is trying to point the way for a county with a lot to gain.[29] Knuepfer was defeated, however, in the March 1990 primary and over three decades later, DuPage remains without home rule.

According to the Illinois Municipal League, there are 219 communities with home rule today.[30] In 1987 James Banovetz and Thomas Kelty surveyed ninety-five Illinois municipalities and found that home rule was used in a wide variety of ways. In descending order of importance, the uses were taking on new debt (89 percent), passing regulations (72 percent), regulatory licensing (61 percent), making intergovernmental agreements (58 percent), levying new taxes (57 percent), executing property transactions (43 percent), exploiting new sources of nontax revenues (36 percent), making changes in government structure (28 percent), and consolidating property tax levies (26 percent).[31]

Banovetz and Kelty found that once these home rule powers are used, most municipalities prefer to keep them; when the question to retain home rule was put to the voters in twenty-five municipalities, twenty-one voted for its retention. The four municipalities abandoning home rule were Lisle, Villa Park, Lombard, and Rockford. The Illinois Supreme Court also has been "pro-home rule," according to Banovetz and Kelty. They classify thirty-one court decisions handed down between 1972 and 1987 as favorable to home rule and twenty as unfavorable. Last, the General Assembly has reacted cautiously to bills that preempt home rule; only a handful of such bills have been approved since 1972.

Two-thirds of the state's population is now governed by home rule because, with a few exceptions, it is in place for the state's largest municipalities and its most populous county. Still, that leaves a lot of downstate and suburban counties and about six thousand other government units that remain subject to the common law principle known as Dillon's Rule, the cornerstone of municipal law since 1872, which holds that a local government has only that authority specifically granted by the state constitution and its statutes.

The flip side of home rule is state mandates that direct local governments and school districts to provide a benefit or service. Mandates come in five categories: local government organization and structure, due process, service, tax exemption, or personnel mandates. Service, tax exemption, and personnel are reimbursable by the state. However, the General Assembly has gotten in the habit of exempting the mandates from reimbursement when they are passed.[32] For example, the state legislature from time to time increases pension benefits for local government employees—without providing the funds to pay the benefits.

Cooperation and Regional Governance

Allowing this wide freedom of choice in the way local government organizes itself and conducts its affairs remains at the philosophical core of the decentralized approach, key in Illinois. Yet because of varying approaches to management and widely divergent agendas, it is no wonder that local governments have a difficult time presenting a common front in Springfield. Most government units in Illinois are organized into separate statewide lobbying groups—for cities, townships, and villages—with the overall aim of improving the local governments' authority vis-à-vis the state government.

The Illinois Municipal League is one such organization. But even with a strong financial base, it has a hard time representing the needs of the rapidly growing northeastern cities along with the problems of the many declining municipalities downstate. Chicago, East St. Louis, Aurora, and Naperville all have their own sets of problems. In order to address these differences, separate regional groupings of municipalities have been developed for lobbying purposes. For example, there are strong mayors' and managers' organizations in DuPage and Will Counties, in the southern Cook County suburbs, and in other regional groupings throughout the state.

In 1997 Chicago mayor Richard M. Daley created the Metropolitan Mayors' Caucus. Each of the nine metropolitan mayors' and managers' associations sends delegates to the caucus, which represents 275 municipalities. The caucus has worked on economic development, reliability of electricity, affordable housing, emergency preparedness, and other topics. It only works, however, because the caucus agrees to avoid topics of conflict such as expansion of O'Hare International Airport and a possible third airport. For instance, in 2022 its agenda focused on how to address the regional needs of an aging population.

These arrangements have laid the groundwork for increased cooperation between governmental entities. The independent-minded local governments generally share the individualistic values discussed in this book, that is, they tend to be skeptical of or outright opposed to comprehensive, collective policies for the region that would override the objectives of the individual governments. But large-scale issues, most notably the dispersion of jobs away from areas with affordable housing, the disparity in spending by school districts, and the worsening problem of traffic congestion throughout the metropolitan area, beg for regional solutions. Problems do not stop at jurisdictional boundaries.

The Metropolitan Planning Council (MPC), which has been around since the 1930s, is a nonprofit designed to assist with planning and development, and it expanded its services toward the end of the century. In 1991 the council wrote that it "helps members save money through joint purchasing, training programs for municipal employees, and joint testing of police and fire candidates. Special programs address issues that cross jurisdictional boundaries, including solid waste, cable franchising, and storm-water management."[33] Today it has expanded its services to assist with research, governance, environment and sustainability, transportation, equitable development, and housing.[34]

In 1958 the MPC helped establish the Northeastern Illinois Planning Commission (NIPC), which for decades served the region as a toothless tiger that planned for the region yet lacked any enforcement authority. According to one business newspaper writer, "Such plans in the past have been routinely disregarded, as municipal officials exert their authority to make decisions about zoning and land use in their towns."[35]

NIPC was eventually replaced in 2005 with the Chicago Metropolitan Agency for Planning (CMAP), consolidating it and the Chicago Area Transportation Study, another longtime planning unit. As with the predecessor units, appointments to the seventeen-member CMAP board are carefully doled out in a balanced fashion to people from Chicago, Cook County, and suburban county subregions.[36] CMAP declares that it "will provide leadership by taking a comprehensive, collaborative approach that gives decision makers a new regional context for their choices regarding land use and transportation."[37]

The problem of lack of power over the separate governments remains, however. "The new agency faces the same legal obstacles as CATS and NIPC," declared one observer. "Under pressure from municipal officials, lawmakers [in 2005] insisted the bill creating CMAP avoid anything that could be construed as giving the new agency control over land use decisions."[38] A decade and a half later, planning proponents have still failed to convince lawmakers to provide this power to CMAP. Cooperation and collaboration are fine, say lawmakers, but not coercion of local governments.

CMAP has instead developed its own coping mechanism. Because it cannot coerce, it helps, and helps very well. Take the example of south suburban Calumet Park. Like other south suburbs, Calumet Park never really recovered from the loss of the manufacturing economy, and by the 2000s led the region in poverty. The municipality could not invest in economic development; it didn't have enough for basic infrastructure. Enter CMAP staff in 2019, who listened and helped the struggling municipality apply for millions in grants from the state and federal government.[39] It has now become a model for other struggling municipalities. In this way, CMAP has adapted as source of expertise and a support for local governments willing to use its services.

It is not that Illinois residents and their leaders do not recognize the inefficiencies of the current system. Rather, they accept them as part of the state's personality and way of doing business. Instead of trying to dismantle something so integral—and in the process disrupting longstanding webs of jobs and allegiances—they develop mechanisms to try to improve relations among the multitude of competing governments.

Lack of planning and cooperation are not peculiar to northeastern Illinois. The problem is statewide and is particularly intense in growing areas such as Champaign County, where uncontrolled urban growth forced a clumsy and inefficient reaction by three neighboring municipalities: Champaign, Urbana, and Savoy. Each recognized the need for an annexation agreement, but because each had its own interests, negotiations were prolonged and complex.

The three cities decided to sign agreements among themselves so that they could divide up unincorporated areas just outside their boundaries. But they needed the help of a fourth entity, the Champaign-Urbana Sanitary District, so that they could withhold sewer connections to developers in areas refusing to be annexed to a city. What was the advantage for the sanitary district? Champaign and Urbana would assume the district's liability for the frequent flooding of Boneyard Creek, which runs through the twin cities. When the district agreed to that approach, Champaign County had to be convinced because it appoints sanitary district board members. Once the county came on board, the deal went through in 1993, but only after the three cities agreed to reimburse the county for sales tax on any commercial properties that they annex for the next few years. All this negotiation was needed to address what would seem to be a simple matter of providing orderly growth.[40]

The Chicago Approach

Even if regional cooperation could be developed, the state is likely always to be affected by difficult relations between its biggest city and the state government. As by far the largest municipality in Illinois at almost 2.7 million people, Chicago wields a level of political power disproportionately greater than its numbers. Legally, Chicago is a subunit of the state, but politically, the city often tries to operate independently.[41] Prior to the provision of home-rule powers to cities by the Illinois constitution of 1970, Chicago and its disciplined legislative bloc frequently were successful in generating special legislation for the city through classification; that is, ensuring that a state statute would either apply to or exempt cities of more than 500,000. This applied, of course, only to Chicago since no other town or city had a population of this size. Nonetheless, the lack of home-rule powers spurred recommendations to make Chicago and the metropolitan area a separate state; in 1933, for example, a University of Chicago study said, "There is much to be said for the separate statehood of Chicago, especially in view of the inability of the city to obtain proportional representation in the state legislature, or a degree of home-rule adequate to deal with the needs of a growing metropolis."[42] The city has since gained home-rule powers it sought, and in any case such proposals are not taken seriously because Illinois without its only large city would be a much more modest state with a fraction of its current national profile and power.

The career ladder for Chicago politicians illustrates the confusion about the relation between local government and the State of Illinois. Several former legislators (plus two former congressmen) have served in the Chicago city council, but few former city aldermen have been elected subsequently to the state legislature. In other parts of the state, the pattern of upward mobility for a local government official is to be elected to the legislature. In Chicago, the legislature has more often been a stepping-stone not only to the City Council but also to more powerful local offices. Both the late Chicago mayor Richard J. Daley and his son Mayor Richard M. Daley served in the Illinois General Assembly early in their political careers. In 1979, powerful Illinois Senate president Thomas Hynes resigned his office so that he could run for the office of Cook County assessor (which he won).

Chicago uses its home-rule powers extensively. It started the home-rule movement in 1954, when Mayor Martin Kennelly created a Home Rule Commission. Kennelly's successor Richard J. Daley continued to carry the home-rule banner, and Richard M. Daley helped create the home-rule provisions as a member of the 1970 Constitutional Convention's Local Government Committee.

Home-rule authority has increased Chicago's bargaining power with the legislature and governor. Prior to 1970, Chicago had to present a laundry list of changes it wanted from the legislature and then negotiate and make trades to achieve its aims. Not having to negotiate items that can be changed under home-rule authority increases the city's negotiating strength in matters not covered by home rule.

In theory, Chicago is a "weak mayor" city, with much power lodged in the city council and numerous other elected citywide officials. In practice, however, most recent Chicago mayors have had very strong political power. Richard J. Daley was chairman of the Cook County Democratic Central Committee, which controlled more than twenty-five thousand patronage jobs at the time, as well as mayor. As a result he developed legendary power and was known as "Boss

Daley" by supporters and opponents alike. The mayors who served after his death (Michael Bilandic, Jane Byrne, Harold Washington, and Eugene Sawyer) did not hold the party office and were not as strong, but they were often able to steer the city council.

Mayor Richard M. Daley eschewed the party office but was able to steer the city council, still known as a "rubber stamp council," with more ease. Studies by the University of Illinois at Chicago show that he often enjoyed more support from city council in his twenty-two years as mayor than his father. King of so-called "pinstripe patronage," he modernized machine politics by trading contracts and favors for votes instead of just jobs and building a gleaming downtown that would bring upper-echelon service economy jobs to donate to his reelection fund.[43] His successor, Rahm Emanuel, former chief of staff to President Barack Obama, was also adept at this.

Emanuel was perhaps too good at developing Chicago as a "global city," and thus provoked a progressive backlash that earned him the moniker Mayor 1% for catering only to downtown interests while the rest of the city languished.[44] In 2015, he narrowly survived a primary challenge from then county commissioner and now U.S. congressman Chuy Garcia, who is a key leader of the Chicago progressive movement. Emanuel's rubber-stamp city council started to assert itself, and in 2018 he announced he would not seek another term. This paved the way for Lori Lightfoot, a former assistant U.S. attorney, to become the first female, Black, and gay mayor not just of Chicago, but any major city in America.

The Chicago city council is large. Aldermen are elected from each of the fifty wards on a nonpartisan ballot, as is the mayor, although the partisan affiliations of the aldermen are well known. In 2007 all but one were Democrats, though they came from different factions of the party. The Chicago wards of roughly 50,000 people each are the building blocks for the county political organization, in many instances the elected Democratic ward committee member is also the alderperson This combination makes the alderman a very potent political actor because Chicago ward committee members appoint party precinct captains.[45]

The Chicago city council has the potential to wield great power, and it used it at the start of Mayor Harold Washington's first term in 1983. The majority of the council members at the time were not supporters of Washington, the city's first Black mayor. By voting as a bloc for more than three years, the opposing aldermen were able to prevent the bulk of Washington's program from being implemented. Called the "council wars" by the media, this conflict had strong racial overtones, with Blacks generally supporting Washington and most of the council's white majority opposing him.

There have been calls to reform the city council, most recently a 1989 report titled "Chicago City Council Reform" by the City Club of Chicago. Some changes have been made in the council and its procedures. But the size of the council has not been changed, although it could be done using the city's home-rule powers. Apparently, the classic remark of colorful alderman "Paddy" Bauler, uttered with gusto in 1955, still prevails: "Chicago ain't ready for reform."

One of the most dramatic and revealing investigations of institutionalized corruption was splashed on the front pages of the *Chicago Sun-Times* for a solid month in 1978, after the newspaper and the Better Government Association (BGA) had opened and operated a tavern named the Mirage less than a mile from city hall.

That Chicago's inspectors were on the take had been well known for decades, but because business owners needed licenses to operate and could cut a few corners with a fifty-dollar bribe, they rarely came forward to fight the system. Investigative reporter Pamela Zekman and the BGA's William Recktenwald decided the best way to gather hard evidence was to open a real business and let the inspectors walk in. As they prepared to open the tavern and during the four months it was in business, the purported tavernkeepers encountered repeated payoff demands. Plumbing, electrical, and fire inspectors and a sign inspector all looked the other way or expedited paperwork in exchange for payoffs of ten dollars or more. The owner of a neighborhood delicatessen already knew the pattern. "The name of the game in Chicago is baksheesh. That's Arabian. It means payoff, bribe. This is the city of baksheesh."[46]

From 1976 to 2020, the Department of Justice recorded 1,792 criminal convictions for corruption in the federal Northern District of Illinois (the district that encompasses the Chicago metropolitan region). This is the highest in the nation. Indeed, Chicago was not ready for reform—yet. However, there is hope in the numbers. While overall they are the highest, when disaggregated by decade and compared to other regions, Chicago's numbers are actually declining.[47]

Corruption aside, Chicago looks good when its spending is compared to that of other big American cities. This is possible because functions that would belong to the city elsewhere are performed by other governmental units in Chicago. These arrangements were made by the legislature and are in line with the decentralized nature of local governments throughout Illinois. Public hospitals are a county, not a city, function in Chicago. The public schools, as in other parts of the state, are a separate government unit with taxing powers. The Chicago Housing Authority has considerable independence. Public transportation is the purview of the Chicago Transit Authority and the Regional Transportation Authority. The park district, too, is fiscally independent of the city.

This decentralization helped Chicago, or at least masked its symptoms, during the 1970s, when New York City faced fiscal disaster. As one reporter noted, "Today the effect of these differences [between the two cities] is striking. Cook County, not the city of Chicago, operates the city's public hospitals and the state legislature picked up most of the city's transportation and social welfare costs. By contrast, New York is the only city in the country whose state legislature requires it to pay a substantial share of its own Medicaid and welfare bills."[48]

Although some Chicago governmental agencies are legally independent and do not appear on the organization chart as city functions (such as the Chicago Public Schools, Park District, Transit Authority, and Housing Authority), the mayor can have considerable impact on their decision-making. Recent mayors have exercised influence through their appointment powers. This is best illustrated by the Chicago Park District, for which the mayor appoints the board members and the top administrative officer. Legally, all of these separate governments are outside the jurisdiction of the mayor. In reality, their independence depends on whether the mayor has the political strength to control his appointees.

Beyond the Borders

States cannot afford to be shy in dealing with the national government in Washington, D.C. Nor has Illinois been, although dollar figures of revenue returned to the state suggest otherwise, as we will see.

Even before the state's incorporation in 1818, the territory's delegate to the U.S. Congress, Nathaniel Pope, was working hard in Washington, D.C. Through Pope's efforts, Congress pushed the northern border of Illinois forty-one miles up from Lake Michigan's southern tip, capturing the port of Chicago from Wisconsin and setting a precedent for the state's aggressiveness to this day.

Pope's advocacy to expand Illinois's original borders has been followed by a steady stream of leaders who went before the U.S. Congress, the federal bureaucracy, the president, and even foreign governments to assert the state's needs. Members of the Illinois congressional delegation played lead roles, but governors, mayors, state legislators, and business leaders also had a part in the ongoing efforts.

External relations are typically pursued for a simple reason: to bring back money or jobs. From the 1950s to the 1970s, Chicago mayor Richard J. Daley was a master of this art, trading his ability to generate votes for hundreds of millions of dollars' worth of building projects and federal human service programs. In the 2000s, Rahm Emanuel did the same as he had been chief of staff to then President Barack Obama. Governor Jim Thompson (1977–90) traveled frequently to foreign cities and helped generate thousands of jobs backed by export sales and foreign investments. Governor Rod Blagojevich maintained foreign trade offices in nine foreign cities, including Hong Kong, Shanghai, Warsaw, and Johannesburg. Former Speaker of the U.S. House Dennis Hastert (R-IL, 1999–2006) continued to bring home the bacon, as has U.S. Senate majority whip Dick Durbin (D-IL).

Washington is the focus of each state's external relations because that is where the money is. Federal payments to Illinois state and local governments in FY2023 will amount to $38 billion plus another $14 billion in COVID-19 relief funds.[49] The money from Washington comes via 356 categorical grants (for specific purposes) and block grants (groupings of grant programs in a functional area such as health or community development). Other dollars flow directly to the research universities, particularly the University of Chicago, the University of Illinois, and Northwestern University via agencies such as the National Institutes of Health, the National Science Foundation, and the Department of Defense.

Federal aid to the states has been shifting, however. General, unrestricted revenue sharing with the states was terminated in 1980 and for local governments in 1986. There were reductions in numerous categorical aid programs to the states during the Carter and Reagan administrations in the late 1970s and early 1980s. But there have been massive infusions of federal dollars to Illinois since the late 1980s to match state dollars for the rapidly expanding federal-state Medicaid program, which provided health coverage for 2.5 million of Illinois's 12.8 million residents in 2007. In 2022 and 2023, state and local governments received billions in aid from the federal government to help recover from the COVID-19 pandemic.

Although the amount of federal monies that come to the state is huge, the state ranks forty-fifth among the states in the amount of federal aid it receives on a per capita basis. In 2018 Illinois received $7,006 per person, significantly below the national average of $10,077 per person and far below the amount received by other big states such as New York ($8,972) and Florida ($9,073).[50] Illinois also consistently sends more tax dollars to Washington than it receives back. This is all the more reason that the state's political leaders feel pressure to increase Illinois's slice of federal funding.

Several factors explain the state's low ranking in terms of federal largesse. First, state social service program expenditure dollars are often matched by the federal government on formula bases—the more the state spends, the greater the match in federal dollars. In 2018, Illinois state and local governments spent

$1,681 per person (including federal dollars) on public welfare programs, whereas New York spent $3,624 and California, $2,840.[51]

Illinois, along with New York and California, receives the lowest percentage match from the federal government for the immense Medicaid program, which provides healthcare for low-income residents. Because of a formula created in 1965 that was based on the wealth of the state and welfare needs at that time, Illinois receives only a 50–50 match from the federal government for Medicaid, while neighboring Indiana and Iowa receive 63 cents for each 37 cents expended by those states. If Illinois received the match of these neighbors, it would generate about $2 billion more in federal funds per year from that program alone. Because of the huge cost to the national government in increasing the match for states such as Illinois, New York, and California, even Illinois's well-placed members of Congress have been unable to achieve a higher federal match. The federal stimulus funding from the American Recovery and Reinvestment Act of 2009 temporarily increased the reimbursement rate for Illinois to 61 percent but that was short-lived.

Other factors include transportation and military expenditures. Illinois has a rich highway network, yet it ranks lower in miles of highway per person than sparsely populated states in the West. Illinois also has fewer military installations than do a number of many southern and coastal states, so it receives fewer dollars than many states to support children of these installations in local schools.

With structural factors such as these working against the state, Illinois officials are expected to devote a significant part of their time to winning projects and funding for the state. For example, the Illinois congressional delegation holds monthly luncheon meetings that are chaired by Senator Dick Durbin. The delegation works on a bipartisan basis to lobby for projects for their state. Illinois governors maintain a state office in Washington for the same purpose, as does the City of Chicago. Many smaller cities and entities such as hospitals retain lobbyists in Washington as well to seek funding from the hundreds of grant programs sprinkled across the federal agencies as well as from special project "earmarks" of funding sponsored by individual members of Congress.

Friends in High Places

The most significant factor in external relations is the human one. Simply put, a state that provides effective political leaders will do better in Washington than one that does not. Considering its size, Illinois has not supplied many presidential candidates. Prior to the 2008 election of Barack Obama as president,

Institutions

one other Illinois resident, Abraham Lincoln, was elected president, defeating a fellow Illinoisan, Stephen A. Douglas, in 1860. Governor Frank O. Lowden was a leading candidate for president in 1920, losing out to Warren G. Harding at the Republican convention. Another governor, Adlai E. Stevenson, was the unsuccessful Democratic candidate for president in 1952 and 1956. (Ronald Reagan lived in Illinois until age twenty-two, but was a resident of California when he ran for president.)

However, Illinois has played an important role in presidential elections. In 1960, John F. Kennedy narrowly defeated Richard M. Nixon in Illinois on the strength of Richard J. Daley's organization. Daley knew that the downstate vote would be pro-Nixon and that he had to deliver a surplus of four hundred thousand or more votes to put his man in the White House. That was a tall order, even for Daley. "At no time . . . had the Democratic ward bosses been subject to the pressure he [Daley] applied for Jack Kennedy," wrote television commentator Len O'Connor. "There was not the slightest doubt in the minds of the ward bosses, in advance of the 1960 election, that the man who failed to deliver a massive vote was going to be permanently maimed politically."[52] Every vote counted. Daley delivered a plurality of 456,312 votes in Chicago, and Kennedy squeaked through by a margin of 8,858 votes out of 4.65 million cast. In appreciation, Kennedy was always responsive when Daley called for help.

Illinois is at the heart of a sticky web of governments. The federal and local governments constrain, support, complement, and frustrate the state government. Each level of government—federal, state, and local—tries to maximize and apply financial resources to achieve its respective objectives.

PART III
POLICY

.

10

BUDGETING, TAXING, AND SPENDING IN ILLINOIS

The Illinois state budget is a plan for spending scarce financial resources, including revenues from taxes, fees, lottery profits, riverboat casinos, recreational cannabis, interest income, the federal government, and borrowed money. The budget reflects, in effect, an allocation of public values. Each spending item competes with all others because the dollars available are always scarce relative to demand. Aid to college students competes not only with spending for prisons and county fairs but also with programs for mentally disabled adults and poor children.

Elected officials, who often want to be reelected, like to do things *for* people, as in spending on programs that would appear to benefit people, but they don't like to do things *to* people, as in taxing them more to pay for the programs. Thus, budgets are difficult to balance.

In 2023, according to statista.com, federal (national government) spending equaled 36 percent of our nation's gross domestic product (GDP). Add to that the approximately 10 percent of GDP represented by state and local government spending, and we appear to be edging toward half of all our annual national economic product (value of goods and services) flowing through our governments. We're actually closer to four in ten dollars of GDP flowing through governments, as about one-quarter of state and local spending comes to the states and localities comes from the federal government, and you should not count that as spending twice. Any way you look at it, government is really big business.

Where Does the Money Go in Illinois, and Where Does It Come From?

Figures 10.1 and 10.2 are pie charts that represent spending shares (termed appropriations in Illinois budget making) and the revenues to pay for the spending. We use the FY2020 budget for Illinois, because the pandemic started late in that fiscal year, when the national government began infusing extraordinary amounts of money on a temporary basis into state and local governments, to protect the citizenry and stimulate the economy. Thus, the budgets for 2021 to 2023 (the year this book went to press) are atypical.

The nearly $77.8 billion budget for FY2020 represented about $6,000 *per person* in Illinois and obviously has major impact on the lives of residents. For example, Medicaid is the federal-state program that provides healthcare and nursing home services for more than 3 million generally low-income Illinois citizens (out of nearly 13 million total population). In 2020, this program absorbed almost one-third of the total state budget, at a cost of $24 billion, or almost $8,000 *per beneficiary* on average. Almost 2.6 million students were enrolled in school in Illinois in 2020, from pre-K all the way up through two-year or four-year public and private colleges and universities, seminaries, and technical schools, at a total cost to the state of $21.5 billion, or about $8,360

2020 Illinois state government revenues, all funds

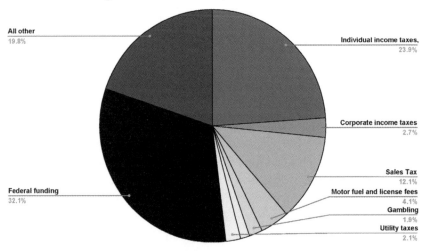

Figure 10.1. Revenues. Note: "All other" includes hundreds of fees, licenses, and small revenue sources. Source: FY 2020 Illinois State Budget, https://budget.illinois.gov/budget-books.html.

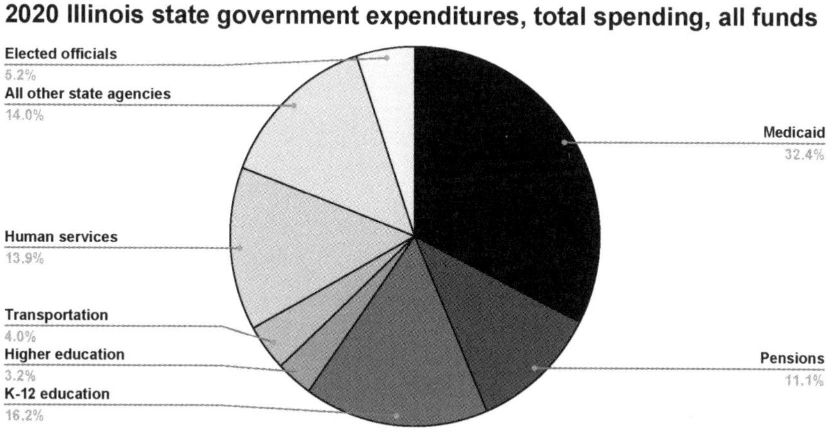

2020 Illinois state government expenditures, total spending, all funds

Elected officials
5.2%
All other state agencies
14.0%
Human services
13.9%
Transportation
4.0%
Higher education
3.2%
K-12 education
16.2%
Medicaid
32.4%
Pensions
11.1%

Figure 10.2. Expenditures. Source: FY2020 Illinois State Budget, https://budget.illinois.gov/budget-books.html.

per student.[1] Healthcare and education together represent more than half of all state spending.

There have been dramatic changes over the past half century in the allocation of our values, or priorities, as can be seen in figure 10.3. From 1970 to 2020, Medicaid costs *per capita* (all citizens), and adjusted for inflation, have increased more than ten times, from $165 per person to $1,937. At the same time, annual spending for pensions for our state public employees has risen almost as dramatically, from $64 to $664 per every Illinois citizen. It would appear from the bar chart that funding for our public colleges and universities has suffered significantly as a possible result, on a per capita basis, adjusted for inflation, from $455 to $188 per capita.

Smaller groups of state government "beneficiaries" absorb even larger amounts per person. For example, Illinois had over 30,400 male and 1,700 female incarcerated prisoners in June 2020, and more than 26,400 were on supervised parole, at a cost in state budget dollars of $1.5 billion, or about $25,600 per adult inmate.[2]

Until 2021, the Illinois state budget had been plagued for decades by what economists call a "structural deficit," that is, perennial increases in spending at rates higher than the annual growth rate of revenues. This is a deficit that occurs without adding any new programs. From 2002 to 2021, the net assets (total assets [dollar and capital resources] minus liabilities) of the State of Illinois declined from negative $5.7 billion to negative $199.0 billion, an asset decline of more than $10 billion a year on average, a negative amount equal to about twice that of the total budget of the State of Illinois for 2021.[3]

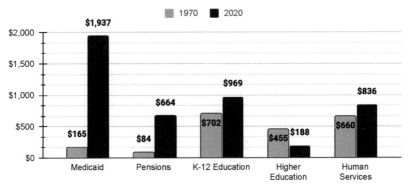

Per Capita Spending by Illinois state government

Selected major categories

Source: Annual Illinois State Budgets, respective years; some calculations by authors

Figure 10.3. Per Capita Spending. Notes: 1. 1970 figures inflation adjusted to 2020. 2. Year 2020 used rather than 2023 because the pandemic of 2020 resulted in dramatic, temporary increases in federal funding to state governments, which are unrepresentative of normal years 3. Over the decades of this chart, federal funding for the Medicaid program in Illinois has varied, from 50 percent of the total in the early decades of the chart, to as much as 60 percent during the 2020–22 pandemic.

How could the state get so far behind? Because *rates* of growth for major state programs are generally higher than those for state revenues, and because of understandable reluctance on the part of governors and legislators to increase taxes. For example, pension obligations and employee health benefits have been growing at about 12 percent per year for some years and Medicaid has grown at a rate of about 9 percent per year. Unfortunately for the state budget, state revenue growth has been about 4 percent per year on average.[4] Thus, the structural deficit.

In the short term, these deficits can be hidden by underfunding long-term obligations to the state's pension and healthcare systems. In other words, because future retiree benefits don't have to be paid for *this* year, state government can appropriate (invest) less this year than will be needed to pay future obligations.

From 2020 to 2023, the federal government injected about $26 billion into Illinois state and local governments via numerous programs.[5] This unprecedented infusion of federal government pandemic stimulus funds to Illinois state and local governments alleviated some of Illinois state budget woes, in the short term. The authors sense, however, that once the pandemic stimulus "pig" has worked its way through the government python, Illinois will once again face its old structural deficit, which will ultimately result, we predict, in either, or both, budget reductions or tax increases.

The Illinois Revenue System
and the Search for Pain-Free Revenues

Governments basically tax what you own (property), buy (sales), and earn (income). In addition, state and local governments levy literally hundreds of fees on licenses and government services. In Illinois, the tax on property is reserved for local governments, especially public schools, and the tax generates, at $33.8 billion in 2020, significantly more than any other tax source. The revenue budget pie for Illinois government (excluding the state's local governments) in figure 10.1 shows that the tax on individual citizen incomes is the largest single source of state revenue for Illinois. The state tax on sales generates only half as much, which is a lesser slice of the pie than in many states. This is because Illinois taxes sales on goods such as automobiles and appliances, yet has resisted imposing taxes on scores of services, such as lawyers and barbers. Since World War II, sales of services have grown faster than those of goods, with services in 2021 representing 83 percent of our nation's gross domestic product, and goods representing just 17 percent.[6]

Twenty-seven taxes are listed in the 2021 edition of the *Illinois Tax Handbook for Legislators*, including taxes for car rentals, pinball machines, and pull-tab and jar games.[7]

As noted at the beginning of the chapter, elected officials enjoy doing things *for* people such as appropriating money for programs that benefit voters. They do not like to do things *to* people, in particular to levy taxes on them. But the bills have to be paid and the operating cash budget has to be balanced. To meet this responsibility, public officials search for revenues that are either: voluntary payments, such as taxes on gambling, tobacco usage, and in 2019, recreational cannabis; or least painful (for example, a quarter-percent increase in the sales tax would add only a small amount to each purchase); or tied to use of a product (such as the motor fuel tax), and nontax revenue, such as state lottery tickets (thirty-three cents of each dollar gambled is net profit for the state).

The state's five public employee pension systems (teachers, universities, state employees, judges, and legislators) represent another source of funding for future beneficiaries that in the past has been diverted to meet current spending needs. Painless, in the short term; costly in the future. For decades, Illinois officials put less money into investments than would be needed in the future for pension payments. As a result, according to Pew Charitable Trusts, in 2019 Illinois had developed unfunded pension liabilities equal to 19.4 percent of the state's annual personal income, higher than for any state but New Jersey (20.4 percent), and a nationwide average of 6.8 percent. By another measure, unfunded state pension liabilities (not counting those for Illinois's 8,923 local governments) is the equivalent of $11,600 per person in the state.[8]

The pension funds currently have balances large enough to pay for the current year's obligations, so it is possible to reduce the annual appropriation for pensions without shorting anyone *at the moment*. This often happens when money is tight, as in the FY1991 budget, when the legislature authorized the Chicago Board of Education to take $66 million that was to be invested in the Chicago teachers' pension system and appropriate it instead for teachers' salaries.

Because of this history of underfunding, in order to rebuild its pension funds asset base while also meeting its annual payouts to retirees, Illinois has had to devote about 13 percent of its annual total budget to pension funding, which is about twice what it would otherwise need to do.

Fees for services and for the privilege of doing business make up another significant category of revenue, including university tuition charges, drivers' licenses, carnival amusement ride inspection fees, fishing and hunting licenses, and professional licenses for physicians, architects, and beauticians. In 2020, the State of Illinois collected $11 billion from 1,598 fees administered by eighty-five agencies, which represented about 14 percent of overall revenues.[9] If fees were tracked as a single revenue source, they would represent more revenue than that generated by the Illinois state sales tax.

The issue of who should pay the taxes, and thus how much of their respective income and wealth, becomes complicated. Should governments impose taxes on property, income, goods, services, gasoline, utilities, or the "sins" of consuming tobacco and alcohol? If it is to be property, should farmland, residential, and business property be treated the same, or differently, and if so, why? Who should bear the greater burden—individuals or corporations, the wealthy, middle class, or poor? These are tough questions for governors and lawmakers who want to be reelected. For example, if you tax business too heavily, businesses might leave the state. If you tax wealthy individuals at a higher rate, they too might flee to other states.

The Other Budget: Capital Projects

In addition to expenditures for immediate purposes, the state makes long-term investments in highways, university laboratories, wastewater treatment plants, prisons, and other projects that will last many years. The Illinois capital budget for 2023 authorized $45 billion for various projects, most of them for transportation projects, an amount equal to almost one-quarter of all proposed appropriations dollars. Only about one-quarter of this amount was actually spent in 2023, as most infrastructure projects require several years to complete, yet the total project amount is appropriated, that is, authorized to be spent.[10]

Just as individuals pay for a home with a mortgage, the state borrows money and retires the debt by paying off principal and interest over the course of ten to thirty years. Illinois has authorized a number of agencies to borrow money by issuing bonds. The primary authorities are the Capital Development Board and the Illinois Finance Authority. Others include the Metropolitan Pier and Exposition Authority (for Chicago's McCormick Place and Navy Pier) and the Sports Facilities Authority (which built the White Sox stadium).

Bonds cannot be sold to investors without assurances that streams of revenue are in place to pay the principal and interest for up to thirty years. Although capital spending is separate from operating expenses, the two budgets are nevertheless in competition because state borrowing generally requires the identification of a revenue source or sources to make principal and interest payments.

Sometimes the revenue source is insufficient. For example, a special tax on used cars was to be a primary source of revenue for the Build Illinois bonds, but in FY1990 that source generated only $41 million of the $83 million needed. As a result, an additional $42 million in general revenues had to be deposited in the Build Illinois account, money that might otherwise have been available for education or child care services.[11] Similarly, in 2007 the Metropolitan Fair and Exposition Authority took $30 million from general revenue funds to meet annual payments on bonds because the designated revenue sources for new capital projects of the authority, such as the new McCormick Place West building, were inadequate.[12]

Budgeting: Simple Math, Difficult Decisions

According to Robert L. Mandeville, budgeting is a simple five-step process: (1) find out what you have in the bank; (2) estimate your receipts for the budget period; (3) decide what you want to have in the bank at the end of the budget period; (4) subtract item 3 from the sum of the first two items; and (5) allocate the remaining amount among programs. "That's all there is to it. That's the truth," says Mandeville, who served as director of the Bureau of the Budget from 1977 to 1990.[13] Simple, perhaps, but never easy, because of step 5.

There are several fundamental points to keep in mind about budgeting in Illinois. First, major changes are difficult because most funding is already committed. This means that unless some new revenue stream is available, most of the spending for the coming year's budget will mirror that of the previous year. Education, transportation, healthcare, assistance to the poor and abused, and state agencies consume most of the budget every year and leave little room for dramatic changes.

Second, demands will nearly always outstrip resources; and third, the growth generated primarily by inflation will not be enough to cover any new programs as well as the increased costs of ongoing programs caused by that inflation.

A balanced budget is required by the Illinois constitution, which says that "proposed expenditures shall not exceed funds estimated to be available for the fiscal year as shown in the budget."[14] Budgeting frustrates a new governor, who wants to do for his constituents all the good things he might have promised in his campaign. Coauthor Nowlan recalls a scene from the transition to office in 1976 of James R. Thompson, who had been holding sessions with his budget director, Robert Mandeville. As they prepared to review the education budget, Thompson looked at Mandeville and said, with some exasperation, "Okay, Bob, how much *can't* I spend today?"[15]

There are always more demands than available resources can satisfy. Full funding of the pension systems is a noble goal. To take funding from the poor to pay for state pensions is not. Restructuring Medicaid to make poor children healthier is a noble goal. A cut in funding for poor children's education to fund Medicaid is not.[16]

Under this pressure from areas of growing need, lawmakers must seek other ways to fund their pet projects, and they often latch onto inflation-induced "natural growth" in revenue. This growth is the revenue increase that occurs even when there is no change in the tax rates. It is generated primarily by inflation and generally does not represent a windfall, for the costs of salaries and healthcare and goods purchased by state government also increase with inflation.

Although it might seem self-evident that natural growth is not a dependable source of new money, Thompson in his FY1989 budget book listed twenty-one new initiatives adopted either by the legislature or by administrative action of the governor since 1985. They included education reforms, expanded probation services, expanded circuit breaker (property tax) relief for the elderly, searches for missing children, AIDS research, and asbestos removal in schools.[17] There had been little change in the state's tax structure during this period; Thompson and the legislature were counting on inflation-induced natural growth to carry the budget forward. Finally, in 1989 the legislature found it necessary to increase the individual income tax from 2.5 percent to 3 percent to accommodate increased spending for new programs and growth in Medicaid and education.

Natural growth might suffice to fund new initiatives if simultaneous minor cutbacks in various program areas were considered a normal part of budgeting. In reality, the opposite is true: the tendency is for programs to cost a little bit more each year. Governors, budget staff, and legislative leaders basically accept what was spent during the preceding year, on the assumption that it was reasonable—after all, they voted for it. Then they focus on how much of an increase, or increment, is proposed for the coming year. Specialists in public management have criticized this "incremental" approach as less than rational, saying that it lacks comprehensiveness and leaves most of the budget outside review. They often call for "zero-base budgeting," in which every budget line item—thousands of them—is reviewed every year, from the base up.

Yet the time pressures of an annual budgeting cycle and the size and complexity of the budget make the zero-base approach almost impossible. As budget analyst Raymond F. Coyne pointed out, incremental budgeting has the benefit of limiting political conflict.[18] If the whole budget were opened up, and the budgeteers were allowed to start from scratch each year, they might feel compelled to joust over the whole budget pie, rather than just the small slice represented by the increment. It would be politically treacherous and impractical, given the limited legislative session time available, and thus it is almost never done.

Workings of the Governor's Office of Management and Budget

After the annual budget process is complete, the chief executive has the responsibility of matching spending with revenue. Budgeting at this stage is basically cash management, and it is a challenging task. The monthly balance in the state's general funds "checkbook" has often fallen into the fiscal "danger zone" of less than $200 million, sometimes for a year or more at a time. Management of the budget falls to the Governor's Office of Management and Budget (GOMB), which must ensure that budget commitments are being met, and to the state comptroller, who holds the state checkbook and must often delay payments of valid claims to avoid overdrawing the accounts. As former budget division chief Craig Bazzani put it: "The [office of management and budget] is also something of an 'efficiency engineer.' As a protagonist in the budgeting process, it is GOMB's job to help departments find a more efficient way to 'build a better mousetrap'—that is, educate more students at less cost, improve management, or save more agricultural land."[19]

The checkbook balance of cash on hand generally gives a misleading picture of the state's fiscal situation because the balance is subject to manipulation.[20] For example, the governor and his GOMB often find it necessary to hide the true budget deficit situation by delaying payment requests for nursing homes, hospitals, and school districts and by speeding up collections of certain taxes. In

"AW, THAT'S NOT A GHOST—THAT'S SOMEONE OPENING THEIR PROPERTY TAX BILL".

Figure 10.4. "That's Not a Ghost." Cartoon by Bill Campbell.

2008, for example, healthcare providers were owed $3.8 billion that was deferred from one fiscal year to the next.

Political Dynamics of Budgeting

In the 1960s the political scientist Thomas Anton saw budgeting in Illinois as a ritualized game in which each interested party played its part and, if all went well, everyone came out a winner.[21] The agencies would request more than they needed, and the governor and legislature would each make some cuts. The final budget would provide the agencies what they actually wanted—sometimes more than expected—and the politicos could claim to have cut the budget.

Players in the budget game still anticipate the actions of others. Since the 1960s, however, the process has become more professional with the addition of GOMB, legislative staffing, the Illinois Board of Higher Education (which recommends university budgets), and the reduction veto provided to the governor by the 1970 constitution. As a result, the state agencies probably have less influence than they had in an earlier era, and the legislature has become more involved in the substance of budgeting negotiations.

In simplified form the process is as follows. State agencies make budget requests to the GOMB, which makes its recommendations for each agency to the governor. If an agency head feels strongly that the budget level recommended by GOMB is unreasonably low, the agency head might be able to appeal directly to the governor, who resolves the differences. The final budget document, often up to seven hundred pages in length, is presented in March via a formal budget address by the governor to the General Assembly.

Throughout the process, the interest groups and beneficiaries of state spending press their claims. If budget recommendations are seen as inadequate, cries of catastrophe erupt. University presidents cite a brain drain of faculty who are leaving for higher salaries elsewhere. The rhetoric often heats up, as in this 1989 statement in a press release from the state school superintendent: "School districts are going down the financial tube; Chicago school reform is jeopardized before it gets underway. We are in disgraceful condition and it's time for the people of this state to say we've had enough."[22]

Governors generally dominates the budget process because they construct the original budget and later can impose line-item and reduction vetoes on spending requests outside the budget that are sent to them by the legislature. The legislature has, however, shown the capacity to impose its own spending priorities. In 2007, the legislature basically took over the task of crafting a final state budget, although the governor had the final word. In a different era, Republican governor Bruce Rauner (2015–19) was at constant war with the Democrat-controlled legislature throughout his term. Rauner refused to sign an annual budget during his first two years in office. Several state agencies, including public universities, went without annual funding during that period. Unpaid bills reached more than $15 billion. The legislature finally enacted a tax increase over the governor's veto. Budget conflict is expected, yet the failure to adopt a budget for two years in a row was unprecedented nationally.[23]

Possibly because the rank-and-file lawmakers sometimes chafe at playing such a small role in budgeting, legislative leaders in the 1990s began a program of "member initiatives," in which each lawmaker was allocated an amount of money for projects identified by the lawmaker for their district. This is similar to the ear-marking process in the federal budget. The amount of money, often $1 million or more per lawmaker, has varied from year to year, generally depending upon the funds legislative leaders feel is available. The member initiatives also increase the power of leaders over their members because lawmakers can be punished or rewarded by the allocation process.

In summary, the budget represents accommodation. Participants apply their power and influence, such as expert information, a key vote in committee, veto action, campaign support, or editorial comment. Yet rarely does any participant or group get all that it wants, whether agency head, GOMB analyst, governor, lawmaker, legislative staffer, or interest group. Nevertheless, the final appropriations, after the legislature responds to the governor's vetoes, roughly approximate the will and values of the political society of Illinois.

Politics of Taxation

As the old saw goes, "The only good tax is one you pay, and I don't." In 1978, Jim Thompson was running for his second term as governor, shortly after a property tax limitation known as Proposition 13 was adopted by California voters. To show his concern about taxes, he led a petition drive to put a nonbinding advisory referendum on the ballot. This so-called Thompson Proposition asked voters whether they favored ceilings on their state and local taxes. As might have been expected, 82 percent favored the idea. Yet no ceilings ensued from either governor or legislature.

Voters can be convinced to support tax increases, though it often takes time. In elections held between 1972 and 1993, one-half of all referendums for school tax rate increases were ultimately passed by the voters. Many rejected issues went back to the voters again and again until they were ultimately passed.

Illinois state finance is a cyclical affair, according to budget expert Michael D. Klemens: "Spending increases have preceded gubernatorial elections; then tax increases followed elections. Tax increases have prompted spending increases; then revenues have lagged and more tax increases are needed."[24] In a display of candor, Governor Thompson acknowledged in 1987 that he had signed into law dozens of programs without funds to pay for them:

> Many of them I signed against the advice of my director of the Bureau of the Budget [Robert Mandeville], who for 11 years has stood for fiscal integrity and 'don't sign a bill unless you can pay for it, regardless of how good it is.' And I'd say to him, 'Doc, this is a good idea.' And he'd say, 'You can't pay for good ideas with no money.' . . . And I'd sit and say to myself, well, maybe the economy will pick up. Maybe they'll [the legislature] do the right thing next year. Maybe prosperity is around the corner. Maybe, maybe, maybe should have listened to Dr. Bob.[25]

In part because of his actions, Thompson sought tax increases in 1987 and 1988, each time leading the ritual dance with legislators and interest groups. For two years, the legislature rejected the governor's pleas for more revenue.

In 1989, however, following the lead of Speaker of the House Michael Madigan, lawmakers enacted a temporary 20 percent increase in the state income tax. It was less than Thompson wanted and in a different format, but he signed the bill and moved on, the crisis averted for the time being.

As noted above, in 2018 the legislature enacted, over the governor's veto, an increase in the individual income tax rate from 3.75 percent to 4.95 percent.

In 2019, new governor JB Pritzker led an effort to put on the ballot a referendum that, if enacted by the voters, would authorize a graduated rate income tax, that is, higher rates on high incomes than on lesser incomes. Democrat billionaire Pritzker spent $56.5 million of his own money in advocacy for the "Fair Tax Amendment," as he styled it. Republican billionaire Ken Griffin also spent more than $50 million in opposition to the proposal, which was defeated, with only 45 percent of voters supporting the amendment.

For elected officials, raising taxes represents the most politically sensitive votes they make in office.

Politics of "Shift and Shaft"

As can be seen from the revenue budget pie in figure 10.1, about one-quarter of the Illinois state budget revenue comes as distribution from the federal, that is, national government. Similarly, big shares of local government revenue are provided by transfers from the state government.

The politics of fiscal (tax and spend) federalism (interactions among federal, state, and local governments) can be seen in large part as a serious game in which each level of government—federal, state, and local—tries to expand its authority over programs while inducing the others to pay for most of the changes. For example, through such education programs as the former No Child Left Behind Act, the federal government asserted extensive authority over local education, even though federal funding amounts to only about 10 percent of all spending by local public schools. The State of Illinois has also imposed mandates for the way its local schools must operate, while imposing the costs of compliance on local property taxpayers. Local government leaders are also skilled at playing the game. In 1993, municipal leaders negotiated an increase—from one-twelfth to one-tenth—in the share of state income tax revenues automatically distributed to cities and counties, thus reducing the amount available to be spent in the state budget. This game has been aptly labeled the politics of "shift and shaft."

One argument for shifting money from one government to another is that the receiving government can deliver the service more effectively. These monies can also act as a carrot to induce state or local governments to initiate or change programs. Prominent examples of the hundreds of federally supported but state-administered programs in Illinois include Medicaid, education, Temporary Assistance to Needy Families, and highway construction.[26]

Nevertheless, Illinois will continue to receive less from the federal government on a per capita basis than do most states, because many federal programs allocate funds on the basis of per capita wealth, with poorer states receiving more support. Being above average in wealth, Illinois receives less per capita for many programs. Illinois is required, for example, to provide 35 percent of the cost of the basic Medicaid program, whereas neighboring Indiana pays 22 percent and Iowa 27 percent.[27]

There is a close working relationship between Illinois and its local governments on matters of finance, with the state government collecting local sales taxes and distributing them back to the local governments; the state also shares with local governments part of the income and motor fuel taxes. Major state appropriations are made for local education and social services; about 60 percent of all state expenditures are distributed in the form of grants and awards to school districts, nongovernment social service agencies, and individuals.[28]

The single largest source of revenue for Illinois governments continues to be the local property tax. In 2020, the property tax generated $33.8 billion for local governments, more than was generated that year for state government by the personal income tax, the state sales tax, and lottery profits combined.[29] Schools receive 60 percent of total property tax revenues; municipalities about 20 percent; special districts, 10 percent; counties, 6 percent; and townships, 3 percent.

The property tax has been a revenue mainstay since the state and its local governments were established, and today Illinois relies somewhat more heavily on the property tax to fund local services than do most states. In 2019, the average residential property tax bill in Illinois was $4,942, with the highest average bills of $6,285 in Lake County, to the north of Chicago, and the lowest of $447 in Hardin County, in the far south of the state.[30] The great differences are largely a reflection of variations of wealth, in this case the overall market value of property, from county to county.

Heavy reliance on the property tax has caused problems. First, citizens consider the property tax the least fair tax in Illinois, according to an annual opinion survey by Northern Illinois University.[31] The tax is, for example, generally paid in two large lump-sum payments each year, which can mean two payments of up to $10,000 *each* (or more) on a $1 million home. Second, property wealth is not spread evenly across the state, as can be seen in the residential property tax bills noted in the paragraph just above. Third, property owners are often skeptical that their property is being assessed fairly in comparison with other similar properties.

Governors and lawmakers try to be sensitive to the impact that taxes might have on politically important groups such as senior citizens, and on the state economy. They do this by exempting persons from paying certain taxes they would otherwise have to pay. These exemptions, obviously popular with recipients, are called "tax expenditures" by public finance specialists, because they represent the expenditure, or loss, of tax revenue that would otherwise be generated for the state treasury. In 2019, tax expenditures in Illinois totaled $10.2 billion, or about one-eighth of the total all funds budget for that year. The exemption of all pension income from income taxation, at $2.8 billion in foregone revenue to the state, represented the largest tax expenditure.[32]

In each session of the legislature, several bills are proposed that would exempt certain services and economic development activities from taxation. The 2021 *Illinois Tax Handbook for Legislators* lists fifty-five items exempted from the sales tax, including newsprint and ink, coal gasification machinery, semen used for artificial insemination of livestock, and goods sold to not-for-profit music or dramatic arts organizations.[33]

During the same period, other taxes went up. To build and maintain the state's 137,000 miles of roads and 25,000 highway bridges, the state motor fuel tax on gasoline rose from 11 cents per gallon in 1983 to 20.1 cents in 1996, and to 39.1 cents in 2019, one of the highest rates in the nation.[34] The flat-rate income tax on individuals and corporations was increased in 1989 from 2.5 percent to 3 percent for individuals and from 4 percent to 4.8 percent for corporations. In 2019, Governor Pritzker and the legislature increased the flat-rate individual income tax rate to 4.95 percent, and to 7 percent for corporations.

In the quest for relatively painless revenue sources, policymakers in Illinois have been attracted by sin taxes. The state tax on cigarettes rose from 20 to 30 cents per pack in 1990, to 98 cents in 2002, and to $2.98 per pack in 2019.[35] The lottery was the big revenue success story of the 1980s. Created in 1974, it got off to a slow start, generating net revenue of only $33 million in 1979, but by 2022, with steady promotion and regular introduction of new types of game cards, the lottery was netting $833 million on sales of $3.4 billion annually. This was more net revenue than the amount brought in by the income tax on corporations.

Riverboat gambling was approved in 1989. In 2019 (before the pandemic), revenue from the ten riverboats (no longer all on rivers) to the state totaled $464 million, plus additional revenues for the municipalities where the boats were docked.[36] The "drop" (total amount of wagering) came to more than $1.39 billion in 2018, or $108 for every man, woman, and child in Illinois; this is a bit misleading, however, because each dollar bet returns about ninety cents on average, so the same dollar can be wagered several times, on a declining basis, before becoming lost.

Legal gambling does not come without other costs to the state. It is widely assumed that poor families spend higher percentages of their income than the wealthy on the lottery and other state-sanctioned games. Jack R. Van Der Slik contends that the biggest negative is that the state legitimizes the making of new gamblers: "The state's slick television ads sustain hope among many, especially the poor, of a big hit, a jackpot, and then let the good times roll. Forget hard work. Saving is for suckers. Why sacrifice for the future when the future is now? And, like alcohol, widespread gambling reveals more and more people for whom it is an addiction. What a regressive way to serve the public."[37] Indeed, state-authorized and -operated gambling is the only function of state government in which its citizens must lose overall for the state to win. (See chapter 11, "State Regulation of Our Behavior," for further discussion of gambling in Illinois.)

Is Illinois a High Tax State?

In 2019, Illinois total state and local tax revenue was $6,643 per capita, versus a national average of $5,679. Only ten states had higher per capita tax revenue.[38] As figure 10.5 shows, Illinois state and local taxes as a percent of personal income were below the national average in 1977, but have moved above the nation on that basis by 2020.

The local property tax burden in Illinois as a percentage of gross state product is significantly higher than in all but ten other states, at 3.39 percent versus a national average of 2.74 percent. On the other hand, the Illinois state and local sales tax imposes less burden than in all but eight states, at 1.71 percent of gross state product against 2.06 percent nationwide. The property tax is the least popular of taxes whereas the sales tax is less objectionable, probably because it is generally extracted in small amounts per transaction.[39] Thus, while readers might think it logical for lawmakers to broaden the sales tax and reduce the property tax, efforts to do so have failed or, more often, simply not been tried. This appears to be the case because lawmakers think voters are highly skeptical that an increase in one tax would actually result in a reduction of another tax.

Advocates in Illinois for higher taxes seek to address education reform, healthcare, and infrastructure issues. There are equally intense opponents to tax boosts. Each side makes its arguments, one on behalf of improving work-force quality and social justice, the other in the interests of trying to maintain an attractive business climate.

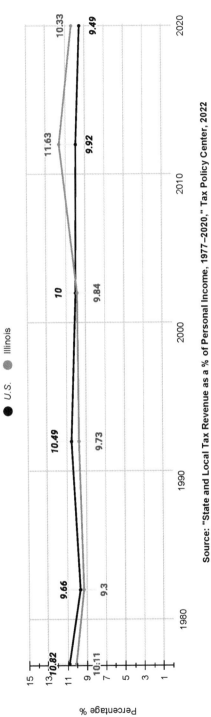

State & Local Taxes as a % of Personal Income
U.S. vs. Illinois, 1977–2020

● *U.S.*   ● Illinois

Source: "State and Local Tax Revenue as a % of Personal Income, 1977–2020," Tax Policy Center, 2022

Figure 10.5. State and Local Taxes as a Percentage of Personal Income. Source: "State and Local Tax Revenue as a % of Personal Income, 1977–2020," Tax Policy Center, 2022, https://www.taxpolicycenter.org/statistics/state-and-local-tax-revenue-percentage-personal-income.

Now, You Balance the Budget!

In figure 10.6, we offer an exercise for balancing the budget, using hypothetical figures, yet in the ballpark of reality. This proposed budget for FY2024 calls for spending $88 billion from all funds. Yet, proposed revenues are expected to generate only $83 billion. Make decisions below that will balance the budget, or at least come as close as you can. Consider yourself to be a member of the Illinois House who is seeking reelection in 2024.

The Illinois Budget Game
Task: Eliminate $5 billion deficit in proposed annual total state spending of about $88 billion.
Select among the following options, then total deficit reductions and any budget additions (Remember: You have primary and general re-elections coming up next year.)

Expenditure reductions/additions: $ change

Reduce spending for K-12 education, from $20 billion, or add spending   ____

Reduce spending for colleges and universities, from $3 billion   ____

Reduce spending for Medicaid (low income health care),
from $24 billion, or add spending   ____

Reduce spending for prisons, from $1.8 billion   ____

Reduce pension spending, from $10 billion (court says cannot cut for present
retirees and active workers, but tweaking possible, through buyouts, for
example, saving maybe $0.5 billion)   ____

Reduce "waste and corruption" (possible reductions, at most, of $0.5 billion) ____

Total expenditure changes (use minus sign for reductions) $ ____

Revenue increases:
Re-impose sales tax on food for home consumption, $1.5 billion   ____
Tax retirement income, $2.8 billion   ____
Eliminate 5% property tax credit on income tax. $0.5 billion   ____
Impose sales tax on nonprofit organizations, $0.4 billion   ____
Eliminate 70 sales tax exemptions, $3.2 billion   ____
Tax scores of services, as in Iowa, e.g. pet grooming, plumbing, $4 billion ____
Expand gambling, e.g. more casinos, sports gaming, more video gaming, $0.5billion ____
Increase individual flat-rate income tax from 4.95 to 5.95%, $4.0 billion ____
Increase corporate income tax from 7% to 8.6%, $0.5 billion   ____
Increase fees on hundreds of licenses, e.g. on driving, hunting, etc., $1.0 billion ____

Total revenue changes $ ____

**Total of actions to eliminate $5.0b deficit: budget cuts/additions + revenue
increases** $ ____

Figure 10.6. Budget Game.

11

STATE REGULATION
OF OUR BEHAVIOR

"Poor, nasty, brutish, and short"—that is life in the absence of government constraints on the actions of man, according to seventeenth-century English political philosopher Thomas Hobbes.[1] Americans cherish our freedoms to do, act, and say as we wish, yet these freedoms are not unlimited. The freedom to swing our fists stops just before the point of another's nose. Thus, our political society grants governments, often after lengthy conflict and disputes, the authority to regulate our actions. States and their local governments, not the national government, prescribe most of this regulation of what we can and cannot legally do.

The challenge is, we aver, for state and local governments to impose or intrude as lightly as possible on our freedom of action all the while maintaining, even enhancing, the public safety, health, and economic well-being of society, according to the predominant values of its citizens.

These values, or learned behaviors of a society, vary across our fifty states, and so the regulations of what we can do legally are somewhat different from state to state and among local governments.

The 2023 Illinois *Budget Book* lists fifty-five agencies of the governor. At least seventeen of these agencies seek to protect our safety and health. During the pandemic of 2020–23, the governor and his Department of Public Health obviously regulated our actions related to mask wearing and of places we could physically congregate. The Department of Financial and Professional Regulation examines, licenses, and oversees more than 1 million Illinois citizens who need state licenses to practice medicine and a number of healthcare professions, as well as architecture, plumbing, even boxing and wrestling; the department oversees 129 different professions and occupations. In addition, the Illinois secretary of state is responsible for licensing our right to drive and as well as the vehicles we drive.

Local municipalities and counties often enforce state regulations within their bounds via their public safety departments. In addition, localities typically impose (or some opt not to impose) zoning and land-use regulations, which can limit the types of construction of buildings, and of access to home ownership. For example, several high-income suburbs in the Chicago area limit the size of building lots to no less than three, or even five, acres.

Table 11.1 offers a display of how the top five states in population (Illinois is no. 6), and our neighboring states, regulate behavior across six important, mostly lifestyle issues. As of 2022, it appears that Illinois tends to side in its regulations of our behavior with liberal, Democratic states such as California and New York, and in contrast to conservative states like Texas and those on our borders, including Kentucky and Missouri.

These regulatory policies are hammered out by elected officials in our state and local governments. Elements at play in the politics of regulation include the political skills of the officials, lobbyists, and citizen groups; the intensity of feeling of proponents and opponents of a proposed regulation; campaign contributions; the influence, even power, of participant groups, such as organized labor and business; and of course, the respective, generally dominant social values that groups bring to a topic.

Following are several snapshots of the politics of regulation for abortion, recreational cannabis, and gambling, and of how Illinois regulations are often different from those of many other states.

Abortion. Throughout American history, the regulation of abortion has largely been a state function of its "police powers" (the fundamental power of the state to enact laws to coerce its citizenry for the public good). In 1973, however, in *Roe v. Wade*, the U.S. Supreme Court declared that a woman's right to abortion was a right conferred by the U.S. Constitution, which largely removed the states from a role in the matter. In 2022, however, in *Dobbs v. Jackson*, the nation's high court reversed itself, which returned the responsibility to the fifty states.

In the years leading up to the *Dobbs* decision, Illinois had become liberal on legal abortion policies and support. In the wake of the *Dobbs* decision, Illinois repealed a decades-old law that would have reinstated a ban on abortion—if

Table 11.1. State Regulation of Behavior 2022

State (in order of population)	No. of current laws regulating firearms?	Abortion access Y/N	Recreational cannabis Legal Y/N, Medical, M Recreational, R, or R/M if both	Online sports betting Legal Y/N; Pending, P	Ban on indoor smoking Y/N (#) is 100% smokefree in how many public places: bars, worksites, restaurants	Minimum wage amount *Effective 2023 †Federal amount, no state minimum
California	107	Y	Y (R/M)	N	Y (3)	$15.00*
Texas	18	N	N	N (P)	N	$7.25†
Florida	30	Y	Y (M)	N (P)	Y (2)	$12.00*
New York	75	Y	Y (R/M)	Y	Y (3)	$13.20 (fast food: $15.00)
Pennsylvania	37	Y	Y (M)	Y	Y (1)	$7.25†
Illinois	65	Y	Y (R/M)	Y	Y (3)	$13.00
Indiana	12	N	N	Y	Y (2)	$7.25
Missouri	2	N	Y (M)	N	N	$12.00*
Wisconsin	23	Y	N	N (P)	Y (3)	$7.25†
Kentucky	7	N	N	N	N	$7.25
Iowa	24	Y	Y (M)	N	Y (3)	$7.25

Sources: "State Firearm Laws," State Firearm Laws Database, last updated 2020, https://mail.statefirearmlaws.org/state-state-firearm-law-data; "After Roe Fell: Abortion Laws by State," Center for Reproductive Rights, last updated 2023, https://reproductiverights.org/maps/abortion-laws-by-state/?state=IN; "Where Marijuana Is Legal in the United States," *MJBizDaily*, last updated August 2023, https://mjbizdaily.com/map-of-us-marijuana-legalization-by-state/; "Where Is Online Sports Betting Legal in the USA?" World's Sports Network, last updated July 2023, https://www.wsn.com/sports-betting-usa/; "STATE System Smoke-free Indoor Air Fact Sheet," CDC, last updated March 31, 2023, https://www.cdc.gov/statesystem/factsheets/sfa/SmokeFreeIndoorAir.html; "Minimum Wage by State and 2023 Increases," Paycor, last updated July 10, 2023, https://www.paycor.com/resource-center/articles/minimum-wage-by-state/; State population numbers from "US States—Ranked by Population 2023," *World Population Review*, last updated 2023, https://worldpopulationreview.com/states.

Note: Generally speaking, the states that have more laws regulating guns tend to have stricter gun control overall. According to Giffords Law Center, an organization focused on ending gun violence, Illinois ranks eighth in the nation for the strength of its gun control laws.

ever the U.S. Supreme Court reversed itself on the *Roe v. Wade* decision. (These so-called "trigger laws" existed in other states as well, and caused some state bans to be automatically reinstated after *Dobbs*.)

Earlier, in 2017, Republican Governor Bruce Rauner signed legislation that expanded coverage under the state's Medicaid program to provide abortion care for low-income women. Since the federal government decades earlier prohibited the use of federal funds for abortion, Illinois pays the total amount of such procedures for Medicaid recipients. This action angered many fellow Republicans, and Rauner lost his subsequent bid for reelection, in 2018, in part at least because of this action.

Rauner's successor JB Pritzker and the legislature further expanded the state's abortion rights in 2021, by repealing a law that required a parent or legal guardian to be notified before an individual under the age of 18 could have an abortion.

The politics of these decisions are rather straightforward. Illinois is considered a "blue," that is, Democratic state, and this party is strongly supportive of a woman's right to legal abortion. The party's position is backed politically by Planned Parenthood, a national organization, and PersonalPAC, an Illinois political action committee. From its inception in 1979 until January of 2023, PersonalPAC was headed by Terry Cosgrove, who was highly effective at raising money for use in support of prochoice candidates for the legislature. In 2022, PersonalPAC contributed more than $750,000 in support of prochoice candidates for state offices.

The prolife, anti-abortion position in Illinois is staunchly supported by the Federalist Society and the Thomas More Society, the latter a Catholic nonprofit law firm based in Chicago. The Thomas More Society was in 2022 challenging the Illinois law that required health insurance plans, including those offered by Catholic organizations, to include abortion services in their policies.

Gambling. People love to gamble, or so it would seem. To illustrate, in 2022, each Illinois household (of, say, three people) on average plunked down more than $800 on Illinois Lottery tickets, a state government-operated enterprise (how $800 per household: $3.4 billion in lottery purchases divided by 4.25 million households). Even more dramatic, in the period January–October 2022, wagers on professional and college sports at Illinois gambling licensees (nearly all online) totaled more than $5 billion.[2]

Over the past century, gambling in Illinois has moved from illegal games in the back rooms and basements of taverns to the comfort of your home, where you can make legal (and illegal) wagers online in Illinois for your favorite sports teams. As the money involved has increased significantly in recent decades, the ownership of gambling venues in our state has evolved from individual, small-time roadhouse owners and regional equipment suppliers to global, multibillion-dollar companies.

The progression of legal gambling has been, in the following order: horse racing (1927)>lottery (1975)>riverboat casinos (1992)>land-based casinos (2019)>video gaming (2013)>online sports betting (2020). Of course, old-fashioned bingo parlors and even pull-tab and jar games are also legal, yet they generate minuscule revenue for the state.

Revenue to the state from gambling has increased from $672 million in 1975 (adjusted to 2022 dollars) to $1.89 billion in 2022.[3] In 2022, the lottery was still the highest-grossing revenue source from gambling in Illinois. However, video gaming and online sports wagering are expected to rival or surpass the lottery in revenue in years to come, because they are so handy, literally on your handheld smartphone.

According to the Illinois Gaming Board's revenue report of September 2022, 8,107 establishments across the state offered access to 44,110 video gambling terminals, an increase of 2,453 terminals since January 2022. Data from August 2022 show the state surpassing the $1 billion mark in gross video gaming revenue since its legal inception in 2009.[4]

And according to the *Chicago Tribune*, in 2022, driven largely by sports and video gambling, Illinois became second only to Nevada in gambling revenues.[5] The newspaper also reported that 4 percent of adults in Illinois are considered to have a gambling problem and that an additional 8 percent (761,000 residents) are at risk for developing such a problem.

Although nearly $2 billion in annual net state revenue from gambling is a big figure, it represents just over 2 percent of a state budget of $88 billion (as of 2023).

Gambling is the only state-sanctioned or operated activity in which citizen gamblers must lose overall for the state to achieve its objective of generating "painless" (nontax) revenue. For much of American history, gambling was seen by many, especially the churches, as a "sin," because of the societal costs of gambling in terms of addiction, loss of household income, and the resulting harm to family life. Persons of a more libertarian philosophy counter that individuals should have the freedom to do what they wish. And the gambling industry sees big profits in legal gambling; its campaign contributions are simply a cost of doing business.

Casino gambling was sold by the deep-pocketed gambling industry as economic development for depressed downstate communities. Video machine gambling was sold as a lifeline to bars and veterans' posts in the wake of the ban on indoor smoking in 2009, which dampened attendance in those venues, or so the proprietors contended. More gambling is also sold as an option preferable to extending the sales tax to services to fund government operations.

Ask any Illinois lobbyist, and they will tell you that the gambling industry is one of the most influential in our State Capitol. A number of state legislators have made their political livelihoods via receipt of campaign contributions from and, after their legislative service, in jobs as lobbyists for the industry. As head of the Illinois Church Action League Against Alcohol and Addiction from 1992 to 2022, Anita Bedell fought legal betting, and then marijuana. As a rather lonely one-woman band, her plaints ultimately fell on deaf ears. Known around the State Capitol as the "Church Lady," Bedell never wavered in her quixotic efforts to block the advances of legal gambling. But her reasoned arguments about the social costs of gambling were the equivalent of a popgun against a 155-millimeter howitzer that spewed cash all over the Capitol. Expect gambling in Illinois to be expanded in the years to come.

Marijuana. Legal use of a drug like marijuana, better known today as cannabis, offers an excellent illustration of how public attitudes, and thus the laws of governments, have changed over the course of American history. Prior to the twentieth century, opiates, cocaine, and cannabis were common ingredients in patent medicines and over-the-counter concoctions, such as cocaine in the original formula for Coca-Cola, and unregulated by governments.[6] Smoking marijuana leaf in cigarettes or pipes was largely unknown in the United States until it was introduced by Mexican immigrants in the first few decades of the twentieth century. About this time, and maybe encouraged in part by anti-Mexican xenophobia, at least with regard to cannabis, a crusade to rid the nation of drug and alcohol use swept the nation. In 1920, Americans prohibited legal use of alcohol by adoption of the Eighteenth Amendment to the U.S. Constitution. Between 1914 and 1925, twenty-six states passed laws prohibiting the growing and use of cannabis.

Prohibition of alcohol by the national government was abolished in 1933. But drugs continued to be generally under attack as bad for users and, because of the crimes that drug opponents associated with drug use, for society, and thus generally illegal. Presidents Richard Nixon (1969–74) and Ronald Reagan (1981–89) waged "war" on drug use. And even as of 2023, cannabis remains on the federal government's list of Schedule 1 drugs, defined as the most dangerous of the controlled substances, and is labeled as posing a severe risk of addiction, although many physicians don't believe that to be true.[7]

Views of cannabis use began to change in the 1960s, as smoking "dope" became increasingly popular on college campuses. Smoking seemed like harmless fun, and perhaps a little more fun because it was against the law.

Beginning around 1970, there were rather desultory, grassroots, and ineffective efforts for cannabis legalization in state capitals by pot users and NORML (National Organization for the Reform of Marijuana Laws). About 2010, and more important to legal use, entrepreneurs began to see huge, multibillion-dollar markets for marijuana from younger generations, which had been using the product extensively, if illegally, considering it less harmful than alcohol. So, contract lobbyists began representing growers and sellers in Springfield, and other state capitals.

In 2014, Illinois joined twenty other states in legalizing use of marijuana, or cannabis, for medicinal purposes. This was the gateway policy wedge into legal use for recreational purposes, which was enacted in 2019, always the long-term objective of the marijuana industry. Arguments for broader, recreational usage included the libertarian case for letting people do what they wish, and the significant "painless" revenue to the state from licensing and taxing the product. As of 2023, Illinois was the only state that has legalized marijuana for recreational use by legislative action, rather than by referenda of voters.

According to Stephen Siff, writing in 2014: "Although black Americans smoke pot at a nearly identical rate as whites, they are nearly four times more likely to be arrested because of it."[8] Because people of color had also been disproportionately incarcerated for possession and sale of drugs, leaders of minority communities in the legislature were concerned that mostly white businesses would come to dominate the profits from legal drugs. Thus, extensive efforts were made to ensure licenses for minorities for the growing and retail sale of cannabis. As of 2023, minorities continued to feel they were mostly being patronized, if not indeed pushed aside, in the marijuana business in Illinois. Prospective minority owners of cannabis dispensaries appeared to lack either the capital or the management experience necessary.[9]

Conclusion

As these very brief snapshots suggest, state legislative policies that regulate legal individual behavior are guided largely by a combination of (1) changing social values, (2) the infusion of investor money devoted to lobbyists and campaign contributions, and (3) the skill of legislative sponsors in persuading fellow lawmakers that behavior which for decades had been prohibited had become in the best interests of both individuals and the state.

12

EDUCATION

In the fall of 2022, the Illinois State Board of Education released its annual *Report Card*, the first full year of reporting since the COVID-19 pandemic began. The news was not good: scores on standardized tests were lower than prepandemic levels for all grades and all groups.[1] While students showed some improvement from 2021, clearly the pandemic and school shutdowns had taken a toll.

In March of 2020, the pandemic threw the entire state's educational structure into remote learning. After being told to close, public schools across the state took several weeks to rewrite lesson plans and redesign courses, and then, from preschool to graduate school, students were told to log in and complete their education from home. For the duration of spring semester 2020, schools remained online. The rigor suffered: it was impossible to transition eight-hour days in a classroom to eight-hour days in front of a screen, so times were shortened. Students were given instructions and told to do work from home, often requiring the assistance of parents who were working from home themselves.

Success assumed perfect access, but the truth was, going remote exposed a digital divide among students, with as many as half in some districts not having the equipment needed to do remote work. Districts scrambled to provide laptops and tablets, only to find that students didn't always have internet access. Even if they did, multiple students and adults in one house tested the best connections.

After a spring of stay-at-home orders and a summer limited by capacity restrictions everywhere in the state, in June of 2020 Governor JB Pritzker's office released reopening instructions for schools in the fall.[2] Students could attend on staggered schedules following safety guidelines like masking and social distancing called for by the Illinois Department of Public Health (IDPH). But he also gave districts the option to submit remote-only plans. Some districts, like Geneva on the western fringe of the Chicago suburbs, opted for the reopen. But many more opted to remain fully remote due to fears of a fall and winter surge by parents, teachers, and teachers' unions.

Pressure was mounting on the other side from parents who wanted their children back in school. They started showing up at school board meetings, also held remotely, to demand that all schools reopen. So in March of 2021, after the first dose of vaccine was made available to teachers and school personnel, most did reopen although there were remote options. Schools were still required to mask, use social distancing, and be on staggered schedules. The debate in communities then moved to masking. School board meetings in some areas became even more raucous and the municipal elections in April 2021 were, for many districts, a referendum on pandemic mitigations. For example, the consolidated school district in Wheaton, a conservative pocket in DuPage County that recently has been seeing some change, had ten candidates for four seats. Some were motivated explicitly by opposition to the mandates.

In the fall of 2021, schools returned to their prepandemic schedules. However, the mask mandate was now joined by an executive order that required teachers and staff to be vaccinated or undergo weekly testing. Most school personnel accepted this; however, some quit in protest. Parents and community members on both sides held rallies and formed groups. Parents in 170 of the school districts went further: they joined together in a lawsuit saying Governor Pritzker and the IDPH did not have the authority to do this. And in early February 2022, a Sangamon County judge agreed, issuing a temporary restraining order against mandatory masking, vaccinations, and testing. While the governor appealed the ruling, the Illinois General Assembly also backed off a rule that required masking, meaning the IDPH no longer had the authority to make these requirements.

The reactions were mixed. While supporters were elated, state officials were not. Said Governor Pritzker, "The grave consequence of this misguided decision is that schools in these districts no longer have sufficient tools to keep students and staff safe while COVID-19 continues to threaten our communities—and this may force schools to go remote."[3] Attorney General Kwame Raoul said, "This decision sends the message that all students do not have the same right to safely access schools and classrooms in Illinois, particularly if they have disabilities or other health concerns."[4]

As a result of the lawsuit, some schools dropped the mandates entirely and others kept them. Peoria's school district opted to keep the mandates, while Metro East schools dropped them. Elgin's school district opted to follow the mandates only if positivity rates were 8 percent or more. Chicago Public Schools decided to phase out masks by the end of February.[5] A week after the ruling an appeals court agreed, and Pritzker eventually decided not to go to the Illinois Supreme Court. Instead, mask mandates for the entire state were dropped at the end of February.

Throughout the pandemic and the politics, student learning was suffering. In 2019, 39.4 percent of third graders met or exceeded standards in reading on the state's mandated Illinois Assessment of Readiness (IAR) test, compared to 17.3 percent in 2022. For the math section of the IAR, these numbers were 32.9 percent and 19.5 percent respectively. Scores for highschoolers, who take the SAT, fell similarly. State Superintendent Carmen Ayala stated, "The student could have started the school year multiple years behind grade level or already been on grade level. Proficiency doesn't factor in that information."[6] But what the reader should take away is that the scores were already low to begin with, and couldn't afford to drop. The pandemic exacerbated an already tenuous state of education in Illinois when communities were forced to trade health and safety for proficiency at basic skills.

K–12 Education in Illinois

If politics is about who gets what, how, and why, then clearly education funding is political. Other educational issues that are clearly political include that of who governs education (the local, state, or national government), whether children and parents should have choices in the schools they attend, and whether all children should have equal educational resources.

Education is arguably the most important function of state and local government. Illinois enrolls more than 2.8 million students from prekindergarten through higher education, about one in every four of the state's 12.7 million people. Illinois governments spend about $38 billion annually, about 5 percent of the state's gross domestic product, on education.[7]

After decades in which Illinois ranked in the middle or lower rungs among the states in financial support for kindergarten through high school (K–12) public education, the state and local school districts showed strong support from the 1990s to 2022. In 1992, for example, Illinois state and local governments spent $4,866 per pupil versus a national average of $5,097 and ranked twenty-third among the fifty states. By 2008 Illinois spending per pupil had jumped to $11,428, fourteenth in the nation, and significantly higher than the national average of $10,259, and by 2018 that number and ranking jumped to $15,547 and eleventh, respectively.[8] The figure is misleading, however, because spending for Illinois schools is spread unevenly across property-rich and property-poor districts; as a result, two-thirds of Illinois school districts actually spend less than the national average.[9]

Since 1998, in contrast, state general funds spent for higher education actually declined until a historic increase in the 2023 budget, breaking a tradition in Illinois budgeting in which state increases for the two sectors of education went together.

These two issues—uneven spending for K–12 and weak support for higher education—are central to understanding the dynamics of the politics of education in Illinois, including regional differences, individualistic as opposed to collective approaches to spending, and state budgetary constraints imposed by the demands of healthcare and pension obligations.

"Fourth Branch" of Government

Many educators like to think of education as an independent fourth branch of government, and in many ways it is. In 1941, public university employees in Illinois were placed in their own civil service system, and job openings have been mostly exempt from the political patronage pressures that have affected state government otherwise. University, community college, and school employees have their own separate retirement systems, and on the organization charts, education is distinctly separate from other state agencies.

Governors and lawmakers traditionally viewed education as a major responsibility, but they did not consider it as important politically as transportation, regulation, criminal justice, and capital spending for a lawmaker's district. Since the 1970s, education has become more important politically because it has been linked to economic development and workforce quality. The growth since World War II of the twelve public universities and thirty-eight public community colleges has also made higher education a part of pork barrel politics because a lawmaker seeking reelection can pick up votes by delivering an auditorium or law school to their district. The trend toward full-time service by lawmakers has played a role as well. It increased the amount of time legislators and their staffs could devote to education and encouraged a tendency to keep constituents happy by addressing parochial needs rather than trying to institute comprehensive statewide change.

The Illinois constitution of 1970 devotes only three short sections to education, but a few clauses are often quoted and debated hotly. "The State shall provide for an efficient system of high quality public educational institutions and services," the constitution says, and the state "has primary responsibility for financing the system of public education."[10] Various critics have charged repeatedly that the state government neither provides an efficient system of high quality nor fulfills its primary responsibility for financing schools, which we discuss below. There is no mention of higher education in the state charter, in contrast to most other state constitutions.

Public school enrollment reached a high of 2.37 million pupils in 1972, declined to 1.93 million in 1994, and leveled off in 2022 at almost 1.9 million.[11] Minorities represented 28.8 percent of enrollees in 1981, yet two generations later, in 2022, nonwhites represented 53.3 percent. The largest growth was in Latino enrollment, which in 1981 represented about 20 percent, but in 2022 grew to about 27 percent. Black enrollment declined from about 20 percent in 1981 to about 16.5 percent in 2022. And now about 5 percent are Asian. Nearly three in every ten public school students came from low-income families in 1991; today half of our public school children are coming into classrooms from low-income homes.[12]

Many families eschew the public system. However, this number has been declining and the large role that private schools used to play has been shrinking greatly. Private schools enrolled 14 percent of all elementary and secondary students in 1994, but twenty-five years later in 2018 this number is less than 5 percent. This means the number of students enrolled in private schools has declined sharply from 320,290 in 1994 to 215,524 in 2018.[13] Much of the decline has been in Catholic schools: the Archdiocese of Chicago enrolled 98,000 students in 2008 but only about 50,000 in 2022.[14] Declining engagement with the Catholic Church and the sex abuse scandals explain much of this; however, in mushrooming suburbs public schools are thought to be good and private education unnecessary.

The number of families educating their children at home has grown sharply in recent years according to the National Center for Education Statistics. Nationally, it had almost doubled in 2018 to 1.7 million from about 900,000 in 1999.[15] If Illinois is close to the national average, the state would have about 70,000 students who are homeschooled. But Illinois requires families who homeschool only to register their children with their regional office of education; there is no assurance that all do so.

Illinois public schools are organized into a tangle of state, intermediate, and local administrative units. The governor appoints the nine-member board of education from the state's five appellate court districts; the Illinois State Board of Education (ISBE) in turn appoints a state superintendent of education who oversees a staff of five hundred in Springfield, Chicago, and Mount Vernon. In addition, forty-one independent, elected regional office of education superintendents throughout the state support the ISBE and operate their own independent programs in support of local school districts. At the local level, 852 school districts elect seven-member boards, which operate K–12, elementary, or high school districts.

In 1942 there were 12,000 elementary school districts in Illinois, most with a single one-room schoolhouse per district.[16] Some counties had more school board members than teachers. Increased state aid and persistent efforts by groups including the Illinois Farm Bureau cut the number of districts in half by 1948. Consolidation continued in the 1950s with the total falling to 2,000 districts, and this number fell to 852 in 2018, still more than every state except Texas and California.[17]

Who Governs?

"Local control" of schools is the mantra of elected officials at all levels, because that plays best with voters, who generally treasure their local schools. In fact, control of the schoolhouse is a continuing struggle among the local, state, and national governments, as well as the business community and education unions, among other interests. The reality of the situation is more complex. School districts, like any other local government, are creatures of the state, and have no inherent constitutional rights. And the federal government has been fond of passing sweeping legislation that looks like a mandate but instead uses the power of the purse to obtain compliance. Since early in the twentieth century, control of local schools has been a tug of war among local boards, the state, and the federal government.

The day-to-day activities and operations of schools are handled by the district, the head of which is the superintendent. The superintendent is selected by an elected school board from within that district's boundaries.[18] Although we have come to know school boards for much more, and many do much more, this is really their sole responsibility. The superintendent is responsible for budgets; the structure of the district; filling various other roles including principals of the schools, teachers themselves, support staff, and maintenance personnel; future planning; and much more. This is why the selection of this individual is so important. Attend a board meeting and you will see members approve contracts to renovate million-dollar buildings and hire a mom who will be supervising the lunch at an elementary school on a daily basis.

The State School Code, located in chapter 105 of the *Illinois Compiled Statutes*, used to be issued in a book of 600 pages of dense, small type on large double-columned pages. Today it can be found online, with the same small type, replete with over one hundred mandates about what the schools must do.[19] For example, instruction must be provided in patriotism, honesty, kindness, consumer education, the Holocaust, prevention of steroid abuse, and the avoidance of abduction. The state mandates that internet safety education be taught including "safe and responsible use of social networking websites, chat rooms, electronic mail, bulletin boards, instant messaging, and other means of communication on the Internet." Legislative efforts to remove instructional mandates, such as the requirement of four years of physical education in high school, are quickly buried as the unions rally teachers to the cause. Even efforts to reform education tend to create new mandates; the 1985 requirement of "learning assessments" and school improvement plans created lengthy exercises in paperwork that may or may not translate into better schools.

In the 2022 session of the legislature, lawmakers added several new mandates including instruction on mental health and illness, including where and how to find help. Also added was sexual abuse education, Asian American history, media literacy, and computer literacy.[20]

Who Pays for Schools? Local Wealth and Inequities

Illinois spends about $38 billion per year in total on its public K–12 schools, which as noted at the beginning of this chapter is significantly higher than the national average on a per-pupil basis.[21] Illinois is, however, significantly different from national norms both in where the money comes from and how the money is allocated. These differences have sparked decades-long efforts to reform the school finance system in Illinois, to no avail as yet.

School funding comes from state, local, and federal sources. In the 2019–20 school year, schools nationwide derived 47 percent of funding from state sources, 45 percent from local sources, and 8 percent from the federal government.[22] In fiscal year 2020, however, state revenues provided a much smaller share of school funding in Illinois than was the case in most states, with 27 percent coming from state sources, 65.9 percent from local school districts, and 7.1 percent from the federal government.[23] This share puts Illinois at last place for state funding.[24]

Property wealth, the primary source of local school revenue, is spread unevenly in Illinois. In 2020, median property taxes per household ranged from a high of $7,724 in Lake County to a low of $601 in Pulaski County (see figure

12.1). As a result, districts with high property wealth can fund their schools extravagantly without any state funding, while many property-poor districts fund their schools inadequately, even with significant state revenue assistance. For example, the per-pupil operating expenditures of elementary school districts in Illinois in 2020 ranged from $6,502 to $38,917, with a median of $13,437.[25] Even with the extremes taken out, some districts spent more than twice as much as others across the state. A random perusal of school districts using the Illinois School *Report Card* data shows that Aviston elementary school district in downstate Illinois spent $6,900 in 2020–21 while the Salt Creek district in suburban DuPage County expended $22,000, and Lake Forest High in Lake County spent $24,000 per pupil. (The Illinois School *Report Card* is an annual public report of test scores and related data about each public school in the state. The *Report Card* is easily available on the internet at the site of the Illinois State Board of Education.)

For many years, the Illinois state government attempted to reduce the differences between the richest districts and the poorer ones by funding the difference between what property wealth provides and a "foundation level" of support. Determining this difference was accomplished by means of a complicated formula. Property-poor districts, generally those downstate, could not reach the foundation level with their property taxes alone, so they received significant monies from General State Aid to bring their funding up to the foundation level. Property-rich districts, generally those in the Chicago suburbs, could generate more than the foundation level, often much more, from local property taxes alone, so they received little from the General State Aid formula.

In 1997 the state board of education created the Education Funding Advisory Board (EFAB), made up of school experts, for the purpose of establishing an objective level of per-pupil funding that would be adequate to provide a minimally acceptable education. The idea was that the "adequacy level" would become the foundation level, which would improve but still not eliminate the big disparities between the poorer and the richest districts.

But state aid fell short of the recommended adequacy level and state foundational levels never met this target simply because the state never paid its share. Speaking at a meeting of poor school districts, former University of Illinois education professor James Ward declared, "If you folks spent a couple of days in a top-flight school in DuPage or Lake Counties and saw what they had that you don't, there would be a revolution."[26] No revolution occurred during the 1980s, when the per-pupil spending gap was widening, for two basic reasons. First, the fragmented education community could not agree on a course of action. Second,

2020 Median household property taxes,
by county
Source: "Illinois Property Taxes Among Highest in Nation,"
Civic Federation, September 22, 2022

Figure 12.1. Median Household Property Taxes. Source: Civic Federation, "Illinois Property Taxes among Highest in Nation," September 22, 2022.

huge infusions of state funding for local schools would have been required to reduce the disparities significantly. The option of taking property tax money away from rich districts and giving it to poor districts was politically unacceptable. State lawmakers have appeared paralyzed by the magnitude of the action needed to reduce the variance, such as a shift in the primary mechanism for funding schools from the local property tax to state sources such as the income tax, which would require a major statewide tax increase.

Efforts have been mounted to reverse the inequities, but none has been successful. The legislature in 1985 tried to institute a no-pain approach by passing a law requiring that all profits from the Illinois lottery go to education. The law turned out to be the equivalent of a shell game: the lottery profits *replaced* general revenue funds rather than supplementing them. Poor districts have also tried to sue, saying the constitutional requirements of funding were not being met, but the courts would not take the case. Schools then tried to change the constitution in 1992 to assign the state "preponderant responsibility," as opposed to the current "primary responsibility," for financing local schools. But it was defeated when opponents successfully convinced residents it would lead to a doubling of taxes. Finally, in 1997 Governor Jim Edgar backed an increase in the income tax, but it also failed.

In 2008, the Chicago Urban League and the high-profile Chicago law firm of Jenner & Block tried the courts again by filing a suit aimed at overthrowing the longstanding variances in financing between rich and poor districts. The suit contended that the civil rights of minority groups were being violated because these groups tend to be in districts that receive less in total school funding than do the generally white, more affluent school districts.[27] After nine years of fighting, the ISBE eventually settled with the group as part of a complete overhaul of school funding.

This overhaul came in August of 2017, when Governor Bruce Rauner signed a bill that enacted Evidence Based Funding (EBF) to allocate new state resources to school districts. The General Aid formula was scrapped, and five grant programs—General Aid, three for Special Education, and one for English language learners—were combined into one.

EBF represents a radical shift from the old model in that it calculates an adequacy level for each district based on its own unique factors, instead of a one-size-fits-all per pupil amount. These unique factors can be the number of students in special education, English language learners, and from poverty level households. After the adequacy level is calculated, the district's resources are determined and then the amount of state aid needed to make up the difference. This allocation is for new state dollars only; a hold-harmless provision in the law states that no district will get less money as a result than it has in the past from the state. The law requires the state to add $350 million in new funding every year, to address more equitably the fact that some districts have far less property tax revenues than others. The schools with the most need are designated Tier 1, and are prioritized for funding. In the first year of the new law, 2017–18, over 89 percent of new funds went to Tier 1 schools.[28] Almost all these districts educate students in poverty and/or have overwhelmingly minority students.

This meant a lot for property tax-poor districts such as DeKalb, in western Illinois. "We received an additional $2.8 million because of that Tier-1 status, because the whole point is the districts that are in the lower tiers should get additional funding to get them to better adequacy," said Cindy Carpenter, who is the school district's director of business and finance.[29] Because of this, and the hold-harmless provision, Carpenter says DeKalb is better off.

And DeKalb is not alone. Many rural and poor districts that already had high tax rates could not tax themselves into better schools because the values of the properties just weren't there. East St. Louis, which has low property values and a student population with high need, is now funded at 96 percent of adequacy as a result of the new legislation.[30] Going into the 2022 school year, only two districts in the state of Illinois are below 60 percent funding adequacy: Washington Community High School District 308 in Tazwell County and Chaney-Monge School District 88 in Will County. This is compared to 300 districts under 60 percent when the formula was implemented.[31]

While great strides have been made, it will take a lot more money to bring all schools to adequacy. The state would need to add another $3.6 billion in order to bring all districts just up to 90 percent.[32] The unequal property tax system remains, with no reform in sight. And this is devastating for education, because this discussion should make clear that finance is the most intransigent education problem in Illinois. And while EBF shows promise, the problem still is that the majority of funds for K–12 schools comes from property taxes. With disparities in a state like Illinois where the highest median property tax bill is over ten times that of the lowest, without massive cash infusions, parity will never be reached.

Exacerbating funding obstacles is the fact that Illinois spends double the national average in administrative costs, $544 per pupil; the next highest is New York, at $349.[33] The multiplication of governments is to blame. Combining school districts or otherwise sharing administrative costs would save millions that could be used in the classroom.

Charter Schools

Illinois also has charter schools, which are publicly funded but privately managed and serve kindergarten through twelfth grade. Entities that wish to found a charter school are granted special "charters" by the state of Illinois for an initial five years, which then may be renewed in increments of ten years.[34] These charters lay out specific items for which the school will be held accountable, and the district can shut down a charter for not meeting them. Existing public schools may convert themselves to charters. Any child may attend, but preference is given to students in the geographic boundaries of the school, and if there are more applicants than seats a lottery is used. Because demand has been so high, lotteries are almost always used.

While these schools receive public funds, they do so only on a per pupil basis. The idea is that this will make them more competitive—they need to seek out students in order to remain financially afloat. They are bound by the same academic standards, but not the same laws and mandates that traditional public schools must follow. Students may meet for longer days or over the summer. A school may focus its curriculum on a specialty such as math and science or college prep or choose to do entirely home-based delivery. Ball Charter School in Springfield does not issue letter grades.

The Illinois legislature first passed legislation authorizing charter schools in 1996, and that same year the Peoria Alternative Charter School opened in Peoria. Caps are placed on the number of charters that may operate in the state of Illinois; however, demand has caused that number to increase over the past twenty-five years. Thus, while initial legislation only authorized a few dozen, today there are 137, of which 122 are located in the city of Chicago, for a total statewide enrollment of almost 55,000.[35]

Charter schools are controversial for several reasons. First, some people oppose a private organization running a public school that receives public money. Second, others say charter schools steal money from public schools. When that per pupil stipend is allotted to the charter, the district doesn't have it to do the things it needs. Third and related, many public schools argue charters siphon off the best students, leaving already underresourced public schools with student populations that are needier. Finally, charters, especially in Chicago, are seen as a primary way to circumvent the teachers' unions.

When Rahm Emanuel became mayor of Chicago in 2011, he campaigned on a promise to turn around Chicago Public Schools. He did this in part by fighting the Chicago Teacher's Union and committing to charter schools. In all, more than forty were opened under his watch—but it came at a cost of almost fifty public schools, mostly in Black neighborhoods.[36] The charters did not necessarily perform better than the public schools, and under his tenure the worst-performing school was a charter.

What's more, the city's largest charter school network, USCN, came under fire for improper use of funds. The United Neighborhood Organization, or UNO, is a nonprofit organization with the mission of improving the lives of Latinos in Chicago. In support of that, the UNO School Charter Network was founded in 1998 and eventually ran sixteen charter schools in predominantly Latino neighborhoods, the largest network in the city.[37] It was so powerful that its chief, Juan Rangel, was co-chair of Rahm Emanuel's first campaign for mayor. In 2013, however, a *Chicago Sun-Times* investigation revealed that many of UNO's top executives were spending lavishly on meals and trips of dubious need and contractors with insider ties were profiting—all at the expense of the taxpayer. Many of its top executives were ousted, and in 2014 it was charged by the SEC of defrauding investors (UNO also issued bonds to pay its bills). That case was eventually settled. The schools still operate, now under the name Acero.

It is not clear whether charters perform better than public schools. While charters are often in the list of best performing, it is worth remembering that they have disproportionately fewer of the district's students in need, and thus the averages are not truly representative. They are also in the list of worst-performing schools. In 2023, twenty-two of the thirty-five charter schools due for contract extension in Chicago were only granted two- and three-year contract extensions instead of the normal ten due to deficits in performance and financial management.[38] Most research actually shows that charters perform about the same as public schools.[39]

Unions Show Their Muscle

The strength of the teachers' unions should not come as a surprise, but it was not always so. Until the 1970s, Illinois education policy tended to be shaped by small groups of education elites and legislators.[40] Teachers' organizations were passive. Governors were not closely involved, except in setting overall budget limits, nor was the federal government active. Most funding came from the local taxes. Those days are over. Today the state and national governments have greater funding at risk, and the U.S. Congress and the Illinois legislature have large and active education staffs. Governors now see education as central to economic prosperity. Most importantly, the teachers' unions have become assertive and highly protective of their gains.

The Illinois Education Association (IEA) is a teachers' union with 135,000 members in suburban and downstate school districts that dominate the politics of education outside Chicago. The other major union is the Illinois Federation of Teachers/Chicago Teachers Union (IFT/CTU), with 103,000 members in Chicago and in several downstate cities, including Champaign and East St. Louis.[41] Beginning in the late 1960s, the IEA transformed itself from an apolitical, milquetoast group of teachers and administrators into a political powerhouse that can strike terror into a lawmaker. Ken Bruce served as director of government relations for the IEA for more than two decades, stepping down in 1993. "When I started, we would not take a stand on any—not any—piece of legislation," recalls Bruce.[42] Today, the IEA tracks and takes a position on any bill that it feels may potentially affect its members and/or education.[43] These bills vary from district consolidation to pensions, employee rights and benefits, to COVID-19 and even driver's education standards.

The IEA contributes to favored candidates, assigns lobbyists to elected officials, sends staff professionals to help manage campaigns, and organizes teachers to get involved in local races. It formed its political action committee, IPACE, in 1974 and two years later endorsed Republican governor James R. Thompson early in his first campaign. IPACE contributed $80,000 to his candidacy (about $416,000 in 2022 dollars), more than any other group that year. Its teachers were active in each of Thompson's four successful campaigns. Not surprisingly, Thompson's first assistant for education reported that he consulted with the IEA on education issues as a matter of standard operating procedure.[44]

IPACE later endorsed Republican Jim Edgar in 1990 and his successor Republican George Ryan in 2000, who also received its endorsement for secretary of state in 1996. These endorsements meant large donations of up to $33,000 for Ryan.[45] This was no match for Democrat Rod Blagojevich, who beat Jim Ryan in 2002 and won the endorsement and subsequent campaign cash of the IEA to the tune of half a million dollars.[46] Blagojevich bested Ryan who, by then, was under a cloud of suspicion after many of his associates had been indicted for corruption. When Blagojevich was impeached in 2010, the IEA reluctantly supported his lieutenant governor, Pat Quinn, after endorsing another candidate in the primary. This meant almost $700,000 for Quinn's reelection bid.[47]

The IEA's (and IFT's) biggest beef with Quinn was his support for pension reform. Since arriving in office he had made it a top priority and was one of the only governors to be able to fund the liabilities completely in his annual budgets. In 2013 Quinn worked with party leaders and eventually signed a bipartisan bill that, among other things, reduced cost-of-living adjustments (COLAs) for retirees and increased contributions for newer members. Although the reductions were small, made statewide they had great effect on reducing the unfunded pension liability. However, the Illinois state constitution guarantees pensions and so the IEA (along with the IFT) rallied its membership to call, write, and rally against the legislation. The law was eventually struck down by the Illinois Supreme Court, but it was enough to completely sour education unions on Quinn, who would no longer enjoy their support.

In the 2014 gubernatorial election the IEA decided to embark on a different strategy when anti-union Republican Bruce Rauner announced he was running for the nomination. The IEA donated $450,000 to the campaign of Republican Kirk Dillard, a former member of the Illinois State Senate but, more importantly, the man who was the chief of staff to former governor Jim Edgar. The IEA had endorsed Dillard previously, when he ran for the Republican nomination in 2010 against Bill Brady. Brady won, but would lose in the general election to Democrat Pat Quinn.

This time the IEA was encouraging all members, both Republican and Democratic, to support Dillard by pulling Republican ballots in the primary.[48] The IFT, however, continued to support Quinn, to the tune of almost half a million dollars.[49] Together with other unions, both the IEA and IFT funneled funds to pro-union Illinois Freedom PAC, which would eventually receive over $2 million from the IEA, by far its largest donor.[50] The group ran thousands of anti-Rauner ads on TV, cable, and radio stations ahead of the primary elections. In the end, it was not successful, and some believe this publicity had the opposite effect of associating Dillard with unions when in general by the 2010s many Republicans were anti-union.[51] Not only did Rauner win the primary, but also the general election.

This hardly spelled the end of the IEA's influence. Instead, the IEA kept its eye on the prize elsewhere, namely the statehouse where it also interviews and endorses candidates. An IEA endorsement for its most favored candidates can bring in tens of thousands of dollars, sometimes more. Speaker of the House Emanuel "Chris" Welch (D-Westchester) has received over $313,000 from IPACE. Representative Sue Scherer (D-Decatur) has received over $327,000. Sam Yingling (D-Round Lake Beach) has received almost $390,000, with the average between twenty and thirty thousand.[52] The IFT's donations are also along these lines. Endorsements from unions usually come with mailers to members in the district advocating for the candidates as well as social media promotions.

Both the IEA and IFT also "rebate" money back to the individual school unions that make up the organization (known as "locals") so that they may set up their own PACs or other organizations and be influential in local elections.

While this has traditionally meant that individual school district or community college faculty unions use the funds to affect their particular board races, the IEA will hold endorsement meetings for any office that any local requests. For instance, this year for the first time ever, the IEA held endorsement meetings for the candidates running in the DuPage County board chair's race—even though the county board government has no jurisdiction over the schools.

The IEA has become involved in judicial contests as well, endorsing and providing contributions to candidates for the appellate and supreme courts. It makes sense to see friends of the IEA succeed to the state's high courts, because many issues of importance to teachers are resolved by lawsuits.

The IEA has had more influence than other education interests because the union has invested heavily in Illinois elections. It assesses each of its 135,000 members $30 per year for dues for its political action committee. Today it is the third most powerful regular political action committee in Illinois, with almost $4.5 million, ahead of realtors, bankers, and attorneys.[53] The IFT ranks fourth, with over $2.8 million cash on hand.[54]

Nonmonetary contributions are made as well, typically by local affiliates for rallies and other campaign activities. Attracting hundreds of teachers to a rally generates media coverage and increases enthusiasm among teachers to go out and do telephoning and other campaign work, particularly canvassing. Using union teachers from the local school has been a great way for incumbents to show a connection to the community and more importantly, support. This increases credibility for the candidate, spurring support and contributions from elsewhere.

The IEA has long linked contribution decisions to legislative performance. Even legislators who are confident that they could beat an election challenge from the IEA would just as soon avoid the increased time, effort, and money needed to do so. Thus, whenever a legislator can give the IEA a vote in committee or on the floor, they generally try to do so. As a result, the IEA has dominated education action in the House and Senate. Its five full-time lobbyists meet with committee members before every hearing, testify in committee, and organize teachers and specialists to provide testimony. Several observers of the legislative process say they have watched IEA lobbyists give "thumbs up" and "thumbs down" signals from the committee hearing room audience and House and Senate galleries as cues to legislators about how to cast votes. The IEA has even provided written colloquies for legislators to read into the record on the chamber floor, thus establishing a record of legislative intent for use later when the resulting statute is being interpreted by lawyers and judges in court cases.

On the two hundred or more bills introduced each session that are specifically related to school matters, the IEA generally—but not always—gets what it wants. The IEA beats back with apparent ease efforts to reduce instructional mandates. The union has progressively restricted the authority of local boards. In 1987, for instance, it was successful in extending seniority protection to all nonteaching personnel, including bus drivers, food service workers, aides, and secretaries. Further, teachers are almost never successfully fired for incompetence. In an award-winning investigative series, Scott Reeder of the Small Newspaper Group found that between 1985 and 2005, on average only two teachers per year—of ninety-five thousand tenured teachers—were fired for incompetence.[55] The average cost in legal fees to school boards for each of the firings came to $219,000. Part of the reason for the small number of firings for incompetence is believed to be the unions' effectiveness at bargaining for detailed, protective procedural elements in the dismissal process.

There are, nonetheless, limits to the union's power. On the issue that most seem to agree on as the most important facing the education community—state financing of education—the IEA has had little effect. State government provides only 45 percent of total funding for local school districts in Illinois, one of the lowest percentages in the nation. The IEA's lack of aggressiveness may be the result of its internal dominance by teachers from the collar counties, where schools generally have strong property tax bases and thus need relatively little state funding. The IEA also has had more influence on narrow education issues than on broader questions such as school funding, which involves taxes and thus transcends the education arena.

Management Fights Back

School administrative and management interests have had much less influence than the IEA, in part because of the fragmentation created by regional differences—primarily differences in wealth—across the 852 school districts. The Illinois Association of School Boards (IASB) and Illinois Association of School Administrators (IASA) find it difficult to represent all their members satisfactorily with regard to contentious issues such as funding and school consolidation. Thus, many sub-state organizations have been created to represent categories of interests. These include the Large Unit District Association, Education Research and Development (an organization of 135 north suburban school districts), South Cooperative Public Education (representing 35 districts in southern Cook

County), Legislative Education Network of DuPage, and FAIRCOM, an organization of school districts that have utility power plants in their boundaries and thus great property wealth that is coveted by other districts.

School management groups appear to have more potential clout than they have historically wielded. Each district elects seven board members, so more than six thousand individual board members could conceivably be rallied to support issues. But this has not happened, perhaps because the board members serve as volunteers and thus lack the vested interests that spur teachers to action. In addition, the school board members often devote long hours to their local schools, leaving little time or energy for lobbying the government.

The IASB staff nonetheless presents well-developed testimony in legislative committees and in other communications with lawmakers. The legislators and their staff listen respectfully and sometimes act on the basis of a case well made. But because the group has not produced votes at the polling place, lawmakers do not fret much when they cast a vote against the IASB or the IASA.

In 1994 school management groups began to play political hardball. They forged the Illinois Statewide School Management Alliance (ISMA), a single lobby representing the statewide organizations of board members, administrators, principals, and school business officials. The ISMA developed unified positions with regard to bills, coordinated its lobbying efforts, and created a political action committee to raise money for contributions to legislative candidates.

The ISMA is joined by the Illinois Association of School Administrators (IASA), the Illinois Association of School Business Officials (ASBO), and the Illinois Principals Association (IPA). Yet since Edgar's time, none have had the clout or the reach to do the same type of work. Sprouting up instead are right-wing conservative advocacy groups such as the Illinois Policy Institute (IPI), created in 2002, which bills itself as a nonpartisan research organization that works on behalf of taxpayers. The IPI is funded by prominent conservatives such as Richard Uihlein, the Rauner Family Foundation, the Mercer Family Foundation, and Donors Trust.[56]

These groups are able to raise the cash and carry the influence to sell a different kind of message: that education problems would be resolved by the reduction of administrative bloat and dissolution of unions. On the latter point, after the *Janus v. AFSCME* case determined fair share union dues were unconstitutional, the IPI sent several rounds of mailers to teachers (as well as other public union members) encouraging them to quit their union and instructing them how.[57] The IPI even sent canvassers to people's homes to discuss quitting with them.

Illinois Higher Ed: Bounceback or Continued Decline

In 1989, education expert Harold Hodgkinson wrote of Illinois, "While the schools are in some difficulty, there is no doubt that Illinois has, over the years, built a major system of higher education, diverse and of high quality, including both public and private institutions."[58] Yet thirty years later, after decades of divestment, Illinois now has the dubious distinction of having the worst higher education enrollment declines in the country.

In 2021, almost 680,000 students were enrolled at 12 Illinois public university campuses, 48 community college campuses, 111 private, nonprofit colleges and universities, 11 for-profit colleges, and 20 out-of-state institutions offering programs in Illinois or online.[59] This is well over one hundred thousand fewer than just fifteen years ago. The greatest number of students seeking higher education attend the state's community college system with more than one third of the total—over 230,000—enrolled, and 40 percent of those students attended part-time.

In 1947, before expansion of the public system, two-thirds of Illinois students attended private institutions. By the 1990s, private students made up 29 percent of the total. Since 1992, however, private nonprofit and for-profit institutions have once again surpassed the number of students enrolled in four-year

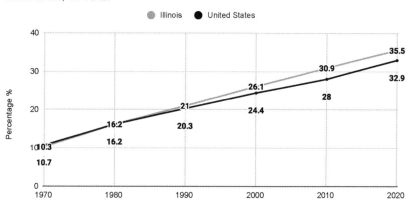

% of Adults, 25 years or Older, Completing 4 years of College or More
Illinois vs. U.S, 1970-2020

Figure 12.2. College Completion. Sources: "Educational Attainment for Adults Age 25 and Older for the U.S., States, and Counties, 1970–2019," USDA, Economic Research Service, February 24, 2020; U.S. Census Bureau, American Community Survey, 1 year estimate, 2010; U.S. Census Bureau, American Community Survey, 5 year Estimates, 2016–2020; "Status and Trends in the Education of Racial and Ethnic Groups," National Center for Education Statistics, February 2019.

institutions; as of 2020, private institutions enrolled 207,000, compared with 186,500 in the public four-year category.[60]

Following strong funding increases in the late 1990s, Illinois General Revenue Fund support for public universities decreased every year for the next two decades. Since 2003, direct state support to the U of I system was cut in half: from almost $1.4 billion to less than $700 million.[61] Back then, the state provided three dollars for every dollar in tuition revenue. Today, there is two dollars of tuition for every dollar of state support.[62] The four other state university systems tell a similar story.

James D. Nowlan recalls being told as a young member of the Illinois House appropriations committee in the late 1960s that "we" (lawmakers) always provided one dollar for the "big kids" in higher education for every two dollars that went to the "little kids" in K–12 education. In contrast, the new funding formula for K–12 meant in fiscal year 2022 those schools received over $360 million in new money, while the big kids received about $28 million, a ratio of 12:1.

The number of students enrolling in colleges outside of the state of Illinois has jumped 73 percent since 2000.[63] By 2019, half of all high school students were leaving the state to go to college.[64] Illinois exported 32,000 students, second only to California.[65] Most of these exports went to top-rated schools, such as neighboring flagship public universities in Iowa, Indiana, Wisconsin, and Michigan, which offered them full-ride scholarships Illinois schools could ill afford.

Politics has played a part in the development of higher education in Illinois since 1863, when the Illinois General Assembly accepted 480,000 acres of land from the federal government through the Morrill Land Grant Act for the establishment of programs of higher learning.[66] Presidents of the sectarian colleges immediately lobbied to seek division of the proceeds among a select number of private institutions. This approach was resisted by legislators, however, and the communities of Lincoln, Bloomington, Kankakee, Jacksonville, and Urbana entered into competition as prospective sites for the new institution, each city bidding for the prize. Urbana's $285,000 was among the low bids, but through political manipulation, it garnered the campus, which would become the University of Illinois.

From 1867 until World War II, the University of Illinois was the sole state university. There were five teacher education, or "normal," schools that struggled with whatever appropriations were left after the university had been funded. After the war, public higher education in Illinois blossomed into five multicampus systems coordinated at the top by a statewide Illinois Board of Higher Education (IBHE) created in 1961.

Four years later, in 1965, the legislature created the Illinois Community College Board (ICCB) to create a unified system of public community colleges that would be available to every resident. Junior colleges and legislation for them had existed as a patchwork since 1901, the brainchild of William Rainey Harper, president of the University of Chicago. Harper and his successors sought part-time and in-community alternatives to traditional universities that would also offer vocational training. Originally under the jurisdiction of the Board of Education, this legislation moved community colleges under the IBHE, via the ICCB. The IBHE would now see that the same credentials, standards, and rigors of higher education were applied.

Funding for community colleges differs in that in addition to tuition and state funding, they draw from their local district tax base, a luxury that the five public university systems do not have. The property tax base for community colleges subsidizes the cost of tuition so that it is as little as one-fifth the cost of a state school's average tuition rate. However, this reliance on property taxes also means that the community colleges are subject to disparities akin to—although not as bad—as those in public schools. Additionally, community colleges have been the victim of the state's decades-long cuts to higher ed, making them rely on local taxation and tuition even more.

Facing Stagnation: New Markets, New Players

When enrollment demand is strong, growth comes easily and all can benefit, as happened in Illinois between 1951 and 1967, when total college enrollment grew from 127,000 to 344,000 students.[67] During the 1980s, however, full-time-equivalent enrollments were basically flat for public universities, community colleges, and private colleges, and state appropriations grew at less than the rate of inflation. While community colleges enjoyed a bump in the 2000s, the slide downward both in terms of enrollment and appropriations continues for all Illinois colleges and universities. This combination has created understandable concern within the world of higher education and forced private colleges and public universities to seek additional markets to ensure stability or growth.

The old system had been slow to respond and for-profit and out-of-state online universities have become aggressive in marketing their wares to Illinois students. For-profit colleges and universities almost quadrupled their enrollments between 1992 and 2021 in Illinois, from 13,500 students to 54,000. DeVry University alone more than doubled its enrollment from 7,000 to 17,000 students on three campuses. National Louis University (NLU), a small college of education until the 1980s, responded to the market by transforming itself to a full-fledged university that eventually bought Kendall Culinary College and absorbed students and staff of two other for-profits when they were disbanded.

DeVry and NLU show two very different paths that make this route tricky for students. NLU's Kendall College is home to James Beard Award winners, a national prize for excellence in culinary arts. DeVry, by contrast, has been sued by its students for fraud saying they were misled by recruiters and enrollment specialists into paying tens of thousands of dollars for degrees that would ultimately be useless.[68] DeVry is not alone: many other for-profit institutions have been sued and/or have gone out of business as a result of lawsuits for failure to abide by the Department of Education's "gainful employment" rule, a rule that says these schools must publish accurate statistics about costs, time to graduation, and job prospects after graduation. Some schools closed seemingly overnight. Westwood College, Corinthian Colleges, ITT Tech College, Le Cordon Bleu, and Everest Colleges all had campuses in Illinois that have shuttered.

In 2021, out-of-state institutions enrolled just over 5,600 students in Illinois. These are mostly online-only schools. Some, like Western Governors University, are nonprofit. Others, such as the University of Phoenix, the largest online institution in the nation, were also subject to federal deceptive practices lawsuits and have recently entered into settlements with the federal government.[69]

The increasing competition between the public and private institutions comes as the two sides become more like each other. Corporate grants to public universities have been growing such that by 1989 public and private institutions received roughly equal shares of corporate donations.[70] Public institutions have also become more aggressive in generating support from alumni, as the private colleges have been doing since their origins. This makes up somewhat for the recent decline in state funding, which, for example, dropped at the University of Illinois at Urbana-Champaign from 49 percent of total 1979 revenues to only 11 percent in 2022.[71]

Tuition charges have tripled since 1980, outpacing inflation at both public and private institutions, striking fear in the hearts of parents and students alike. Tuition charges are set by the individual university governing boards, in contrast to states where the legislature and governor have a hand in setting the rates. The Illinois Truth in Tuition Law (2003) may have made it easier for public universities to raise tuition and easier for state lawmakers to ignore the increases. The law requires that the tuition for entering first-year students not change during their four-year college enrollment. As a result, only one class of students and parents becomes upset each year, rather than all of them as was the case when everyone's tuition went up each year.

In order to remain competitive, the public universities fight to keep their tuition low but feel forced to increase student charges for such things as room and board and fees in the face of declining state funding. At the University of Illinois at Urbana-Champaign, for example, tuition and fees have increased from $4,374 in 1998 to up to $22,324 in 2022.

Though their stated tuition rates are still significantly higher than at the public institutions, the private colleges try to structure financial aid packages that bring their costs close to those of the public ones. For example, when admissions officers at Knox College, a private college in Galesburg, find that their prospective students are considering both Knox and the University of Illinois at Urbana-Champaign, the college officials can often build packages of federal, state, and Knox financial assistance and loans to bring out-of-pocket costs for Knox prospects close to those for students at the University of Illinois.

Community colleges have tried to keep up with universities and for-profit alternatives not just with their reduced tuition rates but by easing transfer to four-year institutions by creating 2+2 and 3+1 programs with universities. These allow students to take the first two or three years at the community college and then guarantee transfer acceptability of courses for specific programs of study. The drawback to these programs is that students need to know immediately when starting which school they are transferring to, and must start taking the proper courses immediately. It also creates an environment at the community college that encourages only general education requirements to be taught and discourages electives.

Community colleges have also tried to keep up by increasing the number of certificates they offer. In addition to occupational-vocational degree and certificate programs traditionally offered, such as HVAC, nursing, automotive repair, and cosmetology, for example, most also offer certificates in liberal arts or social sciences. At the College of DuPage in western suburban Glen Ellyn, for instance, students can get certificates in business anthropology, creative writing, professional writing, and data science in sociology. Faculty are often encouraged to create more certificate programs to make the college more competitive regardless of market demand or usefulness.

Hope for Education in Illinois?

In the past five years, there has been some hope for education in Illinois. The new EBF funding formula for K–12 schools has shown results. Increases in higher education funding are finally here. As a result of the American Rescue

Plan, designed to provide direct relief from the effects of the pandemic, Illinois has received $1.3 billion in Higher Education Emergency Relief Funds (HEERF). Colleges and universities were required to use half to provide direct aid to students. The legislature has approved more funding for MAP grants, including a historic $122 million increase for FY2023. A scholarship program to encourage high school students to attend Illinois state schools, AIM HIGH, is now in its fourth year and has seen some success. More importantly, the FY2023 budget also increases state appropriations to universities (and community colleges) 5 percent over FY2022.[72]

But the hope should be tempered with a realistic understanding of the landscape Illinois schools are facing. That half of the funding for K–12 schools comes from property taxes doesn't just create inequality, it perpetuates it. The poorest schools in the poorest communities are already serving those with the most need. The state must move away from this model. Continued divestment in the state's great universities must end. Historic funding increases for the 2023 fiscal year must continue to be matched. Yet it will also take structural changes as well: increases in funding will not translate to improvement so long as administrative bloat continues to siphon money away from students and teachers. In fact, if this latter problem would be addressed, we would probably find the funding issues far less daunting.

13
PEOPLE SERVICES

As temperatures started to climb in the spring of 2020, Illinoisans started to chafe under the stay-at-home orders issued by the state of Illinois in the wake of the COVID-19 pandemic. Growing weary of life online and indoors and looking for safe alternatives, residents turned out in droves to forest preserves and state parks. Some forest preserves in the collar counties saw crowds so large they had to limit guests to only residents of their county. Some of most popular campgrounds in Illinois had holiday-sized crowds year-round that caused congestion that rural parts of the state were simply not used to.

Forest preserves do not have ways to record attendance, but website traffic was three times higher than the daily record for Cook County preserves. Suburban camping spots were almost full as early as April—even though restrictions prevented outdoor grilling. In the middle of the state at Starved Rock Campground, near Matthiessen State Park, trail congestion was so heavy people were walking in roadways.[1] Chicago decided to keep the beaches closed, but many more state parks and recreation areas, such as Kickapoo State Recreation area in Vermillion County, were recording the highest numbers they had ever seen.[2]

The Illinois Department of Natural Resources (IDNR) manages 145 state parks that vary greatly. The agency is also not new—state parks (and county systems) have been around for at least a century. Fort Massac, the very first state park in one of the southernmost parts of Illinois near Metropolis, recounts the Native American and colonial experience. The Chain O'Lakes, near the Wisconsin border, by contrast, is made up of exactly that—a chain of lakes—and caters to those who enjoy water-oriented recreation such as boating and fishing. James

"Pate" Phillip State Park is a sprawling expanse in the far western suburbs with open fields and walking trails and even a place where you can fly radio-controlled airplanes and helicopters.

But state parks are only part of what the IDNR does—in fact its charge is to protect and enhance all of the state's natural resources and this includes fish and wildlife management, water resource management (including Lake Michigan), and management of invasive species, and mining, oil, and gas resources. And it does so rather cheaply. Although its enacted budget was $460 million in 2022, it generated about two-thirds of its own revenues through fees and received about $60 million from the federal government.[3] The pandemic has led not just to a new appreciation for the majestic natural resources of the state, but also to what an agency can do for its residents.

The largest part of the Illinois budget is spent on people services. That is, services that touch ordinary people of the state of Illinois living their daily lives. These vary from agencies like IDNR that provide and protect natural resources, to health and human service agencies, to those that keep roads and people moving. This chapter discusses the functions of the state dedicated to these endeavors.

Healthcare in Illinois

Prior to the mid-1960s, healthcare in Illinois was like that in other states—if you didn't have private insurance, you paid for it yourself. Hospitals for the poor existed, but primarily in urban areas and not commonly until the mid to late 1800s in Chicago. Rural areas continued to be underserved. The American mentality at the time was that healthcare was more of a privilege, and not necessarily a right.

Several things began to change the minds of Illinoisans. First, in Chicago especially, successive outbreaks in the mid- to late 1800s of communicable diseases such as cholera and smallpox stimulated huge demand for the city and the county to build medical facilities.[4] This, and the excesses of the Industrial Revolution, also caused an outcry for more to be done for public health. Slowly, the idea of state regulation was taking hold. As the Chicago area suburbanized in the early and mid-1900s, this attitude expanded, and suburban counties established their own health departments.[5]

While regulation had become routine and hospitals and clinics more common, the cost of healthcare was becoming an issue for many. In the 1950s medicine really began to advance and modernize when doctors discovered, for instance, how to stop and restart the human heart.[6] But all of this was really expensive.

And by 1960, only 70 percent of all Americans had health insurance. A full one-third of the population was left out.[7]

Enter the federal government. In 1965 the Medicare Act was passed and incorporated into the Social Security Act, which would create an insurance program for those aged sixty-five and over. It included another provision known as Medicaid that would assist low-income individuals. Medicaid is state-sponsored but jointly funded by the state and federal government (initially a 50–50 cost-sharing arrangement). Medicaid has several coverage groups: Moms and Babies, All Kids, Aid to the Aged, Blind, and Disabled (AABD), and Affordable Care Act (ACA) Adult.

Today, 2.7 million adults and children are enrolled in the first three categories. Although only 16 percent of Medicaid clients are seniors or persons with disabilities, they account for 55 percent of the cost. The majority of Medicaid clients are poor children, accounting for 1.7 million.[8] The expansion of Medicaid allowed under the Affordable Care Act meant that in fiscal year 2021, another approximately 774,000 adults were covered under the Illinois Medicaid program, for a total enrollment just under 3.4 million. This reduced the uninsured population by 46 percent to only 6.5 percent.[9]

The Medicaid numbers translate to one in seven adults aged nineteen to sixty-four, three in eight children, four in seven nursing home residents, one in three disabled individuals, and one in six Medicare beneficiaries. Of all adult Medicaid recipients, 68 percent are working.[10] Medicaid is a huge program in Illinois, and has changed lives.

Problems with Medicaid

Since its inception, Medicaid has been controversial and for several reasons. First, many simply did not agree with state-funded services for the poor. Illinois had a history from the very beginning of generous coverage, especially in comparison to southern states. The legislature tried to enact residency requirements, but in 1968, a federal court struck them down.[11] Without this protection, fears were that the poor would flock to Illinois. In 1969, then Speaker of the House Ralph Smith already was proposing cuts to the program because of increased claims after the court ruling.

Another criticism was rogue doctors. A 1969 investigation by the *Chicago Tribune* found that some "welfare doctors" saw as many as 150 patients a day, for an average of three minutes each. Offices became mills for the purpose of collecting government payments.[12] The investigation also found illegal solicitation by doctors, doctors who sent patients to certain pharmacies, and the overprescription of medications and procedures. All this combined meant that in the four years after the legislation was enacted, costs to the State of Illinois for Medicaid rose 300 percent.[13]

Beyond the financial abuses, however, were very real abuses in the system affecting those it was designed to help. Loyola University Chicago professor Pierre de Vise, a sociologist, had been in front exposing these disparities. For de Vise, the system was simply not effective because it created a two-tiered system of medical care for Blacks and whites in Illinois. Blacks, who tended to be urban and poorer, relied more on Medicaid and received services at the Cook County Hospital. Whites, who tended to be suburban and have more means, received services at private hospitals and with private insurance. Black neighborhoods also had fewer general practitioners, giving them less choice.[14]

Compounding this, the state was not paying its bills. Three years into Medicaid, the State of Illinois already owed hospitals $10 million. In today's money, that is the equivalent of close to $81 million. This lack of payment has caused doctors to flee the program, exacerbating the already drastic disparities in care. David Daniel, then director of the Cook County Department of Public Aid, said that this situation amounted to discriminatory practices by the state and had "resulted in more money to doctors in outlying white areas of Chicago that to doctors practicing in black communities."[15]

But the crunch was not just felt in the city. The expansion in access to medical care by Medicaid and the problems caused by the state's inability to pay its bills on time also meant that rural areas of Illinois faced a doctor shortage as well. By 1970, 150 towns in Illinois with populations of 1,000 or less did not have a doctor at all, and four counties—Johnson, Pope, Hamilton, and Hardin—only had one apiece.[16]

The state's retort was, predictably, that the costs were much higher than it had anticipated. By 1972, Medicaid was already 42 percent of all public aid spending in the state.[17] Not even ten years in and the conversations around the program focused on how to control costs and cut the budget. From shortening hospital stays to limiting who qualifies to creating a mandatory fee structure for hospitals, lawmakers became obsessed with controlling what they felt was an uncontrollable program.

But by the 1980s at the federal level, then-President Ronald Reagan's Council of Economic Advisers was heralding it as a success. "Medicaid has successfully met its legislated objectives," its 1985 report said.[18] The council acknowledged some fraud, but argued reports were overblown. Still, the 1980s were a time for trimming budgets and as this was a federal matching program, the federal government continued to cut the amount it was giving the states. But state demand did not change. Governor James Thompson along with the Illinois legislature were dealing with their own budget crisis and could not cut their way out of this one. They would have to institute two temporary tax increases—one in 1983 and one in 1989—in order to generate funding to stay afloat.

Federal programs to the states are thus a double-edged sword: they have much potential for states to be able to do so much good, but when the largess dries up, most states simply cannot just stop what they are doing. And Illinois could not either. It was more than a matter of finding the money—it was a fight between the Democrat-controlled legislature led by Speaker of the House Mike Madigan, who in the 1980s was rising, and Governor James Thompson, a Republican. Fights over how, when, and how much money should be appropriated, and to whom it should go, and which providers should be prioritized, played into decisions just as much as need.[19] By 1990, the system seemed unsustainable. But at least in urban and suburban areas there were doctors to wait for payments. Pregnant women on Medicaid in twenty-six of Illinois's rural counties did not even have a doctor willing to take their insurance because so many had fled.[20]

When Jim Edgar became governor in 1991, he agreed to borrowing to help catch up on payments, which generally worked. While he of course had his share of woes, a better economy in the 1990s led to fewer problems. In 1998 he joined other states in the Medicaid expansion for children through a program created by Congress called the State Children's Health Insurance Program (SCHIP). This allowed coverage up to 185 percent of the federal poverty level; however, of the 200,000 children it aimed to cover, only 30,000 enrolled.[21] When George Ryan became governor, he implemented a waiver that allowed caretakers of these children to also obtain coverage—the waiver being granted as a result of Illinois's higher than average uninsured rate. This also helped working families who met certain conditions get reimbursed for purchasing coverage on their own.[22]

Going much further, however, was Governor Rod Blagojevich in 2006 after the Illinois Legislature passed All Kids—an entirely state-funded plan to insure all children in Illinois regardless of parental income or citizenship on a sliding scale. Funding came from savings in other managed-care initiatives, so no new money was needed. About 50,000 children were immediately enrolled.[23] By all measures the program was a success and Illinois became a model for other states to emulate.

Kids are generally cheap and easy to insure, and are a sympathetic population. But Illinois still had a large population of adults that needed coverage, and the next expansion was not far off. The federal Patient Protection and Affordable Care Act (ACA) was passed in 2010, and was designed to provide all Americans with insurance. One way was an expansion of Medicaid for the poor by increasing eligibility to 133 percent of the federal poverty level starting in 2014, although states could apply for a waiver to do this earlier, and Illinois did so.

However, ACA *required* states to do this, and would only be reimbursing them for 100% of the increased cost in 2014, decreasing to 90 percent by 2020 and all subsequent years.[24] Some states did not like that, called it coercion, and the U.S. Supreme Court agreed and dismantled that provision. States could opt to remain in, and Illinois did.

Today, these expansions mean that over 3,330,000 Illinoisans are covered by Medicaid in some form. The Affordable Care Act expansion is responsible for almost a quarter of it, with over 700,000 new enrollees signed up between 2013 and 2021. The uninsured rate dropped 46 percent from 2010 to 2019. The ACA expansion of Medicaid coverage has also been good for rural hospitals such as Franklin Hospital in southern Benton, about an hour southeast of St. Louis. It was on the verge of closing its doors for a decade, but as one of the only Medicaid providers in the county, coverage expansion changed all of that.[25] Patients now are more likely to have coverage, and those with coverage are now more likely to have better coverage, which means more revenue.

But the expansion did nothing to increase the actual number of providers willing to take Medicaid, and so it is still largely left to public hospitals like Franklin to do so. The pandemic multiplied the burden on public hospitals exponentially, and after a while, it became less about the money and more about the staffing. In June of 2021, National Nurses United, the union that represents nurses in Cook County's health system, went on a one-day strike to announce their plight: understaffing has made conditions too dangerous. They had been working seven months without a contract and wanted people to know it was about safety. While they eventually signed a deal, today at least a quarter of all nursing positions in Cook County Health go unfilled.[26]

The FY23 state budget includes monies dedicated to healthcare workforce development, including specifically nursing and community health workers. The idea is that the pandemic has caused the loss and burnout of so many that there needs to be adequate replacement. Additionally, our aging population has caused a greater demand. A challenge will be ensuring that these new healthcare professionals will not only materialize, but will then want to go to the rural and urban areas to serve the populations where they are most desperately needed.

Child Welfare and Foster Care

In Governor JB Pritzker's 2023 budget address he announced an increase of $250 million over the previous year for the Illinois Department of Children and

Family Services (DCFS). Priorities included the foster homes program, adoption, and guardianship but also a focus on hiring 360 new employees to address the extreme staffing shortage.

Just mention DCFS and eyes roll and people shake their heads. Very few have a good word for the agency, and many recall the terrible stories they have heard either from those who have had contact with the system or in the media. The department now is responsible for approximately 15,000 children, not an unusually high number given Illinois's population. However, its director, Marc Smith, currently has eleven contempt charges against him from Cook County judge Patrick Murphy for not placing children in proper homes. One child, for instance, currently remains locked in a psychiatric ward of a hospital, even though she has been discharged, because there is no home to take her.[27]

But this is not even the worst—the department is currently under fire for several deaths of children who either were not removed or were returned to their homes when they should not have been. DCFS has been in the news for several high-profile deaths of children by parents who had contact with the agency.[28] According to most recent audits, the department has failed in an overwhelming majority of cases to ensure homes are properly prepared to receive their children back, and in over half has failed to check on them once they did.[29]

It's hard to lay the blame squarely at the feet of Director Smith. When he joined the agency in May of 2019, he was the fifteenth director in as many years (including acting and interim) to run the agency. And as has become the forever woe of the agency, it was and is underfunded and understaffed. But it wasn't always this way.

Illinois was on the forefront of child welfare. In 1865 the first state-supported home for the children of Civil War soldiers opened in Normal. Private agencies, however, took care of most needy children, and in 1869 the State Board of Commissioners of Public Charities was created to oversee them. In 1899 this State Board was granted inspection authority by the state.[30] In 1905 the task of supervising visitation of foster children and licensing and inspecting foster facilities became so great that a Department of Visitation was created.[31]

In 1917 a Department of Public Welfare absorbed all these responsibilities and a new state mandate: annual inspection. But lack of adequate funding prevented the new department from being as effective as it could be.[32] In addition, the public's attitude was changing, and there were more and more calls from Illinoisans to do away with the private system and create one that would be more accountable.

The early twentieth century shift mirrored national politics. The Progressive era reforms had made their way to childcare, and the Children's Bureau was created as a part of the United States Department of Health and Human Services in 1912. At the time the main concern was child labor, so the next year the bureau was transferred to the Department of Labor.[33] As this became less of a problem, the Children's Bureau was placed within the Social Security Administration, which kept it until the 1960s when it was transferred again to the renamed Department of Health, Education, and Welfare.

Back in Illinois, in 1964 the state created the first-ever cabinet-level state child welfare agency, now named the Department of Child and Family Services.[34] While some states had by this time created their own departments, they were all housed in other agencies. For Illinois, however, elevation to the cabinet level meant more resources and more importantly more money to help children. In its first year 4,000 children were served, compared to about 15,000 today and 51,000 at its peak in 1997.[35] Today, the job of DCFS is multifaceted. In 2020, it responded to calls for investigation of abuse or neglect involving more than 111,000 children, cared for over 15,000 foster children, and handled the licensing and oversight of daycare facilities that served more than 290,000 children.[36]

Controversy

DCFS has one of the toughest missions in all of government. And because of that, the agency faces two simultaneous yet opposite problems: charges that it removes children too easily, and charges that it does not remove children frequently enough.

Critics contend on the one hand that sometimes children were removed simply because their parent ran in the house to get something when the children were outside. The parent was not a danger to the child, and the intervention was based on judging the parenting itself. Even when children might have been removed on suspicion of abuse or neglect, there was no immediate hearing or agreement as to what might be done to rectify the situation. Children were often moved from one foster home to another, even over the objection of the foster parent, sometimes for unknown reasons. Siblings' relationships were not always honored. On the other hand, in cases where children were not removed, critics decry the obvious instances of abuse and neglect that should have kept a child from returning home. Had the state swung too far in taking children from families, only to swing too far in returning them?

In 1988, the American Civil Liberties Union (ACLU) filed a federal class action lawsuit on behalf of the then 14,000 children in DCFS care alleging that DCFS failed to provide basics such as adequate food and shelter.[37] Funding was at the crux of these allegations, as the ACLU alleged the then-director, Gordon Johnson, did not ask for additional money in appropriations and let his opportunities

whither. The ACLU also blamed then-governor James Thompson for not prioritiz-
ing the agency. The lawsuit further alleged that children were moved too frequently
between foster homes and reunification efforts were sorely insufficient as children
were too easily removed from their homes. The ACLU said this was the result of
neglect by DCFS bosses who responded, in ACLU's opinion, more to headlines
than real crises.[38] (The ACLU was not the only litigant. Others had filed both in
federal and state courts in cases on similar issues.)[39]

In 1989 the federal courts ruled against the ACLU in part, determining that
children in foster care do not "have rights to be reunified with their families,
to visit siblings and to be placed 'in the least restrictive setting.'"[40] But other
issues in the lawsuit remained to be decided. At the same time, the numbers
of children in DCFS care were rising at an astronomical rate. By 1990 there was
20,000 (up from 14,000). The number of reports to the agency also jumped to
100,000 from the 70,000 when the lawsuit was filed.[41]

In 1991, Jim Edgar became governor of Illinois and the lawsuits against DCFS
created pressure on his incoming administration and their promise not to raise
taxes. A ruling in favor of the ACLU on parts of the case not decided in 1989
could mandate changes that were very costly. In March of that year Edgar appointed a panel to recommend changes.[42] A few months later he took those
recommendations and entered into a consent decree with the federal courts,
agreeing to make changes by 1994. These changes included:

- Reduction in caseloads for caseworkers;
- Reduction in the number of personnel that a supervisor is responsible for;
- Specialized caseloads for all caseworkers to handle either children in foster
  care or in an intact family;
- Increased services to intact families;
- Better assessment for children removed from their homes;
- Dedication to more stable placement (ending constant movement); and
- Ensuring health and dental care would be provided to all children in cus-
  tody.[43]

There was great hope that the reforms would bring the necessary changes
to the beleaguered department. However, a year later the director, Sue Suter,
resigned suddenly after she was asked to lay off 300 staff amid budget cuts.[44]
The consent decree created additional responsibilities for the agency, and it
could not perform them without people. By this time, the number of children
in DCFS care had swelled to 29,500.[45] The ACLU threatened court action, and the
Illinois General Assembly agreed to provide more funds and commit to hiring
more people.[46]

Amid the problems DCFS was facing, the *Chicago Tribune* began documenting the deaths of children in care. In 1993 a three-year-old boy was hanged with a telephone cord by his mother after being returned to her three times, despite her long and documented history of mental illness. Even her own family did not understand why she was allowed to have her children. Said the foster father, "No one protects the children, only the biological mother's rights."[47] This toddler was one of thirty-six deaths that year, which was not an outlier according to *Tribune* reporting. More harrowing, the numbers kept rising: in 1993 there were almost 34,000 in the system.[48] The system was broken but it was handling more kids than ever. Increasing funding and hiring would only go so far. The state could not find enough foster families to house all the children. And now DCFS was facing new claims—children were sleeping and practically living out of its offices instead of being quickly placed into homes or centers.[49]

In 1994 retired Cook County judge Joseph Schneider, appointed by the federal court to oversee the consent decree, issued a preliminary report that stated what was already on the front pages of the newspapers at the time: DCFS would not be able to comply with at least half of its promises.[50] Despite Governor Edgar's nearly doubling funding to more than $1.1 billion in 1994, there was still too much pressure on the agency. And the numbers of children just kept rising—in 1994 it added another 7,400 children to its rolls for a total of 41,200. There just was no breathing room. In 1997 the agency would reach its peak of 51,300 children in care—three times the amount as when the ACLU had originally filed suit in 1988. This meant 17 of every 1,000 Illinois children were in the custody of DCFS, the highest of any state in the nation.[51]

However, the numbers belied a fact that did not pertain to many other states. As one of the reforms implemented by DCFS, many of these "foster" children were actually in "kin care," or in the care of extended family such as aunts, uncles, and grandparents. Registering these families with DCFS made them eligible to get services from the state, consequently preventing children from going to unrelated foster families. Illinois did, in fact, have one of the highest permanent placement rates.[52]

DCFS was also reducing the number of administrators and hiring more caseworkers, another important change. Yet nothing was done to change the way cases came to it or were processed through the agency. Calls to the child abuse hotline in Springfield was averaging 300 calls per day. And while DCFS and call center workers said reports must meet guidelines, it was up to the investigator assigned to the case to decide if the claim was well founded. The investigator just had to determine if the event happened, not if the parent was currently dangerous, and that was enough to remove a child.[53]

As a result of the continued issues, in 1997, the ACLU worked with DCFS to present a new plan to the judge in the case for settlement that was eventually accepted in 1998.[54] The changes were implemented, and the number of children in care began to plummet. In 2000 the number was down to 31,300, and DCFS was accredited by the New York–based Council on Accreditation of Children and Family Services.[55]

In 2003, still under the consent decree, DCFS was continuing to have a hard time when it came to moving foster children between placements and an even harder time with incompetent caseworkers in private agencies. That year the Cook County public guardian, Patrick Murphy, who had been involved and outspoken in the original ACLU case, filed his own.[56] DCFS agreed to create a plan of action and to work with both Murphy and the federal judge to create enhanced monitoring of private agencies. Responding to additional criticisms, DCFS also agreed to create a special program for high-risk youth, including those who run away.[57] Helping matters was that the number of children in custody was down to 20,500.[58]

By the mid-2000s, DCFS was still in need of work but seemed to be turning a corner. That was until charges that its most difficult children could not be placed in homes and were being left to languish in foster placements that were unsafe, mental health facilities when they could be discharged, or even jail.[59] While reforms had been made and numbers dropped, the children that were left were the state's most vulnerable and hardest to place. The state just did not have proper facilities for these children. Furthermore, charges were being leveled that the state was simply moving children from juvenile court, where foster cases are heard, into probate court, where general guardianship cases are heard, a technique that keeps them from being counted as foster children and keeps them off the DCFS rolls. The real problem was that this tactic was keeping resources from the caregivers as well.[60]

But in 2011, any progress came to a screeching halt as the state's back-to-back governor indictments and singular budgetary focus on the pension crisis took its toll. Making matters worse, then-director Erwin McEwen stepped down after accusations he failed to properly monitor grants to a friend. This friend, George Smith, later would be sentenced to two years in prison and made to pay $500,000 restitution after pleading guilty to defrauding several Illinois state agencies under contracts for work he did not do.[61]

The 2014 election of Bruce Rauner meant yet another fiscal crisis—this time no budget for two years. As hiring froze, DCFS caseloads swelled again to almost double what the 1991 consent decree had ordered.[62] Calls to the hotline went unaddressed. It is hard to underestimate the stress of underfunding on an agency with this kind of mission and this kind of public scrutiny, especially under a consent decree. And then, one by one, directors left after sometimes only months of tenure, never finishing a year.

The election of JB Pritzer brought hope, and cash—over $100 million new funding to the agency each year since his 2018 election and $250 million for 2023, which includes earmarks for better technology and better training. But then the new problems with the new director brought new ire and it was like déjà vu all over again. In fact, in the opinion of Charles Golbert, the public guardian, "DCFS is in the worst shape it's been in 30 years."[63]

Others agree. State Representative Steve Reick, a Republican from Woodstock in McHenry County, said, "I don't care how much money you throw at it, there are just way too many problems with DCFS that make me think it is an agency that can't be fixed."[64] Representative Rita Mayfield, a Democrat from north Suburban Waukegan, agreed. "Your budget is one of the largest budgets in the state of Illinois . . . and we're just not getting our money's worth."[65] State Senator Chapin Rose (R-Mahomet), who is on the DCFS oversight committee, believes its mission is too large and things like childcare licensing need to be given to other agencies. "It needs to be completely restructured in terms of its duties, management functions, and certainly in terms of its personnel," he said.[66]

There is no easy solution. Even hard ones are not working. DCFS is a necessary agency—there are children in homes that are not safe and children who have no homes at all. But it is also a prime example of how very difficult it is for "street-level bureaucrats"—those human beings who represent the frontlines of government policy—to actually effectuate policy when they work with the highest expectations from lawmakers and residents but the fewest resources in the most daunting of circumstances.

Department of Human Services

The Department of Human Services (DHS) has a big and varied job in Illinois: low-income support, crisis prevention, rehabilitation services. But in comparison to Medicaid and DCFS, its budget is small at $11.6 billion.[67]

Many may know DHS as the place low-income Illinoisans apply for cash or food assistance, known as Temporary Assistance to Needy Families (TANF) and Supplemental Nutrition Assistance Program (SNAP). Both of these are federal programs that the State of Illinois administers and then gets reimbursed for by the federal government. Applicants must fill out a universal twenty (yes, that says twenty)-page form that automatically goes to all aid programs (including Medicaid). Questions are extremely detailed and require information about the household, citizenship/immigration status, health conditions, expenses, job/

income history, any current health coverage, previous history with aid, any other possible source of income, and then there are two pages detailing penalties for false information.

The amount of benefit varies depending on family size and senior/disabled status. And it is not easy to qualify. For a family of four in Illinois, the maximum monthly gross income to receive SNAP benefits as of October 2021 is $3,364 and the maximum benefit is $835. That may sound like a lot but that is pretax income, and average rent for a two-bedroom apartment in the city of Chicago can be half of that. A single senior or a disabled person with an income of $2,147 can apply for a benefit up to $250.[68] That also may sound like a lot but if that senior or disabled person has decided to live with a roommate to save money, the state will require them to disclose and count all of the financial information of the roommate because they are a "household member," which may completely disqualify the applicant.

The TANF calculation is a little trickier—it depends on the number of adults and children in the household and for how many days the cash assistance is received, and clients usually cannot have any income. Pregnant, breastfeeding, or mothers of children under five can also apply for a supplemental benefit under the Women, Infants, and Children (WIC) program. Even this program isn't as simple as it looks because of the requirements on brands, sizes, and forms of foods and formulas purchased with WIC vouchers.

These programs can draw ire from some in the public, but in Illinois TANF benefits a little less than 20,000 people, the overwhelming majority of whom are children.[69] And among the states, Illinois ranks exceptionally low for TANF recipients overall—only 1.5 percent of the population compared to the nationwide average of 5.3 percent of the population. Or compare Illinois to our southern neighbor Kentucky, that has the same number of TANF recipients, but only a third of the population, making its rate three times ours at 4.5 percent. It's not just small, poor states that rank high. New York has about 115,000 TANF recipients with a population of about 20 million, putting its rate at about 5.75 percent.[70]

Perhaps it is DHS's wraparound services that make the cash assistance less necessary. Low-income Illinoisans can also apply through DHS for a program that will pay for their daycare if they qualify. Affordable, quality daycare is often what stops parents from being able to work and all licensed daycares participate in this program. Families can earn between 225 percent and 275 percent of the federal poverty level, depending on circumstances, to qualify.[71] DHS also helps disabled Illinoisans find rehabilitation services. It is a place where you can report fraud, abuse, or neglect of any kind, even running a special hotline for those persons with mental illness or developmental disability (1-800-368-1463). The DHS also has suicide and crisis counseling and prevention. Human services mean just that.

Secretary of State

In Illinois the Office of the Secretary of State is synonymous with driver's services. Indeed, it is this office where you obtain a driver's license/state identification card, registers your vehicle, and get license plates. Until 1939, a driver's license was not even required in the state. Today, there are about 8.26 million licensed drivers on the streets, representing almost two-thirds of all Illinoisans.[72] It's hard to imagine that many people hitting the road with no training and no regulation, so even though most people have a story about a long line or a bad photo, most agree licensure and registration requirements serve important safety goals.

But the Department of Motor Vehicles (DMV) is only part of what the Secretary of State does. As the state's official record keeper, in 1992 Illinois became one of only three states to create a computerized organ and tissue donor registry and add a donor consent feature to its driver's license. Illinois did this in response to a national shortage—every year hundreds of people die waiting for donors and the state hoped this could help. Employees were encouraged to promote organ and tissue donation and by the end of that year, 22 percent of those applying for or renewing driver's licenses opted to become part of the registry. Later laws changed to mandate first-person consent and the signatures on the back of the licenses went away. However, the popularity of the campaign did not, and in 2018, legislation allowed sixteen- and seventeen-year-olds to consent to the registry. Today, about half of the people in the state are registered organ and tissue donors.[73]

In 1993, as part of the National Voter Registration Act (NVRA), the federal government required states to create a regime for registering voters while they were seeking services at the DMV. The NVRA created a uniform registration, deemed valid those registrations completed thirty days prior to the election, and required states to inform voters if their registration was accepted or rejected. At first the state refused to comply, on constitutional grounds, and was sued by the federal government. However, a settlement was reached and full implementation was achieved by the 1996 election. After, when people went to access services at the DMV they could register to vote or update their registration. The thinking was that residents had identification documents in hand at the time, so why not get this important step done as well. And it worked—registration numbers were higher than ever.

The Secretary of State also maintains the State Library in Springfield, and the official state archives. If you want to start a business in Illinois you must register first with the Secretary of State, and properly file a report yearly. Lobbyists must also file paperwork with the Office of the Secretary of State for the public to view. And if you would like to become a notary public, this is where you go.

Finally, as a service to the people, every year the Secretary of State prints (and now publishes online) a *Blue Book*, with "up-to-date information about state officials and government agencies, as well as a snapshot of Illinois facts and history."[74] It is a veritable encyclopedia on everything Illinois—very handy for students of all ages and kinds.

Serving the People

One of the great charges of the Illinois constitution is to provide for the welfare of the people. Sometimes, as in the case of IDNR and even the DMV, the mission is fairly straightforward and relatively uncontroversial. In other cases, such as DCFS, it can be really difficult to balance the interests of residents and lawmakers' budgets and make sure that the primary objective—to take care of the children—is being carried out.

In all these instances, agencies are trying to solve problems. Defining something as a problem assigns it social importance, and says to a larger audience, this should be at the top of the political agenda. But once it is there, it is subject to different opinions as to how best to solve it. Sometimes the solutions are straightforward: house the records somewhere that water and air cannot decay them so they will be safe for future generations, and put copies online for accessibility. Sometimes the solutions look straightforward: ensure poor people have access to food, clothing, and medical care. Most of the time for most people, there is general agreement that the state should step in and provide public services.

But sometimes, and especially when breakdown occurs, effectuating solutions requires a deep dive into intellectual, philosophical, and moral questions about what the state is and should be, and how it can best address the problem it set out to solve. This doesn't necessarily mean agency abandonment; as we've seen with Medicaid expansion it has saved some rural hospitals. But it will, as in the case of DCFS, require more than just cash infusions to ensure it provides for the welfare of Illinois's most vulnerable children.

14

BUFFETED BY CHANGE, ILLINOIS CONTINUES AS THE HUB OF THE MIDWEST

This brief chapter draws from what we have written to this point, and also offers observations about Illinois based on the authors' 130 cumulative years of analysis and participation in our state's politics and government.

Over the past half century, crosscurrents of major demographic change have washed over Illinois. Significant numbers of whites left the state in the period, replaced by new residents of various hues. In 1970 the state had 9.8 million white residents; in 2024 there were but 7.6 million. In 1970, so-called minorities (Latino, Black, Asian) represented 11 percent of the state population; in 2022, the U.S. Bureau of the Census reported they account for 38.8 percent of all residents.

The "changing faces of Illinois" contributed to a transformation of partisan politics in the state. The whites who left tended Republican; those who came, Democratic. Half a century ago, Illinois had a fiercely competitive two-party political system. In 2024, political analysts count the state as strongly "blue," that is, Democratic. Fourteen of the seventeen members of the U.S. House from Illinois are Democrats, and the Democratic Party dominates all three branches of government.

Following World War II, Illinois's wealth and population both grew rapidly, making Illinois a robust, prosperous state. Since about 1970, however, rapid growth has shifted largely to the South and Southwest, while such in Illinois has been slower than for the nation as a whole, and slower even than in the rest of the Midwest. In 1958, Illinois had per capita income that was 116 percent of the national average; in 1970, 110, and 2021, 106 percent.

Within our state, wealth and average per capita income downstate (the ninety-five counties outside metropolitan Chicago) have been declining relative to the seven counties that encompass Chicago and its suburbs. Political party power and influence have also shifted. In 1970, downstate was a powerful political region. Elections were often decided downstate (its cities Democratic; the rural parts GOP), as Chicago (Democratic) and the suburbs (then heavily Republican) often roughly balanced one another. In 2024, elections are often now decided in the suburbs, which have become racially and ethnically diverse, and now overall lean Democratic.

Downstate is now the "weak sister" among the three geopolitical regions of Illinois (Chicago—Cook County; the six suburban "collar counties," and downstate). Democrats have little need to bargain with downstate GOP leaders, who represent but a third of all lawmakers.

Power within political parties has shifted as well. In 1970, party organizations, especially the Cook County Democratic Party, basically selected the candidates. In 2024, patronage jobs for parties are largely gone, and court decisions limit contributions to party organizations. Instead, often-wealthy candidates select themselves and self-fund their campaigns, or seek big independent expenditures in their behalf from billionaire contributors. State legislative leaders have generally replaced party chairs as the leading powers in state's party politics.

Political influence among interest groups has also shifted somewhat. Business interests, as represented by chambers of commerce, manufacturers, and medical groups, now operate largely in the shadows of an array of politically powerful unions, including craft unions, teachers, and government employees. The unions are major funders of Democratic political campaigns, with unions also contributing to some Republican political campaigns.

For decades, the authors have been waiting, in vain it appears, for the state's national reputation for political corruption to subside. In 2023–24, major bribery trials of certain legislative leaders, lobbyists, and a major corporation kept public corruption in the news.[1] The collective, learned behavior of too many Illinoisans has treated, or has at least tolerated, government as an enterprise in which it is acceptable to do well while doing good. The costs to the state are hard to quantify yet, we believe, significant—in loss of trust in government and forgone economic development, when companies interested in relocating to Illinois may see corruption as a possible cost of doing business they prefer not to incur.

The emphasis on the expensive political game of getting elected seems to take energy away from the task of managing government well. To cite but one example, Illinois has been under a federal court consent decree for more than three decades (!) to manage its Department of Children and Family Services more effectively, with little if any apparent success. In other words, government and policy seem less important in Illinois than politics.

In 2028, Illinois voters will be asked if they favor holding a state constitutional convention. This activity will rather force Illinoisans to confront their state's future, at least through the lens of our governing charter. A written constitution provides both the ballpark and some of the rules of the game of politics and government. As dictated by the 1970 state constitution, this question of a convention was on the ballot in 1988 and 2008, and the prospect was rejected each time by voters.

However, the pile-up of challenges that Illinois faces—persistent fiscal woes; economic and population growth that continually lags the nation; unacceptable levels of street crime violence, both in Chicago as well as downstate cities; and embarrassing national media coverage of frequent public corruption trials in our state—may induce citizens to take a new look at a rewrite of our state's charter.

We have long felt that leaders, and followers, in Illinois need to address our fundamental challenges more forcefully. And, on the other hand, to trumpet more loudly the many strengths and advantages that Illinois offers. As noted in the first chapter, in each of the six Rs that are critical to economic development—roads, rails, rivers, routers, runways, and research—Illinois is arguably among the top three states. These strengths should, especially when combined with the state's copious water supplies and our location at the very center of the world's largest economy, make Illinois a powerhouse of activity and creativity. Unfortunately, we don't think Illinoisans, the nation, and the world appreciate all this.

The authors have great affection for the State of Illinois. We hope this book helps readers understand our state better, especially its politics, government, and policies. You and other readers will have to set the course for the future of Illinois.

Notes

Chapter 1. Illinois in Perspective

1. Robert Sutton, "The Politics of Regionalism Nineteenth-Century Style," in *Diversity, Conflict, and State Politics: Regionalism in Illinois*, ed. Peter F. Nardulli (Urbana: University of Illinois Press, 1989), 97.

2. Cullom Davis, "Illinois: Crossroads and Cross Section," in *Heartland: Comparative Histories of the Midwestern States*, ed. James H. Madison (Bloomington: Indiana University Press, 1988), 133.

3. For a good discussion of the internal improvements effort, see Robert P. Howard, *Illinois: A History of the Prairie State* (Grand Rapids, MI: Eerdmans, 1972), chap. 9.

4. Richard J. Jensen, *Illinois: A Bicentennial History* (New York: Norton, 1978), chap. 2.

5. Ibid., 86

6. For an excellent discussion of the settlement of Illinois, see Frederick M. Wirt, "The Changing Social Bases of Regionalism: People, Cultures, and Politics in Illinois," in *Diversity, Conflict, and State Politics: Regionalism in Illinois*, ed. Peter F. Nardulli (Urbana: University of Illinois Press, 1989) 31; Davis, "Illinois: Crossroads."

7. James Simeone, *Democracy and Slavery in Frontier Illinois* (DeKalb: Northern Illinois University Press, 2000).

8. Jensen, *Illinois: A Bicentennial History,* throughout.

9. Ibid., 52–53.

10. Ibid., 53–54.

11. Ibid., 48–49.

12. William Cronon, *Nature's Metropolis: Chicago and the Great West* (New York: Norton, 1991), chap. 8.

13. Kristina Valaitis, "Understanding Illinois," *Texas Journal* 14 (Fall-Winter 1992): 20–22.

14. Cronon, *Nature's Metropolis*, 208–9.

15. Ibid., chap. 7, "The Busy Hive," provides an assessment of the business dynamics of Chicago and the Midwest.

16. Quoted in ibid., 3, citing Frank Norris, *The Pit*, 1903.

17. Howard, *Illinois: A History*, chap. 21.

18. Cronon, *Nature's Metropolis*, 347. A few years after the 1893 fair, the architect Daniel Burnham produced "The Chicago Plan," a design for a city of wide boulevards, spacious parks, and an unobstructed lakefront. Much of the audacious plan was implemented.

19. Jensen, *Illinois: A Bicentennial History*, 162.

20. Nelson Algren, *Chicago: City on the Make* (New York: McGraw-Hill, 1951), 56.

21. Stephen Ohlemacher, "Early Presidential Primary States Are Far from U.S. Average," *Associated Press*, May 17, 2007.

22. "US GDP by State—2022 Rankings," *MoneyTransfers.com*, accesses October 10, 2023, https://moneytransfers.com/news/2022/12/14/gdp-by-state.

23. "The World's Largest Economies," *WorldData.info*, accessed October 10, 2023, https://www.worlddata.info/largest-economies.php#:~:text=With%20a%20GDP%20of%2025.46,ninth%20place%20in%20this%20ranking.

24. United States REAProject, "Illinois vs. United States Comparative Trends Analysis: Per Capita Personal Income Growth and Change, 1958–2021," accessed June 2, 2022, https://united-states.reaproject.org/analysis/comparative-trends-analysis/per_capita_personal_income/tools/170000/0/.

25. Geoffrey J. D. Hewings, "Economic Challenges for the Illinois Economy" (Paper presented at the Institute of Government and Public Affairs, University of Illinois at Urbana-Champaign, March 8, 2007).

26. Heartland Alliance, "Illinois County Well-Being Dashboard: Poverty Rate, 2019," accessed June 2, 2022, https://www.heartlandalliance.org/illinois-poverty-data-dashboards/.

27. Daniel J. Elazar, "Series Introduction," in *Illinois Politics and Government: The Expanding Metropolitan Frontier,* Samuel K. Gove and James D. Nowlan (Lincoln: University of Nebraska Press, 1996), xi.

28. See the map in Robert Sutton, ed., *The Prairie State: A Documentary History of Illinois*, 2 vols. (Grand Rapids, MI: Eerdmans, 1976), 1:369.

29. Chicago Historical Society, "Chicago as a Modern World City," *Encyclopedia of Chicago*, last modified 2005, http://www.encyclopedia.chicagohistory.org/pages/962.html.

30. Davis, "Illinois: Crossroads," 147–48.

31. Marek Kepa, "How Chicago Became a Distinctly Polish American City," *Culture.Pl*, April 27, 2020.

32. For a lyrical essay on the diversity of people in Illinois, see Paul Gapp, "Chicagoans All—Our 'Melting Pot' Is Really a Savory Stew," *Chicago Tribune Sunday Magazine*, September 25, 1988.

33. Howard, *Illinois: A History*, 103.

34. Elazar, *Cities of the Prairie*, 181.

35. St. Clair Drake and Horace R. Clayton, *Black Metropolis: A Study of Negro Life in a Northern City* (Chicago: University of Chicago Press, 1993), 47. The material that follows is based in part on chapters 2–5 of this book.

36. U.S. Census Bureau, "QuickFacts: Illinois," accessed June 3, 2022, https://www .census.gov/quickfacts/IL.

37. Hansi Lo Wang, "These 14 States had Significant Miscounts in 2020 Census," *NPR. com.*, May 19, 2022, https://www.npr.org/2022/05/19/1099810793/census-undercount -by-state-arkansas-florida-illinois-mississippi-tennessee-texas.

38. U.S. Census Bureau, "1970 Census of Population, Characteristics of the Popula-tion: Illinois," Volume 1, Part 15, Section 1, page 14, accessed June 4, 2022, https:// www2.census.gov/prod2/decennial/documents/1970a_il1–01.pdf; see also U.S. Census Bureau, "QuickFacts: Illinois."

39. Pew Research Center, "Hispanic Population, Share Hispanic and Intercensal Growth Rate for Counties 1980–2020 Censuses," accessed June 5, 2022, https://www .pewresearch.org/hispanic/wp-content/uploads/sites/5/2022/01/RE_2022.01.31 _Hispanic-population-and-ranks-for-counties-1980–2020_FINAL.xlsx; see also U.S. Census Bureau, "QuickFacts: Illinois."

40. Leon F. Bouvier, "Shaping Illinois: The Effects of Immigration, 1970–2020," Cen-ter for Immigration Studies, March 1, 1996; see also U.S. Census Bureau, "QuickFacts: Illinois."

41. Extrapolation by the authors from Cheng H. Chiang and Richard Kolhauser, "Who Are We? Illinois' Changing Population," *Illinois Issues*, December 1982, 6–8.

42. U.S. Census Bureau, 1970 Census; see also U.S. Census Bureau, "QuickFacts: Illinois."

43. U.S. Census Bureau, "QuickFacts: Illinois."

44. William Scarborough, Amanda E. Lewis, and Ivan Arenas, "Shifting Population Trends in Chicago and the Chicago Metro Area," Report for the MacArthur Foundation, UIC Institute for Research on Race and Public Policy, June 2022; see also U.S. Census Bureau, "Quick Facts: Chicago," accessed August 24, 2022, https://www.census.gov/ quickfacts/fact/table/chicagocityillinois/PST045221.

45. U.S. Census Bureau, "QuickFacts: Lake County, Illinois," last modified July 1, 2022, https://www.census.gov/quickfacts/fact/table/lakecountyillinois/PST045222.

46. Ibid.

47. This is as recalled by Nowlan, who represented Bureau, Carroll, Henry, Stark, and Whiteside Counties in the Illinois House of Representatives from 1969 to 1972.

48. Bocce is a lawn bowling game enjoyed by many Italian Americans. Bud Billiken is a mythical hero of Blacks on the South Side of Chicago who is celebrated each year in a parade that is obligatory for local and some statewide politicians.

49. Chicago Metropolitan Agency for Planning (CMAP), Community Data Snapshot, Cook County, July 2022.

50. Gregory D. Squires, Larry Bennett, and Philip Ryder, *Chicago: Race, Class, and the Response to Urban Decline* (Philadelphia: Temple University Press, 1987), 98.

51. Chicago Metropolitan Agency for Planning (CMAP), Community Data Snapshot, Chicago, August 2021, https://www.cmap.illinois.gov/documents/10180/102881/Chicago.pdf.

52. Ibid.

53. U.S. Census Bureau, "QuickFacts: Chicago."

54. Scarborough, Lewis, and Arenas, "Shifting Population Trends in Chicago and the Metro Area," 22–23.

55. Michael B. Preston, "Political Change in the City: Black Politics in Chicago 1871–1987," in *Diversity, Conflict, and State Politics: Regionalism in Illinois,* ed. Peter F. Nardulli (Urbana: University of Illinois Press, 1989), 180–87.

56. See Lawrence J. McCaffrey, Ellen Skerrett, Michael F. Funchion, and Charles Fanning, *The Irish in Chicago* (Urbana: University of Illinois Press, 1987), 90.

57. Edward R. Kantowicz, *Polish-American Politics in Chicago* (Chicago: University of Chicago Press, 1975), 41–42.

58. Milton Rakove, *We Don't Want Nobody Nobody Sent: An Oral History of the Daley Years* (Bloomington: Indiana University Press, 1979), 318.

59. John Herbers, *The New Heartland* (New York: Times Books, 1986); "Look Out, Wasco, Here Comes the Suburban Sprawl," *Chicago Tribune*, March 18, 1994.

60. U.S. Census Bureau, "QuickFacts: Frankfort Village; Naperville City, Illinois," accessed August 24, 2022, https://www.census.gov/quickfacts/fact/table/frankfortvillageillinois,napervillecityillinois/PST045221.

61. Great Cities Institute, University of Illinois at Chicago, "Fact Sheet: Black Population Loss in Chicago," July 2019, 1, 9, https://greatcities.uic.edu/wp-content/uploads/2019/08/Black-Population-Loss-in-Chicago.pdf; see also U.S. Census Bureau, "QuickFacts: Chicago" and "QuickFacts: Cook County."

62. Chicago Metropolitan Agency for Planning (CMAP), Community Data Snapshot County Series, August 2021, https://www.cmap.illinois.gov/data/community-snapshots.

63. U.S. Census Bureau, "QuickFacts: Elgin City; Aurora City; Cicero Town," accessed June 3, 2022, https://www.census.gov/quickfacts/fact/table/elgincityillinois,auroracityillinois,cicerotownillinois/PST045221.

64. Chicago Metropolitan Agency for Planning (CMAP), Community Data Snapshot County Series, Cook County, https://www.cmap.illinois.gov/documents/10180/102881/Cook+County.pdf.

65. U.S. Census Bureau, "QuickFacts: Chicago" and website for Village of Olympia Fields, Illinois, https://olympia-fields.com/.

66. Paul Green, interview with Nowlan, April 4,1994, Chicago.

67. *1993 Metro Survey Report* (Chicago: Metro Information Center, 1993).

68. Mary Patrice Erdmans, "New Chicago Polonia: Urban and Suburban," in *The New Chicago: A Social and Cultural Analysis,* ed. John P. Koval, Larry Bennett, Michael I. J. Bennett, Fassil Dimissie, Roberta Garner, and Kiljoong Kim (Philadelphia: Temple University Press, 2006), 125.

69. "DuPage County IL Churches," *Illinois Gazetteer, Hometown Locator,* last modified 2022, https://illinois.hometownlocator.com/features/cultural,class,church,scfips,17043,startrow,151.cfm.

70. John Foster and John Jackson, "The Politics of Public Budgeting in Illinois," Paper #53, July 2018, Paul Simon Public Policy Institute, Southern Illinois University, Carbondale, 20–24.

71. U.S. Census Bureau, American Community Survey 5-Year Data (2009–2021), Cairo, Illinois, accessed August 25, 2022, https://www.census.gov/data/developers/ data-sets/acs-5year.html.

72. Heartland Alliance, "Illinois County Well-Being Dashboard: Poverty Rate, 2019."

73. In 1895, Chicago's downtown was enwrapped within a rectangle of elevated commuter train tracks, still in use, and thus called "the Loop."

74. Email discussion with Kent Redfield, week of June 29–July 5, 2008.

75. See chapter 12, "Education," for detailed discussion of these issues.

76. Rich Miller, *CapitolFax.com*, Springfield, May 19, 2009.

Chapter 2. Power and Influence in Illinois Politics

1. Kent D. Redfield, "What Keeps the Four Tops on Top?: Leadership Power in the Illinois General Assembly," *Almanac of Illinois Politics*, Institute for Public Affairs Publications Unit, University of Illinois Springfield, 1998, 1–8.

2. Ray Long, *The House That Madigan Built: The Record Run of Illinois' Velvet Hammer* (Urbana: University of Illinois Press, 2022).

3. Mike Royko, *Boss: Richard J. Daley* (New York: Plume, 1988). Milton Rakove, *Don't Make No Waves—Don't Back No Losers: An Insider's Analysis of the Daley Machine* (Bloomington: Indiana University Press, 1975).

4. The author of the chapter has been constructing databases from campaign committee receipt and expenditure records since the early 1990s, first through data entry and since 1995 through downloading data. Unless otherwise noted, all data on contributions and expenditures reported in this chapter are based on the author's analysis of campaign committee records filed with the Illinois State Board of Elections.

5. Anne Freedman, *Patronage: An American Tradition* (Chicago: Nelson-Hall, 1994).

6. Cindi Canary and Kent Redfield, "Lessons Learned: What the Successes and Failures of Recent Reform Efforts Tell Us about the Prospects for Political Reform in Illinois," Paper #33, Paul Simon Public Policy Institute, Southern Illinois University Carbondale, October 2012, 40–50.

7. Robert E. Hartley, *The Dealmakers of Downstate Illinois: Paul Powell, Clyde L. Choate, John H. Stelle* (Carbondale: Southern Illinois University Press, 2016).

Chapter 3. Elections

1. National Conference of State Legislatures NCSL, "Election Administration at the State and Local Levels," November 1, 2011, accessed December 10, 2022, https:// www.ncsl.org/research/elections-and-campaigns/election-administration-at-state -and-local-levels.aspx.

2. Illinois State Constitution, art. 3, sec. 5.

3. Illinois State Board of Elections, "Election Operations," accessed December 10, 2020, https://www.elections.il.gov/ElectionOperations/ElectionAuthorities.aspx.

4. Illinois State Board of Elections, "Running for Office," accessed December 10, 2020, https://www.elections.il.gov/RunningForOffice.aspx?MID=rOlNCTNZd9A%3d.

5. Prior to 2014 the lieutenant governor ran separately from the governor. The law was changed to have the governor and lieutenant governor run as a team in the partisan primaries with the primary winners running in the general election.

6. Commission on Government Forecasting and Accountability Research Unit, *1970 Illinois Constitution: Annotated for Legislators*, 5th ed., December 2018, accessed December 10, 2020, https://www.ilga.gov/commission/lru/lru_home.html.

7. Ibid.

8. Illinois State Board of Elections, "Information for Voters," accessed December 10, 2022, https://www.elections.il.gov/InformationForVoters.aspx?MID=IocuvBFuZRw%3d.

9. Sangamon County Clerk, "Voting," accessed December 10, 2020, https://countyclerk.sangamonil.gov/Elections/Vote/Default.aspx.

10. *Buckley v. Valeo*, 424 U.S. 1 (1976); *Nixon v. Shrink*, 528 U.S. 377 (2000); *McConnell v. FEC*, U.S. 540 U.S. 93 (2003); *Randall v. Sorrell*, 548 U.S. 230 (2006); *Davis v. FEC*, 554 U.S. 724 (2008); *Citizens United v. FEC*, 588 U.S. 310 (2010).

11. Cindi Canary and Kent Redfield, "Lessons Learned: What the Successes and Failures of Recent Reform Efforts Tell Us about the Prospects for Political Reform in Illinois," Paper #33, Paul Simon Public Policy Institute, Southern Illinois University Carbondale, October 2012, 33–40.

12. The author of the chapter has been constructing database from campaign committee receipt and expenditure records since the early 1990s, first through data entry and since 1995 through downloading data. Unless otherwise noted, all data on contributions and expenditures reported in this chapter are based the author's analysis of committee records filed with the Illinois State Board of Elections.

13. Data aggregated from reports of the U.S. Census for Illinois counties for 1990, 2000, 2010, and 2020.

14. Rob Paral and Associates, *What Does the 2010 Census Tell Us about Metropolitan Chicago?* (Chicago: Chicago Community Trust, May 2011).

15. Illinois Election Data, "Regional Share of General Election Vote," accessed December 10, 2022, https://illinoiselectiondata.com/.

16. Illinois State Board of Elections, "Candidate Filing, Downloadable Vote Totals, Candidate Total by County," accessed December 10, 2022, https://www.elections.il.gov/CandidateFilingAndResults.aspx?MID=kvBopx3%2bckA%3d. Author's analysis of votes by county and region for 2014 and 2018 gubernatorial elections.

17. *Reynolds v. Sims*, 377 U.S. 533 (1964); also *Baker v. Carr*, 369 U.S.186 (1962); *Wesberry v. Sanders,* 376 U.S. 1 (1964).

18. *Rucho v. Common Cause*, 588 U.S. 139 (2019).

19. Kent Redfield, "Drawing Congressional Districts in Illinois: Always Political, Not Always Partisan," in *The Political Battle over Congressional Redistricting*, ed. William J. Miller and Jeremy D. Walling (Lanham, MD: Lexington Books, 2013), 376–92.

20. Ibid.

21. Author's analysis of 2021 congressional districts created by Illinois General Assembly, available from https://ilhousedems.com/redistricting/; map at https://www.google.com/maps/d/u/1/viewer?mid=1qfnRiuOZ3yok6WGvBHZ9P6u3EMy_LwRv&ll=39.79510521942542 %2C-89.50414500000001&z=6.

22. Cindi Canary and Kent Redfield, "Partisanship, Representation, and Redistricting: An Illinois Case Study," Paper #38, Paul Simon Public Policy Institute, Southern Illinois University Carbondale, September 2014.

23. Author's analysis of 2021 House and Senate districts created by the Illinois General Assembly, available from https://ilhousedems.com/redistricting/ and https://www.ilsenateredistricting.com/.

24. Kent D. Redfield, "What Keeps the Four Tops on Top?: Leadership Power in the Illinois General Assembly," *Almanac of Illinois Politics*, Institute for Public Affairs Publications Unit, University of Illinois Springfield, 1998, 1–8; Kent Redfield, *Money Counts: How Dollars Dominate Illinois Politics and What We Can Do About It* (Springfield, IL: Institute for Public Affairs, University of Illinois Springfield, 2001), chap. 4.

25. Kent D. Redfield, "Electing Supreme Court Judges in Illinois 2000–2014" (Unpublished paper prepared for expert witness testimony in civil case, October 2015; rev. January 2020).

26. Ray Long and Rick Pearson, "New Illinois Supreme Court Justices Got Major Boost from Hidden Spending by Democratic Group," *Chicago Tribune,* February 4, 2023, https://www.chicagotribune.com/politics/ct-supreme-court-money-helps-dem-justices-20230204-gntd3tx6qbd47hbyxz7u5z6glu-story.html.

27. Illinois State Constitution, art. 14, sec. 2.

28. Illinois State Constitution, art. 14, sec. 3.

29. *Hooker v. Ill. State Bd of Elections* (63 N.E. 3rd 824; Ill. 2006).

Chapter 4. Political Corruption

1. Dick Simpson, Marco Rosaire Rossi, Thomas J. Gradel, University of Illinois at Chicago Department of Political Science, *Anti-Corruption Report* #14, May 11, 2022, 4–8, https://pols.uic.edu/chicago-politics/anti-corruption-reports/.

2. U.S. Attorney's Office, Northern District of Illinois, "Former Dixon Comptroller Rita Crundwell Sentenced to Nearly 20 Years in Federal Prison for $53.7 Million Theft from City," press release, February 14, 2013, https://www.justice.gov/usao-ndil/pr/former-dixon-comptroller-rita-crundwell-sentenced-nearly-20-years-federal-prison-537.

3. U.S. Attorney's Office, Northern District of Illinois, "City of Chicago Alderman Indicted on Federal Racketeering and Bribery Charges in Connection with Alleged Corruption Schemes," press release, May 30, 2019, https://www.justice.gov/usao-ndil/pr/city-chicago-alderman-indicted-federal-racketeering-and-bribery-charges-connection/; U.S. Attorney's Office, Northern District of Illinois, "Superseding Federal Indictment against Former Illinois Speaker of the House Adds Charge for Alleged Corruption Scheme Related to AT&T Illinois," press release, October 14, 2022, https://www.justice.gov/usao-ndil/pr/superseding-federal-indictment-against-former-illinois-speaker-house-adds-charge.

4. Jim Nowlan, "Corruption in Illinois: An Enduring Tradition" (Paper presented at the Ethics and Reform Symposium on Illinois Government, September 27–28, 2012, Union League Club, Chicago).

5. Robert E. Hartley, *The Dealmakers of Downstate Illinois* (Carbondale: Southern Illinois University Press, 2016); James L. Merriner, *The Man Who Emptied Death Row: George Ryan and Politics of Crime* (Carbondale: Southern Illinois Press, 2008).

6. Cindi Canary and Kent Redfield, "Lessons Learned: What the Successes and Failures of Recent Reform Efforts Tell Us about the Prospects for Political Reform in Illinois," Paper #33, Paul Simon Public Policy Institute, Southern Illinois University Carbondale, October 2012, 20–25.

7. Elrod v. Burns, 427 U.S. 347 (1976); *Rutan v. Republican Party of* Illinois, 497 U.S. 62 (1990).

8. Thomas J. Gradel and Dick Simpson, *Corrupt Illinois: Patronage, Cronyism, and Criminality* (Urbana: University of Illinois Press, 2015).

9. "The 12 Most Corrupt Public Officials in Illinois History: The Complete List," NBC5 Chicago, January 26, 2012, https://www.nbcchicago.com/news/local/the-12-most -corrupt-public-officials-in-illinois-history-the-complete-list/1938347/.

10. Mike Royko, *Boss: Richard J. Daley* (New York: Plume, 1988); Milton Rakove, *Don't Make No Waves—Don't Back No Losers: An Insider's Analysis of the Daley Machine* (Bloomington: Indiana University Press, 1975).

11. Ron Grossman, "Vintage *Chicago Tribune*: 50 Years before Track's Final Race, Arlington Park Was in Middle of a Scandal That Ousted a Former Governor," *Chicago Tribune*, August 7, 2022; Bill Barnhart and Gene Schlickman, *Kerner: The Conflict of Intangible Rights* (Urbana: University of Illinois Press, 1999).

12. Hartley, *Paul Powell of Illinois.*

13. William C. Hidlay, "Former Attorney General, Once Convicted of Tax Fraud Dies," *Associated Press*, June 23, 1986, https://apnews.com/article/6984ba7010137d1dada3 afed3e16e001.

14. Mike Lawrence, "Corruption in the Legislature: Cement Bribery Trial," *Illinois Issues,* December 1976.

15. Elrod v. Burns, 427 U.S. 347 (1976).

16. Anne Freedman, *Patronage: An American Tradition* (Chicago: Nelson-Hall Publishers, 1994); Dave Byrnes, "Seventh Circuit Ends 50 Years of Federal Oversight of Illinois Governor's Office," *Court House News Service*, August 5, 2022, accessed December 10, 2022, https://www.courthousenews.com/seventh-circuit-ends-50-years-of-federal -oversight-of-illinois-governors-office/.

17. The material in this section draws on the *Anti-Corruption Reports* produced by Dick Simpson and his associates at the University of Illinois Chicago to establish the basic timeline for the political corruption activities and events that are highlighted. *Anti-Corruption Reports* #1–14, https://pols.uic.edu/chicago-politics/anti-corruption -reports/. See also Austin Berg, "2019–2020 Illinois Corruption Tracker," *Illinois Policy*, last updated September 8, 2020, https://www.illinoispolicy.org/reports/2019-illinois -corruption-tracker/.

18. City of Chicago Board of Ethics, *A Guide for the Public*, https://www.chicago.gov/ city/en/depts/ethics/supp_info/general_guide_forthepublic.html.

19. Christi Parsons, "Ex-MSI Exec Found Guilty of Laundering," *Chicago Tribune*, November 14, 1997; Ray Long, "MSI Scandal Link to Aides of Edgar, Philip Revealed," *Chicago Tribune*, August 24, 2000.

20. Mike Lawrence, "Mission Impossible: Illinois Officials Chose to Reform Campaign Finance," *Illinois Issues*, September 1998; Canary and Redfield, "Lessons Learned," 22–28.

21. *Rutan v. Republican Party of* Illinois, 497 U.S. 62 (1990). Freedman, *Patronage*.

22. U.S. Attorney's Office, Northern District of Illinois, "Former Staff Chief to Leading Illinois Republican Indicted for Diverting State Employees to Campaign Work," press release, May 19, 2005; Editorial Board, "A Lesson in Contrasts: How the GOP Purged Its Leader amid Corruption Allegations," *Chicago Tribune*, August 7, 2020.

23. Merriner, *The Man Who Emptied Death Row*.

24. Canary and Redfield, "Lessons Learned," 29–32 and 81.

25. Ibid., 33–40 and 82–83.

26. "Transcript: Justice Department Briefing on Blagojevich Investigation," *New York Times*, December 9, 2008, https://www.nytimes.com/2008/12/09/us/politics/09text-illinois.html.

27. Bernard Sieracki, *A Just Cause: The Impeachment and Removal of Governor Rod Blagojevich* (Carbondale: Southern Illinois University Press, 2016).

28. Adriana Colindres, "Illinois House Passes Measure to Curb 'Pay to Play,'" *State Journal Register*, May 21, 2009, https://www.sj-r.com/story/news/2009/05/21/illinois-house-passes-measure-to/48768644007/.

29. Canary and Redfield, "Lessons Learned," 40–50.

30. Stephan Roth and Jeannie Romas-Dunn, "Freedom of Information Act—Recent and Proposed Changes," *Public Servant* 12, no. 4 (June 2011), https://www.isba.org/committees/governmentlawyers/newsletter/2011/06/freedomofinformationactrecentpropos.

31. Hal Dardick, "Emanuel Ethics Reforms Back on Track at City Council," *Chicago Tribune*, July 28, 2011, https://www.chicagotribune.com/politics/chi-emanuel-ethics-reforms-back-on-track-at-city-council-20110728-story.html.

32. Heather Cherone, "Ald. Ed Burke 'Thoroughly Corrupt': Federal Prosecutors," *WTTW*, April 21, 2021, https://news.wttw.com/2021/04/21/ald-ed-burke-thoroughly-corrupt-federal-prosecutors.

33. U.S. Attorney's Office, Northern District of Illinois, "Commonwealth Edison Agrees to Pay $200 Million to Resolve Federal Criminal Investigation into Bribery Scheme," press release, July 17, 2020, https://www.justice.gov/usao-ndil/pr/commonwealth-edison-agrees-pay-200-million-resolve-federal-criminal-investigation.

34. U.S. Attorney's Office, Northern District of Illinois, "Former Commonwealth Edison Executives and Consultants Charged with Conspiring to Corruptly Influence and Reward State of Illinois Official," press release, November 18, 2020, https://www.justice.gov/usao-ndil/pr/former-commonwealth-edison-executives-and-consultants-charged-conspiring-corruptly.

35. U.S. Attorney's Office, Northern District of Illinois, "Former Illinois Speaker of the House Indicted on Federal Racketeering and Bribery Charges in Connection with Alleged Corruption Schemes," press release, March 2, 2022, https://www.justice.gov/usao-ndil/pr/former-illinois-speaker-house-indicted-federal-racketeering-and-bribery-charges,

36. U.S. Attorney's Office, Northern District of Illinois, "Superseding Federal Indictment against Former Illinois Speaker of the House"; Ray Long, *The House That Madigan*

Built: The Record Run of Illinois' Velvet Hammer (Urbana: University of Illinois Press, 2022).

37. Dean Olsen, "Package of Government Ethics Reforms Passed by Illinois Legislature, Sent to Pritzker," *State Journal-Register*, June 1, 2021, https://www.sj-r.com/story/news/2021/06/01/illinois-ethics-bill-aims-to-interrupt-lawmakers-returning-as-lobbyists/5276147001/.

38. Heather Cherone, "Chicago City Council Unanimously Passes Ethics Overhaul, Boots Fines to $20K," *WTTW*, July 20, 2022, https://news.wttw.com/2022/07/20/chicago-city-council-unanimously-passes-ethics-overhaul-boosts-fines-20k.

39. Jon Seidel and Tina Sfondeles, "In Closing Arguments, Feds Hammer at 'Stunning' Stream of Benefits to Madigan While Defense Calls Bribery Charges 'Collateral Damage,'" *Chicago Sun-Times*, April 2, 2023, https://chicago.suntimes.com/2023/4/24/23696308/comed-prosecutors-hammer-stunning-stream-of-benefits-to-michael-madigan.

40. Janson Meisner, Ray Long, and Megan Crepeau, "Defendants Found Guilty on All Counts in 'ComEd Four' Trial; Juror Says Panel Wanted 'Politics to Run in a Correct Manner,'" *Chicago Tribune*, May 2, 2023, https://www.chicagotribune.com/news/criminal-justice/ct-comed-four-bribery-trial-verdict-madigan-20230502-ykjanxkczveudny7v4fci5bsqy-story.html.

41. Daniel J. Elizar, "Series Introduction," in *Illinois Politics and Government: The Expanding Metropolitan Frontier*, ed. Samuel K. Gove and James D. Nowlan (Lincoln: University of Nebraska Press, 1996), xx–xxv.

Chapter 5. Constitutions

1. Janet Cornelius, *Constitution Making in Illinois, 1818–1970* (Urbana: University of Illinois Press, 1972), 34. The sections about early constitutions rely heavily on this work.

2. Illinois allows for public initiative only for matters pertaining to the Legislative Article of the constitution. This petitioning process was used in the successful 1980 amendment that reduced the size of the House and eliminated cumulative voting in Illinois. Later, State Treasurer Patrick Quinn initiated a successful petition to require term limits for state legislators, but the Illinois Supreme Court in 1994 ruled that the petition was invalid because it did not address structural or procedural subject matter as required by the constitution.

3. For further discussion of the slavery issue, see Cornelius, *Constitution Making*, 15–24.

4. Robert P. Howard, *Illinois: A History of the Prairie State* (Grand Rapids, MI: Eerdmans, 1972), 333.

5. Daniel J. Elazar, *American Federalism: A View from the States* (New York: Crowell, 1966), 20.

6. *Bachrach v. Nelson*, 349 Ill. 579, 182 N.E. 909 (1932).

7. Elmer Gertz and Joseph P. Pisciotte, *Charter for a New Age: An Inside View of the Sixth Illinois Constitutional Convention* (Urbana: University of Illinois Press, 1980), 6. This book provides a detailed and readable summary of the workings of the convention.

8. Elmer Gertz and Edward S. Gilbreth, *Quest for a Constitution: A Man Who Wouldn't Quit; A Political Biography of Samuel W. Witwer* (Lanham, MD: University Press of America, 1984), 76–77.

9. Quoted in Samuel K. Gove and Thomas R. Kitser, *Revision Success: The Sixth Illinois Constitutional Convention* (New York: National Municipal League, 1974), 15.

10. James D. Nowlan and Samuel K. Gove, *Illinois Politics: A Citizen's Guide* (Urbana: University of Illinois Press, 2010), 76–77.

11. Elazar, *American Federalism*, 20.

12. Daniel J. Elazar, introduction to *Illinois Government and Politics: The Expanding Metropolitan Frontier*, by Samuel K. Gove and James D. Nowlan (Lincoln: University of Nebraska Press, 1996).

13. Neal R. Peirce, *The Megastates of America: People, Politics, and Power in the Ten Great States* (New York: Norton, 1972), 393–94.

14. Quoted in James D. Nolan, "Con Con 30," personal files, n.d.

15. Illinois Constitution, 1970, art. 1, sec. 25, on workers' rights. Adopted November 8, 2022.

16. *Klinger v. Howlett*, 50 Ill. 2d 242, 278 N.E.2d 84 (1972); *Continental Illinois National Bank and Trust v. Zagel*, 78 Ill. 2d 387, 401 N.E.2d 491 (1979); *City of Canton v. Crouch*, 79 Ill. 2d 356, 403 N.E.2d 242 (1980).

17. Ann Lousin, *Illinois State Constitution: A Reference Guide* (Santa Barbara, CA: Praeger, 2010).

18. Ibid., 31–32.

Chapter 6. The Legislature

1. Stacey St. Clair, "An Only-In-Illinois Story: ComEd Bribery Scheme Hearing Is Run by Daughter-in-Law of Alleged Key Player in the Case," *Chicago Tribune*, July 29, 2020.

2. Illinois State Board of Elections, "Election Results, 2022 Primary," accessed November 3, 2022, https://elections.il.gov/electionoperations/VoteTotalSearch.aspx?ID=63aIZoIunYs%3d.

3. Theresa Mah, "Asian Americans Are Making a Big Mark in Illinois Politics," *Chicago Sun-Times*, November 9, 2022.

4. Until the mid-1960s, an Illinois legislator had no office, no staff, no telephone, and insignificant pay. The constitution authorized only fifty dollars per biennium for postage for lawmakers, and they traditionally met only in the spring of odd-numbered years. For a thorough assessment of the Illinois General Assembly, see Jack R. Van Der Slik and Kent D. Redfield, *Lawmaking in Illinois* (Springfield: Office of Public Affairs Communication, Sangamon State University, 1986). An earlier yet still useful work is Samuel K. Gove, Richard W. Carlson, and Richard J. Carlson, *The Illinois Legislature: Structure and Process* (Urbana: University of Illinois Press, 1976).

5. Patrick Keck, "Pritzker Signs Pay Increase Bill for Legislators, Statewide Office-holders," *State Journal-Register*, January 9, 2023.

6. Office of Management and Budget, Executive Office of the Governor, "Illinois State Budget, Fiscal Year 2023," accessed October 1, 2022, https://budget.illinois.gov/.

7. See Illinois Constitution, 1970, art. 4, sec. 2, which requires that redistricting for all Senate seats take place every ten years and that in the year following the redistricting, all seats be up for election. After that, the seats go through two- and four-year terms in stages so there will be some Senate seats up for election every two years. A statute divides Senate seats into three groups, with the secretary of state to draw cards at random after each redistricting to determine which group of senators will have terms of four, four, and two years, which will have terms of four, two, and four years, and which will have terms of two, four, and four years. 10 Illinois Compiled Statutes 5/29C-5 ff.

8. As a result of rule changes that concentrate power in the leaders, since 2003, legislators have not been allowed to consider a "floor amendment" until the leader first assigns it for a hearing in committee. If the sponsor receives a favorable recommendation from the committee, it then goes back to the whole body for further consideration. Previously, legislators considered and voted on floor amendments *on the floor* without having to resort to committees.

9. Illinois Constitution, 1970, art. 14, sec. 2, provides for constitutional amendments by the legislature. The 1994 amendment to change the effective date of laws amended, art. 4, sec. 10.

10. Governor Bruce Rauner vetoed this bill; however, both houses voted to override the veto.

11. See Gove, Carlson, and Carlson, *Illinois Legislatures*, chap. 4, for a thorough discussion of lawmaking and legislative action relating to vetoes.

12. U.S. Constitution, art. 1, sec. 7: "If any Bill shall not be returned by the President within ten Days (Sundays excepted) after it shall have been presented to him, the Same shall be a Law, in like Manner as if he had signed it, unless the Congress by their Adjournment prevent its Return, in which Case it shall not be a Law."

13. House Rule 10 (b) (102nd General Assembly).

14. National Conference of State Legislatures, "Legislator Compensation," accessed September 3, 2022, https://www.ncsl.org/Portals/1/Documents/About_State_Legislatures/Legislator_Compensation_2021_House.pdf.

15. Ibid.

16. Rick Pearson and Ray Long, "'Present' Votes Emerging from the Past," *Chicago Tribune*, February 3, 2008.

17. This observation is provided by James D. Nowlan, who served in the House of Representatives from 1969 to 1972.

18. Senate Rule 8–4 (a), 102nd General Assembly.

19. Elmer Gertz and Joseph P. Pisciotte, *Charter for a New Age: An Inside View of the Sixth Illinois Constitutional Convention* (Urbana: University of Illinois Press, 1980), 230.

20. Illinois Constitution, 1920, art. 4, secs. 8–10.

21. Kent R. Redfield, "What Keeps the Four Tops on Top?: Leadership Power in the Illinois General Assembly," *Almanac of Illinois Politics*, Institute for Public Affairs Publications Unit, University of Illinois Springfield, 1998, 2.

22. "Party Funds in Illinois," Reform for Illinois' Sunshine Database, accessed October 6, 2022, http://illinoissunshine.org/. These figures will likely grow by a few million by Election Day.

23. Ibid.

24. This section is drawn largely from James D. Nowlan, "Redistricting: The Politics," in the series *A Media Guide to Illinois REMAP '91*, no. 5 (Urbana: Institute of Government and Public Affairs, March 1991).

25. Illinois Constitution, 1970, art. 4, sec. 3 (b).

26. Jennifer Halperin, "The Walking Giant," *Illinois Issues*, December 1994, 24.

27. Daniel C. Vock, "Latino Power: A Rising Population Is Pushing for Political Change," *Illinois Issues*, May 2004.

28. Charles N. Wheeler, "A Democratic Decade?" *Illinois Issues*, April 10, 1982, accessed October 6, 2022, https://www.lib.niu.edu/1982/ii820410half.html.

29. Ibid.

30. Ibid.

31. Rick Pearson, "What Is Mike Madigan Up To?" *Illinois Issues,* April 12, 1997, accessed October 3, 2022, https://www.lib.niu.edu/1997/ii970412.html.

32. Ray Long, *The House That Madigan Built* (Urbana: University of Illinois Press, 2022).

33. "Friends of Michael J Madigan," Reform for Illinois' Sunshine Database, accessed October 6, 2022, http://illinoissunshine.org/committees/665/.

34. Long, *The House That Madigan Built.*

35. Ibid.

36. Dave McKinney, "Breaking Down the ComEd Patronage Scandal," *NPR*, July 20, 2020.

37. Grace Perry, "The Madigan Indictment," *Chicago Magazine*, April 11, 2022.

Chapter 7. The Executive

1. Isaac Ghinai et al., "First Known Person-to-Person Transmission of Severe Acute Respiratory Syndrome Coronavirus 2 (SARS-CoV-2) in the USA," *Lancet*, March 13, 2020, https://www.ncbi.nlm.nih.gov/pmc/articles/PMC7158585/.

2. Dave Davies, "Reckoning with the Dead: Journalist Goes Inside an NYC COVID-19 Disaster Morgue," *NPR*, May 28, 2020, https://www.npr.org/sections/health-shots/2020/05/28/863710050/reckoning-with-the-dead-journalist-goes-inside-an-nyc-covid-19-disaster-morgue.

3. See Executive Order 2020–47.

4. Alisha Haridasani Gupta, "How Do You Lead a State's Coronavirus Response? Ask Her," *New York Times*, May 27, 2020.

5. Edward McClellan, "How Chicago Dealt with the 1918 Spanish Flu," *Chicago Magazine*, March 17, 2020.

6. This section draws heavily on the highly readable profiles of Illinois governors by Robert P. Howard, *Mostly Good and Competent Men: Illinois Governors, 1818–1988* (Springfield: Illinois Issues, Sangamon State University, and Illinois State Historical Society, 1988).

7. Ibid., 79.

8. Ibid.

9. For Thompson's version of his years in office, see James R. Thompson, *Illinois, State of the State, 1977–1991: The Thompson Administration* (Springfield: State of Illinois, 1991).

10. Ibid., 21.

11. Ibid., 188.

12. Ibid., 340.

13. Dave McKinney, "Ryan's Paradox," *Illinois Issues*, November 2002, 15–19. This is an excellent summary of the career of Governor George Ryan.

14. "Former Illinois Governor Ryan Enters Prison," *Reuters*, November 7, 2007.

15. David Bernstein, "Mr. Un-Popularity," *Chicago Magazine*, January 17, 2008.

16. Taylor Pensoneau, "Rod Blagojevich," in *The Illinois Governors: Mostly Good and Competent Men*, rev. and ed. Taylor Pensoneau and Peggy Boyer Long (Springfield: Illinois Issues, 2007), 314–25 (update of the 1988 book edited by Robert P. Howard).

17. "Illinois Governor Signs Preschool for All," *New York Times*, February 13, 2006.

18. Charles N. Wheeler III, "The Governor's Lawsuits Are the Latest Signs of a Toxic Environment at the Statehouse," *Illinois Issues*, October 2007, 33–34.

19. Jim Fletcher, conversation with James D. Nowlan, Springfield, IL, May 28, 2008.

20. Harvey Berkman, "Electing Illinois' Other Executives," *Illinois Issues*, August/September 1990.

21. Carol Felsenthal, "Does Pat Quinn Have a Personal Life?" *Chicago Magazine*, October 20, 2014.

22. Katherine Barrett and Richard Greene, "Grading the States 2008: The Mandate to Measure," *Governing: The Future of States and Localities*, March 2008, http://governing .com/gpp/2008/index.htm.

23. Rick Pearson, "Quinn Job Approval Rating Just 26%," *Chicago Tribune*, October 12, 2012.

24. Patrick Rehkamp and Andrew Schroedter, "Will Quinn Cash In on Pension Front?" *Better Government Association*, November 23, 2014, https://www.bettergov.org/author/patrick-rehkamp/page/5/.

25. Hunter Schwartz, "GOP Governors Call for State Employee Hiring Freezes," *Washington Post*, January 19, 2015.

26. Monique Garcia, Kim Geiger, and Hal Dardick, "Rauner Signs a Stopgap Budget, School Funding Bill—But Relief from Stalemate Proves Temporary," *Chicago Tribune*, June 30, 2016.

27. "Illinois Finally Has a Budget," *WBEZ*, July 6, 2017, accessed September 22, 2022, https://www.wbez.org/stories/illinois-finally-has-a-budget/ff3e45e6-ac06-4221-aef7 -ef0d3626c587.

28. Quoted in Carol Marin and Don Mosely, "Dollars and Sense: Here's How Much Bruce Rauner and J.B. Pritzker Spent," *NBC News*, November 5, 2018.

29. Rick Pearson, "Gov. J.B. Pritzker Gave Democratic Governors Group $24 Million to Fund Ads that Helped Nominate His GOP Opponent," *Chicago Tribune*, July 22, 2022.

30. Edward McClelland, "Mr. Competent," *Chicago Magazine*, May 26, 2022.

31. For more complete descriptions of the duties of the executive officers, see the *Illinois Blue Book*, published every two years by the Illinois secretary of state. This is a comprehensive, though sometimes self-serving, guide to state government. For more balanced articles about the offices and the personalities and politics therein, see the annual index to *Illinois Issues*, a monthly magazine of public affairs published by the University of Illinois in Springfield.

32. Andy Grimm, "Illinois to Spend Up to $760 Million from Lawsuit Settlement to Confront Opioid Crisis," *Chicago Sun-Times*, July 29, 2022.

33. Nika Schoonover, "Mendoza Pushes for Law Requiring Greater Deposits to 'Rainy Day' Fund," *WQAD8* (ABC), accessed May 23, 2023, https://www.wqad.com/article/news/politics/illinois-politics/illinois-rainy-day-fund-automatic-deposits/526-691eb460-14e2-413c-85bc-ba589314c693.

34. Ibid.

35. David Miller, "Vetoes Could Cause Controversy," *First Reading* 4, no. 9 (October 1989): 11. This is a publication of the Legislative Research Unit of the Illinois General Assembly.

36. Ibid.

37. Mark Brown, "It Doesn't Take Quantum Physics to Understand Pritzker's 'Rebuild Illinois' Program, but Just in Case . . . ," *Chicago Sun-Times,* June 5, 2019.

38. Anecdote related by James D. Nowlan from the period when he was a member of the Illinois General Assembly, 1969–73.

39. Alan Rosenthal, *Governors and Legislatures* (Washington, D.C.: CQ Press, 1990), 11.

40. Ibid.

41. Ibid., 170.

42. Governor's Office of Management and Budget, *Illinois State Budget, Fiscal Year 2023* (Springfield: Governor's Office of Management and Budget, 2022).

43. Tom Berkshire and Richard J. Carlson, "The Office of the Governor," in *Inside State Government in Illinois*, ed. James D. Nowlan (Chicago: Neltnor House, 1991), 18–40.

44. Quoted in James D. Nowlan, "An Introduction to State Government," in *Inside State Government: A Primer for State Managers*, ed. James D. Nowlan (Urbana: Institute of Government and Public Affairs, University of Illinois, 1983), 5.

Chapter 8. The Courts and Criminal Justice Policy

1. Maya Dukmasova, "Bail Abolition Is Just the Tip of the Iceberg," *Chicago Reader*, March 19, 2021.

2. Briana Payton, "Why Ending Cash Bail in Illinois Is a Win for Racial Justice and Community Safety," Metropolitan Planning Council, accessed September 27, 2022, https://www.metroplanning.org/news/10082/Why-ending-cash-bail-in-Illinois-is-a-win-for-racial-justice-and-community-safety/.

3. Ibid.

4. Quoted in Jerry Nowicki, "Illinois Pretrial Detention Reforms Go Beyond No Cash Bail," *Illinois State Journal-Register*, September 19, 2022.

5. Phillip Marcelo, "Illinois Law Doesn't Make Murder, Other Crimes 'Non-Detainable,'" *Associated Press*, September 15, 2022.

6. Nowicki, "Illinois Pretrial Detention Reforms Go Beyond No Cash Bail."

7. Tony Preckwinkle, Cook County president, Lecture delivered to POLS 211, "Chicago's Future" class, Fall 2014, University of Illinois at Chicago.

8. Civic Federation, "Pretrial Reform Efforts in Illinois and Outcomes from Other States," February 22, 2021, https://www.civicfed.org/iifs/blog/pretrial-reform-efforts-illinois-and-outcomes-other-states.

9. Frank Main, "Cash Bail Reform: A Lesson for Illinois?" *Chicago Sun-Times*, January 16, 2021.

10. Maureen Foertsch McKinney, "Ending Cash Bail Doesn't Increase Crime: Report," *NPR Illinois*, accessed September 27, 2022, https://www.nprillinois.org/equity-justice/2020–11–23/ending-cash-bail-doesnt-increase-crime-report.

11. Andy Grimm, "Cook County's Top Judge Defends Bond Reform, Juvenile Courts," *Chicago Sun-Times*, January 27, 2022.

12. Ibid.

13. Ibid.

14. Emanuel Camarillo, Kade Heather, Mary Norkol, Jon Seidel, and Andy Grimm, "A Judge Ruled the Portion of the SAFE-T Act Ending Cash Bail Is Unconstitutional," *WBEZ*, December 29, 2022, accessed May 30, 2023, https://www.wbez.org/stories/safe-t-act-ending-cash-bail-is-unconstitutional-judge/5fd5bb70-6fd0-43a2-b797-a6241ecac3b5.

15. Shannon Heffernan, "Five Things to Know as the SAFE-T Act Goes to the Illinois Supreme Court," *WBEZ*, March 12, 2023, accessed May 30, 2023, https://www.wbez.org/stories/safe-t-act-cash-bail-illinois-supreme-court/3bbc71c4-d3b1-4c55-80aa-1fc2ff818ffc.

16. *2021 Annual Report of the Illinois Courts* (Springfield: Supreme Court of Illinois, 2021).

17. Illinois Courts, "State and Local Funding for the Illinois Courts," accessed September 23, 2022, https://www.illinoiscourts.gov/public/state-and-local-funding-for-the-illinois-courts/.

18. Ibid.

19. Adamas, County, Illinois, "Illinois Court Structure," accessed on May 30, 2023, https://www.co.adams.il.us/government/departments/judicial/illinois-court-structure.

20. Ibid.

21. *2021 Annual Report of the Illinois Courts*.

22. Illinois Constitution, 1970, art. 6, sec. 16.

23. Amanda Vinicky, "New Illinois Supreme Court Districts Bring Competition," *WTTW*, May 17, 2022, accessed September 23, 2022, https://news.wttw.com/2022/05/17/new-supreme-court-districts-bring-competition.

24. "Ann Burke Retiring from the Illinois Supreme Court," *Crain's Chicago Business*, September 12, 2022.

25. James Tuohy and Rob Warden, *Greylord: Justice, Chicago Style* (New York: Putnam, 1989).

26. Illinois Constitution, 1970, art. 6, sec. 12 (d).

27. Nancy Ford, "From Judicial Election to Merit Selection: A Time for Change in Illinois," *Northern Illinois University Law Review* 8, no. 3 (1988): 665–707.

28. *Caperton v. A. T. Massey Coal Company*, 129 S. Ct. 2252, 173 L. Ed. 2d 1208 (2009).

29. Lawyers are encouraged to participate by canon eight of the American Bar Association code: "Generally, lawyers are qualified by personal observation and investigation to evaluate the qualifications of persons seeking or being considered for such public offices, and for this reason they have a special responsibility to aid in the selection of those who are qualified."

30. "Our Picks for Subcircuit Judges," *Chicago Sun-Times*, October 8, 1994.

31. Dan Mihalopoulos, "The Illinois State Bar Association Rates ShawnTe Raines Welch 'Not Qualified' for Bench," *WBEZ Chicago*, May 28, 2022.

32. Ibid.

33. "Check Your Judges," *Injustice Watch*, accessed September 23, 2022, https://www.injusticewatch.org/interactives/judicial-election-guide/2022-primary/en.

34. Illinois Supreme Court, Special Commission on the Administration of Justice, *Solovy Report*, February 12, 1987, pt. 1, 51.

35. Illinois Constitution, 1970, art. 2, sec. 1. See *Kunkel v. Walton*, 179 Ill. 2d 519, 533, 689 N.E.2d 1047, 1053 (1997) ("The separation of powers provision does not seek to achieve a complete divorce between the branches of government; the purpose of the provision is to prevent the whole power of two or more branches from residing in the same hands. There are areas in which separate spheres of governmental authority overlap and certain functions are thereby shared [citation omitted].").

36. Illinois Constitution, 1970, art. 8, sec. 3.

37. Supreme Court of Illinois, "Amended Responses to the Financial and Compliance Audit Report" (Springfield: State of Illinois, October 4, 1989).

38. Ken Armstrong and Rick Pearson, "Heiple's Pyrrhic Victory—Panel Assails Him, Rejects Impeachment," *Chicago Tribune*, May 16, 1997.

39. Legislative Research Unit, "Articles Voted in 1833 Impeachment Proceedings" (Research response prepared by George Fox Rischel, staff attorney, File 10–833, April 22, 1997): "The only impeachment proceedings previously held in Illinois were the 1832–33 impeachment and trial of Theophilus W. Smith, a justice of the Illinois Supreme Court. The House of Representatives voted to impeach Justice Smith on January 5, 1833, and then prepared seven articles of impeachment and exhibited them on January 9, 1833, to the Senate (which failed to convict)."

40. Illinois Constitution, 1970, art. 6, sec. 14.

41. *Jorgensen v. Blagojevich*, 211 Ill. 2d 286, 811 N.E.2d 652, 285 Ill. Dec. 165 (2004).

42. 730 Illinois Compiled Statutes 5/3-3-13.

43. *People ex rel. Madigan v. Snyder*, 208 Ill. 2d 457, 804 N.E.2d 546 (2004).

44. *People ex rel. Madigan*, 208 Ill. 2d 457, 804 N.E. 2d546 (2004).

45. *Kunkel*, 179 Ill. 2d 519, 533, 689 N.E.2d 1047, 1053 (1997). See generally Abner J. Mikva and Eric Lane, *An Introduction to Statutory Interpretation and the Legislative Process* (New York: Aspen Law and Business, 2002), 95–144 (chap. 3, "The Interpretation of Statutes"); William N. Eskridge, Philip P. Frickey, and Elizabeth Garrett, *Cases and Materials on Legislation: Statutes and the Creation of Public Policy*, 4th ed. (St. Paul: Thomson/West, 2007), 689–846 (chap. 7, "Theories of Statutory Interpretation").

46. *Kunkel*, 179 Ill. 2d 519, 533, 689 N.E.2d 1047, 1053 (1997).

47. *Johnson v. Edgar*, 176 Ill. 2d 499, 680 N.E.2d 1372 (1997).

48. *Geja's Café v. Metropolitan Pier and Exposition Authority*, 153 Ill. 2d 239, 606 N.E.2d 1212, 1220 (1992).

49. Michael J. Kasper, "Using the Single-Subject Rule to Invalidate Legislation: A Better Approach?" *Illinois Bar Journal* 87, no. 3 (March 1999): 146.

50. Ibid.

51. *Johnson v. Edgar*, No. 81019 (Cir. Ct. Cook Co. 1996).

52. *People v. Pitts*, 295 Ill. App. 3d 182, 691 N.E.2d 1174 (4th Dist. 1998); *People v. Reedy*, 295 Ill. App. 3d 34, 692 N.E.2d 376, 383 (2d Dist. 1998).

53. Kasper, "Using the Single-Subject Rule," 146.

54. *Illinois State Chamber of Commerce v. Filan*, 216 Ill. 2d 653, 837 N.E.2d 922 (2005).

55. *Illinois State Chamber v. Filan*, Case No. 2004-CH-06750, Circuit Court of Cook County, Illinois, accessed July 4, 2009, https://w3.courtlink.lexisnexis.com/cook county/FindDock.asp?NCase=2004-CH-06750&SearchType=0&Dateabase=3&case_no =&=&=&=&PLtype=1&sname=&CDate=.

Chapter 9. Local Government and the Intergovernmental Web

1. Civic Federation, "An Inventory of Local Government in Illinois," February 25, 2021, accessed August 30, 2022, https://www.civicfed.org/sites/default/files/inventory _of_local_governments_report__0.pdf.

2. Ibid. For a complete discussion of methodology and definition of governments, see pages 10–22 of the report.

3. It has been argued that Illinois also could do without townships, at least outside of the Chicago metropolitan area.

4. "Regional Revenue and Spending Project," in *Seeking a New Balance: Paying for Government in Metropolitan Chicago* (Chicago: Regional Partnership, 1991), executive summary, 2.

5. "An Inventory of Local Government in Illinois." Previous counts include road and bridge districts in townships.

6. James F. Keane and Gary Koch, eds., *Illinois Local Government: A Handbook* (Carbondale: Southern Illinois University Press, 1990), ix. Another estimate in the same book puts the figure at one hundred thousand.

7. As recounted by State Representative Chris Welch and River Forest village president Catherine Aducci, in presentations to PSC 286, "State and Local Government" class, Dominican University, September 12 and October 10, 2013, respectively.

8. Ibid.

9. "Rep. Welch Pulls Bill Calling for Binding Referendum on River Forest Township's Future," *The Patch*, March 25, 2014, accessed September 2, 2022, https://patch .com/illinois/oakpark/rep-welch-pulls-bill-calling-for-referendum-on-river-forest -townships-future.

10. Marie Wilson, "Naperville Township Roads Debate Is Not Just about Money: City Would Need to Add 2 Employees, Fill Vacant Position," *Daily Herald*, April 11, 2016.

11. Marie Wilson, "Naperville Township Road Issue Solved in Deal with Lisle Twp.," *Daily Herald*, August 12, 2016.

12. Joseph Diebold, "Evanston Votes to Abolish Township," *Daily Northwestern*, March 18. 2014.

13. Kristen Taketa, "Belleville Council Votes to Dissolve Township, Absorb Services," *St. Louis Post-Dispatch*, May 2, 2016.

14. Robert P. Howard, *Illinois: A History of the Prairie State* (Grand Rapids, MI: Eerdmans, 1972), 479.

15. Dick Simpson, Marco Rosaire Rossi, and Thomas J. Gradel, "Corruption Continues through the Covid-19 Pandemic," University of Illinois at Chicago Department of Political Science Anti-Corruption Report #14, May 11, 2022, accessed August 30, 2022, https://pols.uic.edu/wp-content/uploads/sites/273/2022/05/Corruption-Rpt-14-on-5-7-22-final.pdf.

16. Ibid. As of this writing, Mario DePasquale, McCook police chief, has been indicted, and pled not guilty, and was placed on administrative leave.

17. Better Government Association, "Public Salary Database," accessed September 3, 2022, https://salary.bettergov.org/person/joseph-c-vallez-44d862f0/; Bensonville Park District, https://salary.bettergov.org/unit/bensenville-park-district-343d72d0/?data_year=2019; Justice Park District, https://salary.bettergov.org/unit/justice-park-district-e429e8b5/?data_year=2019.

18. Samuel K. Gove, *The Illinois Municipal Electoral Process* (Urbana: Institute of Government and Public Affairs, 1964).

19. Dick Simpson, Marco Rosaire Rossi, Constance A. Mixon, and Melissa Mouritsen, *Twenty-First Century Chicago* (San Diego: Cognella, 2022).

20. Jefferson County Clerk, "Election Statistics," accessed September 3, 2022, http://www.jeffersoncountyillinois.com/sites/default/files/Voting%20Stats_0.pdf; Sangamon County Clerk, "Consolidated Election Results," accessed September 3, 2022, https://results.enr.clarityelections.com/IL/Sangamon/108900/web.276013/#/summary; Rock Island County Clerk, "Previous Election Results," accessed September 3, 2022, https://www.rockislandcounty.org/PreviousElections/.

21. DuPage County Clerk, "April 6, 2021, Consolidated General Election," accessed August 4, 2021, https://www.dupageresults.gov/IL/DuPage/108904/web.276603/#/summary.

22. Ibid.

23. DuPage County Clerk, "April 4, 2017, Consolidated General Election," accessed August 4, 2021, https://www.dupageresults.gov/IL/DuPage/71873/Web02.194085/#/.

24. Illinois City/County Management Association, "ICMA-Recognized Jurisdictions," accessed September 6, 2022, https://www.ilcma.org/why-professional-management/local-government-management-resources/icma-recognized-jurisdictions/.

25. Steve Sadin, "Waukegan Officials Debate Merits of Nonpartisan Elections, City-Manager Form of Government; 'I've Never Had to Vote on Anything Along Party Lines,'" *Chicago Tribune*, December 17, 2021.

26. Ibid.

27. "Annual Financial Reports: Unused and Unusable," *Tax Facts*, October 1990, 7.

28. Illinois Constitution, 1970, art. 71, sec. 6.

29. Editorial, *Chicago Tribune*, June 17, 1990.

30. Illinois Municipal League, "Purpose of Home Rule," accessed August 31, 2022, https://www.iml.org/homerule.

31. James Banovetz and Thomas W. Kelty, *Home Rule in Illinois* (Springfield: Illinois Issues, Sangamon State University, 1987).

32. Illinois Municipal League, "State Mandates," October 20, 2021, iii, accessed May 30, 2023, https://www.iml.org/file.cfm?key=16607.

33. Regional Revenue and Spending Project, *Seeking a New Balance*, executive summary, 25.

34. Metropolitan Planning Council, "Home," accessed September 6, 2022, https://www.metroplanning.org/index.html.

35. Bob Tita, "Looking to Add Teeth to Planning," *Crain's Chicago Business*, October 16, 2006.

36. Chicago Metropolitan Agency for Planning, *About CMAP* (pamphlet), 2007.

37. Chicago Metropolitan Agency for Planning, *About CMAP*.

38. Tita, "Looking to Add Teeth to Planning."

39. Judith Crown, "Hiring a City Planner Helped Calumet Park Get Beyond Surviving 'Day to Day,'" *Crain's Chicago Business*, March 11, 2022.

40. Philip Bloomer, *Champaign-Urbana News Gazette*, March 2, 1990.

41. An exception to this statement is found in Samuel K. Gove, "State Impact: The Daley Legacy," in *After Daley: Chicago Politics in Transition,* ed. Samuel K. Gove and Louis H. Masotti (Urbana: University of Illinois Press, 1982), 203–16. The political literature about Chicago is voluminous, but little attention has been given to the city's relationship with the state because the authors do not believe that the relationship is important for an understanding of Chicago politics.

42. Charles E. Merriam, Spencer D. Parratt, and Albert Lapawsky, *The Government of the Metropolitan Region of Chicago* (Chicago: University of Chicago Press, 1933), 179.

43. For a comprehensive analysis of voting patterns of the Chicago city council from Mayor Daley to Lori Lightfoot, see the University of Illinois at Chicago Department of Political Science's numerous reports located at https://pols.uic.edu/chicago-politics/.

44. The progressive resistance was in the making during the last of the Richard M. Daley years. However, in Kari Lydersen's excellent work, *Mayor 1%: Rahm Emanuel and the Rise of Chicago's 99%* (Chicago: Haymarket, 2014), she details how his almost singular focus on downtown interests at the expense of the rest of city created a focal point for Chicago progressives.

45. In the suburbs of Cook County, township committee members are elected to serve on the county central committee. Outside Cook County, precinct committee members are elected, and they then select the county chairs.

46. Zay N. Smith and Pamela Zekman, *The Mirage* (New York: Random House, 1979), 39–40.

47. Simpson et al., "Corruption Continues through the Covid-19 Pandemic."

48. Malcolm Gladwell, "Paring the Big Apple," *Washington Post,* national weekly edition, March 21–27, 1994, 33. The authors relied heavily on the study by Ester R.

Fuchs, *Mayors and Money: Fiscal Policy in New York and Chicago* (Chicago: University of Chicago Press, 1992).

49. "Illinois State Budget Fiscal Year 2023," Office of Management and Budget, accessed September 6, 2022, https://budget.illinois.gov/content/dam/soi/en/web/budget/documents/budget-book/fy2023-budget-book/fy23-budget-in-brief-final-1.31.22.pdf.

50. Kathleen O'Leary Morgan and Scott Morgan, eds., *State Rankings 2020: A Statistical View of America* (Washington, DC: CQ Press, 2020), 197–99.

51. Ibid.

52. Len O'Connor, *Clout: Mayor Daley and His Chicago* (Chicago: Henry Regnery, 1975), 150–57.

Chapter 10. Budgeting, Taxing, and Spending in Illinois

1. Matt Masterson, "Student Enrollment Down across Illinois, Education Officials Say," *WTTW*, October 29, 2021; Illinois Board of Higher Education, "Degree Granting College and Universities Schools," last updated 2020, https://www.ibhe.org/institutionsByL.asp; "College Search," College Simply, last updated 2022, https://www.collegesimply.com/.

2. Illinois Department of Corrections, "Annual Report Fiscal Year 2020," https://www2.illinois.gov/idoc/reportsandstatistics/Documents/FY20%20Annual%20Report%20FINAL.pdf.

3. Illinois State Comptroller's Office, "Annual Comprehensive Financial Report 2021," and various earlier years, https://illinoiscomptroller.gov/__media/sites/comptroller/ACFR%20Final%202021.pdf.

4. *Facing Facts: A Report of the Civic Committee's Task Force on Illinois State Finance* (Chicago: Civic Committee of the Commercial Club of Chicago, December 2006), 23.

5. Authors' best estimates, drawing upon various government reports.

6. "Share of Value Added to the Gross Domestic Product (GDP) of the United States in 2021, by Industry," Statista Research Department, March 2022, published by Bureau of Economic Analysis, U.S. Department of Commerce, 2021.

7. *Illinois Tax Handbook for Legislators*, 37th ed. (Springfield: Illinois General Assembly, Commission on Government Forecasting and Accountability, 2021).

8. Joanna Biernacka-Lievestro and Joe Fleming, "State's Unfunded Pension Liabilities Persist as Major Long-Term Challenge," Pew Charitable Trusts, July 7, 2022. The number of local governments is from "An Inventory of Local Governments in Illinois," Civic Federation of Chicago, February 23, 2021.

9. Illinois Comptroller's Office, *Fiscal Focus*, May 2007.

10. *Capital Budget Fiscal Year 2023* (Springfield: Governor's Office of Management and Budget, 2022).

11. "Nearly $43 Million Diverted from General Revenue Fund in FY89," press release, Office of the Comptroller, Springfield, IL, May 14, 1990.

12. "McPier Set to Tap Sales Tax for 1st Time," *Crain's Chicago Business*, May 14, 2007.

13. For a delightful, highly instructive essay on budgeting, see Robert L. Mandeville, "It's the Same Old Song," in *Illinois State Budget, Fiscal Year 1991* (Springfield: Illinois Bureau of the Budget, March 1990), 1–14.

14. Illinois Constitution, 1970, art. 8, sec. 2 (a).

15. As observed by James D. Nowlan, who was a member of the 1976 transition team.

16. Mandeville, "It's the Same Old Song," 5.

17. As reported in James D. Nowlan, *New Game Plan for Illinois* (Chicago: Neltnor House, 1989), 113.

18. Raymond F. Coyne, "The Legislative Appropriations Process: Selective Use of Authority and Tools," in *Illinois: Political Processes and Governmental Performance*, ed. Edgar Crane (Dubuque, IA: Kendall-Hunt, 1980), 287–305.

19. For an informative look at the Bureau of the Budget (renamed the Governor's Office of Management and Budget), see Craig Bazzani, "The Executive Budget Process," in *Inside State Government in Illinois*, ed. James Nowlan (Urbana: Institute of Government and Public Affairs, 1982). The quotation in the text is found on 42.

20. Coyne, "Legislative Appropriations Process," 144.

21. Thomas Anton, *The Politics of State Expenditure in Illinois* (Urbana: University of Illinois Press, 1966).

22. Illinois State Board of Education, press release, Springfield, January 19, 1989.

23. Maggie Thomas, "Public Health without a Budget: Budget Crisis in Illinois," *Public Health Post*, December 2, 2016.

24. Michael D. Klemens, "An Overture to Overcome Overspending," *Budget Watch Reporter*, no. 5 (June 1990): 1–8.

25. Quoted in Michael D. Klemens, "Budget Crisis: The Seeds and the Harvest," *Illinois Issues*, August-September 1987, 46.

26. *Federal Funds to State Agencies FY2007–2009*, 18th ed. (Springfield: Legislative Research Unit, May 2009), xiii.

27. "Federal and State Share of Medicaid Spending FY 2021," Kaiser Family Foundation, Last updated 2022, https://www.kff.org/medicaid/state-indicator/federalstate -share-of-spending/?currentTimeframe=0&sortModel=%7B%22colId%22:%22Location %22,%22sort%22:%22asc%22%7D.

28. Randy Erford, *Illinois State Spending: The Thompson Years* (Springfield: Taxpayers' Federation of Illinois, 1998), 9.

29. Illinois Department of Revenue, *Property Tax Statistics* (Springfield: Illinois Department of Revenue, 2020).

30. Taxpayers' Federation of Illinois, *Tax Facts* (May 2022).

31. *The Illinois Poll, 1991* (DeKalb: Center for Governmental Studies, Northern Illinois University, 1991).

32. *Tax Expenditure Report Illinois, Fiscal Year 2019*, Illinois State Comptroller's Office, March, 2021).

33. *Illinois Tax Handbook for Legislators*, 2021.

34. Ibid.

35. Ibid.

36. "Wagering in Illinois—2018 Update," Commission on Government Forecasting and Accountability, Illinois General Assembly, Springfield, Illinois, 2021.

37. Jack R. Van Der Slik, "Legalized Gamblers: Predatory Policy," *Illinois Issues*, March 1990, 30.

38. Maurice Scholten, "Overall State and Local Taxes—How Does Illinois Compare?" *Tax Facts* (January 2022), and as well from other monthly *Tax Facts* during the first half of 2022, also authored by Scholten.

39. Sean Williams, "America's 5 Most Hated Taxes," *Motley Fool*, November 2, 2013.

Chapter 11. State Regulation of Our Behavior

1. Thomas Hobbes, *The Leviathan* (1651).

2. Illinois Gaming Board, *Sports Wagering Report*, January-October 2022, accessed October 31, 2022, https://www.igb.illinois.gov/SportsReports.aspx.

3. Commission on Government Forecasting and Accountability, *Gaming in Illinois* (Springfield, 2022), https://cgfa.ilga.gov/Upload/2022_Wagering_in_IL.pdf.

4. "Statewide Allocation Summary for January 2022–September 2022," Illinois Gaming Board Video Gaming Revenue Report, accessed October 24, 2022, https://www.igb.illinois.gov/videoreports.aspx; Dave Briggs, "Illinois Sportsbooks Rank 2nd in the USA, Surpass $1 Billion in Online Bets," *PlayIllinois*, October 19, 2022.

5. Robert McCoppin and Steve Lord, "Casinos Hope Convenience Counts as Chicago Antes Up," *Chicago Tribune*, October 31, 2022.

6. Stephen Siff, "The Illegalization of Marijuana: A Brief History," *Origins* (May 2014), https://origins.osu.edu/article/illegalization-marijuana-brief-history?language_content_entity=en.

7. Ibid.

8. Ibid.

9. Amanda Vinicky, "The Illinois Marijuana Industry Was Supposed to Bring Equity. Advocates Say Those Promises Are Falling Short," *WTTW*, September 28, 2022.

Chapter 12. Education

1. "State Snapshot," *Illinois Report Card*, 2022, accessed October 31, 2022, https://www.illinoisreportcard.com/State.aspx.

2. Executive Order 2020–15.

3. Jacob Kuerth, Sam Clancy, and Holden Kurwicki, "Metro East Schools Make Policy Changes after Illinois Judge's Ruling Blocks School Mask Requirements," *NBC 5*, February 6, 2022, accessed October 31, 2022, https://www.ksdk.com/article/news/education/metro-east-schools-policy-changes-illinois-judges-ruling-blocks-school-mask-mandates/63-dc425825-c348-42ed-a622-8c67d61fdcac.

4. Ibid.

5. Susie An and Caroline Kubzansk, "School Districts across Illinois Are Going Mask Optional," *WBEZChicago*, February 18, 2022.

6. Susie An, "Illinois Student Test Scores Are In. They Remain Far Below Pre-pandemic Levels in Reading and Math," *WBEZChicago*, October 27, 2022.

7. Kathleen O'Leary Morgan and Scott Morgan, eds., *State Rankings 2020: A Statistical View of America* (Washington, DC: CQ Press, 2020), 113–66. Data in the state rankings book are from federal government sources, unless otherwise noted below, and sources are provided therein.

8. Ibid.

9. Peter Mulhall, "Illinois K–12 Education," *Illinois Report 2007* (Urbana: Institute of Government and Public Affairs, University of Illinois, 2007), 24–29.

10. Illinois Constitution, 1970, art. 10.

11. *Illinois Report Card 2022.*

12. Ibid.

13. O'Leary Morgan and Morgan, *State Rankings*, 2020.

14. Karen Ann Cullotta, "Frustrated by Chicago Public Schools' Union Battles, a Growing Number of Weary Parents Enroll Kids in City's Catholic Schools," *Chicago Tribune*, January 14, 2022.

15. "School Choice in the United States," National Center for Education Statistics, 2019, accessed August 13, 2022, https://nces.ed.gov/pubs2019/2019106.pdf#page=24.

16. For an excellent discussion of education in Illinois before 1975, see Martin Burlingame, "Politics and Policies of Elementary and Secondary Education," in *Illinois: Political Processes and Governmental Performance*, ed. Edgar Crane (Dubuque, IA: Kendall-Hunt, 1980), 370–89. See also Cullom Davis, "Illinois Crossroads and Cross Section," in *Heartland: Comparative Histories of the Midwestern States*, ed. James H. Madison (Bloomington: Indiana University Press, 1988), 154.

17. Danish Murtaza. "Too Many School Districts in Illinois? What You Should Know About Consolidation," Better Government Association, January 17, 2018, accessed June 28, 2022, https://www.bettergov.org/news/too-many-school-districts-in-illinois -what-you-should-know-about-school-consolidation/.

18. The exception to this is Chicago, which has a school board appointed by its mayor.

19. Illinois Constitution, 1970, art. 10. See specifically section 105, the Illinois School Code, and 105 ILCS 5/27, mandated study.

20. "Illinois Instructional Mandates 2022–2023," Illinois State Board of Education, accessed August 29, 2022, https://www.isbe.net/Documents/IL-Mandated-Units-of -Study.pdf.

21. O'Leary Morgan and Morgan, *State Rankings*, 2020.

22. "Public School Revenue Sources," National Center for Education Statistics, May 2022, accessed September 13, 2022, https://nces.ed.gov/programs/coe/indicator/cma/ public-school-revenue.

23. *Illinois Report Card 2022.*

24. "Public School Revenue Sources."

25. "Finance, Budget, and Funding," Illinois State Board of Education, accessed October 18, 2022, https://www.isbe.net/Pages/Operating-Expense-Per-Pupil.aspx.

26. James Ward, remarks before a meeting of Voice of the Prairie, Galesburg, IL, October 28, 1989.

27. *Chicago Urban League and Quad County Urban League, Plaintiffs v. State of Illinois and Illinois State Board of Education, Defendants,* complaint filed August 20, 2008, in the Circuit Court of Cook County, Illinois.

28. "Moving Forward: Illinois' Evidence-Based School Funding Formula Can Reverse Decades of Inequity Created by the Foundation Formula It Replaced," Center for Tax and Budget Accountability, accessed September 28, 2022, https://www.ctbaonline .org/reports/moving-forward-illinois-evidence-based-school-funding-formula-can -reverse-decades-inequity.

29. Quoted in Peter Medlin, "Has Evidence-Based Funding Made Education in Illinois More Equitable?" *Illinois News Room*, accessed September 29, 2022, https://illinoisnewsroom.org/has-evidence-based-funding-made-education-in-illinois-more-equitable/.

30. Peter Hancock, "As Evidence-Based Funding Formula Turns 5, Lawmakers Reflect on Historic Legislation," *Illinois Public Media*, accessed September 29, 2022, https://illinoisnewsroom.org/as-evidence-based-funding-formula-turns-5-lawmakers-reflect-on-historic-legislation/.

31. Ibid.

32. Ibid.

33. Adam Slade, "How Can Illinois School Districts Address Funding Woes? Share Administrative Costs," Metropolitan Planning Council, accessed October 18, 2022, https://www.metroplanning.org/news/8716/How-can-Illinois-school-districts-address-funding-woes-Share-administrative-services.

34. 105 Ill. Comp. Stat. Ann. § 5/27A-1 et seq.; 105 Ill. Comp. Stat. Ann. §5/27A-9.

35. "Charter Schools," Illinois Network of Charter Schools, accessed May 30, 2023, https://www.incschools.org/.

36. Lauren FitzPatrick, "Rahm Emanuel's Schools Legacy: Record Grad Rates, But He Also Closed 50 Schools," *Chicago Sun-Times*, May 10, 2019.

37. Dan Mihalopoulos, "THE WATCHDOGS: UNO's Secret Spending Spree," *Chicago Sun-Times*, January 30, 2017.

38. Nereida Moreno, "35 Chicago Charter Schools Approved to Stay Open, but with CPS Closely Watching Over Them," *WBEZ*, January 26, 2023, accessed May 30, 2023, https://www.wbez.org/stories/35-chicago-charter-schools-approved-to-stay-open-but-with-cps-closely-watching-over-them/439f0bf0-cf97-47b9-ae20-8f1d59fccbd7.

39. Jon Valant, "What Are Charter Schools and Do They Deliver?" Brookings Institution, October 15, 2019, accessed May 30, 2023, https://www.brookings.edu/policy2020/votervital/what-are-charter-schools-and-do-they-deliver/.

40. Burlingame, "Politics and Policies," 370–89, provides a thorough discussion of the development and central role played by the School Problems Commission, which consisted of legislators and members of the public, from about 1950 until 1971.

41. "Strength in Numbers," Illinois Federation of Teachers, accessed August 29, 2022, https://www.ift-aft.org/iftstrong; and "Our Members," Illinois Education Association, accessed August 29, 2022, https://ieanea.org/members/.

42. Ken Bruce, interview James D. Nowlan, February 1, 1990, Springfield, IL.

43. See the IEA's online bill tracker available at https://ieanea.org/legislative/capitol-watch/.

44. Reflection of James D. Nowlan, who was special assistant to the governor in 1977.

45. "Citizens for George Ryan," Illinois Sunshine Database, accessed September 13, 2022, http://illinoissunshine.org/committees/21/.

46. "Friends of Rod Blagojevich," Illinois Sunshine Database, accessed September 13, 2022, http://illinoissunshine.org/committees/1169/.

47. Mark Ritterbusch, "IEA Recommends Hynes, Dillard for Governor," Illinois Education Association, last updated January 23, 2010, accessed September 13, 2022,

https://archive.ph/20120715055712/http://illinoiseducationassociation.org/featured/iea-recommends-hynes-dillard-for-governor/#selection-601.5–601.16.

48. Reflection of Melissa Mouritsen, IEA member since 2010, who also received many communications encouraging this strategy.

49. "Illinois Federation of Teachers (COPE)," Illinois Sunshine Database, accessed September 21, 2022, http://illinoissunshine.org/committees/185/.

50. "Illinois PAC for Education," Illinois Sunshine Database, accessed September 13, 2022, http://illinoissunshine.org/committees/1169/.

51. Greg Hinz, "Anti-Rauner Group Pulls Plug on TV Ad Campaign," *Crain's Chicago Business*, March 11, 2014.

52. "Illinois PAC for Education (IPACE)," Illinois Sunshine Database, accessed September 13, 2022, https://illinoissunshine.org/committees/1169/.

53. "Political Action Committees," Reform for Illinois' Sunshine Database, accessed August 30, 2022, http://illinoissunshine.org/committees/?type=action.

54. Ibid. These figures are from August 2022, after many dues have been collected from members and before disbursements are made for the November general elections. They are subject to change and likely increase when figures from third quarter reporting is released at the end of September and reflects donations made ahead of the November elections.

55. Reeder, "Teacher Unions Have A+ Clout."

56. Mick Dumke and Tina Sfondeles, "As Conservative Group Grows in Influence, Financial Dealings Enrich Its Leaders," *Chicago Sun-Times*, February 8, 2018.

57. As an IEA member, author Melissa Mouritsen received at least four of these mailers.

58. Harold L. Hodgkinson, *Illinois: The State and Its Educational System* (Washington, DC: Institute for Educational Leadership, 1989), 7.

59. "Preliminary Fall Enrollment 2021–22," Illinois State Board of Higher Education, accessed September 22, 2022, http://www.ibhe.org/EnrollmentsDegrees/search.aspx.

60. Ibid.

61. "Budget 101: Fiscal Year 2022," University of Illinois System, accessed September 30, 2022, https://www.uillinois.edu/about/budget#:~:text=The%20total%20FY%202022%20operating,Illinois%20System%20is%20%247.2%20billion.

62. Ibid.

63. Dawn Rhodes, "Growing Brain Drain," *Chicago Tribune*, April 6, 2018.

64. "When Illinois Students Leave the State for College, Who Reaps the Rewards?" *Illinois Public Media*, August 8, 2019, accessed September 30, 2019, https://will.illinois.edu/news/story/when-illinois-students-leave-the-state-for-college-who-reaps-the-rewards.

65. Jon Boekenstedt, "Freshman Enrollment and Migration from 30,000 Feet," *Higher Ed Data Stories*, accessed September 30, 2022, https://www.highereddatastories.com/2021/11/freshman-enrollment-and-migration-from.html. Jon Boeckenstedt is the vice provost for enrollment at Oregon State University and compiles data using the Integrated Postsecondary Education Data System (IPEDS) database.

66. This background is taken from James D. Nowlan, *The Politics of Higher Education: Lawmakers and the Academy in Illinois* (Urbana: University of Illinois Press, 1976), chap. 1.

67. *Strengthening Private Higher Education in Illinois* (Springfield: Commission to Study Non-Public Higher Education in Illinois, 1969), 5.

68. Quill Lawrence, "Debt Relief for Veterans Who Say They Were Cheated by For-Profit Colleges," *NPR*, accessed September 30, 2022, https://www.npr.org/2022/06/27/1107961508/debt-relief-for-veterans-who-say-they-were-cheated-by-for-profit-colleges.

69. "$50 Million in Refund Checks for University of Phoenix Students," U.S. Federal Trade Commission, accessed September 30, 2022, https://www.ftc.gov/business-guidance/blog/2021/03/50-million-refund-checks-university-phoenix-students.

70. From an Ameritech Foundation study, as reported in the *Bloomington Pantagraph*, January 18, 1990.

71. "Budget 101: Fiscal Year 2022," University of Illinois System, 2022.

72. "Budget in Brief," Illinois Office of Management and Budget, 2022, accessed September 30, 2022, https://budget.illinois.gov/budget-books.html.

Chapter 13. People Services

1. Patrick O'Connell, "'Unprecedented' Surge in Visitors at Forest Preserves, Natural Areas during Pandemic," *Chicago Tribune*, June 19, 2020.

2. Vivian La, "State Parks Officials See Increase in Visitors amid Understaffing, Encourage Compliance with Rules," *Illinois Newsroom*, July 29, 2021, accessed September 20, 2022, https://illinoisnewsroom.org/state-parks-officials-see-increase-in-visitors-amid-understaffing-encourage-compliance-with-rules/.

3. "Illinois State Budget Fiscal Year 2023," Illinois Office of Management and Budget, accessed September 20, 2022, https://budget.illinois.gov/.

4. Paul Buelow, "Hospitals," *Encyclopedia of Chicago*, accessed June 22, 2022, http://www.encyclopedia.chicagohistory.org/pages/602.html.

5. Jennifer Koslow, "Public Health," *Encyclopedia of Chicago*, accessed June 22, 2022, http://www.encyclopedia.chicagohistory.org/pages/602.html.

6. "1950's: The Golden Age of Innovation," the Cleveland Clinic, accessed June 22, 2022, https://my.clevelandclinic.org/about/history/1950s.

7. Michael Morrisey, *Health Insurance*, 3rd ed. (Washington, DC: AUPHA/HAP 2020).

8. Illinois Department of Healthcare and Family Services, "Medicaid 101," accessed June 16, 2022, https://www2.illinois.gov/hfs/SiteCollectionDocuments/medicaid101.pdf.

9. Illinois Department of Healthcare and Family Services, "Number of Persons Enrolled in the Entire State," accessed June 22, 2022, https://www2.illinois.gov/hfs/info/factsfigures/Program%20Enrollment/Pages/Statewide.aspx.

10. "Medicaid in Illinois," Kaiser Family Foundation, October 2019, accessed June 22, 2022, https://files.kff.org/attachment/fact-sheet-medicaid-state-IL.

11. Michael Killian, "Illinois House Receives Bill to Cut Public Aid," *Chicago Tribune*, April 29, 1969.

12. Thomas Powers and Ronald Kotulak, "Medicaid Cost up 300 Percent in 4 Years," *Chicago Tribune*, June 16, 1969.

13. Ibid.

14. Joseph Boyce, "'Dual Medical Aid' of Blacks, Whites Ripped," *Chicago Tribune*, July 10, 1969.

15. Ibid.

16. Ronald Kotulak, "Crisis: The Disappearing Doctors," *Chicago Tribune*, May 17, 1970.

17. Sheila Wolfe, "Program Begun to Shorten Hospitalizing under Medicaid," *Chicago Tribune*, February 24, 1972.

18. "Medicaid Gets a Booster Shot; Reagan Advisers Say Program Meets Its Mandate," *Chicago Tribune*, February 9, 1985.

19. Daniel Egler, "Medicaid Bailout Deal Approved Compromise Frees $60 Million for Overdue Doctor Bills," *Chicago Tribune*, June 3, 1988.

20. Rob Karwath and Dan Culloton, "Severe Lack of Obstetricians Afflicts Rural Illinois," *Chicago Tribune*, June 6, 1991.

21. Teresa Coughlin and Mindy Cohen, "A Race to the Top: Illinois' All Kids Initiative," Kaiser Commission on Medicaid and the Uninsured, August 2007, accessed September 8, 2022, https://www.kff.org/wp-content/uploads/2013/01/7677.pdf.

22. Ibid.

23. Ibid.

24. "How Health Reform's Medicaid Expansion Will Impact State Budgets," Center on Budget and Policy Priorities, July 11, 2012, accessed September 8, 2022, https://www.cbpp.org/research/how-health-reforms-medicaid-expansion-will-impact-state-budgets.

25. Beth Kutscher, "Where Medicaid Expansion Makes a Difference," *Modern Healthcare* 45, no. 23 (June 8, 2015): 20.

26. Kristen Schorsch, "Cook County Health Struggling to Fill Thousands of Jobs," *Chicago Sun-Times*, August 29, 2022.

27. Beth Hundsdorfer, "Death Puts DCFS under Scrutiny Again: Agency Timeline Shows," *Daily Herald*, June 14, 2022.

28. Dan Petrella, "Pritzker Used Own $50k to Fund DCFS Director Search," *Chicago Tribune*, May 17, 2019.

29. "For the Sake of Ta'Naja Barnes, Pritzker Must Take a Hard Look at DCFS Leadership," *Chicago Tribune*, May 16, 2022.

30. Illinois Department of Children and Family Services, "DCFS Serves Children and Families," accessed June 23, 2022, https://www2.illinois.gov/dcfs/lovinghomes/fostercare/Documents/FP_Handbook_Section_1_2014.pdf.

31. Ibid.

32. Ibid.

33. "The Children's Bureau," Social Security Administration, accessed 6/23/22, https://www.ssa.gov/history/childb1.html.

34. Illinois Department of Children and Family Services, "About DCFS," accessed June 23, 2022, https://www2.illinois.gov/dcfs/aboutus/Pages/ab_about.aspx.

35. Ibid.

36. Illinois Department of Children and Family Services, "DCFS Serves Children and Families."

37. Jean Davidson, "ACLU Taking State's Child Welfare System to Court," *Chicago Tribune*, June 30, 1988.

38. Ibid.

39. Rob Karwath, "Tiff Threatens Settlement of Suits against Child Welfare Agency," *Chicago Tribune*, August 14, 1990.

40. "DCFS Wins Part of Lawsuit," *Chicago Tribune*, May 21, 1989.

41. Gordon Johnson, "Give DCFS the Credit It Deserves," Op-Ed, *Chicago Tribune*, March 22, 1990.

42. Rob Karwath, "As Lawsuit Looms, Edgar Names Panel to Study DCFS Woes," *Chicago Tribune*, March 26, 1991.

43. Jennifer Smith, "Overhaul at DCFS: Lawsuit Prompts Change," *Illinois Issues*, October 16, 1991.

44. Rob Karwath, "DCFS Chief Quits, Blames Budget Cuts," *Chicago Tribune*, August 6, 1992.

45. "Children in Substitute Care in Illinois," Ann E. Casey Foundation, accessed June 23, 2022, https://datacenter.kidscount.org/data/tables/.

46. Rob Karwath, "State Keeps DCFS Out of Court on Reform Plan," *Chicago Tribune*, November 16, 1992.

47. Rob Karwath, "State Must Juggle Rights of Kids, Abusive Parents," *Chicago Tribune*, April 25, 1993.

48. "Children in Substitute Care in Illinois," Ann E. Casey Foundation.

49. Rob Karwath, "Abused Kids Sleep in DCFS Office '91 Settlement Violated, ACLU Says," *Chicago Tribune*, June 29, 1993.

50. Rob Karwath, "DCFS Stung for Unkept Promises, Deadline for Reform May Be Pushed Back," *Chicago Tribune*, February 2, 1994.

51. Alysia Tate, "DCFS Defends Foster Care Figures," *Daily Herald*, August 9, 1997.

52. Ibid.

53. Gail Vida Hamburg, "When Parents Fail," *Chicago Tribune*, November 9, 1997.

54. Sue Ellen Christian, "Judge Rejects Change in DCFS Reform Agreement," *Chicago Tribune*, January 25, 1997.

55. Christi Parsons, "Upgrades Earn DCFS National Recognition," *Chicago Tribune*, July 10, 2000.

56. Ofelia Casillas, "DCFS Tells its Flaws to Court; Plan to Improve Services Outlined," *Chicago Tribune*, December 7, 2003.

57. Ofelia Casillas, "Boost in Foster Homes in Works; Court Hears Plan to Aid Kids Who Need Special Care," *Chicago Tribune*, June 29, 2004.

58. "Children in Substitute Care in Illinois," Ann E. Casey Foundation.

59. Ofelia Casillas and Steve Mills, "Shortage Leaves Some DCFS Kids in Limbo: Children Wait in Hospitals, Other Sites for Homes," *Chicago Tribune*, December 22, 2008.

60. Ofelia Casillas and Dahleen Glanton, "Is DCFS Diverting Cases to Cut Costs?" *Chicago Tribune*, April 6, 2010.

61. "Chicago Businessman Gets Two-Year Prison Sentence in Fraud Scheme," *Chicago Sun-Times*, September 23, 2016.

62. Gutowski, Christy, "Perilous Caseloads at DCFS: Investigators Strain as Caseloads Exceed Limits, *Tribune* Finds," *Chicago Tribune*, March 4, 2012.

63. Quoted in Claire Spaulding, "Some Say Ill. Child Welfare in Worse Shape Than Ever," *Chicago Tribune*, March 22, 2022.

64. Ibid.

65. Ibid.

66. Chris Tye, "'Numbers Don't Lie': After 10th Child on the DCFS Radar Dies in the Last 9 Months, Lawmakers Demand Change," *CBS Chicago*, September 1, 2022.

67. Illinois Department of Human Services, "FY23 Budget IDHS Budget Presentation," accessed September 7, 2022, https://www.dhs.state.il.us/page.aspx?item=140951.

68. Department of Human Services, "SNAP Program, Effective October 2021," accessed August 4, 2021, https://www.dhs.state.il.us/page.aspx?item=33412.

69. "United States Department of Human Services TANF Caseload Data 2022," United States Department of Human Services, August 2, 2022, accessed September 7, 2022, https://www.acf.hhs.gov/sites/default/files/documents/ofa/fy2022_tanf _caseload.pdf.

70. Ibid.

71. Illinois Department of Human Services, "Income Guidelines, 2022–07–01," accessed September 7, 2022, https://www.dhs.state.il.us/page.aspx?item=118832.

72. Bureau of Transportation Statistics, "Licensed Drivers," accessed September 28, 2022, https://www.bts.gov/content/licensed-drivers.

73. Secretary of State Jesse White Organ/Tissue Donor Program, "History of the Illinois Organ/Tissue Donor Program," accessed September 20, 2022, https://www .lifegoeson.com/about_us/historyofodnov19.pdf.

74. Jesse White, *Illinois Blue Book*, 59th ed. (Springfield: Illinois Secretary of State, 2022), accessed September 20, 2022, https://www.ilsos.gov/publications/illinois_bluebook/ message.pdf.

Chapter 14. Buffeted by Change, Illinois Continues as the Hub of the Midwest

1. In May 2023, three lobbyists and one utility company president were found guilty in federal court on all nine counts of conspiracy, bribery, and falsification of records, that is, public corruption. In August 2023, the longtime top aide to former Illinois Speaker of the House Michael Madigan was found guilty of lying to a federal grand jury. Madigan and former Chicago alderman Edward Burke were scheduled to go to trial in 2024, in separate cases, on federal charges of political corruption.

Index

Melissa Mouritsen is an associate professor of political science at the College of DuPage and the coeditor of *Twenty-First Century Chicago*.

Kent D. Redfield is emeritus professor of political science at University of Illinois Springfield and the author of *Money Counts: How Dollars Dominate Illinois Politics and What We Can Do About It*.

James D. Nowlan has for decades written columns about "Understanding Illinois" for newspapers across the state. He is the author of *Politics, the Starter Kit: How to Succeed in Politics and Government*.

The University of Illinois Press
is a founding member of the
Association of University Presses.

———————————————

Composed in 12/14 Chaparral Pro
with Georgia display
by Lisa Connery
at the University of Illinois Press
Manufactured by Versa Press, Inc.

University of Illinois Press
1325 South Oak Street
Champaign, IL 61820–6903
www.press.uillinois.edu